Reading Success
for Struggling Adolescent Learners

SOLVING PROBLEMS IN THE TEACHING OF LITERACY
Cathy Collins Block, *Series Editor*

RECENT VOLUMES

Reading Success for Struggling Adolescent Learners

edited by
Susan Lenski
Jill Lewis

THE GUILFORD PRESS
New York   London

© 2008 The Guilford Press
A Division of Guilford Publications, Inc.
72 Spring Street, New York, NY 10012
www.guilford.com

Printed in the United States of America

This book is printed on acid-free paper.

Last digit is print number: 9 8 7 6 5 4 3 2 1

Library of Congress Cataloging-in-Publication Data
Reading success for struggling adolescent learners / edited by Susan Lenski
and Jill Lewis.
    p. cm.—(Solving problems in the teaching of literacy)
  Includes bibliographical references and index.
  ISBN 978-1-59385-676-2 (pbk. : alk. paper)
  ISBN 978-1-59385-677-9 (hardcover : alk. paper)
  1. Reading (Middle school) 2. Reading (Secondary) 3. Reading—Remedial
teaching. I. Lenski, Susan Davis, 1951– II. Lewis, Jill, Ed.D.
  LB1632.R375 2008
  428.4′2—dc22
                                                            2008002138

To my husband, Fran Lenski,
for his unwavering support
—Susan Lenski

To my grandmother, Marie Viner,
for her encouragement and optimism
—Jill Lewis

About the Editors

Susan Lenski, EdD, is Professor of Curriculum and Instruction at Portland State University, where she teaches graduate reading and language arts courses. Previously, Dr. Lenski taught school for 20 years, working with children from kindergarten through high school. During her years as a teacher, she was awarded the Nila Banton Smith Award from the International Reading Association (IRA) for integrating reading in content-area classes and was instrumental in leading her school to receive an Exemplary Reading Program Award. Dr. Lenski was inducted into the Illinois Reading Hall of Fame in 1999, and she served on the IRA Board of Directors from 2004 to 2007. Her research interests focus on strategic reading and writing, adolescent literacy, preparing teacher candidates, and social justice education. She has published more than 65 articles and 14 books, including *Reading and Learning Strategies: Middle Grades through High School*, *Reading Strategies for Spanish Speakers*, and *Becoming a Teacher of Reading: A Developmental Approach*.

Jill Lewis, EdD, is Professor of Literacy Education at New Jersey City University, where she teaches graduate courses in reading, and reading development courses to underprepared freshmen. Previously she taught high school English and reading in public schools and at a community college. Dr. Lewis is a past member of the IRA's Board of Directors (2004–2007), chaired IRA's Government Relations Committee, is an IRA Volunteer Education Consultant for a secondary school literacy project in Macedonia, and volunteered in IRA's Reading and Writing for Critical Thinking project. She served on several state-level task forces, including the New Jersey Task Force on Middle School Literacy, and co-chaired New Jersey's Task

Force for Curriculum Framework for Language Arts Literacy. Dr. Lewis was a Princeton University Faculty Fellow for policy studies and directed community leadership programs in New Jersey. The New Jersey Reading Association awarded her its Distinguished Service Award in 2002. She has authored numerous articles on adolescent literacy, professional development, advocacy, and content-area reading, and has published the books *Adolescent Literacy Instruction: Policies and Promising Practices; Educators on the Frontline: Advocacy Strategies for Your Classroom, Your School, and Your Profession;* and *Academic Literacy: Readings and Strategies.*

Contributors

Peter Afflerbach, PhD, Department of Curriculum and Instruction, University of Maryland, College Park, Maryland

Rita Bean, PhD, Department of Instruction and Learning, University of Pittsburgh, Pittsburgh, Pennsylvania

Micki M. Caskey, PhD, Department of Curriculum and Instruction, Portland State University, Portland, Oregon

Kathleen Crawford-McKinney, PhD, Department of Teacher Education, Wayne State University, Detroit, Michigan

Avivah Dahbany, PhD, Department of Professional Psychology and Family Therapy, Seton Hall University, South Orange, New Jersey

Fabiola P. Ehlers-Zavala, PhD, Department of English, Colorado State University, Fort Collins, Colorado

Laurie Elish-Piper, PhD, Department of Literacy Education, Northern Illinois University, DeKalb, Illinois

Nancy Farnan, PhD, School of Teacher Education, San Diego State University, San Diego, California

Leif Fearn, PhD, School of Teacher Education, San Diego State University, San Diego, California

Gay Fawcett, PhD, independent consultant, Akron, Ohio

Teresa A. Fisher, PhD, Department of Counseling, Adult and Higher Education, Northern Illinois University, DeKalb, Illinois

Dana L. Grisham, PhD, Department of Teacher Education, California State University at East Bay, Hayward, California

Kattie Hogan, MSEd, Warren Woods Middle School, Warren, Michigan

Erexenia Lanier, MSEd, Kingsley Junior High School, Normal, Illinois

Susan Lenski, EdD, Department of Curriculum and Instruction, Portland State University, Portland, Oregon

Jill Lewis, EdD, Department of Literacy Education, New Jersey City University, Jersey City, New Jersey

Becky McTague, EdD, Department of Language and Literacy, Roosevelt University, Chicago, Illinois

Timothy Rasinski, PhD, Department of Teaching Leadership and Curriculum Studies, Kent State University, Kent, Ohio

Margaret Ann Richek, PhD, Department of Reading, Northeastern Illinois University, and Department of Language and Literacy, Roosevelt University, Chicago, Illinois

Alfred W. Tatum, PhD, Department of Curriculum and Instruction, University of Illinois at Chicago, Chicago, Illinois

Thomas DeVere Wolsey, EdD, College of Education, Walden University, Minneapolis, Minnesota

Acknowledgments

We would like to thank the editorial team at The Guilford Press for their wisdom, encouragement, and counsel. We also acknowledge New Jersey City University for granting Jill Lewis release time to work on this project.

Contents

Reading Success
for Struggling Adolescent Learners

Introduction

Susan Lenski
Jill Lewis

One of the most complex problems in education today is how to address the needs of struggling adolescent readers. There are many programs and interventions focused on elementary readers, but once students reach middle grades, reading support often decreases. There are several factors that interact to make it difficult to help middle and high school students become proficient readers, which include the following:

- Title I support and special education services often decline after elementary school.
- Reading is typically not one of the core subjects taught in middle and high schools. Although it may seem logical to teach reading skills and strategies in language arts classes, most secondary English teachers are not trained in teaching reading and do not view that as their responsibility (Ericson, 2001).
- Literacy instruction has not been incorporated into many content-area classes (Biancarosa & Snow, 2004).
- The range of reading achievement increases through the grades, so that it is harder for teachers to find texts that students can read and that challenge more proficient readers.
- Secondary teachers typically spend more time instructing in whole groups, rather than in small groups, which could facilitate teaching reading (Tomlinson, 2004).

The factors that are obstacles to adolescents' reading achievement can be addressed through changes in classroom instruction and school infra-structures, according to Biancarosa and Snow (2004) in *Reading Next: A Vision for Action and Research in Middle and High School Literacy*. And they should be addressed, according to a position statement published by the International Reading Association (Moore, Bean, Birdyshaw, & Rycik, 1999), which states that all adolescents deserve texts, classroom instruc-tion, and school organizations that promote literacy achievement. Strug-gling adolescent readers *do deserve* more access to literacy, and the recom-mendations of the *Reading Next* report should be implemented in every classroom, school, and district so that a greater number of adolescent read-ers learn to read proficiently.

As editors of this book, we agree that changes need to occur in most schools to address the large numbers of middle and high school students who struggle with literacy. Although we have come to the same place in the discussion about struggling adolescent readers, our journeys to this topic are very different. We bring different backgrounds and experiences to this book, which we believe have made the book stronger and richer. What fol-lows is a brief description of our individual backgrounds and explanations of our deep passion for helping adolescent readers.

Susan's Experiences

It all started with Brian Riggazi (a pseudonym), a student in my eighth-grade language arts class. I had no idea that Brian couldn't read proficiently until it was almost too late. Brian always looked as though he was on task when I gave students time to read in class; he handed in all of his home-work; and he passed every quiz and test. Brian received a C+ in language arts for the first semester, but he had failing grades in social studies, science, and math. When I looked at Brian's standardized reading scores, I found that he scored in the bottom quarter of the norming group. I knew what trouble with reading could mean for young teens. In the evenings, I taught at an alternative high school. Most of the high school dropouts whom I taught could read at only a fourth-grade level and considered their reading problems as a primary cause of their school failures.

Fortunately, our building principal called a meeting to discuss the fail-ing grades that many students had received in the first semester and encour-aged us, the teachers, to incorporate reading strategies in our classroom in-struction. At that time, I didn't have many ideas about ways to help struggling readers, but I did implement some strategies that I found in an early edition of Readance, Bean, and Baldwin's (1989) content-area reading book. Reading that book changed me and my outlook on teaching. I did what I could for Brian and all the other struggling readers in my classroom that year, and I vowed to learn more so that I could help all of my students learn to read proficiently.

The realization that Brian couldn't read spurred me on to consider the reasons why so many adolescents have trouble with academic reading. I began taking reading classes at a nearby university and immediately learned strategies that helped me assess and instruct all students in reading. I also learned strategies to work with content-area teachers, which I used when I later became a reading specialist. My instructional practices began to change, and I saw the difference in the achievement of my students. Eventually, I completed a doctorate in reading and began teaching, researching, and writing in the field of literacy. I grew especially interested in instructional strategies and have written several books on the subject, including *Reading and Learning Strategies: Middle Grades through High School* (Lenski, Wham, Johns, & Caskey, 2007).

I still remember Brian Riggazi, though, and I often think of him. I continue to look for answers to the complex question of what teachers can do to help struggling adolescent readers. This book contains many of those answers.

Jill's Experiences

Like many of our readers, I have always wanted to teach. Since childhood I had imagined that there was something magical about being able to share ideas, create learning opportunities, and see students' eyes beaming with excitement as they participated with fellow students. What I didn't realize until I began teaching high school was that some students never have these experiences. For them, school is a struggle.

My first teaching job was teaching English to 7th and 8th graders, mostly children of farmers in the tiny town of Canastota, New York. I quickly learned that many of my students could not read very well. They also really didn't know how to "do school" and were not much interested. Thus I began my professional journey, asking myself, "How can I help struggling students to become better readers and to have more promising futures?" I ransacked the school's book room for appropriate teaching materials; took course work and received an MA in reading while directing a Title I theme-based cross-content program at a high school in Arlington, Virginia; conducted research on struggling readers; directed a reading lab at a Virginia community college after several years of high school teaching; moved to university teaching and teacher education; and pursued a doctorate, which allowed me to look more closely at how the sociopolitical context impacts school and classroom structures and student outcomes. I joined professional communities: the International Reading Association (IRA), American Reading Forum, National Reading Conference, and New

Jersey Reading Association (NJRA). I wrote books for students who struggled with literacy in academic environments and for teachers who sought evidence-based information about teaching adolescents, the most recent being *Academic Literacy: Readings and Strategies* (4th edition, 2007) published for students by Houghton Mifflin, and *Adolescent Literacy Instruction: Policies and Promising Practices* (Lewis & Moorman, 2007), an IRA publication for teachers. I also met with policymakers to advocate for students, teachers, and schools, for better teacher preparation, more school funding, and purposeful assessment.

I know the instructional strategies I use with my students do not exist in a vacuum. Their appropriateness and usefulness are always dependent on the in- and out-of-school contexts each student experiences. Thus, there has been a moving forward and then pulling back for me, shifting from large societal concerns about education to a more intense focus on individual students, classrooms, and teachers. The constant in my journey has been my desire to be a better teacher, to have workable albeit tentative answers for students, and to motivate each student to achieve to the maximum. I remember my students in Canastota and the many who followed and am grateful for what I have learned from them and from my colleagues about what struggling adolescent readers need and how I might help. Like others who have contributed to this book, I share some possibilities with you.

Purposes of This Book

This book grew out of a desire to put together a group of experts who would think about ways to make substantial changes in classroom and school contexts to help students learn to read proficiently. As we conceptualized this book, some of us took the *Reading Next* principles into account and considered the various instructional and infrastructure improvements that are needed before change can be accomplished. (See Chapter 2 for a list of the principles.) Others developed equally important frameworks (see Chapter 1) that drew from their research and experiences with struggling readers.

Reading the individual chapters of this book can be helpful to pinpoint specific areas to improve a school program, but the book in its entirety needs to be taken into account for serious change to take place. We advise teachers and administrators to consider all of the ideas in this book together, implementing a range of ideas from a few chapters at a time. For example, if a school has a large number of students who do not speak English, educators may want to first implement the ideas in the chapters on teaching English language learners (ELLs), reading fluency, comprehension, and increasing parental involvement. Schools that have a large number of students who are not motivated to read may find the chapters on fostering resilience, independent reading, critical literacy, and workplace literacy to be of special importance. Educators interested in making systemic changes that really make a difference in the lives of struggling readers may want to revisit additional chapters of this book after they implement their first priorities.

Organization of the Book

We have organized this book into four parts. Part I, "Understanding Struggling Adolescent Readers," deals with our knowledge of adolescents as it relates to struggling readers. In Chapter 1, Lewis and Dahbany explain how adolescents develop and learn and offer a framework for literacy instruction with struggling readers that is based on our knowledge of adolescent development. Chapter 2, by Lenski, describes what we know about struggling readers and the complexity of meeting their literacy needs. In Chapter 3, Tatum and Fisher explain why some students are more resilient than others and are better able to take advantage of school instruction. Part I concludes with principles for instructing ELLs in Chapter 4, by Ehlers-Zavala.

"Organizing Classroom Contexts that Promote Literacy," Part II, addresses changes in classroom contexts that can make a difference for struggling readers. In Chapter 5, Grisham and Wolsey discuss the role of technology in supporting struggling readers. Chapter 6, by Crawford-McKinney and Hogan, details ways to engage students in texts. Lenski and Lanier conclude Part II with Chapter 7 on ways in which independent reading can be implemented in middle and high schools.

Part III, "Implementing Classroom Instruction for Struggling Adolescent Readers," contains practical instructional strategies that teachers of all disciplines can use in their classroom instruction. Fawcett and Rasinski begin the section with Chapter 8 on fluency strategies. Caskey writes about comprehension strategies in Chapter 9, and Richek explains how to incorporate vocabulary strategies in Chapter 10. Chapter 11, by Fearn and Farnan, explains how to teach writing to students who struggle with literacy. Part III concludes with Chapter 12, written by Lenski, which contains ideas and strategies for critical literacy and taking social action.

The topic of Part IV is "Developing Schoolwide Contexts to Support Literacy." Afflerbach begins this part with Chapter 13, which discusses the topic of classroom assessment in middle and high schools. Chapter 14, written by Bean, focuses on ways literacy coaches can work in middle and high schools. Chapter 15, by Elish-Piper, explains how to keep parents involved during the middle and high school years. Lewis concludes Part IV with Chapter 16, which discusses ways we can incorporate literacy for the workplace in content classes to meet the needs of struggling adolescent readers.

References

Biancarosa, G., & Snow, C. (2004). *Reading Next: A vision for action and research in middle and high school literacy.* Washington, DC: Alliance for Excellent Education.

Ericson, B. (2001). *Teaching reading in high school English classes.* Urbana, IL: National Council of Teachers of English.

Lenski, S. D., Wham, M. A., Johns, J. L., & Caskey, M. M. (2007). *Reading and learning strategies: Middle grades through high school* (3rd ed.). Dubuque, IA: Kendall/Hunt.

Lewis, J. (2007). *Academic literacy: Readings and strategies* (4th ed.). Boston: Houghton Mifflin.

Lewis, J., & Moorman, G. (Eds.). (2007). *Adolescent literacy instruction: Policies and promising practices.* Newark, DE: International Reading Association.

Moore, D. W., Bean, T. W., Birdyshaw, D., & Rycik, J. A. (1999). Adolescent literacy: A position statement. *Journal of Adolescent and Adult Literacy, 43*(1), 97–112.

Readance, J. E., Bean, T. W., & Baldwin, R. S. (1989). *Content area reading: An integrated approach* (3rd ed.). Dubuque, IA: Kendall/Hunt.

Tomlinson, C. A. (2004). Differentiating instruction: A synthesis of key research and guidelines. In T. L. Jetton & J. A. Dole (Eds.), *Adolescent literacy research and practice* (pp. 228–248). New York: Guilford Press.

PART I

Understanding Struggling Adolescent Readers

CHAPTER 1

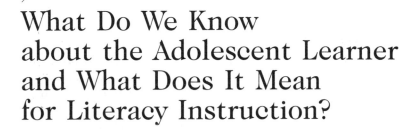

What Do We Know
about the Adolescent Learner
and What Does It Mean
for Literacy Instruction?

Jill Lewis
Avivah Dahbany

T he experiences of adolescents of the 21st century are quite different
from those of young people who grew up in the early 1900s. Public education in the United States has shifted from what was a highly local endeavor
to one that has become increasingly systemized and regulated by state and
federal agencies. Today's teenagers, sometimes referred to as Millenials
(Howe & Strauss, 2000) or Generation Y, live in more diverse communities; are fluent in the language, customs, and values of the digital world;
often grow up in one-parent families; and generally expect to go to college.
These differences also give rise to multiple literacies that our students experience, identified by 21st Century Schools (2007) as aural literacy, business
literacy, civic or social literacy, computer literacy, ecoliteracy, emotional lit-
eracy, financial literacy, information literacy, media literacy, multicultural
literacy, political literacy, print literacy, and visual literacy. Although many
of these types of literacies clearly overlap, identifying them as individual
subsets enables us to acknowledge the complexities of preparing students to
be literate today. The focus of this chapter, therefore, is on what we refer to

as academic literacy (Lewis, 1996, 2007a, 2007b). It is a combination of several of the literacies identified above that collectively make up the literacy skills students need to succeed with the academic content that typifies the core curriculum of most middle and high schools.

The differences in today's adolescents' experiences and what will be expected from them in the future require that we adjust school literacy curricula from the more traditional practices that have served some students well for decades to those that benefit all students, helping them to achieve their potential and leading them to purposeful and fulfilling lives.

To make these adjustments, we first need to look beyond programs, assessments, and regulations and to learn more about the students we teach. For students throughout the world, adolescence is typically the transition from childhood to adulthood in terms of cognitive, social, emotional, and physiological behaviors. Thus, we begin this chapter by reviewing what we know about the psychology of adolescence, providing a brief review of the various factors affecting adolescents as they make this transition and reviewing theories of motivation, one of the issues of greatest concern to teachers of adolescents. Then we identify literacy practices for adolescents that are both developmentally appropriate and instructionally sound.

Transition to Adolescence

The changes students experience as they move from childhood, to adolescence, and then to adulthood are often tumultuous. All children go through these changes, with variations based on the rate of development, the child's culture, and a number of other factors. It is important to know the various theories of development to help us understand our students in the context of our changing times. Theories can be considered as a framework that guides our understanding of our students. However, theories alone do not provide all the answers we need to understand how to teach students to read. Nor are theories static and unchanging; current and future research will influence theoretical understanding. Theories do, however, provide us with the knowledge we need to understand adolescents, especially struggling readers. What follows are some cognitive, psychosocial, physical, and motivational developmental theories to inform our understandings.

Brain and Cognitive Development

Cognitive ability is defined as "the skill of, or aptitude for, perception, learning, memory, understanding, awareness, reasoning, judgment, intuition, and language" (VanderBos, 2007, p. 187). To teach reading skills to adolescents, especially struggling readers, we need to understand their brain development and functioning. During adolescence the brain continues to develop, which enables teens to process information faster and increase reaction time. The prefrontal cortex of the brain controls executive functioning, which is defined as "higher level cognitive processes that organize and order behavior, including (but not limited to) logic and reasoning, abstract thinking, problem solving, planning, and carrying out and terminating goal directed behavior" (p. 350). Some research has found that adolecents' behaviors are the result of immature prefrontal cortex development (Sabbagh, 2006). Does brain development precede learning, or can learning enhance brain and cognitive development? This question continues to be explored in the literature. However, knowledge of adolescent cognitive development enhances our ability to teach struggling readers.

Piaget's Stages of Cognitive Development

Piagetian concepts influence the ways we teach, especially in the primary grades. Piaget's main premise is that "development precedes learning" (Piaget & Inhelder, 1969/2000). However, more current research has indicated that some aspects of object permanence can be displayed at younger ages (Baillargeon, Graber, DeVos, & Black, 1990), some of the Piagetian tasks can be taught to children at younger ages of development (Case, 1997; Siegler, 1998), and perspective taking can be displayed in simple situations (Siegler, 1998).

Analytical Thinking

In Piaget's (1969/2000) stages of development, adolescents transition from the concrete operational stage (6–11 years of age) to the formal operational stage (11 years of age and above). In the concrete operational stage, children are able to think inductively and reason from the specific to the general. However, they are able to deal with things only within their own experiences.

In the formal operational stage, adolescents are able to think about possibilities that are outside their experiences. They develop deductive reasoning, whereby they can start with an idea and use their logic to develop specific conclusions. They can test hypotheses and reason logically. They develop metacognition, which is the ability to think about their own thinking. Adolescents can assess how to accomplish a task and can learn the best way to complete it. They can monitor their own performance as they work on a task and adjust their performance to complete it successfully. These skills develop between 11 and 15 years of age in many adolescents. Some students, however, never develop such reasoning abilities.

The demonstration of these analytical skills is not generally consistent. These abilities are situational and depend on the adolescents' familiarity with the concepts, their knowledge base, and individual differences. As adolescents become more familiar with a specific concept, they are more likely to use their analytical skills. In unfamiliar tasks, however, adolescents tend to use more concrete operational and less metacognitive skills (Cobb, 1995).

Intuitive Thinking

To counterbalance the analytical thinking skills, intuitive thinking skills also develop and increase in importance in adolescence. Here, thoughts derived from previous feelings and memories are applied to a problem-solving task. This type of thinking is quick and emotional, which frequently results in wrong conclusions. The combination of their newly developed metacognitive skills and intuitive skills makes adolescents think a great deal about themselves. Adolescent egocentrism results, as they think they are always being noticed and believe they are much more socially important than they actually are. They think that others are very interested in their activities and that they are always at "center stage" (Elkind, 1967; Vartanian, 2001). Teenagers are self-absorbed and believe that their experiences, feelings, and thoughts are unique. They believe that they are invincible and cannot be harmed or suffer consequences for their inappropriate behaviors. They worry about their conflicting feelings, such as dependence on their parents and a desire to be independent from them. They worry about how their peers perceive them, about their appearance, and about their future. Most adolescents are extremely self-conscious, which may be their way of coping with their social discomfort.

Vygotsky: Sociocultural Cognitive Development

Vygotsky (1978), a contemporary of Piaget, had different ideas about cognitive development. He believed that cognitive development can be understood only within the context of children's cultural and historical experiences. He believed that development is dependent on the "sign symbols" children learn that enable them to think, communicate, and solve problems. Sign symbols are the language, counting, and writing skills within their culture. Children learn these sign symbols in interaction with others, internalize these symbols, and then use these skills in problem-solving tasks. To foster such development, adults or more able peers work with children on tasks that are not yet learned but can be learned with assistance. These skills need to be just above the children's current level of functioning, which is called the zone of proximal development. In order to assist the children, "scaffolding" is used. Scaffolding includes giving clues and/or examples, reminders, encouragement, breaking a task into steps, and so on.

Bloom's Taxonomy of Educational Objectives

Bloom's (1956) taxonomy of educational objectives, which was developed to guide curriculum planning, has been revised since Bloom first introduced his theory (Anderson et al., 2001). Active cognitive processing is required for meaningful learning. The current cognitive domain consists of six cognitive processes: remembering, understanding, applying, analyzing, evaluating, and creating. Although no specific age ranges are noted, the last five cognitive processes have relevance to adolescent cognitive development. For teenagers to understand what they are learning, they need to develop meaning and to apply their skills in given situations. In order to analyze, they need to break down materials into their various parts and determine how these parts relate to each other and to the whole. When students are given criteria and standards, they need to be able to evaluate and make judgments. To create, adolescents need to reorganize elements into a new pattern or structure. Teenagers need the educational opportunities to develop these skills.

Erikson's Stages of Psychosocial Development

Erikson (1968) believed that there are eight stages in developing one's psychosocial maturity throughout the life span. In each stage, there are psychosocial crises that need to be resolved to successfully take on the new challenges of the next stage. Adolescents would be emerging from the industry versus inferiority stage (6–12 years of age) into the identity versus role confusion stage (12–18 years of age).

In the industry versus inferiority stage, the influence of parents decreases as the importance of school increases. When students are able to tackle academic tasks and are successful, their self-image increases. If they are unable to do these things successfully, they feel inadequate and inferior, which results in a negative self-image. Sometimes a negative self-image is not based on a student's accurate assessment of his or her skills. It can be based on a student's inability to measure up to his or her own unrealistic standards or the standards of parents, teachers, and relevant others.

As adolescents transition into the identify versus role confusion stage, they are trying to answer the question "Who am I?" They are pressured to form their own psychosocial identities and make career and educational plans, which include gender, sexual, and ethnic identities. As adolescents try to develop greater autonomy and independence, they turn to their peer group for support as they turn away from their parents. The ultimate goal is identity achievement, whereby they establish their own identities based on their own selection of values and goals after consideration of parental and society influences.

Adolescents try out various "possible identities" through their teenage years, which are images of who they are or who they might like to become. Their identities change with the social groups, settings, and circumstances they encounter. They can also develop "false selves," which are reflected in behaviors they adopt in order to be accepted by their peer group. There are three kinds of false selves. One is the "acceptable false self," which results when the real self is rejected by peers or parents. This leads to feelings of worthlessness and hopelessness as teens betray their real selves. Another is the "pleasing false self," which results from the desire to please or impress others—a common occurrence. There is also the "experimental false self," whereby they try out various behaviors to see how they make them feel (Harter, Waters, & Whitesell, 1997).

Identity achievement is a difficult task to master, owing to the questioning and analyzing it requires. Some adolescents try to cope with this task by identity foreclosure, which occurs when they prematurely adopt parental or societal roles and values for themselves. Others adopt a negative identity, which is the total opposite of parental expectations, because they cannot find alternatives of their own that are appealing (Marcia, 1966; Marcia, Waterman, Matteson, Archer, & Orlofsky, 1993). A variant of the negative identify is an oppositional identity, in which a negative stereotype is adopted and exaggerated and the dominant culture is rejected (Ogbu, 1993). Other adolescents experience identity diffusion, in which they are apathetic about developing an identity, have few if any goals or commitments, and lack self-definition (Marcia, 1966; Marcia et al., 1993). Probably the best process of finding one's identity is to have an identity moratorium. This enables the adolescent to try out various identities or possible selves. Attending college, joining the military, or other activities enable the adolescent to fulfill a temporary identity while buying time to form his or her final identity.

Physical Development

The hallmark of physiological development for an adolescent is puberty. Changes occur in the physical shape and size of a person's body, leading to sexual maturation. Hormones signal these physiological changes and have direct and indirect effects on a teenager's emotions. The direct effects of the hormonal changes result in the rapid arousal of emotions and emotional extremes. In girls, the menstrual cycle affects their mood; they are usually happy in mid-cycle and frustrated and angry prior to menstruation. Boys' hormonal levels increase their thoughts about sex and masturbation. Although hormones have lifelong effects on both genders, they have a more potent effect on adolescents because teenagers have no prior experience with these physiological changes. This results in less control and more erratic behaviors (Susman, 1997). The timing and rate of puberty are other factors to consider. Most adolescents want to develop at the same rate as their peers so as to remain part of their social group. In general, girls mature 1 to 2 years earlier than boys. Girls mature between 8 and 16 years of age, whereas boys mature between 9 and 18 years of age. Once males and females start to develop, they achieve maturation within 2 to 6 years (Berk, 1996).

There are indirect consequences for both early- and late-maturing adolescents (Downs, 1990). Early-maturing girls can feel out of place socially or can be shunned by their same-age peers. The attention they arouse in others because of their physical development may cause discomfort, resulting in their varied emotional reactions. Teenage girls who mature early can develop lower self-esteem, more depression, and poorer body images than their peers (Siegal, Yancey, Aneschensel, & Schuler, 1999). Late-maturing boys may not experience similar issues. They can compensate with their academic and intellectual strengths if these traits are valued by their families, schools, and cultures (Downs, 1990).

Interestingly, family stress can have an effect on the timing of puberty, especially for girls. Stress affects hormonal production. Girls can enter puberty at a younger age if they have conflicted relationships with their families and/or there is an unrelated man (stepfather, mother's boyfriend) living with their mothers. Apparently, the longer the unrelated man has lived in the household, the earlier the onset of puberty (Ellis & Garber, 2000).

Motivation

Motivation is defined as an internal process that activates, guides, and maintains behavior over time and varies in intensity and direction (Schunk, 2000). Motivation is important because it helps students achieve their goals. This is especially important for struggling readers who have experienced many failures. Understanding and implementing strategies to help students maintain their motivation when they face obstacles are essential skills. Depending on the theory of motivation one uses, there are a variety of ways to enhance adolescent motivation for learning.

Behavioral Learning Theory

Behavioral learning theory indicates that pleasurable consequences following a behavior increase that behavior, and negative consequences decrease the behavior. Reinforcement, or pleasurable consequences, is the most powerful shaper of behavior. A consequence hierarchy needs to be developed, starting with giving adolescents something they desire in order to maintain or increase their motivation. If this is not successful, then taking away something they do not like is the next step (e.g., "homework, passes," which can be used to excuse them from doing their homework for one night, etc.). If these reinforcement steps do not work, then negative consequences follow, giving adolescents something they do not like (e.g., extra homework) to decrease their inappropriate behaviors. The last step in the hierarchy is to take away something they like in order to decrease behaviors (e.g., preventing them from participating in a desired activity). For this theory to work, it is essential to select reinforcements that are meaningful to the individual adolescent (Bandura, 1986; Skinner, 1953).

Extrinsic versus Intrinsic Motivation

Behavioral theory focuses on providing extrinsic incentives (reinforcements) for learning in order to help maintain a student's motivation. These reinforcements include things such as good grades and positive recognition but are not generally related to the subject content (Brophy, 1998). However, courses that students enjoy provide them with intrinsic motivation that enables them to learn without the need for external reinforcement. Accomplished readers have already developed the intrinsic motivation they need to read, which is reinforced by the satisfaction that reading provides. However, because of the frustrations struggling readers experience, it is important to provide them with even more external reinforcement for the smallest gains they make. Such reinforcement supports their continuing efforts and helps them cope with their frustrations in their journey to become accomplished readers.

Maslow's Hierarchy of Needs

Maslow (1954) proposed a concept of motivation that is related to the satisfaction of needs. In his hierarchy, deficiency needs are defined as the basic requirements for psychological and physical well-being. They include physiological needs (food, clothing, shelter, etc.), safety needs, belongingness and love needs, and esteem needs. Once these needs are met, adolescents can progress to the growth needs, including the need to know and understand, aesthetic needs, and self-actualization, which refers to the ability to develop to one's full potential and achieve good psychological health. What is germane here is that if struggling readers are developing low self-esteem due to their difficulties, they will be less likely to have the motivation to develop the "need to know and understand" their struggles. Without such an understanding, they will be less likely to be able to overcome their reading obstacles.

Attribution Theory

Attribution theory concerns the rationales people give for their successes or failures in order to maintain a positive self-concept (Graham, 1991). Locus of control (Rotter, 1954) is a personality trait that enables people to attribute their success or failure to internal or external factors. Internal factors include those within the person, and external factors are generally viewed as outside the person's control. Stable traits include one's ability and the task difficulty, whereas unstable traits include one's effort and luck. A person with an internal locus of control attributes success or failure to his or her own efforts and abilities. Self-efficacy, or a person's belief that a his or her behavior can make a difference, comes from an internal locus of control (Bandura, 1997). A person with an external locus of control attributes success or failure to factors beyond his or her control such as luck, task difficulty, and so forth. Learned helplessness, or the expectation of failure based on experience, results from the feeling of lack of control (Seligman, 1972). Struggling readers are more likely to develop an external locus of control. This helps them cope by attributing their reading difficulties to things they cannot control. Learned helplessness, coupled with an external locus of control, makes these students feel that nothing they do can help them learn to read. We need to provide struggling readers with feedback indicating that their lack of success is due to a lack of effort, rather than a lack of ability. If we are successful, then these students can start to develop a more internal locus of control that will provide them with the motivation needed to continue to struggle and overcome their reading difficulties.

Goal Orientation

Students are motivated toward either performance or learning goals (Dweck, 1986). Those with performance goal motivations want to obtain approval for their academic competence from others. They want to get good grades by taking easy courses that do not challenge their skills. However, students with learning goals want to develop academic competence, so they seek challenges by taking difficult courses.

A Developmentally Considerate Framework for Promoting Adolescent Literacy

We can use the features of adolescents' psychological development to organize a program for adolescent literacy instruction. In this section, Lewis outlines five themes and suggests they be used as a literacy curriculum planning framework, referred to here as the Promoting Adolescent Literacy (PAL) framework. She also provides ideas to illustrate how each of its five themes can be used in schools: Literacy for Developing Cognition, Literacy for Self-Assessment and Self-Monitoring, Literacy for Understanding Multiple Perspectives and Flexible Thinking, Literacy for Building Relationships, and Literacy for Developing Autonomy and Identity

There are literally hundreds of strategies for improving adolescents' literacy. Those discussed here have been selected because they clearly illustrate the themes. Other chapters in this volume offer more strategies, and as you read them consider where in the PAL framework each strategy falls. This process can enable teachers to create a developmentally appropriate and comprehensive plan for developing adolescent literacy in their classrooms.

Literacy for Developing Cognition

During adolescence, as students encounter more difficult texts in school with more complex ideas, they sometimes need to expand the meanings and relationships they attach to these ideas. They will need to, at least momentarily, let go of their personal opinions to allow for a consideration of other viewpoints. In this section, several activities are suggested for engaging students in such cognitive experiences.

Critical Literacy

Critical literacy is central to helping students to develop mature cognitive processes, and it is essential for educating citizens of a democratic society. Shor (1992) defines critical literacy as

> Habits of thought, reading, writing, and speaking which go beneath surface meaning, first impressions, dominant myths, official pronouncements, traditional clichés, received wisdom, and mere opinions, to understand the deep meaning, root causes, social context, ideology, and personal consequences of any action, event, object, process, organization, experience, text, subject matter, policy, mass media, or discourse. (p. 129)

Thus, critical literacy is understood as "learning to read and write as part of the process of becoming conscious of one's experience as historically constructed within specific power relations" (Anderson & Irvine, 1993, p. 82).

When students explore how they have been socialized to adopt the ideas and values they hold through such powerful means as the media, school, religion, our political system, and the influence of family and friends, they are better able to put their own ideas into an understandable context and to question which ideas are true for them and which are not. They can also realize the power literacy holds for individuals (Freire,

1984). Chapter 12 in this volume provides a fuller discussion of critical literacy in adolescent classrooms; here we offer just a few examples of instructional possibilities for developing critical literacy.

Artifacts are useful for engaging students in critical literacy discussions, starting with artifacts that are currently popular: the iPod, for instance. This device is something people never knew they needed; now some people feel they can't live without it. How did that happen? Students can explore the evolution of the iPod, beginning with music as a shared experience in early American history to one that is now quite individualistic. They may consider whether this shift in any way parallels larger cultural shifts in American society. What role did the media and/or the music industry play in convincing adolescents that the iPod is something they need? How do friends contribute to this way of thinking? How is this phenomenon similar to or different from the musical experience in other cultures? Other examples of artifacts that are reflective of our culture and that may lead to an examination of influences on individuals in society include fashion trends (particularly notice how these have changed over the years), the school's logo, computers, and the Oscar. They might look at changes over time in such artifacts as Barbie dolls or other children's toys. They should also examine how these artifacts privilege some segments of society while disempowering others.

Once students realize how artifacts reflect and support particular cultural values and forge identities, they can study media, such as newspapers, television, and web pages, to further develop their abilities to take a critical stance. The classroom itself and their textbooks can be analyzed as political texts that are not neutral; some groups benefit from the content and ideas, whereas others are silenced.

Developing Good Questions

In addition to the expansion of students' cognition through critical literacy experiences, more traditional classroom activities can be redesigned to achieve this goal. Questions from students and teachers permeate our classrooms and are used routinely to generate discussion and share ideas, assess comprehension, and learn about each other. But do our questions promote sophisticated thinking?

A survey of classroom teachers conducted by the National Education Association (2002) found that textbooks are the most frequently used teaching tools and that nearly half (47%) of the responding teachers say they use textbooks every day. The average yearly expenditure for textbooks and related materials in public schools is approximately $10,000 per school per year (*Today's School*, 2002). Unfortunately, the textbooks available to most middle and high school teachers are not very good. In fact, Alfie Kohn (1999) writes that textbooks "invariably include a little bit of everything and a thoughtful treatment of nothing. (It can safely be said that any course consisting mostly of reading a textbook, chapter by chapter, is a course worth avoiding)" (pp. 59–60). Questions provided in the text are often unchallenging and only touch the content's surface. What follows is a brief passage from an 8th-grade social studies text.

> Buddhism originated in India around 530 B.C. Traders and missionaries traveling along the Silk Road introduced the religion to China during the Han Dynasty. However, it attracted few followers then, mostly because it was foreign. Now, in the troubled times at the end of the Han Dynasty, the new religion became attractive.
>
> The Buddha taught that life is a cycle of pleasure and sorrow, of death and rebirth. Suffering, he taught, was a basic part of life. It was caused by paying too much attention to material things in life—to what the Buddha referred to as "the world of sensory pleasure."
>
> But a person could escape from suffering, according to the Buddha. Through meditation, he taught, one could achieve enlightenment—a state of complete freedom and peace.
>
> The idea of freedom from the chaos of the earthly world appealed to Chinese people of all classes. It appealed to regional rulers living in constant fear of attack, to landowners worried about crop failure, and to peasants longing for their own plots of land. By the 400s, most regional kings supported Buddhism. Buddhist temples and monasteries thrived throughout China. The Buddhists accumulated much valuable land. They also owned grain mills, and operated hospitals, schools, and inns. (Cordova et al., 1999, p. 195)

The textbook includes only one question pertaining to this passage: "Why did the Chinese find Buddhism more appealing than Confucianism after the fall of the Han Dynasty?" How much sophisticated thinking does this question require? A student could conceivably be considered to have the "correct" answer just by giving the information in the first paragraph.

Recall now Anderson's revision to Bloom's taxonomy, mentioned earlier, that includes six cognitive processes: remembering, understanding, applying, analyzing, evaluating, and creating. What processes are addressed by the text question? Here are two more questions. Think about the processes they address:

1. Why would the Buddhists have accumulated so much valuable land when their philosophy was antimaterialism?
2. Explain whether you agree or disagree with the Buddhist philosophy that "suffering is a basic part of life."

These types of questions could elicit different responses from students. The first question asks students to hypothesize; a variety of answers are possible, and students must use the information they have to create a response. The second question asks students to consider an idea, to call upon their own values and then to evaluate the posed idea. These questions illustrate the kinds of rigorous questions teachers should ask, whether they are created by the students, textbook publishers, or the teachers themselves. If teachers use texts and depend primarily on publishers' comprehension questions for instruction, they must carefully review them to be sure they challenge students' thinking and help them extend meaning.

Concept Maps

Deep meaning for concepts can be derived similarly, by having students create concept maps (Novak, 1991), which are visual/pictorial representations that help students understand verbal/semantic concepts. Concepts are single words that represent high-level (formal operational thinking) conceptual abstractions, and teachers select them for elaboration because they meet the following four criteria:

1. They represent a fundamental (key) concept of a discipline.
2. They have the capacity to synthesize or symbolize large bodies of knowledge.
3. They represent a hierarchy of knowledge that increases in complexity, generality, and abstractness.
4. They are powerful conceptual abstractions; they generally cannot be reduced further as a subset of a more fundamental concept. (Baca, n.d.)

Using concept maps, sometimes referred to as semantic webs or semantic maps, students can elaborate meanings of an idea that may be critical to a subject area, such *democracy, conflict,* or *power* in social studies; they may also be drawn from a novel's theme, such as *heroism, tragedy,* or *friendship*; science concepts of *ecosystem* or *energy* may be elaborated. Students completing maps are better able to visualize relationships between ideas connected to the concept and hence gain a richer understanding of it. Pairs or teams can brainstorm ideas. Maps can enable students to communicate complex ideas, integrate new and old knowledge, and assess understanding or identify misunderstanding of key concepts. With maps, students have opportunities to break down material into parts and determine how these parts relate to each other and to the whole. Students can work creatively, reorganizing ideas into a new structure.

Some concept maps can be drawn simply and yet involve deeper thinking about a term or idea than merely defining the concept would. Figure 1.1 offers a template for such a map.

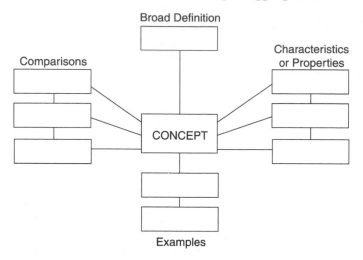

FIGURE 1.1. Concept map.

White (2003) suggests a more elaborate type of map that students can create while working in groups, using a multistage process, as follows:

1. Brainstorming phase, during which students may be able to think of as many as 50 terms related to a concept, and these can be written on Post-it notes.
2. Organizing phase, during which groups and subgroups of related items are created, with attention to hierarchical relationships.
3. Layout phase, when students create an arrangement (layout) that best represents their collective understanding of the interrelationships and connections between groupings.
4. Linking phase, when lines with arrows connect showing relationships between connected items. Students write a word or short phrase beside each arrow to specify the relationship.
5. Finalizing the concept map, when the concept map is converted to a permanent form that others can view and discuss.

As students critique their maps and those of others, they can consider the accuracy and thoroughness and note any misconceptions or any critical ideas that are missing. They should also consider whether the organization reflects higher-order relationships and the quality of the map's appearance as well as the creativity used to show relationships. The resulting map may look like the one shown in Figure 6.2.

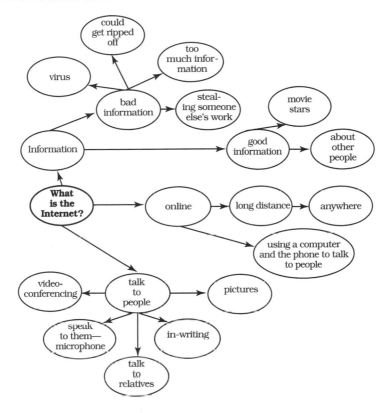

FIGURE 1.2. Elaborated concept map. From Valmont, W. J. (2000. April). *Vignettes from literacy teachers. Reading Online.* Retrieved January 10, 2007, from *www.readingonline.org/electronic/elec_index.asp?HREF=/electronic/valmont_excerpt/ index.html.* Originally published in Wepner, S. B., Valmont, W. J., & Thurlow, R. (Eds.). (2000). *Linking literacy and technology: A guide for K–8 classrooms* (p. 195). Copyright 2000 by the International Reading Association. Figure created with *Inspiration* software (*www.inspiration.com*) by fifth-grade students at Lawrence School in Tucson, Arizona, as part of a workshop conducted by Chris Johnson, of the University of Arizona, and their teacher, Mary Bouley.

Cubing to Explore Concepts

Cubing is another engaging activity for developing multidimensional understandings of concepts. In Cubing, originally suggested for promoting writing (Cowan & Cowan, 1980), students write on each side of a six-sided cube, using each to explain one of the following about an important concept: description (What is it like?); comparison (What is it similar to or different from?); association (What does it make you think of?); analysis

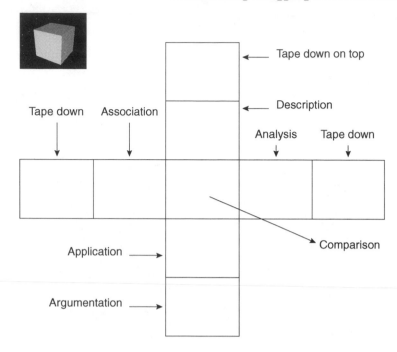

FIGURE 1.3. Cubing activity.

(How is it made? What is it composed of? or What are its features?); application (What can you do with it? How is it used?); argumentation (Take a
stand, arguing for or against it). Students can create cubes individually, in
pairs, or in small groups, and their responses can be entered in one of the
boxes of a precut sheet of paper which, when folded, creates a cube. (See
Figure 1.3.) For older adolescents, Cubing can be done using a six-sided die
and a sheet listing the elements, numbered 1–6 (e.g., "4. Analysis"). In
groups, students take turns rolling the die and have to complete the numbered sheet so that each element has a response.

Literacy for Self-Assessment and Self-Monitoring

One feature that distinguishes adolescents from younger students is their
ability to evaluate and make judgments, including evaluating or judging
their own performance. This ability undergoes refinement during the transition to adulthood, with adolescents being increasingly able to think about
their own thinking and to rule out ideas that conflict with their experiences
or knowledge. The depth of this metacognitive ability, however, varies from
adolescent to adolescent and impacts academic literacy achievement, and it

is thus important to include consideration of its development within the PAL framework.

Developing Fix-Up Strategies through Think-Alouds

We know that more capable readers try to make sense of text by monitoring and verifying their comprehension while they read (Keene & Zimmermann, 1997) and by applying fix-up strategies when they feel they are not comprehending. These strategies, or deliberate plans, include rereading text or looking ahead to see if later text provides explanation, adjusting reading rate, reading text out loud to hear syntax, creating questions and seeking answers for them, creating a visual to outline the ideas or to show relationships between them, and discussing the text with a classmate. Keene and Zimmerman explain:

> When great readers are reading this stuff that has so many ideas in it, they have to listen to that mental voice tell them which words, which sentences or paragraphs, and which ideas are most important. Otherwise they won't get it. Great readers really listen to the voice saying "I think this word or this idea is most important." Then they're able to decide which ideas are most important in the piece. (p. 86)

Thus, students who engage in metacognition and self-monitoring are purposeful and active readers whose reading experiences can be more fulfilling.

We must deliberately teach struggling readers these strategies for self-checking and repairing comprehension. An explicit approach is to model think-alouds. Teachers often tell their students to think while they read, but the opportunity to model how this is done and how fix-up strategies are applied is sometimes missed. We can show students what we do when we don't understand a section of text or realize that something doesn't make sense: how we tell ourselves that something is confusing, ask ourselves questions, and read ahead to verify and clarify meaning. We access prior knowledge and relate it to new information, connect portions of text to each other, adjust our reading rate, make inferences, tackle unfamiliar vocabulary by using context and morphology. We put the text into our own words, identify the most essential information, and try to summarize and visualize the material. We can demonstrate how we set purposes for reading beforehand and check while reading to see if we are achieving these goals.

There are multiple causes for adolescents' struggling with text, ranging from unfamiliarity with subject matter and lack of background knowledge, to complexities of language structure, unfamiliar vocabulary, failure to establish a purpose for reading, and dysfluent reading that disrupts the flow of the text. Students who develop the habit of self-questioning during reading will be better able to recognize when comprehension is disrupted and more information is required through rereading, rethinking the ideas, or seeking additional resources for confusing information. Through modeling, accompanied by scaffolded instruction with students gradually assuming increased responsibility for their own self-monitoring, we can help struggling adolescent readers to develop worthwhile habits to use throughout their lifetimes.

Rubrics for Self-Assessment

Other classroom literacy events can provide adolescents opportunities to self-assess or self-evaluate in order to acknowledge their strengths as well as areas needing improvement. Working with rubrics is a case in point. Rubrics stipulate standards for judging student work. Categories in a rubric outline important components of the work being completed, critiqued, or assessed, and there is a clear description of the criteria that must be met for the student to receive the highest grade possible. A rubric also provides a gradation of levels of completion or competence, with a score assigned to each level, giving students a very clear description of what criteria need to be met to attain the score at each level.

The most valuable rubrics are those that students and their teachers have mutually created, because the students have participated in discussing the criteria for evaluation. Rubrics can be designed for specific projects, such as a learning log, or templates can be developed for ongoing types of classroom activities, such as oral presentations or expository essays. Sometimes students assess their success as individual members of a group, as well as the group work itself. Struggling students benefit from the clearly defined criteria and often use the rubric to guide their production of the assignment. At *ed.fnal.gov/lincon/w01/projects/library/rubrics/presrubric. htm*, teachers can find a useful rubric for presentations. A model rubric for evaluating collaboration in groups can be found at *edweb.sdsu.edu/triton/ tidepoolunit/Rubrics/collrubric.html*. As Kohn (1994) reminds us, "Students acquire a sense of significance from doing significant things, from being active participants in their own education" (¶86).

Literacy for Understanding Multiple Perspectives and Flexible Thinking

We shouldn't be surprised that adolescents tend to be self-absorbed. They are undergoing so many transitions in behavior and thought that they are often impulsive and highly emotional. They also tend to cling to their viewpoints, unable to consider other perspectives. Perspectives may evolve from an individual's culture, knowledge, role, experience, and belief system.

Through deliberate activities we can guide students to the realization that there is more than one way to think about something and that alternative perspectives do not necessarily make one idea right or wrong. Such dispositions can provide entrée to new ideas.

As with previous parts of the PAL framework, it is often best to start developing this element of the literacy framework by using something very familiar to students. An interesting starting point may be for students to share ideas they had when they were very young and how these changed when tested against reality. For instance, some may have believed in Santa Claus. Why do some very young children have this idea? When does it change? Why? Can students identify any changes in their thinking about other beliefs over time, such as beliefs about global warming? Does everyone hold the same viewpoint about this topic? What are some other views? Why might opinions differ?

We can also generate discussion about perspectives by looking at photos or other art forms. We may, for instance, show students a photo of a shiny red sports car and ask them what might be uppermost in the minds of the following persons when they see this car: a mathematician, an environmentalist, an artist, a fiction writer, a teenager. Students can be encouraged to think of other groups of individuals who may have still different perspectives on the car and to discuss how each of these perspectives may have some validity.

Using Corners and Discussion Webs to Promote Flexible Thinking

Teachers often use debate as a strategy to help students to understand the need to provide evidence for their opinions. Although this is an important skill, students can be inflexible, holding rigidly to a single point of view. One way to encourage flexible thinking is through an activity sometimes referred to as *Corners*. In this activity, the teacher presents a controversial topic along with four options or positions that could be taken on this controversy; each option is posted in a corner of the classroom. For example, the topic may be "Students should be able to have computers in their bedrooms to use whenever they want." The options may be (1) Agree completely, (2) Disagree completely, (3) Parents should set a few limits that are agreeable to their children, and (4) This should apply only to children in grades K–6. Each student makes choice and stands in the corner where it is posted. Working with their "corner mates," students develop an argument to defend their choices. Time limits can be set; students prepare arguments, and one person in each corner is selected as presenter. It is important that, during the presentations, students are free to change their positions (move to another corner). Such a shift requires open-mindedness and careful listening, motivates students to develop good arguments, and engages students in literacy refinements. Once all the arguments have been heard and positions changed, the class discusses the reasons for changed positions and the quality of the arguments. In addition to evaluating the original arguments, teachers can evaluate students on the quality of the rationales they provide for changing corners. Corners can be extended into a writing activity that includes research, such as surveys and interviews, as well as using the Internet. More information about this strategy can be found at *www.educationworld.com/a_lesson/03/lp304-04.shtml.*

With a *Discussion Web* (Alvermann, 1991; Duthie, 1986), students have an opportunity to consider two opposing views on an issue before reaching a conclusion. In Alvermann's elaboration of Duthie's work, students begin with a think-pair-share activity in which they respond to a yes–no question, such as "Should scientists be permitted to test new drugs on animals?" Students are given text to read on this topic to find support for their opinions. First they consider the question on their own, then with a partner. Finally, they share their thinking with another set of partners as a small group and reach a consensus, which their spokesperson then shares with the whole class (Figure 1.4). In this process individual students must exercise critical thinking, looking for contradictions and inconsistencies. They learn to create logical arguments and discover how text can be used to support personal viewpoints. To reach consensus, they must also relinquish some of their ideas when others seem more logical or have more support, which makes this strategy quite different from Corners or debate activities.

RAFT (Role, Audience, Form, and Topic) for Learning about Multiple Perspectives

As Santa (2004, p. 186) notes, RAFT was originally conceived by Nancy Vandevanter (1982) as part of the Montana Writing Project. RAFT is another strategy adolescents enjoy and that encourages reflection on multiple perspectives. In this strategy, students write from perspectives different from their own and use alternative discourse modes to create authentic writing projects. Teachers can begin RAFT by illustrating how a particular topic may yield various perspectives. Students can be shown a film, such as *Shower,* a film about how old and new worlds collide in a family that is ultimately brought together by a traditional bathhouse. After viewing the film, the students form small groups related to various aspects of the film, each with a different perspective. For instance, one group represents a tourist bureau; another group includes film critics writing a movie review; a third group is from the film industry, developing a survey to better understand today's film audiences; still another is composed of students who are writing a paper about the generation gap; and so on. For each assignment, students need to consider the following:

YES		NO
	Should scientists be permitted to test new drugs on animals?	
	Conclusions	

FIGURE 1.4. Discussion web.

- R—Role of the writer. The part the writer is playing while composing a particular paper.
- A—Audience for the writer. The people who read the paper. Whom
  the writer is addressing.
- F—Form of the writing. The type of written expression. The paper's
  genre.
- T—Topic to be addressed in the writing. The subject of the paper.

Another possibility, adapted from Lewis (2004) is for students to have
the same assignment insofar as topic, but with each group needing to create
a different written form. For instance, students could be told, "You have

witnessed what Bethany experienced in *All We Know of Heaven*. Recount her experiences in a poem, news account, sermon, or letter." Thus, the assignment would be as follows:

- *Role*—unseen witness
- *Audience*—varies according to form
- *Form*—poem, news account, sermon, letter
- *Topic*—novel—*All We Know of Heaven*

Other forms for RAFT include diaries, directions, encyclopedia entries, interviews, lyrics, memos, news reports, and poems. The possibilities are unlimited.

Literacy for Building Relationships

Although it is critical for adolescents to appreciate individual differences, it is also necessary to their development to build relationships with peers and others. In order to develop this feature of the PAL framework, cooperative learning in the classroom is important. Teachers report that in small groups it is often only one or two students who do the work and that small-group activities sometimes add to the already low self-esteem of weaker students, who often make only limited contributions to the group. The *Jigsaw* strategy (Aronson, Blaney, Stephin, Sikes, & Snapp, 1978) is one way to address both of these issues.

Jigsaw is a highly structured cooperative learning activity that provides each member of a small group with a specific role and builds interdependence among group members. In this cooperative learning strategy, student groups are somewhat like pieces of a puzzle, each with individual responsibilities, which when put together create a cohesive picture. It involves several steps, including several points at which students separate from their "home" groups to work with others. The steps to a Jigsaw activity are usually as follows:

1. The class is divided into small "home" groups. Each group has an assignment, which may be to read a text, such as a chapter of a book, or to conduct research on a topic that the class has chosen or the teacher has assigned.

2. The teacher has divided the text or research topic into small pieces, like a jigsaw puzzle. The chapter may be divided into sections, or the research topic into subtopics. Each person in a home group has one piece and a responsibility to learn/research that particular section or subtopic.

3. To ensure their success, students with the identical text section or topic meet in "expert" groups, sharing their comprehension of the text or findings from research. This meeting greatly benefits struggling readers

because they can check comprehension, learn the material in a supportive environment, and get reinforcement for their ideas.

4. The students return to their home groups to take turns sharing their knowledge. Each student in a home group teaches all its members about his or her area of expertise. Students know they will either be tested on the text material or have to present their research to the class, so motivation to listen to each other is high. In this meeting, group members may request clarifications or decide they need additional information and work together until they all feel they have expert knowledge on all parts of the text or subtopics.

5. The expert for each section/subtopic realizes how important it is to explain the material well. Group success is dependent on individual contributions and efforts and teamwork. An interdependence among students is established, and by students' successfully learning all of the parts, a satisfying whole results.

6. The activity concludes with something that can be graded, such as a test, a presentation, or a written product. Many teachers using Jigsaw give the same grade to each member of a home group, thereby reinforcing the importance of teamwork.

Literacy for Developing Autonomy and Identity

The previous sections included several very motivating small-group activities for developing each feature of the PAL framework. They contribute to adolescents' sense of belonging and promote positive relations among peers, but it is also important for adolescents to have a sense of personal identity and autonomy. This element of PAL, too, can be developed through particular classroom activities.

Rubrics, as discussed earlier, certainly offer the ongoing self-assessment that fosters autonomy and identity. Students can also develop autonomy and self-identity by using *self-paced learning*. Here the curriculum is set up in modules that students study at their own pace, and assessment occurs as they finish each module. The modules can be made up of written and taped material and laboratory or fieldwork, as appropriate. The modules must be well designed, with very clear directions, so that students can work independently for much of the time.

Learning Contracts

The use of learning contracts between students and teachers is another helpful means of developing students' independence. A learning contract is a written plan that describes what an individual will learn as a result of some specified learning activity. It promotes self-directed learning. As they create the contracts, students and teachers negotiate what they believe should be accomplished during a particular time period, such as a marking period. Teachers can identify resources for the project that each student can manage, thus further differentiating for students' needs. Usually negotiation includes specifying which accomplishments will result in what grades. Expectations are very clear when rubrics are used to define the criteria for each accomplishment. Both the content (such as energy-saving devices for the home) and the end product (such as a PowerPoint presentation) are negotiated parts of the contract. Setting a time line for completing each phase of the contract is also critically important, especially for struggling students. Thus, the components of the contract include (1) objectives, (2) project phases and dates for completion of each phase, (3) resources that may be used to complete the project, (4) evidence of accomplishment, and (5) criteria to be used to evaluate the accomplishment.

A contract has built-in accountability, with the student having primary responsibility for achieving the desired results. Although such contracts are sometimes used to modify behavior, the intent here is to use them to promote a positive, satisfying attitude toward learning and to build student confidence. Learning contracts can also have drawbacks. It can be time-consuming for teachers to follow through on each student's contract, and students can become very literal in their translation of expectations (which is why these should be very clearly defined through rubrics). Nevertheless, students often find it satisfying and rewarding to have more control of their learning and to be fully accountable for the end result.

Autonomy, self-direction, and identity can be further extended through classroom activities in which students have opportunities to make choices, including choice of projects, choice of books to read, choice of questions on exams, choices in how they spend their class time and how much they work independently and with others.

Ultimately, what teachers should see evolving through this increased development of autonomy and identity is the students' increased sense of self-efficacy. Bandura (1994) defines self-efficacy as "people's beliefs about their capabilities to produce designated levels of performance that exercise influence over events that affect their lives. Self-efficacy beliefs determine how people feel, think, motivate themselves and behave" (p. 1). Adolescents who have not been given enough independence to begin to recognize their developing capabilities to make decisions and take responsibility will not feel efficacious. Teachers can help enormously with students' maturation in this regard.

Students who have been persuaded that they lack capabilities tend to avoid challenging activities that cultivate potentialities, and they give up quickly in the face of difficulties. By restricting activities and undermining motivation, disbelief in one's capabilities creates its own behavioral validation.

Successful efficacy builders do more than convey positive appraisals. In addition to raising people's beliefs in their capabilities, they structure situations for them in ways that bring success and avoid placing people in situations prematurely where they are likely to fail often. They measure success in terms of self-improvement rather than by triumphs over others. (Bandura, 1994, p. 7)

Concluding Thoughts

We clearly know a great deal about learners' cognitive, social–emotional, and physical development. But what does this mean for literacy instruction? It means that we need to incorporate various literacy strategies that correspond with and enhance the developmental stages that adolescents are navigating. This will require us to use our own self-assessment, self-monitoring, and metacognitive skills to reassess our teaching goals. It will require us to use our own remembering, understanding, applying, analyzing, evaluating, and creating skills to develop lesson plans that are more closely tied to our revised teaching goals and the development of our adolescent learners. It will require our time. If we commit ourselves to these goals, however, we will be preparing our adolescents to be literate, critical adult thinkers.

References

Alvermann, D. (1991). The Discussion Web: A graphic aid for learning across the curriculum. *Reading Teacher, 45,* 92–99.

Anderson, G. L., & Irvine, P. (1993). Informing critical literacy with ethnography. In C. Lankshear & P. L. McLaren (Eds.), *Critical literacy: Politics, praxis and the postmodern* (pp. 81–104). Albany, NY: SUNY Press.

Anderson, L. W., Krathwohl, D. R., Airasian, P. W., Cruikshank, K. A., Mayer, R. E., & Pintrich, P. R. (Eds.). (2001). *A taxonomy for learning, teaching, and assessing: A revision of Bloom's taxonomy of educational objectives.* New York: Longman.

Aronson, E., Blaney, N., Stephin, C., Sikes, J., & Snapp, M. (1978). *The jigsaw classroom.* Beverly Hills, CA: Sage.

Baca, M. L. M. (n.d.). *Key concepts, main and organizing ideas and key questions in the social studies and sciences.* Retrieved January 9, 2007, from *bogota. soehd.csufresno.edu/mariob/ctet150syl/key.htm.*

Baillargeon, R., Graber, M., DeVos, J., & Black, J. (1990). Why do young infants fail to search for hidden objects? *Cognition, 36,* 255–284.

Bandura, A. (1986). *Social foundations of thought and action: A social cognitive approach.* Englewood Cliffs, NJ: Prentice-Hall.

Bandura, A. (1994). Self-efficacy. In V. S. Ramachaudran (Ed.), *Encyclopedia of human behavior* (Vol. 4, pp. 71–81). New York: Academic Press. (Reprinted in

Encyclopedia of mental health [pp. 74–81], by H. Friedman, Ed., 1998). San Diego: Academic Press. Retrieved January 17, 2007, from *www.des.emory. edu/mfp/BanEncy.html.*

Bandura, A. (1997). *Self-efficacy: The exercise of control.* New York: Freeman.

Berk, L. E. (1996). *Infants, children and adolescents* (2nd ed.). Boston: Allyn & Bacon.

Bloom, B. S. (1956). *Taxonomy of educational objectives: Book 1. Cognitive domain.* New York: Longman.

Brophy, J. E. (1998). *Motivating students to learn.* Boston: McGraw-Hill.

Case, R. (1997). The development of conceptual structures. In W. Damon, D. Kuhn, & R. S. Siegler (Eds.), *Handbook of child psychology* (Vol. 2, pp. 851–898). Hoboken, NJ: Wiley.

Cobb, N. (1995). *Adolescence.* Mountain View, CA: Mayfield.

Cordova, J. M., Klor de Alva, J. J., Nash, G. B., Ng, F., Salter, C. L., Wilson, L. E., et al. (1999). *Across the centuries.* Boston: Houghton Mifflin.

Cowan, G., & Cowan, E. (1980). *Writing.* New York: Wiley.

Downs, A. C. (1990). The social biological constructs of social competency. In T. P. Gullotta, G. R. Adams, & R. R. Montemayor (Eds.), *Advances in adolescent development: Vol. 3. Developing social competency in adolescence* (pp. 43– 94). Newbury Park, CA: Sage.

Duthie, J. (1986). The web: A powerful tool for teaching and evaluation of the expository essay. *History and Social Science Teacher, 21,* 232–236.

Dweck, C. S. (1986). Motivational processes affecting learning. *American Psychologist, 41,* 1040–1048.

Elkind, D. (1967). Egocentrism in adolescence. *Child Development, 38,* 1025– 1034.

Ellis, B., & Garber, J. (2000). Psychosocial antecedents of variation in girls pubertal timing: Maternal depression, stepfather presence, and marital and family stress. *Child Development, 71,* 485–501.

Erikson, E. H. (1968). *Identity, youth and crisis.* New York: Norton.

Freire, P. (1984). *Pedagogy of the oppressed.* New York: Continuum.

Graham, S. (1991). A review of attribution theory in achievement contexts. *Educational Psychology Review, 3,* 5–39.

Harter, S. M., Waters, P. L., & Whitesell, N. R. (1997). Lack of voice as a manifestation of false self behavior: The school setting as a stage upon which the drama of authenticity is enacted. *Educational Psychologist, 32,* 153–173.

Howe, N., & Strauss, W. (2000). *Millennials rising: The next great generation.* New York: Vantage Books.

Keene, E. O., & Zimmermann, S. (1997). *Mosaic of thought.* Portsmouth, NH: Heinemann.

Kohn, A. (1994). The truth about self-esteem. *Phi Delta Kappan.* Retrieved January 14, 2007, from *www.alfiekohn.org/teaching/tase.htm.*

Kohn, A. (1999). *The schools our children deserve.* Boston: Houghton Mifflin.

Lewis, J. (1996). *Academic literacy: Readings and strategies.* Boston: Houghton Mifflin.

Lewis, J. (Ed). (2004). *Learning in the classroom (Module 1).* Secondary Education Activity SEA Project. Newark, DE: International Reading Association/ USAID.

Lewis, J. (2007). *Academic literacy: Readings and strategies* (4th ed.). Boston: Houghton Mifflin.

Lewis, J., & Moorman, G. (Eds.). (2007). *Adolescent literary instruction: Policies and promising practices*. Newark, DE: International Reading Association.

Marcia, J. E. (1966). Development and validation of ego identity status. *Journal of Personality and Social Psychology, 3,* 551–558.

Marcia, J. E., Waterman, A. S., Matteson, D. R., Archer, S. L., & Orlofsky, J. L. (Eds.). (1993). *Ego identity: A handbook for psychosocial research*. New York: Springer-Verlag.

Maslow. A. W. (1954). *Motivation and personality*. New York: Harper & Row.

National Education Association. (2002). *2002 Survey on instructional materials*. Retrieved January 15, 2006, from *www.publishers.org/SchoolDiv/research/ research_02/NEA2002InstrMatReport.pdf*.

Novak, J. D. (1991). Clarify with concept maps: A tool for students and teachers alike. *Science Teacher, 58*(7), 45–49.

Ogbu, J. U. (1993). Differences in cultural frames of reference. *International Journal of Behavioral Development, 16,* 483–506.

Piaget, J., & Inhelder, B. (1969/2000). *The psychology of the child*. New York: Basic Books.

Rotter, J. (1954). *Social learning and clinical psychology*. Englewood Cliffs, NJ: Prentice-Hall.

Sabbagh, L. (2006). The teen brain hard at work. *Scientific American Mind, 17*(4), 20–25.

Schunk, D. (2000). *Learning theories* (3rd ed.). Upper Saddle River, NJ: Merrill/ Prentice-Hall

Seligman, M. E. P. (1972). Learned helplessness. *Annual Review of Medicine, 23,* 407–412.

Shor, I. (1992). *Empowering education: Critical teaching for social change*. Chicago: University of Chicago Press.

Siegal, J. M., Yancey, A. K., Aneschensel, C. S., & Schuler, R. (1999). Body image, perceived pubertal timing, and adolescent mental health. *Journal of Adolescent Health, 25,* 155–165.

Siegler, R. S. (1998). *Children's thinking*. Upper Saddle River, NJ: Prentice-Hall.

Skinner, B. F. (1953). *Science and human behavior*. New York: Macmillan.

Susman, E. J. (1997). Modeling developmental complexity in adolescents: Hormones and behavior in context. *Journal of Research on Adolescence, 7,* 283–306.

Today's school: A profile of the site-based public and private school market. (2002). Dayton, OH: Peter Li Education Group. Retrieved January 15, 2007, from *www.peterli.com/global/pdfs/TSSurvey2002.pdf*.

21st Century Schools. (2007). *Multiple literacies*. Retrieved January 9, 2007, from *www.21stcenturyschools.com/Multiple_Literacies.htm*.

Valmont, W. J. (2000, April). *Vignettes from literacy teachers*. Retrieved January 10, 2007, from *www.readingonline.org/electronic/elec_index.asp?HREF=valmont_ excerpt/index.html*. Excerpted from "What do teachers do in technology-rich classrooms?" In S. B. Wepner, W. J. Valmont, & R. Thurlow (Eds.), *Linking literacy and technology: A guide for K–8 classrooms* (p. 195). Newark, DE: International Reading Association.

VanderBos, G. R. (Ed.). (2007). *American Psychological Association dictionary of psychology.* Washington, DC: American Psychological Association.

Vandervanter, N. (1982). *Creating independence through student-owned strategies: A research-based, staff development program.* Dubuque, IA: Kendall/Hunt.

Vartanian, L. R. (2001). Adolescent reactions to hypothetical peer group conversations: Evidence for imaginary audience? *Adolescence, 36,* 347–393.

Vygotsky, L. S. (1978). *Mind in society.* Cambridge, MA: Harvard University Press.

White, H. (2003). *How to construct a concept nap.* Newark, DE: Department of Chemistry and Biochemistry, University of Delaware. Retrieved January 9, 2007, from *www.udel.edu/chem/white/teaching/ConceptMap.html.*

CHAPTER 2

Struggling Adolescent Readers

PROBLEMS AND POSSIBILITIES

Susan Lenski

Far too many students struggle with reading in middle schools and high schools. According to the National Assessment of Educational Progress (NAEP), more than 6 of every 10 adolescents in the United States cannot read grade-level texts proficiently (Perie, Grigg, & Donahue, 2005). Clearly, adolescent reading achievement is a problem.

At the same time that the number of struggling adolescent readers has been increasing, public attention has been captured by teachers who seemingly accomplish the impossible with low-achieving students. A fifth-grade teacher in a high-poverty area inspires his students to perform Shakespeare and writes about his successes in *Teach Like Your Hair's on Fire*. *The New York Times* writes, "Rafe Esquith is a genius and a saint. The American education system would do well to imitate him" (Esquith, 2007, back cover). High school underachievers find their voices by writing about their lives. They take the show on the road and have a movie made about their efforts (The Freedom Writers & Gruwell, 1999). These situations are true, but they are also extraordinary. Reality for most teachers is far different.

In a typical school, at least half of the students have trouble reading, although numbers vary greatly by school, district, and state. In some states, for instance, just over half of the students can be classified as struggling readers. In other states, more than 75% of students need help with reading

(Snow & Biancarosa, 2003). In most classrooms and in most schools the majority of students cannot read the textbooks teachers assign, cannot complete their homework without assistance, and do not read for pleasure.

Can anything be done for struggling adolescent readers? The future appears to be brightening, and the days of ignoring struggling readers are in the past. Before examining the possibilities, though, it is important to understand the severity of the problem. This chapter describes the problem of adolescent reading by providing information about student achievement from a national perspective and then explains some of the root causes for the enormous numbers of struggling readers in middle and high schools. This explanation is followed by a discussion of frameworks for adolescent literacy that have been developed in the past decade. The changes in classroom instruction that show promise of making a difference for struggling readers are then presented. The chapter concludes by making the case that changing the lives of struggling adolescent readers cannot be accomplished on a wide-scale basis without careful attention and systemic change. Concrete examples to invigorate secondary literacy programs, improve classroom instruction, and increase the achievement of struggling adolescent readers are detailed in other chapters of this book.

What Is a "Struggling Adolescent Reader"?

Students who have difficulty reading in schools are often labeled "struggling readers." The term *struggling readers* is an artifact of schooling and can be defined as students who have experienced difficulty with school-based reading (Franzak, 2006). It is important to note that struggling readers have difficulty with *school* reading. The values of school are embedded within the term. Franzak writes, "Because marginalized adolescents are initially identified as such within the school context, the underlying structure and values of school literacy are built into the definitions of struggling readers" (p. 219). An adolescent labeled a struggling reader in school may not necessarily have the same sort of reading problems when reading outside of school. As Dressman and his colleagues (2006) learned when conducting case studies of adolescents' reading identities, some "so-called struggling readers, when given the opportunity, can find their own reasons for becoming literate, reasons that go beyond reading to acquire school knowledge of academically sanctioned texts" (p. 150). For the purposes of this book, however, we discuss struggling readers in the context of their achievement with academic reading, while at the same time recognizing that many students are able to read out-of-school texts proficiently.

Adolescent literacy experts have used a variety or terms to label students who have trouble reading. When students are younger, for example, they are considered "at risk" for school failure, a term derived from the U.S. Department of Education report, *A Nation at Risk* (National Commission on Excellence in Education, 1983). The term *at risk* was borrowed from the insurance industry to describe students who have a high probability of becoming a "loss" with respect to school success (Mueller, 2001). The term *at risk* does not seem to fit secondary students who are at risk of failure; they are already exhibiting low achievement. Other terms that have been used for middle and high school students who have difficulty reading are *aliterate, alienated, marginalized, reluctant,* and *resistant* (Lenters, 2006). Mueller (2001), who studied struggling readers in her classroom, calls them "lifers" as a way of portraying students who have had problems in reading for most of their lives. In this book, however, we have chosen to call students who have difficulty reading in school *struggling readers*.

How Many Adolescents Are Struggling Readers?

One of the best overall measures of reading in the United States is the NAEP. The NAEP is a nationally representative assessment of what students in grades 4, 8, and 12 know and can do in various subject areas, including reading. Scores are categorized as Basic, Proficient, and Advanced. According to the NAEP policy definitions, the Basic level represents a partial mastery of prerequisite knowledge and skills that are fundamental for proficient work. The Proficient level represents solid academic performance, and the Advanced level represents superior performance (*www.nces.ed.gov/nationsreportcard*).

The majority of today's middle and high school students cannot read at the Proficient level. According to 2005 NAEP data, 29% of the nation's eighth graders scored below Basic and another 42% scored at the Basic level (Perie et al., 2005). Only 29% of the eighth graders scored at the Proficient and Advanced levels. (See Figure 2.1.) Using the information on scoring as a gauge, that means that up to 71% of eighth-grade students may be considered struggling readers, because students scoring at the Basic level can read grade appropriate texts but are unable to read them with the depth considered necessary for academic learning.

	Below basic	Basic	Proficient	Advanced
8th grade	29	42	26	3
12th grade	27	38	30	5

FIGURE 2.1. 2005 NAEP reading scores: Percentages by grade level. Data from U.S. Department of Education. (2005). *www.nces.ed.gov/nationsreportcart/*.

The number of students who can be considered struggling readers at twelfth grade is almost as large. According to the 2005 data, 27% of twelfth graders read below Basic, 38% scored at Basic, 30% scored at the Proficient level, and 5% scored at the Advanced level. That means that 65% of the students who reach twelfth grade cannot read well enough to be considered Proficient readers. On the basis of these scores, it appears that more students at twelfth grade read better than do eighth-grade students. That is not necessarily true. The NAEP data at the twelfth-grade level may not accurately reflect the number of students who are struggling readers in high school because they do not include those students who have left the system. More than 3,000 students drop out of high school every day (Biancarosa & Snow, 2004). It is highly likely that the majority of students who do not graduate from high school read at or below the Basic level. Therefore, it is probably more realistic to consider the number of struggling readers in high school to be higher than 65%.

Why Are There So Many Struggling Readers?

There are a number of reasons why so many middle and high school students struggle with reading. If we think about the students of one eighth-grade teacher in a school with the demographics of the NAEP data just cited, this is what we would find. Ms. Mohr teaches at Normal Township Middle School. She teaches a total of 150 different students in three language arts and two social studies classes. According to the national averages, 105 of these students would be able to read the textbooks with only superficial comprehension. Ms. Mohr would have 91 white, 24 black, 24 Hispanic, 9 Asian/Pacific Islander, and 2 Native American/Alaskan Native students. Of the 150 students, 54 would be poor enough to qualify for free/reduced-price lunches. Students would also bring to the classroom their different sociocultural backgrounds, prior experiences with learning, and differing abilities.

There would be a variety of different reasons why the 105 struggling readers in Ms. Mohr's classes have difficulty reading. Some of the students would come from backgrounds not consistent with the school culture or would speak languages other than English. Some would exhibit identified learning problems and may have attended special education or remedial reading classes during their elementary school years. Other struggling readers may have simply been unlucky and had teachers who did not know how to teach reading effectively. Some struggling readers in eighth grade may have done well in elementary school, but when faced with more complex academic texts, began having difficulty in reading. Many of Ms. Mohr's struggling readers may have simply lost their motivation to learn upon reaching early adolescence, and some may have "slipped through the cracks." Each of the reasons that explain why the students failed to learn to read are discussed in the section that follows.

Students from Diverse Backgrounds

In some areas of the United States, middle and high schools have many students from diverse cultures, backgrounds, and languages. Ms. Mohr has 59 students from diverse backgrounds; some teachers have classes in which almost all of their students do not know English. Ms. Mohr speaks some Spanish, which helps her relate to the Spanish-speaking students and parents, but she also has students who speak Russian, Hmong, Arabic, Samoli, Japanese, and Chinese. Ms. Mohr is currently learning the basic words in each language, but because they have different alphabets, she is not making much progress.

Ms. Mohr's makeup of students from diverse backgrounds is typical of eighth grade, but high schools tend to have more English language learners (ELLs) than do elementary schools. Many families wait to emigrate until their youngest children are in school and their oldest children are out of elementary school (Igoa, 1995). A great many students who are learning to speak English also struggle with reading grade-level material. This makes sense. If a student is not proficient in a language, it is extremely difficult to read academic texts that are written at middle and high school levels. In addition, many teachers assume that students will not be able to comprehend academic ideas until they are fluent in English (García & Pearson, 1991). Many secondary teachers, therefore, instruct ELLs only on low-level reading strategies such as accessing background knowledge and rereading (Padrón, 1998). Although these strategies are valuable, ELLs also need to learn more advanced reading and thinking strategies in order to make accelerated gains in reading (Lenski & Ehlers-Zavala, 2004).

Students with Special Learning Needs

Ms. Mohr has 20 students who were identified as learning disabled in elementary school and have received instruction in special education classes. Some of these students have been in special education classes for 6 years, yet they still have difficulty in reading. Although the students have been given extra reading instruction, remedial reading classes have typically not been successful (Allington, 2002). Some researchers theorize that students who have spent years in remedial classes have spent a great deal of time learning reading skills, yet have not spent enough time reading connected texts, possibly because students in special education classes have not spent much time actually reading (Allington & McGill-Franzen, 1989; Kennedy, Birman, & Demaline, 1986) and instruction was focused on acquiring decontextualized reading skills rather than building comprehension (Ivey &

Fisher, 2006). The instruction in remedial reading classes in which students have spent many years is often somewhat limited to the teaching of literal recall and skills that do not promote students' learning how to become strategic readers. This kind of instruction has been tied to slowing rather than accelerating reading progress (Johnston & Allington, 1991). As a result, students who have learning disabilities do not do well in secondary schools, as compared with their peers without disabilities (Fisher, Schumaker, & Deshler, 2002).

Prior Instruction in Reading

Another reason for the large number of struggling adolescent readers is that they have not had reading and writing strategies demonstrated effectively (Cambourne, 2001), and this is the case for several of Ms. Mohr's students. Some teachers are simply better than others at teaching reading. In a study concerning effective language arts teachers, Langer (2002, 2004) found that student achievement was higher when teachers used a combination of explicit and applied instruction, even in schools in which the rate of poverty was high. Other teachers may be effective as elementary teachers, but they do not know what strategies to use when teaching academic texts (Spor & Schneider, 1999). Some teachers have the mistaken belief that students learn to read in the primary grades and then they read to learn. This notion comes from the work of Jeanne Chall (1983), who outlined developmental stages of reading. Recent educational thought, however, has suggested that adolescent readers are "learning to read to learn" (Snow & Biancarosa, 2003). The truth is that as students progress through the grades, they encounter more complex texts with higher reading levels. These readers must be given the skills and strategies needed to comprehend and analyze these more complex texts through explicit instruction.

Text Difficulty

Some struggling adolescent readers are able to read grade-level material in elementary school, but by middle school find academic reading difficult (Guthrie & Davis, 2003). This is true for several students in Ms. Mohr's classes, who exhibited no problem with reading in fourth and fifth grades, but by sixth grade, began having problems reading texts. This is not surprising, because as Snow and Biancarosa (2003) point out, "As content demands increase, literacy demands also increase: students are expected to read and write across a wide variety of disciplines, genres, and materials with increasing skill, flexibility, and insight" (p. 5). Middle and high school students are expected to read texts that have heavy concept loads and much technical vocabulary about topics that are new to the students. Students not only must read these difficult texts with comprehension for initial understanding, but must also be able to think about meaning in such a way as to make inferences, draw conclusions, and acquire new learning (Torgesen et al., 2007). Yet too few students have experiences reading expository texts at this level, because elementary teachers spend much more time teaching fictional stories than teaching students how to read informational texts (Duke, 2000).

In some classes teachers also initiate students into the ways of reading and thinking in the various disciplines; they teach students to read like scientists, historians, and poets (Franzak, 2006). This type of thinking requires students to have a deep understanding of both the texts and the traditions of the different disciplines. According to the National Association of State Boards of Education (2006), "To meet the performance standards across content areas, students need to transact meaning from disciplines that have unique organizational structures and concepts. Students are expected to locate and paraphrase information found in lengthy, complex passages in texts dealing with literature, social studies, science, and math" (p. 12). Students who are not able to read materials of this complexity have trouble succeeding in secondary schools.

Motivation to Read

Lack of motivation to read is one of the most frequent contributors to a struggling reader's lack of achievement. Many of Ms. Mohr's students, especially the boys, began to lose interest in reading when they reached middle school (see Brozo, 2002). According to Pitcher and her colleagues (2007), "Motivation to read is a complex construct that influences readers' choices of reading material, their willingness to engage in reading, and thus their ultimate competence in reading, especially related to academic reading tasks" (p. 379). Motivation is often linked to students' self-efficacy, or their belief in their own ability (Bandura, 1986). According to a research study conducted by Long, Monoi, Harper, Knoblauch, and Murphy (2007), when learning goals and self-efficacy are encouraged to grow, interest in learning and achievement is more likely.

Students with little motivation to read are often disengaged from learning and avoid reading (Beers, 2003). Because these students do not spend time reading, their progress tends to be slower than that of students who do read (Stanovich, 1986). The act of avoiding reading sets the stage for further reading failure, which can result in learned helplessness (Johnston & Winograd, 1985). Learned helplessness occurs when students believe that nothing they can do will help them improve their learning. In the case of adolescents, their past failures in reading have taught them that they cannot succeed no matter how hard they try. Therefore, they lose the motivation to try to read difficult texts. Learned helplessness often occurs when students have entered a negative spiral: They attribute success to luck and failure to themselves; they feel inferior, have low self-esteem and decreased motivation, and eventually feel helpless. Students from diverse minority groups can be especially susceptible to feelings of learned helplessness (Berk, 2001).

The Effects of Poverty

An additional reason for the large number of struggling adolescent readers is that at least one-half of the students in the nation have lived at or near the poverty level by the time they are 15 years old (Taylor, 1996). This means that for Ms. Mohr's 150 students, 75 of them have lived in poverty at some point in their lives, and 54 of them currently are considered poor. The challenges of poverty for these 54 students can prevent many of them from learning to their full capabilities. Some students are homeless—living in shelters, in cars, with relatives, or on the streets. Other students work in part-time jobs that keep them from studying and participating in school events. Still other students have to miss school in order to take care of family members or to act as translators for parents. These and other social factors that go with living in poverty influence students' academic progress (Nichols & Good, 2004).

A Culture of Neglect

What happens to the 105 of Ms. Mohr's students who have difficulty in reading in eighth grade? Even though Ms. Mohr is an excellent teacher who truly cares about her students, some "slip through the cracks." In *The Road to Whatever: Middle-Class Culture and the Crisis of Adolescence*, Currie (2004) writes, "We live in a culture that makes it all too easy for adolescents to define themselves as failures, losers, fundamentally flawed, especially those who do not 'fit' well in their families, schools, and communities—who are out of sync with our dominant conceptions of what adolescents *should* be" (p. 39). He suggests that the United States' culture encourages an inversion of responsibility—adolescents are responsible for their own well-being without adult help. His theory is that the current culture in society and in schools does not allow adolescents to make mistakes without paying a stiff penalty. Currie describes the experiences of students who were often enthusiastic about entering high school, but once they were there and found that their strengths were ignored and any acts of rebellion were magnified, they stopped trying. He describes schools as organizations that classify students according to how well they meet, or do not meet, conventional standards of performance. For students who do not fit the norm, schools do not actively seek to build capacity. In some cases, then, the current structure of schooling does little to nurture struggling adolescent readers.

Policy Documents That Impact Struggling Readers

Struggling adolescent readers have been given increasing amounts of visibility over the past decade. The difficulties that struggling readers face have been recognized, but solutions to their problems are complex. There are indeed no "quick fixes" for struggling readers (Allington & Walmsley, 1995). The hard work of determining how adolescents can achieve higher literacy levels has been the focus of two important organizations: the International Reading Association (IRA) and the Alliance for Excellent Education. Two policy documents and a recent book have been published that have laid the foundation for methods, programs, and initiatives that address the needs of struggling readers and have been the impetus for a renewed emphasis on adolescent literacy.

IRA Position on Adolescent Literacy

In 1997, the IRA brought together adolescent literacy experts to form a Commission on Adolescent Literacy. The Commission developed a position statement delineating what adolescents "deserve" in order to become literate adults (see Figure 2.2). Among its recommendations, the Commission wrote that adolescents deserve instruction that builds both the skill and the desire to read increasingly complex material, that adolescents need well-developed repertoires of reading comprehension strategies, and that adolescents deserve expert teachers who model and provide explicit instruction in reading comprehension across the curriculum (Moore, Bean, Birdyshaw, & Rycik, 1999). The Commission on Adolescent Literacy was at the forefront of making visible the needs of readers in secondary schools by outlining what *should be occurring in middle and high schools.*

Principled Practices

The IRA Commission continued its work by convening a group of adolescent literacy educators, who reviewed the research on adolescent literacy, expert opinions, and observations of highly regarded teachers. The result of this examination is a framework for instruction and policy that details what Sturtevant and her colleagues (2006) have called principled practices. Principled practices are concepts the authors adapted from Smagorinsky's (2002) work. The result is a framework including eight practices that the authors believe should be used for designing adolescent literacy programs. Figure 2.3 lists the eight principled practices.

1. Adolescents deserve access to a wide variety of reading material that they can and want to read.
2. Adolescents deserve instruction that builds both the skill and desire to read increasingly complex materials.
3. Adolescents deserve assessment that shows them their strengths as well as their needs and that guides their teachers to design instruction that will best help them grow as readers.
4. Adolescents deserve expert teachers who model and provide explicit instruction in teaching comprehension and study strategies across the curriculum.
5. Adolescents deserve reading specialists who assist individual students having difficulty learning how to read.
6. Adolescents deserve teachers who understand the complexities of individual adolescent readers, respect their differences, and respond to their characteristics.
7. Adolescents deserve homes, communities, and a nation that will support their efforts to achieve advanced levels of literacy and provide the support necessary for them to succeed.

FIGURE 2.2. Position statement from the International Reading Association. From Moore, D. W., Bean, T. W., Birdyshaw, D., & Rycik, J. A. (1999). Adolescent literacy: A position statement. *Journal of Adolescent and Adult Literacy, 43*(1), 97–112. Reprinted with permission of the International Reading Association.

Principles related to contexts for learning:
1. Adolescents need opportunities to participate in active learning environments that offer clear and facilitative literacy instruction.
2. Adolescents need opportunities to participate in respectful environments characterized by high expectations, trust, and care.

Principles related to instructional practices:
3. Adolescents need opportunities to engage with print and nonprint texts for a variety of purposes.
4. Adolescents need opportunities to generate and express rich understanding of ideas and concepts.
5. Adolescents need opportunities to demonstrate enthusiasm for reading and learning.
6. Adolescents need opportunities to assess their literacy and learning competencies and direct their future growth.

Principles related to connections between literacy in and out of school:
7. Adolescents need opportunities to connect reading with their lives and their learning inside and outside of school.
8. Adolescents need opportunities to develop critical perspectives toward what they read, view, and hear.

FIGURE 2.3. Principled practices for adolescent literacy. Reprinted with permission from Sturtevant, E. G., Boyd, F. B., Brozo, W. G., Hinchman, K. A., Moore, D. A., & Alvermann, D. E. (2006). *Principled practices for adolescent literacy: A framework for adolescent literacy.* Mahwah, NJ: Erlbaum.

Reading Next

The Alliance for Excellent Education viewed adolescent literacy from a different perspective and reported its recommendations in *Reading Next: A Vision for Action and Research in Middle and High School Literacy* (Biancrosa & Snow, 2004). This report makes suggestions for middle and high school educators that fall into two main topics with several subtopics. The first topic is instructional improvements, and it includes the subtopics of direct, explicit comprehension instruction; effective instructional principles embedded in content; motivation and self-directed learning; and ongoing formative assessment of students. The second main topic is infrastructure improvements, which includes such ideas as extended time for literacy, program evaluation, leadership, and a comprehensive and coordinated literacy program. (See Figure 2.4.) Implementing all 15 of these recommendations can overwhelm school personnel, but Biancarosa and Snow (2004) state that implementing only a few of the principles will probably not lead to much improvement. Instead, they recommend that educators use the combination of principles that best fits their situation as the foundation for improvement in literacy.

Changing Perspectives about Classroom Instruction and School Programs

Policy documents that address literacy in middle and high school have been instrumental in changing the direction of adolescent literacy. Most important, experts have emphasized the need for the continued instruction of literacy at the secondary level (Moje, Young, Readance, & Moore, 2000). Currently, three perspectives about classroom instruction and school programs could result in a major shift regarding struggling adolescent readers. First, there is a renewed interest in students as individuals. This perspective sets the stage for new types of assessments and instruction for secondary students. A second change is in how literacy is embedded in the disciplines. The decades of content area reading instruction have not been successful, and a different way of using literacy in the disciplines has been conceptualized. Third, intervention programs for struggling adolescent readers are being developed and examined to reach those students who read far below grade level.

A Renewed Focus on Individual Students

Each of Ms. Mohr's 150 students has his or her own personality, learning background, interests, dreams, and fears. What cannot be captured in these words are the very personal dimensions of teaching. In their work with

Instructional Improvements
 1. **Direct, explicit comprehension instruction,** which is instruction in the
    strategies and processes that proficient readers use to understand what
    they read, including summarizing, keeping track of one's own
    understanding, and a host of other practices.
 2. **Effective instructional principles embedded in content,** including
    language arts teachers using content-area texts and content-area teachers
    providing instruction and practice in reading and writing skills specific to
    their subject areas.
 3. **Motivation and self-directed learning,** which includes building motivation
    to read and learn and providing students with the instruction and supports
    needed for independent learning tasks they will face after graduation.
 4. **Text-based collaborative learning,** which involves students interacting
    with one another around a variety of texts.
 5. **Strategic tutoring,** which provides students with intense individualized
    reading, writing, and content instruction as needed.
 6. **Diverse texts,** which are texts at a variety of difficulty levels and on a
    variety of topics.
 7. **Intensive writing,** including instruction connected to the kinds of writing
    tasks students will have to perform well into high school and beyond.
 8. **A technology component,** which includes technology as a tool for and a
    topic of literacy instruction.
 9. **Ongoing formative assessment of students,** which is informal, often
    daily assessment of how students are progressing under current
    instructional practices.

Infrastructure Improvements
10. **Extended time for literacy,** which includes approximately 2–4 hours of
    literary instruction and practice that takes place in language areas and
    content-area classes.
11. **Professional development** that is both long-term and ongoing.
12. **Ongoing summative assessment** of students and programs, which is
    more formal and provides data that are reported for accountability and
    research purposes.
13. **Teacher teams,** which are interdisciplinary teams that meet regularly to
    discuss students and align instruction.
14. **Leadership,** which can come from principals and teachers who have a
    solid understanding of how to teach reading and writing to the full array of
    students present in schools.
15. **A comprehensive and coordinated literacy program,** which is
    interdisciplinary and interdepartmental and may even coordinate with out-
    of-school organizations and the local community.

FIGURE 2.4. Reading next principles. Reprinted with permission from Biancarosa,
G., & Snow, C. (2004). *Reading Next: A vision for action and research in middle
and high school literacy.* Washington, DC: Alliance for Excellent Education.

struggling adolescent readers, Jackson and Cooper (2007) found that building relationships with students and honoring them as individuals play a crucial role in students' achievement. Many teachers agree with this viewpoint. In a study of 386 high school teachers, 90% of the teachers believed that addressing academic differences was important (Hoostein, 1998, cited in Tomlinson, 2004).

The trend is toward focusing on students as individuals; such a focus is vitally important when developing instruction for struggling readers. According to Tomlinson (2004), the one-size-fits-all classrooms of the past have failed many students. As mentioned earlier in this chapter, Ms. Mohr's classroom has 105 struggling readers, but each of these students has difficulty reading for one or more different reasons. Many students have trouble with the skill of reading and need an intervention program. Many others are resistant readers, students who are not interested in school reading (Lenters, 2006). Students who resist reading and do not read in middle school can fall behind to such an extent that they cannot read high school texts (Bintz, 1993). Still other students are interested in popular culture or are facile with the literacies of technology and can be reached through nonprint reading (Alvermann & Rush, 2004).

There are many reasons why students struggle with reading, and when teachers look at students as individuals, they can more easily determine what can reach the students. Instruction for all students, but especially for struggling readers, should identify students' needs and interests, tailor instruction to their needs, teach skills in the context of authentic texts, and provide opportunities for choice (Primeaux, 2000). In later chapters of this book, many approaches are suggested for struggling readers. It is up to the wise teacher to determine which idea, strategy, or approach meets the needs of the students rather than assuming that all adolescents who struggle with reading need a single approach.

A Changing Perspective on Reading in the Disciplines

Ms. Mohr is like many of her colleagues; she has an undergraduate degree in English, a minor in social studies, and a certificate to teach English and social studies for grades 6–12. During her teaching training, she had one class devoted to teaching reading, in which she heard the mantra, "Every teacher is a teacher of reading." This confused Ms. Mohr. What she knew best were the subjects of English and social studies; she really did not see herself as a teacher of reading. When she began graduate school, however, Ms. Mohr learned how to embed reading and learning strategies in her instruction, and that made perfect sense to her.

The example of Ms. Mohr illustrates how the role of middle and high school teachers is beginning to change with respect to teaching reading.

The well-known saying, "Every teacher a teacher of reading" was coined by William S. Gray in 1937 and has been a popular foundational belief in content-area reading for decades. Recently, however, educators have begun to describe the role of middle and high school teachers in different ways. Shanahan (2004) writes, "Let's avoid the fatuous rhetoric that 'all teachers are teachers of reading' " (p. 44). He goes on to say that content teachers must be committed to teaching their subject matter and that each discipline has its own specialized reading demands.

Torgesen and his colleagues (2007) wrote, "Our current understanding of reading growth indicates that students must continue to learn many new things, and acquire many additional skills, in order to maintain reading proficiency as they move from elementary to middle and high school. If they do not acquire the new skills specific to reading after the initial period of learning to read, they will not leave high school as proficient readers" (p. 4). In a recent study on effective adolescent literacy teachers, Paris and Block (2007) found that teachers who were deemed effective by their administrators and peers were able to embed literacy in their teaching by using critical thinking skills, asking questions, and allowing students to become independent learners. These teachers use reading and learning strategies to help students learn their content, and thus students experience using reading to make sense of complex and varied texts. Lenski, Johns, Wham, and Caskey (2007) suggest that content-area teachers can use reading as one way to help students learn content, but that reading is only one of the many different tools students need to learn.

A Renewed Emphasis on Intervention Programs

Many of Ms. Mohr's eighth-grade students can read only materials written at a third-grade reading level. Using the previously cited NAEP data, we know that 44 of Ms. Mohr's 150 students could benefit from a targeted intervention program. Although all of Ms. Mohr's students can benefit from curriculum-embedded instruction, some students also need to accelerate their reading progress. Additional instruction is necessary for these students to catch up to their peers. According to Shanahan (2004), struggling readers may need 10 additional hours per week in instruction in the foundational components of reading, such as fluency, word knowledge, and comprehension. These intervention programs can be delivered as after-school programs, elective reading classes during the school day, summer academies, weekend seminars, and so on.

There is no agreement in the field about the best intervention models for struggling readers. Snow and Biancarosa (2003) describe 12 of the programs that have the "pedagogically sound approach of scaffolding child learning by providing and gradually withdrawing support to encourage eventual mastery of a taught strategy or skill" (p. 12). Among the programs they describe are the following:

- Short-term, intensive approaches that focus on decoding, fluency, and vocabulary (Boys Town Reading Curriculum)
- Approaches that address literacy needs in the academic disciplines (Concept-Oriented Reading Instruction, Guided Inquiry Supporting Multiple Literacies, Reading Apprenticeship)
- Approaches that focus on students' questioning during reading (Collaborative Reasoning, Reciprocal Teaching, Questioning the Author)
- Computer-assisted reading workshop programs (READ 180)
- Curricular frameworks (Scaffolded Reading Experience)
- Strategy instruction (Strategic Instruction Model, Transactional Strategies Instruction)

Striving Readers Program

The intervention programs for secondary students need more research to determine in what ways they can really make a difference in students' literacy. In response to this need, the U.S. Department of Education created the Striving Readers Program to investigate the programs that work best with middle and high school students who read below grade level. According to its description, "Striving Readers supports the implementation and evaluation of research-based interventions for struggling middle and high school readers in Title I eligible schools that are at risk of not meeting or are not meeting adequate yearly progress (AYP) requirements under the No Child Left Behind Act, or that have significant percentages or numbers of students reading below grade level, or both" (*www.ed.gov/programs/ strivingreaders/index.html*). The goals of the Striving Readers program as described at the website are to:

- Raise student achievement in middle and high schools by improving the literacy skills of struggling adolescent readers, and
- Help build a strong, scientific research base around specific strategies that improve adolescent literacy skills.

Eight Striving Readers awards were given in 2005/2006, each with the following key components: (1) supplemental literacy interventions targeted to students who are reading significantly below grade level, (2) cross-disciplinary strategies for improving students' literacy, which may include professional development for subject matter teachers and use of research-based reading and comprehension strategies in classrooms across subject areas, and (3) a strong experimental evaluation component. For example, Portland Public Schools (PPS) in Oregon was one of the eight school districts to receive a Striving Readers grant in 2005/2006. PPS's project provides research-based and targeted interventions to more than 1,700 struggling readers in grades 6–10 and schoolwide strategies for embedding literacy in all content areas to more than 6,000 students. Portland is partnering with the University of Kansas Center for Research on Learning to implement the Strategic Instruction Model (SIM), with Portland State University for literacy professional development, and with RMC Research to conduct an independent and experimental evaluation of the Striving Readers project.

At the time of the publication of this book, all of the initial Striving Readers projects were in the midst of their 5-year awards, so no results from the projects have yet been reported. Locations of other funded Striving Readers projects and updates on programs and grant awards can be found at *www.ed.gov/programs/strivingreaders/index.html.*

Guidelines for Selecting Intervention Programs

Because there are such a wide variety of intervention programs for struggling adolescent readers, school personnel may have difficulty in selecting the program that best fits their students. Information from Striving Readers projects will eventually provide relevant data to guide educators in making these decisions. However, school personnel also need to look at intervention programs from a wider perspective and to make sure the intervention program they select fits their purposes. As educators consider which intervention is best, they should consider the following questions:

- What are our overarching beliefs about literacy?
- What are the primary literacy needs of the majority of struggling readers (i.e., motivation, decoding, and so on)? What data did we use to arrive at these decisions?
- How are students currently being assessed in literacy? Do the scores accurately reflect students' literacy needs? Do we need more information, such as provided by diagnostic tests? How are assessment data already informing instruction?
- How does the intervention program supplement current classroom instruction in literacy? Is the current intervention program engaging for students?
- How will this intervention make a difference in students' overall literacy progress? How will the intervention program help students become more successful in their academic classes?
- Does the school or district have personnel who are knowledgeable about literacy instruction and can supervise the program?

As school personnel answer these critical questions, they must also remember that intervention programs need to be a supplemental part of an overall school literacy strategy that provides students with significant opportunities to read and that has literacy instruction embedded in academic classes (Allington, 2007). According to Fisher and Ivey (2006), "Without these two nonnegotiable features of the learning environment—access to high-quality, readable texts and instruction in strategies to read and write across the school day—it is doubtful that a specific, limited intervention will make much of a difference" (p. 181). Intervention programs alone will not address the needs of struggling middle and high school readers.

Conclusions

Although individual teachers can inspire their students to great achievements, the needs of the nation's huge number of struggling adolescent readers call for systemic change. According to the National Association of State Boards of Education (2006), "Low levels of adolescent literacy is not a problem that can be solved in isolation with some extra tutoring or supplemental programs for those unable to read well—it will take a concerted statewide policy and program effort that reaches deep into districts and the instructional practices of teachers across the curriculum" (p. 17). Change must occur at the classroom level, as well as at the school, district, and state levels.

As policy and program changes slowly make their way into classrooms, Ms. Mohr is still faced with 105 students who cannot read well enough to comprehend the texts she uses in her classroom. To address the needs of her struggling readers, Ms. Mohr needs to remember that although counting on miracles is seductive, they don't just happen. She can, however, take two actions that can make a difference. Ms. Mohr can begin to incorporate the new perspectives of adolescent literacy that were outlined in this chapter so that she updates her philosophy of teaching struggling readers, and she can immediately try some of the practical ideas described in the following chapters of this book. It is only through both a change in perspective and a change in practice that Ms. Mohr can make a sustained difference in the lives of the struggling readers in her classroom.

References

Allington, R. L. (2002). Research on reading/learning disability interventions. In A. E. Farstrup & S. J. Samuels (Eds.), *What research has to say about reading instruction* (pp. 261–290). Newark, DE: International Reading Association.

Allington, R. L. (2007). Intervention all day long: New hope for struggling readers. *Voices from the Middle*, *14*(4), 7–14.

Allington, R. L., & McGill-Franzen, A. (1989). What's special about special programs for children who find reading difficult? *Journal of Reading Behavior*, *26*, 1–21.

Allington, R. L., & Walmsley, S. A. (1995). *No quick fix: Rethinking literacy programs in America's elementary schools*. New York: Teachers College Press.

Alvermann, D. E., & Rush, L. S. (2004). Literacy intervention programs at the middle and high school levels. In T. L. Jetton & J. A. Dole (Eds.), *Adolescent literacy research and practice* (pp. 210–227). New York: Guilford Press.

Bandura, A. (1986). *Social foundation of thought and action: A social cognitive theory*. Upper Saddle River, NJ: Prentice-Hall.

Beers, K. (2003). *When kids can't read: What teachers can do*. Portsmouth, NH: Heinemann.

Berk, L. E. (2001). *Infants, children, and adolescents* (3rd ed.). Boston: Allyn & Bacon.

Biancarosa, G., & Snow, C. (2004). *Reading Next: A vision for action and research in middle and high school literacy*. Washington, DC: Alliance for Excellent Education.

Bintz, W. P. (1993). Resistant readers in secondary education: Some insights and implications. *Journal of Reading*, *36*, 604–615.

Brozo, W. G. (2002). *To be a boy, to be a reader*. Newark, DE: International Reading Association.

Cambourne, B. (2001). Why do some students fail to learn to read? Ockham's razor and the conditions of learning. *Reading Teacher*, *54*, 784–786.

Chall, J. S. (1983). *Stages of reading development*. New York: McGraw-Hill.

Currie, E. (2004). *The road to whatever: Middle-class culture and the crisis of adolescence*. New York: Metropolitan Books.

Dressman, M., O'Brien, D., Rogers, T., Ivey, G., Wilder, P., Alvermann, D., et al. (2006). Problematizing adolescent literacies: Four instances, multiple perspectives. In J. V. Hoffman, D. L. Schallert, C. M. Fairbanks, J. Worthy, & B. Maloch (Eds.), *National Reading Conference yearbook 55* (pp. 141–154). Oak Creek, WI: National Reading Conference.

Duke, N. (2000). 3.6 minutes per day: The scarcity of informational texts in first grade. *Reading Research Quarterly*, *31*, 62–88.

Esquith, R. (2007). *Teach like your hair's on fire: The methods and madness inside room 56*. New York: Viking.

Fisher, D., & Ivey, G. (2006). Evaluating the interventions for struggling adolescent readers. *Journal of Adolescent and Adult Literacy*, *50*, 180–189.

Fisher, J., Schumaker, J. B., & Deshler, D. D. (2002). Improving reading comprehension of at-risk adolescents. In C. C. Block & M. Pressley (Eds.), *Comprehension instruction: Research-based practices* (pp. 351–364). New York: Guilford Press.

Franzak, J. K. (2006). Zoom: A review of the literature on marginalized adolescent readers, literacy theory, and policy implications. *Review of Educational Research*, *76*(2), 209–248.

The Freedom Writers & Gruwell, E. (1999). *The Freedom Writers diary: How a teacher and 150 teens used writing to change themselves and the world around them.* New York: Broadway Books.

García, G. E., & Pearson, P. D. (1991). Modifying reading instruction to maximize its effectiveness for *all* students. In M. S. Knapp & P. M. Shields (Eds.), *Better schooling for the children of poverty: Alternatives to conventional wisdom* (pp. 31–60). Berkeley, CA: McCutchan.

Gray, W. S. (1937). The nature and organization of basic instruction in reading. In G. M. Whipple (Ed.), *The teaching of reading: A second report. 36th Yearbook of the National Society for the Study of Education, Part I* (pp. 65–131). Bloomington, IN: Public School Publication.

Guthrie, J. T., & Davis, M. H. (2003). Motivating struggling readers in middle school through an engagement model of classroom practice. *Reading and Writing Quarterly, 19,* 59–85.

Igoa, C. (1995). *The inner world of the immigrant child.* New York: St. Martin's Press.

Ivey, G., & Fisher, D. (2006). *Creating literacy-rich schools for adolescents.* Alexandria, VA: Association for Supervision and Curriculum Development.

Jackson, Y., & Cooper, E. J. (2007). Building academic success with underachieving adolescents. In K. Beers, R. E. Probst, & L. Rief (Eds.), *Adolescent literacy: Turning promise into practice* (pp. 243–256). Portsmouth, NH: Heinemann.

Johnston, P. H., & Allington, R. L. (1991). Remediation. In R. Barr, M. L. Kamil, P. Mosenthal, & P. D. Pearson (Eds.), *Handbook of reading research* (Vol. 2, pp. 984–1012). New York: Longman.

Johnston, P. H., & Winograd, P. (1985). Passive failure in reading. *Journal of Reading Behavior, 17,* 279–299.

Kennedy, M. M., Birman, B. F., & Demaline, R. E. (1986). *The effectiveness of Chapter I services.* Washington, DC: U.S. Department of Education, Office of Educational Research and Improvement.

Langer, J. (2002). *Effective literacy instruction.* Urbana, IL: National Council of Teachers of English.

Langer, J. (2004). *Getting to excellent: How to create better schools.* New York: Teachers College Press.

Lenski, S. D., & Ehlers-Zavala, F. (2004). *Reading strategies for Spanish speakers.* Dubuque, IA: Kendall/Hunt.

Lenski, S. D., Johns, J. L., Wham, M. A., & Caskey, M. M. (2007). *Reading and learning strategies: Middle grades through high school.* Dubuque, IA: Kendall/Hunt.

Lenters, K. (2006). Resistance, struggle, and the adolescent reader. *Journal of Adolescent and Adult Literacy, 50,* 138–146.

Long, J. F., Monoi, S., Harper, B., Knoblauch, D., & Murphy, P. K. (2007). Academic motivation and achievement among urban adolescents. *Urban Education, 42*(3), 196–222.

Moje, E. B., Young, J. P., Readance, J. E., & Moore, D. W. (2000). Reinventing adolescent literacy for new times: Perennial and millennial issues. *Journal of Adolescent and Adult Literacy, 43,* 400–410.

Moore, D. W., Bean, T. W., Birdyshaw, D., & Rycik, J. A. (1999). Adolescent literacy: A position statement. *Journal of Adolescent and Adult Literacy, 43*(1), 97–112.

Mueller, P. N. (2001). *Lifers: Learning from at-risk adolescent readers.* Portsmouth, NH: Heinemann.

National Association of State Boards of Education. (2006). *Reading at risk: The state response to the crisis in adolescent literacy.* Alexandria, VA: Author.

National Commission on Excellence in Education. (1983). *A nation at risk: The imperative for educational reform.* Washington, DC: U.S. Department of Education.

Nichols, S. L., & Good, T. L. (2004). *America's teenagers—Myths and realities: Media images, schooling, and the social costs of careless indifference.* Mahwah, NJ: Erlbaum.

Padrón, Y. (1998). Latino students and reading: Understanding these English language learners' needs. In K. Beers & B. G. Samuels (Eds.), *Into focus: Understanding and creating middle school readers* (pp. 105–122). Norwood, MA: Christopher-Gordon.

Paris, S. R., & Block, C. C. (2007). The expertise of adolescent literacy teachers. *Journal of Adolescent and Adult Literacy, 50,* 582–596.

Perie, M., Grigg, W., & Donahue, P. (2005). *The nation's report card: Reading 2005 (NCES 2006-451).* U.S. Department of Education, National Center for Education Statistics. Washington, DC: U.S. Government Printing Office.

Pitcher, S. M., Albright, L. K., DeLaney, C. J., Walker, N. T., Seunarinesingh, K., Mogge, S., et al. (2007). Assessing adolescents' motivation to read. *Journal of Adolescent and Adult Literacy, 50,* 378–396.

Primeaux, J. (2000). Shifting perspectives on struggling readers. *Language Arts, 77,* 537–542.

Shanahan, T. (2004). Improving reading achievement in secondary schools: Structures and reforms. In D. S. Strickland & D. E. Alvermann (Eds.), *Bridging the literacy achievement gap: Grades 4–12* (pp. 43–55). New York: Teachers College Press.

Smagorinsky, P. (2002). *Teaching English through principled practice.* Upper Saddle River, NJ: Merrill Prentice-Hall.

Snow, C. E., & Biancarosa, G. (2003). *Adolescent literacy and the achievement gap: What do we know and where do we go from here?* New York: Carnegie Corporation.

Spor, M. W., & Schneider, B. K. (1999). Content reading strategies: What teachers know, use, and want to learn. *Reading Research and Instruction, 38,* 221–231.

Stanovich, K. (1986). Matthew effects in reading: some consequences of individual differences in the acquisition of literacy. *Reading Research Quarterly, 21,* 360–406.

Sturtevant, E. G., Boyd, F. B., Brozo, W. G., Hinchman, K. A., Moore, D. A., & Alvermann, D. E. (2006). *Principled practices for adolescent literacy: A framework for adolescent literacy.* Mahwah, NJ: Erlbaum.

Taylor, A. R. (1996). Conditions for American children, youth and families: Are we "world class"? *Educational Researcher, 25,* 10–12.

Tomlinson, C. A. (2004). Differentiating instruction: A synthesis of key research and guidelines. In T. L. Jetton & J. A. Dole (Eds.), *Adolescent literacy research and practice* (pp. 228–248). New York: Guilford Press.

Torgesen, J. K., Houston, D. D., Rissman, L. M., Decker, S. M., Vaughn, R. G., Wexler, J., et al. (2007). *Academic literacy instruction for adolescents: A guidance document from the Center on Instruction*. Portsmouth, NH: RMC Research Corporation, Center on Instruction.

U.S. Department of Education. (2007). *Striving Readers program*. Retrieved January 7, 2007, from *www.ed.gov/programs/strivingreaders/index.html*.

CHAPTER 3

Nurturing Resilience among Adolescent Readers

Alfred W. Tatum
Teresa A. Fisher

Many adolescents who have moved beyond the primary grades continue to struggle with reading. Until recently, these students have been ignored, tolerated, reprimanded, or shifted to other environments (e.g., low-level tracks, special education classrooms) to receive skill-focused remediation. This marginalization has occurred without public scrutiny or public debate. Low-level literacy skills generated little discussion because opportunities for low-skill, moderate-wage physical labor within the United States' economic structure were available to a large segment of the American population. Times have changed, however, because of the expansion of technology and its impact on local, national, and international structures. The literacy skills needed to function effectively within these structures have increased.

Policymakers have become increasingly concerned about the "adolescent literacy crisis" (National Governors Association, 2005) in the United States. Their concerns have been fueled by the proliferation of alarming statistics on students' reading and math achievement provided by the National Assessment of Educational Progress (NAEP). Public policy documents, such as *Reading Next* (Alliance for Excellent Education, 2004), remind us that more than 8,000,000 students in grades 4–12 struggle with reading. We also know that roughly 70% of the students entering ninth grade can be considered reading below grade level, and approximately 7,000 students drop out of high school each day. These data suggest that measures must be taken to create conditions to promote the literacy development of struggling adolescent readers.

An adolescent literacy movement is currently underway to increase funding for research and professional development (Alvermann, Hinchman, Moore, Phelps, & Waff, 2006). This movement is calling for more experimental studies to identify best practices for adolescents and a meta-analysis of what we know about adolescent literacy, similar to what occurred with the federally commissioned National Reading Panel. Other researchers, however, have given more attention to students' out-of-school contexts and the molding of adolescents' identities in schools (Davidson, 1996; Hull & Schultz, 2002; Rymes, 2001). There has also been a call to look at cultural–ecological variables and examine how race, class, and gender are interwoven in literacy (Gilbert & Gilbert, 1998; Greene & Abt-Perkins, 2003; Lesko, 2000; Swanson, Cunningham, & Spencer, 2003; Young, 2000). This shift in adolescent literacy and the growing political concern about the literacy development of students in relation to the economy has led to a clear intersection of adolescent literacy and policy focused on struggling readers (Franzak, 2006). Unfortunately, while educators, researchers, and policymakers are working toward solutions, many adolescents continue to remain vulnerable to failing in school and society

In this chapter, we call attention to how instructional practices and contexts can be shaped to nurture reading resiliency among adolescents, particularly for students who experience difficulty with school-based reading. The chapter has a threefold emphasis. Fist, we provide a review of resilience and why it is central to the literacy development of the struggling adolescents. This is followed by a framework that identifies multiple variables for nurturing reading resilience among adolescents. Finally, we discuss how a focus on resilience needs to be considered in the larger conversations about improving the reading achievement of adolescents.

Research on Resilience in Adolescents

Although there are various conceptualizations of what it means to be resilient, most definitions of resilience encompass the capacity for successful adaptations in spite of adverse circumstances or stressful life events (Henderson & Milstein, 2003; Masten, 2001; Masten, Best, & Garmezy, 1990; Werner & Smith, 2001). For many adolescents, having underdeveloped literacy skills is stressful because school demands increase as they progress through school, and they need to use internal and environmental resources to engage with cognitively challenging reading materials. Educators have an instrumental role in helping these adolescents identify, build, and utilize their resources for developing successful reading skills and strategies.

Resiliency research brings attention to individuals' strengths and resources, often referred to as protective factors or protective resources (D'Imperio, Dubow, & Ippolito, 2000; Henderson & Milstein, 2003; Small & Memmo, 2004; Werner & Smith, 2001). Researchers have identified internal factors (e.g., personal attributes) and environmental factors (e.g., home life, community, classroom and school environments) as two sources of these protective resources (Cowen & Work, 1988; Masten, 2001; Werner & Smith, 1992).

Personal attributes such as temperament, self-esteem, self-efficacy, social competence, autonomy, and having a meaningful purpose and goals are individual characteristics researchers have observed among resilient youth. These characteristics are key personal attributes for middle school and high school students. Efforts should be made to acknowledge or honor each of these attributes and combine them with other resources to shape positive literacy and personal trajectories. For instance, educators can help students develop resilient personal attributes or provide strategies that help them adjust to their lack of skills in specific areas. The following list includes a brief description of each attribute and suggestions for how educators can nurture the attributes during reading instruction.

- Self-esteem and self- efficacy are characterized by positive feelings of self-worth combined with the belief that one can succeed at a particular task. Along with teachers working on strategies specifically for reading, students should receive support identifying strengths in other academic or social activities. These activities can provide students with a foundation of confidence before negotiating stressful issues.
- Social competence relates to the skillful combination of knowledge and affect required for social tasks. Students who are socially competent are capable of eliciting positive responses from others and have little difficulty in establishing positive relationships with both adults and peers. These students are also more likely to be receptive to constructive feedback from educators regarding reading improvement.
- Autonomy reflects the belief that self-determined individual actions or behaviors make a difference. Selecting curriculum material to advance a student's identity can enhance autonomous feelings. Reading instructors can be instrumental in selecting books and other materials that students find relevant in relation to their ethnicity, socioeconomic status, gender identity, or adolescent identity.
- Meaningful purposes and goals refer to adolescents' educational aspirations, persistence, and hopefulness. Educators need to help students make connections between the reading curriculum and future possibilities. One such approach is to select texts, both fiction and nonfiction, that include characters who can serve as role models whom students can emulate and from whom they can learn coping strategies.

In addition to the personal attributes described above, there are environmental factors that promote resilience, which include a wide range of influences over which adolescents do not have direct control (e.g., home life, environmental variables, and classroom contexts). These factors impact adolescents' responses to stressful events (Small & Memmo, 2004; Stanton-Salazar & Spina, 2000). There are numerous protective factors in a student's immediate environment that can help him or her to address reading difficulties. A consistently caring adult, positive expectations, and opportunities for meaningful participation are factors that have proven to be effective for nurturing resilience. Adolescents are more likely to be resilient if they feel secure in the presence of adults who clearly communicate high expectations with realistic goals and who support students' meaningful participation by engaging them with authentic tasks and "real-world" dialogue (Henderson & Milstein, 2003; Stanton-Salazar & Spina, 2000).

It is important to recognize that although both personal and environmental resources work together in the process of building resiliency, some factors vary in terms of their importance. For individual students, certain protective resources are in greater demand depending on both the student and contextual factors (e.g., poverty, limited English proficiency, accumulation of failure, school conditions).

The Marginalized Adolescent Reader

National data indicate that approximately 30% of U.S. eighth graders are proficient readers. Almost 40% of students lack the reading and writing skills employers seek by the time they graduate from high school. Roughly 5 out of 10 high school graduates who enroll in college have to take a remedial reading course. Nurturing resilience among adolescent readers is important because poor readers are most at risk of quitting school before high school graduation, which limits their opportunities to fashion positive life outcomes.

In addition to the broader societal implications, poor or underdeveloped literacy skills prevent readers from understanding text beyond a basic level. The inability to understand text affects students' self-perception and self-understanding (Alvermann et al., 2006). Adolescents who struggle with reading also become disconnected from the literacy in classrooms and schools and learn to expect mistreatment and injustice from adults (Ivey, 1999; Miller, 2006). This is problematic because contexts and relationships help to construct students' literacy identities (Triplett, 2004). Arguably, the need to create such contexts is more pronounced among economically disadvantaged students and English language learners (ELLs) because of the likelihood that they will attend schools in which there is a high rate of poverty, with the lowest achievement levels.

In a recent review of literature, Franzak (2006) described adolescents who struggle with reading as marginalized and as having following characteristics:

- They are not engaged in the reading and writing done in school.
- They have language and cultural practices different from those valued in school.
- They are outsiders to the dominant group because of race, class, gender, or sexual orientation.

Within the number of marginalized readers there are three groups, as described in *Reading to Achieve: A Governor's Guided to Adolescent Literacy* (National Governors Association, 2005).

- The first group of marginalized adolescent readers experience some problems with fluency and comprehension, but they are able to read common texts such as newspapers.
- The second group of marginalized adolescent readers have more difficulty with fluency and comprehension. They fail to complete high school or graduate with limited literacy skills.
- The third, and smallest, group of adolescents have difficulty decoding the words on a page.

This wide range of difficulties impacted by personal and environmental factors calls for the need to approach literacy teaching by looking at multiple variables that include, but are not limited to, research-based reading strategies. Educators must also become knowledgeable about students' personal attributes, home life, culture, environment, language, and economics, and instructional environments and how they can be used to support the literacy development of adolescents. We are concerned that an oversimplified approach to literacy teaching that focuses on skill and strategy development alone, without considering the complexity of teaching marginalized adolescent readers, is conceptually thin. In addition, an approach that fails to acknowledge this complexity runs counter to the reconceptualization of adolescent literacy that recommends acknowledging:

- The situational contexts of adolescents' literate identities,
- The ways in which young people are positioned as readers and writers in school,
- Sociocultural and linguistic practices that mediate identity formation in youth,
- The impact of teachers on students' literate identities.

Therefore, in this chapter we are advancing a more comprehensive model of literacy instruction to nurture resiliency among adolescents who struggle with reading.

A Model for Building Reading Resilience among Adolescents

The convergence of adolescent personal identities, in-school and out-of-school experiences, and reading strengths and weaknesses must be accounted for when planning instructional practices aimed to improve students' reading achievement and to nurture their resilience. This accounting suggests the need for a more complete model of literacy instruction informed by theoretical, instructional, and professional development strands, as shown in Figure 3.1 (Tatum, 2005).

The context of students' lives, namely the teenagers' individual, family, and social contexts, forms a web of issues that no education program can ignore (Miller, 2006). Embedded in this premise is the need to pay attention to characteristics of students, educators, and instructional supports that

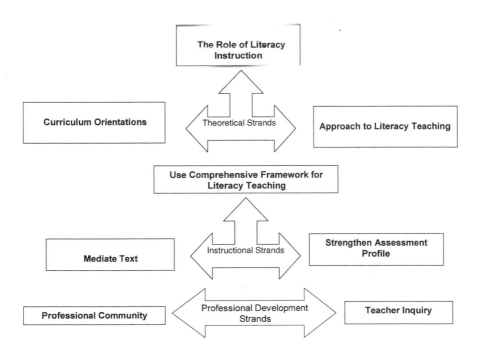

FIGURE 3.1. A more complete model of literacy instruction.

Reading	Readers	Educators	Instructional environments
Vocabulary Fluency Strategy knowledge Language proficiency	Personal attributes Home life Culture Environment Language Economics	Competence Commitment Caring Culpability	Quality instructional support Text Context Assessment

FIGURE 3.2. Vital signs of literacy instruction for improving reading and nurturing resilience.

increase the likelihood of advancing students' literacy development and will allow them to persist in educational settings. Using the analogy of vital signs in patients, as identified by—pulse, weight, temperature, and blood pressure—we have identified the vital signs of literacy instruction as they relate to nurturing reading resilience among adolescents. The vital signs are listed in Figure 3.2 and are described next.

Vital Signs of Reading

In a review of the empirical research on comprehension instruction, Pearson and Fielding (1991) concluded that students' ability to comprehend narrative and expository text points toward four broad generalizations for providing effective comprehension instruction: (1) Build a relationship between students' background knowledge and experiences and the content included in the reading selection, (2) improve students' ability to monitor comprehension, (3) make knowledge of text structure explicit and bring attention to it systematically, and (4) teach students how to recast what they have read by identifying the important versus the unimportant information.

Teaching reading strategies figures prominently in improving adolescents' reading comprehension (Gambrell & Bales, 1987; Greenleaf, Schoenbach, Cziko, & Mueller, 2001; Palinscar & Brown, 1984; Raphael & Pearson, 1985). However, strategy instruction alone can be inadequate for low-achieving students who attribute their reading failures to lack of ability (Carr & Borkowski, 1989). They found that attribution retraining (i.e., getting low-achieving students to attribute their reading-related failures to lack of effort and not lack of ability) led to greater use of comprehension strategies.

When strategies are modeled, many students come to realize that comprehension depends on a combination of their own personal effort and strategy use in searching for understanding (Borkowski, 1992). Students benefit when teachers model, talk aloud, or "make their thinking public." Students also benefit when teachers offer feedback that includes providing clear indications about correctness, repeating correct responses, being encouraging, rehearsing correct information both by speaking and underlining it, and reminding students about important information to learn (Winne, Graham, & Prock, 1993). These behaviors can potentially cause students to use strategies, and to self-regulate their use of the strategies, particularly if they are informed of the benefits and provided with evidence of the contributions of the strategies to their improved performance on comprehension-related tasks.

The research suggests that instruction for adolescents should include explicit strategy instruction. However, explicit strategy instruction for many low-achieving students is inadequate, particularly for those who attribute their failure to lack of ability. Adolescent students benefit when teachers move them toward using comprehension strategies independently and help them understand the value of the strategies. They also benefit when they are given opportunities to use their strategy knowledge and receive corrective feedback and reinforcement about their strategy use.

Vital Signs of Readers

The gaps in reading achievement among today's adolescents, particularly among students of color, are largely attributable to the different components of culture that manifest themselves in varying ways where literacy instruction is taking place. Linguistic differences, cultural differences, inferior education, and the rationales for schooling among different cultural groups can contribute to low student achievement. The perceived rationales of various cultural groups involve their understanding of the significance of school performance to life opportunities. Linguistic differences are prominent when students of diverse backgrounds speak a home language other than standard English. Cultural differences are prevalent when forms of interaction, language, and thoughts of cultural groups conflict with mainstream behaviors generally needed for success in school. The ways each of these factors are mediated through students' daily interactions and experiences in school contribute to literacy achievement, or lack thereof.

To understand the impact of culture in an adolescent's life, one must understand that exploring self-identity is central to adolescence. This is an identity that is structured both inside and outside school. Adolescents bring a cultural knowledge and richness of expression that develop outside school, but often find that these qualities are overlooked in school. When cultural differences are present, teachers and students have to learn how to navigate these borders and boundaries in a respectful way and in an atmosphere of trust.

Patthey-Chavez (1993) describes Latino students and Anglo high school teachers in a particular school who were constantly dealing with issues of cultural boundaries and interpreted the continued reliance on mainstream socialization practices as a cause of increasing conflict when these practices collided with student values. Cultural boundaries are defined as behavioral evidence of culturally different standards of appropriateness, such as different ways of pronouncing final consonants or differing ways of dress. Cultural differences can be an initial source of trouble between teachers and students that can develop over time into entrenched, emotionally intense conflicts.

Research of the past two decades has consistently found that students who are allowed and encouraged to identify with their native languages and cultures in their schools and communities can have improved learning outcomes. Using culturally responsive instructional approaches and infusing culturally responsive materials into reading instruction, so that students do not view their lived experiences outside school as being marginalized, seems to be essential for adolescents. Thinking about possible instructional adjustments that pay attention to adolescents from all groups allows for the following:

- Reconstructing curriculum to incorporate a wider set of interests
- Being personally warm toward, respectful of, and academically demanding of all students
- Spelling out the cultural assumptions on which the classroom (and schooling) operates
- Avoiding the use of direct, overt management strategies and using indirect, private forms of control
- Acknowledging that racism is prevalent in schools and needs to be addressed

These actions require a "wholesale transformation" (Nieto, 1999) that involves a shift in teachers' beliefs and attitudes, and in schools' policies and practices, instead of simply tinkering with a few cultural additions to the curriculum or adopting a new teaching strategy.

Vital Signs of Educators

Students of color and low-income adolescents, who often struggle most with reading, are more likely to find themselves in classrooms staffed by inadequately prepared, inexperienced, and ill-qualified teachers. The vast majority of underprepared teachers are assigned to the most disadvantaged schools with a large percentage of low-performing students of color, where working conditions are least attractive and turnover rates are highest (Darling-Hammond, 1997). These recurring circumstances lead to failure for many adolescents, who find that their right to quality education is not protected or guaranteed.

Ladson-Billings (1995) argued for the centrality of culturally responsive pedagogy in helping students who have not been served well by our nation's public schools, and posited that the conditions for effective learning are created when the role of culture is recognized and used in the activity settings during the actual learning process. Culturally responsive pedagogy is an approach based on using students' cultures as an important source of their education. This type of pedagogy can reduce miscommunication, foster trust, and prevent conflict that can move rapidly beyond intercultural misunderstandings to bitter verbal exchanges between some adolescents and their teachers. Culturally relevant pedagogy rests on three criteria: (1) students must experience academic success; (2) students must develop and/or maintain cultural competence, and (3) students must develop a critical consciousness through which they challenge the status quo of the current social order. Ladson-Billings (1995) also offered that in this approach, instructional activities based on the norms of the students' community are incorporated into the classroom, cooperation is emphasized over competition, and learning is structured as a social activity.

Although multiple research studies reveal a close relationship between a culturally responsive approach to teaching and reading achievement, a call for widespread implementation of culturally responsive teaching has not been made by literacy educators or education reformers as a way to close the reading achievement gap. Gay (2000) identified five notions as to why this is the case: (1) There is a belief that education has nothing to do with culture and heritage, (2) too few teachers have adequate knowledge of how teaching practices reflect European American cultural values, (3) many teachers want to do best for all their students and mistakenly believe that to treat students differently because of their cultural orientation is racial discrimination, (4) there is a belief that good teaching is transcendent; that it is identical for all students and under all circumstances, and (5) there is a claim that education is an effective doorway of assimilation into mainstream society for people from many diverse cultural heritages, ethnic groups, social classes, and points of origin.

Despite these notions, student achievement data on the positive effects of culturally responsive teaching practices used in individual classrooms have emerged (Tatum, 2000). Gay (2000) described several such programs and their achievement effects. For example, 93.8% of African

American eighth-grade students attending the Seattle Academy performed at or above the accepted standard compared to 71.6% of African American students in the district. African American students in grades 6–8 had better achievement results than their ethnic peers in the district when a culturally responsive approach to instruction was adopted.

The implications of the data reviewed in this section point to the following guidelines for improving the reading achievement and nurturing resiliency among adolescents experiencing low-level literacy achievement:

1. Legitimate students' culture and make it a reference for learning.
2. Resist curriculum orientations that stifle or postpone academic growth.
3. Engage students in authentic discussions in which they can analyze their realities in the context of the curriculum and discuss strategies for overcoming academic and societal barriers.
4. Guide students toward academic success and cultural competence.
5. Address students' cognitive, affective, social, emotional, and developmental needs.
6. Require students to meet high academic standards.

Vital Signs of Instructional Environments

Dispositions toward reading are dependent on the kind of instructional environment in which adolescent students are asked to read (Ivey, 1999). Classrooms embodying connections to real-world learning, self-directed activities, direct strategy teaching, and allowance for varied forms of self-expression increase long-term motivation and strategies for reading (Guthrie, Alao, & Rinehart, 1997). Environmental contexts that support adolescent literacy development are characterized by letting students know ahead of time what will be expected, minimizing risks by giving students time to prepare responses; organizing classrooms to meet students' instructional needs; offering choice without sacrificing the intensity of the assignments and activities and identifying ways to negotiate agenda conflicts (Mosenthal, 1998); and engaging students in conversations of how their actions affect the literacy context and how that context affects their literacy development (Moore & Cunningham, 1998). If these environmental strands are mismanaged or ignored, the result may be a series of academic disappointments and failures that can ultimately alienate many students in classrooms and render them powerless to change their literate behaviors.

Students are more likely to engage in classroom activities if they feel supported and valued. The level of student support, opportunities for negotiation, characteristics of discussions, expectations, and the level of interactions between teacher and student, and between students, all have important implications for the daily lives of adolescent readers. Perceived support from teachers is a significant predictor of young adolescents' motivation and academic achievement. According to Wentzel (1997), a democratic interaction style, caring attitudes, and corrective feedback facilitated students' involvement with literate activities.

In summary, classrooms responsive to adolescents' needs are characterized as allowing students' choice, engaging relevant knowledge, and providing opportunities for students to negotiate their needs and desires. Nonthreatening environments in which students are engaged in conversations about the multiple literacies in their lives can help students feel supported and valued. These classrooms have the potential to induce more student participation in literacy-related tasks, increase student motivation, and lead to improved academic outcomes.

In addition, Borkowski, Carr, Rellinger, and Pressley (1990) found that involving students in the evaluation of their literacy learning leads to students' self-regulated assessment behaviors. It has been proposed that adolescents have valuable insights that they should be invited to contribute to any conversation about their literacy education (Alvermann, 1998) and that teachers must come to know individual students through watching them, listening to them, and interacting with them in meaningful literacy activities (Ivey, 1999). Involving students in the assessment process can make their invisible inner dialogue visible, and it can empower them to break down the barriers that disenfranchise them from the reading and writing process (Tatum, 2000).

Constructing a profile of the specific strategies adolescents possess can aid in getting them the specific help they need. A reading assessment plan for adolescents that is effective in assessing their cognitive dimensions (e.g., comprehension, word knowledge) and affective dimensions of literacy (e.g., types of materials student value, attitudes toward reading) has potential benefits. A hallmark of any effective assessment plan is that it is ongoing, involves both formal and informal techniques, and extends across several areas of reading.

From the implications of the discussion in this section, we can generate the following guidelines for teachers of adolescents:

1. Recognize that the concept of adolescent literacy is changing.
2. Work to bridge the gap between adolescents' in-school literacies and out-of-school literacies.
3. Recognize that adolescents are developing a sense of self and that they draw on multiple literacies to define that self.
4. Provide explicit strategy instruction.
5. Structure supportive environments.
6. Involve students in the assessment process and develop an assessment plan that pays attention to their cognitive and affective needs.

Conclusions

In this chapter we identified several vital signs of literacy instruction that should be considered in order to nurture the reading resilience of adolescents who are not performing well with school-based reading. We emphasized that an approach to literacy teaching with a singular focus—to "remediate" struggling adolescent readers—is insufficiently robust. The model we provided gives several entry points for developing students' protective resources and protective factors, largely informed by resilience research. This model frames reading instruction to take into consideration students' personal attributes, their in-school and out-of-school experiences, and their reading strengths and weaknesses. We are advocating for a broader ecological approach that brings attention to the changing concept of adolescent literacy and the growing political landscape to address the adolescent reading crisis in the United States.

Unlike many proposed solutions, the approach we offer here meshes adolescent literacy with the research on resilience because of the potential of this bridging to affect reading achievement, decrease the number of high school dropouts, and shape positive literacy and life outcome trajectories for a nation of adolescents who struggle to read beyond a basic level. In short, we believe that there is a need to develop expert procedures for teaching reading without worrying about the imprecise variables of race, ethnicity, and language, find ways to systematize reading instruction, focus on academic excellence and identity development when planning instruction to improve the reading achievement of adolescents, and question variables that are being undertreated and causing disharmony in the literate lives of a vulnerable population.

We have offered four vital signs of literacy instruction that should be considered while the field of adolescent literacy is going through a productive period of change. We are reminded of two adolescents. One young man stated, "It is scary not to know how to read." A young woman said, "All my grades are bad and nobody can help me." Both of these students are vulnerable in their own right and will continue to be vulnerable unless we find ways to nurture their resilience inside of school in hope that they will become resilient on the outside. It is our hope that teachers, researchers, and policymakers begin to embrace the complexity of nurturing resilience put forth in these pages. Our fear is that if they do not, not only are adolescents vulnerable, but so is the field of adolescent literacy.

References

Alliance for Excellent Education. (2006). *Who's counted? Who's counting? Understanding high school graduation rates.* Washington, DC: Author.

Alvermann, D. (1998). Imagining the possibilities. In D. Alvermann, K. Hinchman,

D. Moore, S. Phelps, & D. Waff (Eds.), *Reconceptualizing the literacies in ado-lescents' lives* (pp. 353–372). Mahwah, NJ: Erlbaum.

Alvermann, D., Hinchman, K., Moore, D., Phelps, S., & Waff, D. (2006). *Reconceptualizing the literacies in adolescents' lives* (2nd ed.) Mahwah, NJ: Erlbaum.

Borkowski, J. G. (1992). Metacognitive theory: A framework for teaching literacy, writing and math skills. *Journal of Learning Disabilities, 25,* 253–257.

Borkowski, J. G., Carr, M., Rellinger, E., & Pressley, M. (1990). Self-regulated cognition: Interdependence of metacognition, attribution, and self-esteem. In B. F. Jones & L. Idol (Eds.), *Dimensions of thinking and cognitive instruction* (pp. 53–92). Hillsdale, NJ: Erlbaum.

Carr, M., & Borkowski, J. G. (1989). Attributional retraining and the generalization of reading strategies with underachieving children. *Learning and Individual Differences, 1,* 327–341.

Cowen, E. L., & Work, W. C. (1988). Resilient children, psychological wellness, and primary prevention. *American Journal of Community Psychology, 16,* 591–607.

Darling-Hammond, L. (1997). *The right to learn: A blueprint for creating schools that work.* San Francisco: Jossey Bass.

Davidson, A. (1996). *Making and molding identity in schools: Student narratives on race, gender, and academic engagement.* Albany: State University of New York Press.

D'Imperio, R., Dubow, E., & Ippolito, M. (2000). Resilient and stress-affected adolescents in an urban setting. *Journal of Clinical Child Psychology, 29*(1), 129.

Franzak, J. (2006). Zoom: A review of the literature on marginalized adolescent readers, literacy theory, and policy implications. *Review of Educational Research, 76*(2), 209–248.

Gambrell, L. B., & Bales, R. J. (1987). Mental imagery and the comprehension-monitoring performance of fourth- and fifth-grade poor readers. *Reading Research Quarterly, 21,* 454–464.

Gay, G. (2000). *Culturally responsive teaching: Theory, research, and practice.* New York: Teachers College Press.

Gilbert, R., & Gilbert, P. (1998). *Masculinity goes to school.* New York: Routledge.

Greene, S., & Abt-Perkins, D. (2003). *Making race visible: Literacy research for cultural understanding.* New York: Teachers College Press.

Greenleaf, C. L., Schoenbach, R., Cziko, C., & Mueller, F. (2001). Apprenticing adolescent readers to academic literacy. *Harvard Educational Review, 71,* 79–129,

Guthrie, J. T., Alao, S., & Rinehart, J. (1997). Engagement in reading for young adolescents. *Journal of Adolescent and Adult Literacy, 40,* 438–449.

Henderson, N., & Milstein, M. (2003). *Resiliency in schools: Making it happen for students and educators.* Thousand Oaks, CA: Corwin Press.

Hull, G., & Schultz, K. (2002). *School's out! Bridging out-of-school literacies with classroom practice.* New York: Teachers College Press.

Ivey, G. (1999). A multicase study in the middle school: Complexities among young adolescent readers. *Reading Research Quarterly, 34*(2), 172–192.

Ladson-Billings, G. (1995). Toward a theory of culturally relevant pedagogy. *American Educational Research Journal, 32,* 465–491.

Lesko, N. (2000). *Masculinities at school.* Thousand Oaks, CA: Sage.

Masten, A. (2001). Ordinary magic: Resilience processes in development. *American Psychologist, 56*(3), 227–238.

Masten, A., Best, K., & Garmezy, N. (1990). Resilience and development: Contributions from the study of children who overcome adversity. *Development and Psychopathology, 2,* 425–444.

Miller, M. (2006). Where they are: Working with marginalized students. *Educational Leadership, 63*(5), 50–54.

Moore, D. W., & Cunningham, J. W. (1998). Agency and adolescent literacy. In D. Alvermann, K. Hinchman, D. Moore, S. Phelps, & D. Waff (Eds.), *Reconceptualizing the literacies in adolescents' lives* (pp. 283–302). Mahwah, NJ: Erlbaum.

Mosenthal, P. (1998). Reframing the problems of adolescence and adolescent literacy: A dilemma-management perspective. In D. Alvermann, K. Hinchman, D. Moore, S. Phelps, & D. Waff (Eds.), *Reconceptualizing the literacies in adolescents' lives* (pp. 325–352). Mahwah, NJ: Erlbaum.

National Governors Association. (2005). *Reading to achieve: A governor's guide to adolescent literacy.* Washington, DC: Author.

Nieto, S. (1999). *The light in their eyes: Creating multicultural learning communities.* New York: Teachers College Press.

Palinscar, A. S., & Brown, A. L. (1984). Reciprocal teaching of comprehension-fostering and comprehension monitoring activities. *Cognition and Instruction, 1,* 117–175.

Patthey-Chavez, G. (1993). High school as an arena for cultural conflict and acculturation for Latino Angelinos. *Anthropology and Education Quarterly, 24,* 33–60.

Pearson, P. D., & Fielding, L. G. (1991). Comprehension instruction. In R. Barr, M. Kamil, P. Mosenthal, & P. D. Pearson (Eds.), *Handbook of reading research, Volume 2.* New York: Longman.

Raphael, T., & Pearson, P. D. (1985). Increasing students' awareness of sources of information for answering questions. *American Educational Research Journal, 22,* 217–236.

Rymes, B. (2001). *Conversational borderlands: Language and identity in an alternative urban high school.* New York: Teachers College Press.

Small, S., & Memmo, M. (2004). Contemporary models of youth development and problem prevention: Toward an integration of terms, concepts, and models. *Family Relations, 53*(1), 3–11.

Stanton-Salazar, R., & Spina, S. (2000). The network orientations of highly resilient urban minority youth: A network-analytic account of minority socialization and its educational implications. *Urban Review, 32*(3), 227.

Swanson, D., Cunningham, M., & Spencer, M. B. (2003). Black males' structural conditions, achievement patterns, normative needs, and "opportunities." *Urban Education, 38*(5), 608–633.

Tatum, A. W. (2000). Breaking down barriers that disenfranchise African American adolescents in low-level reading tracks. *Journal of Adolescent and Adult Literacy, 44,* 52–64.

Tatum, A. W. (2005). *Teaching reading to black adolescent males: Closing the achievement gap.* Portland, ME: Stenhouse.

Triplett, C. (2004). Looking for a struggle: Exploring the emotions of a middle school reader. *Journal of Adolescent and Adult Literacy, 48*(3), 214–222.

Wentzel, K. (1997). Student motivation in middle school: The role of perceived pedagogical caring. *Journal of Educational Psychology, 89,* 411–419.

Werner, E. E., & Smith, R. S. (1992). *Overcoming the odds: High-risk children from birth to adulthood.* Ithaca, NY: Cornell University Press.

Werner, E. E., & Smith, R. S. (2001). *Journey from childhood to midlife: Risk, resiliency, and recovery.* New York: Cornell University Press.

Winne, P., Graham, L., & Prock, L. (1993). A model of poor readers' text-based inferencing: Effects of explanatory feedback. *Reading Research Quarterly, 28,* 53–66.

Young, J. P. (2000). Boy talk: Critical literacy and masculinities. *Reading Research Quarterly, 35*(3), 312–337.

CHAPTER 4

Teaching Adolescent English Language Learners

Fabiola P. Ehlers-Zavala

In public schools in the United States, one student in five is likely to be an English language learner (ELL) (Richard-Amato & Snow, 2005). This proportion will continue to narrow as immigration to the United States steadily rises, contributing to the diverse makeup of many schools. Throughout the United States, ELLs are part of urban, suburban, and rural schools. As any public school official can attest, this reality underscores the need to educate teachers on how to develop advanced levels of academic literacy and academic achievement with ELLs.

Teachers who have ELLs in their classes must have specific kinds of knowledge and expertise for educating learners who are culturally and linguistically diverse (Brisk & Harrington, 2007). At minimum, this enterprise requires that preservice teachers begin their initial teacher preparation programs by taking an introductory course in multicultural/diversity education as required in accredited programs. Teachers who teach ELLs, however, require specialized training that goes beyond this minimum. But currently, many of the accredited teacher preparation programs do not offer a curriculum that meaningfully addresses the new curricular and pedagogical demands of today's diverse classrooms. These programs "are not grounded in the linguistic basis of learning, nor do they typically prepare teachers to help students understand the linguistic challenges of their subject areas" (Schleppegrell, 2004, p. 164). Making matters worse, it is still unclear whether offering this type of training can be realistically accomplished during the initial preparation period. Indeed, given the logistical constraints dictated by state policies, some educational researchers have questioned whether substantially revising the core training of teacher preparation programs is even possible (e.g., Baca & Escamilla, 2002). Therefore, although we may not be able to solve some of these logistical and curricular problems any time soon, those of us involved in bilingual/ESL (English as a Second Language) education and applied linguistics have knowledge and tools we can offer to teachers committed to improving the academic conditions for ELLs in their classrooms, and we look for ways to share them.

This chapter represents such a pathway for supporting teachers who work with ELLs in middle and secondary schools—especially teachers who have ELLs in their mainstream classrooms and may be receiving little or no support in the areas of ESL or bilingual instruction. It offers initial guidance to teachers about the critical elements that influence or mediate ELLs' gains in academic literacy development. This chapter does not, however, offer overnight solutions to mainstream teachers. The best way to assist ELLs in the process of becoming academically successful in schools is by providing them with access to additive forms of bilingual education, that is, bilingual education that supports and develops the ELLs' native language as well as English as an additional language (i.e., biliteracy development; Freeman & Freeman, 2006). What I lay out here is a starting point.

Building the Pathways for ELLs' Academic Success in Middle and Secondary Schools

The centerpiece of this chapter is a series of pedagogical recommendations and implementation accommodations that teachers in mainstream classes may find useful to more effectively work with ELLs. Five core concepts underlie these recommendations. These concepts pertain to our most current understandings of:

1. ELLs,
2. Academic language,
3. Academic literacy,
4. Second-language (L2) academic literacy development, and
5. Approaches that support teachers' ability to advance ELLs' progress in academic literacy development.

These five concepts constitute central tenets and the targeted efforts that middle and secondary school teachers should bear in mind at all times as they prepare to plan and deliver instruction to ELLs.

English Language Learners

While describing the needs of a specific cultural and diverse group of learners, namely, African American students, Delpit (2002) reminds us, "If we are to invite children into the language of school, we must make school inviting to them" (p. 42). She stresses the need to listen to students. ELLs do not differ in this regard. They are likely to feel invited as long as we are willing to listen to them and eager to learn not only *about*, but also *from* them. After all, this is the first step toward working with ELLs effectively (Brisk & Harrington, 2007). It is important to underscore that ELLs come from a diversity of backgrounds (Brisk & Harrington, 2007). The previous educational experiences they bring to the educational process may range from adequate to little or no formal schooling (Freeman & Freeman, 2003). Some ELLs may find themselves immersed in two languages and cultures simultaneously; others may be in contact primarily with their second or foreign language and culture, with little or no contact with their heritage or native language, referred to as L1. Because ELLs are likely to constitute a highly heterogeneous group in a teacher's classroom, helping ELLs acquire the academic competence/literacy needed to survive in classrooms in the United States is frequently an overwhelming challenge for teachers. A beginning point is for teachers to recognize, celebrate, and address the diversity of ELLs in their classrooms.

Academic Language

An academic language is a subcomponent of "language," with a specific register or linguistic forms that are exclusive to, in this case, the academic context. Registers correspond to language variations "associated with particular situational context or purposes" (Biber, 1995). *Academic language* refers to the language that students are expected to use in school subjects. Each content area has its own specific subregister (Freeman, Freeman, & Meyers, 2005). The development of the academic language concept dates back to Cummins (1979), who distinguished between Basic Interpersonal Skills (BICS) and Cognitive Academic Language Proficiency (CALP) in order to raise awareness of the complexities involved in second-language acquisition and bilingual student success in schools. Central to this distinction is the fact that no one is a native speaker of any academic language (Fillmore, 2005). Thus, it follows that academic languages must be taught to students through instruction that explicitly addresses and supports academic literacy development. Although the development of an academic language is contingent upon student differences in linguistic proficiency, it "should not deter teachers from having high expectations, but it should alert them to provide assistance to reach those expectations" (Brisk & Harrington, 2007).

Understanding the Nature of Academic Literacy

Academic literacy, broadly defined, constitutes a specific form of literacy needed to advance learning in the academic context. It is closely tied to an individual's level of proficiency in his or her academic language(s) in the L1 and L2 (Cummins, 1991). It is connected to the concept of academic discourse which, in turn, is highly diverse and dynamic because of its own nature, and it is tied to the features of specific disciplines and types of disciplinary inquiry (Bazerman, 1998). It may, therefore, be preferable to talk about academic literacies, which vary across subject areas, disciplines, or fields of inquiry. Based on this definition of academic literacy, it is possible to suggest that it is part of a larger existing concept: *academic competence.* This term was originally coined by Muriel Saville-Troike (Adamson, 1993) to describe "the knowledge and abilities students do need" (p. 5) to succeed in mainstream classrooms.

Acquiring or developing academic literacy takes time and effort on the part of students (Brisk & Harrington, 2007; Fillmore, 2005). For many ELLs, learning an academic language can practically be equated with learning an additional language. Thus, it is important to understand the additive nature of this phenomenon (Brisk & Harrington, 2007). Unlike the process of first-language acquisition, however, mere exposure to language does not necessarily translate to the acquisition of academic English (Fillmore, 2005). Indeed, ELLs must receive help in becoming conscious of the language used in texts and text materials, and their attention ought to be drawn to language as it is encountered (Brisk & Harrington, 2007; Delpit, 1995, 2002; Fillmore, 2005; Schleppegrell & Achugar, 2003; Schleppegrell & Colombi, 2002; Schleppegrell, Achugar, & Oteíza, 2004). In situations where ELLs may have been exposed to academic English, or even to effective literacy practices in their L1, teachers are likely to find that their ELLs may experience faster progress in school-related tasks and activities, as compared with ELLs who may not have had such experiences in their L2 or L1.

Second-Language (L2) Academic Literacy Development

Unlike monolingual speakers of any language, ELLs may have a unique repertoire of knowledge and strategic resources to utilize for academic literacy development, drawing from their L1-based abilities, knowledge, and experiences to make sense of academic literacy activities in their L2 (Brisk & Harrington, 2007; Cummins, 1991). Their L1, or native language, is particularly important in the early stages of L2 development because it helps students bootstrap into their L2 literacy practices (Genesee, 2005). As learners become more proficient in their L2, their L2 will influence ELLs' performance in L2 academic literacy activities. As Genesee states, an ELL's literacy development is contingent upon how a variety of factors relate to one another:

- Individual differences regarding underlying cognitive abilities, print-related experiences, and oral language abilities,
- Community/sociocultural factors,
- Family literacy,
- Instructional factors, and
- L1 skills, knowledge, and experiences.

With these individual and contextual factors in mind, teachers might naturally question how to identify and best provide ELLs the most effective pathways for L2 academic success, knowing that ELLs must "learn to use literacy in different contexts and for different purposes and how to encode and decode language" (Brisk & Harrington, 2007, p. 3). In the next section, three contemporary approaches are introduced that teachers have available to guide their instruction. The integration of the three approaches can empower teachers to effectively guide and accelerate ELLs' development of academic literacy.

Approaches That Assist Teachers in Promoting ELLs' Academic Literacy Development

There are clearly a number of methods and approaches that have been offered for teachers' consideration in helping ELLs acquire a language (Larsen-Freeman, 2000). These have varied descriptions of language and language acquisition/learning and of the role of cognitive, academic, social, and cultural variables (Richard-Amato & Snow, 2005). Moreover, although some of these approaches (e.g., communicative language teaching, content-based, task-based, and participatory approaches) have been proven to assist the development of ELLs' communicative competence, especially the social component of English, they may not fully help students to attain academic achievement. In fact, ELLs may still need to be guided into what it takes to acquire high levels of academic performance in English. For this reason, it is not surprising that teachers find themselves in need of additional approaches that can get to the core of academic literacy and academic development in L2 teaching/learning. This scenario typically calls for very specialized teacher training, which general education teachers are unlikely to receive in their teacher preparation programs unless they have pursued certification or graduate work in ESL and/or bilingual education. Specialized courses in traditional linguistics, sociolinguistics, and discourse analysis grounded in an educational perspective are typically at the core of this needed type of training.

In light of this possible professional/educational gap, the question becomes what teachers can do. In this section, three key complementary approaches are highlighted that teachers may consider as they prepare themselves to work with ELLs. Each of these approaches offers teachers information from a different angle needed to fully help ELLs in their academic literacy development, contributing to their overall academic competence:

- An ethnographic approach—to learn about what ELLs bring to the learning process, and what they need to be able to produce/comprehend
- A critical socioliterate approach—to learn about the contextual demands of the academic setting
- A systemic functional linguistics approach—to learn to explicitly teach ELLs the conventions of the academic discourse across subject areas

The call for considering an integration of approaches to working with ELLs is primarily framed within the research trends of recent decades. Gersten and Hudelson (2005), for example, noted that "since the 1960s, the study of children's language from a social perspective has taken on an interdisciplinary character" (p. 23). Thus, today's researchers from such diverse fields and disciplines as language studies, literacy, gender studies, and cultural studies are finding themselves collaborating with each other more often than they did previously.

Teachers who use an *ethnographic approach* to helping ELLs work toward providing learners with opportunities to understand their own literacy practices as well as those of others from a variety of discourse communities. The purpose of this approach is to uncover what ELLs bring to the learning process as they further advance their literacy development. It can also help ELLs identify the expectations that they need to be able to meet.

Hence, the use of ethnographic tools, such as observations, interviews, and focus groups with ELLs, can benefit both teachers and students. Their use has been effectively supported by research in the areas of English for academic purposes (EAP) and English for specific purposes (ESP), which target ELLs. Paltridge (2005), for example, has strongly advocated for the use of ethnographies when studying the performance of L2 learners in language learning. He studied *textography,* how students' texts relate to other texts L2 learners are exposed to in order to uncover underlying values that sustain textual production or the composition of texts. Undoubtedly, such an approach is likely to yield greater insights for teachers as they attempt to understand the literacy world of ELLs.

Likewise, ELLs may also benefit from learning to put into practice ethnographic principles and to use ethnographic tools. By doing so, ELLs can become researchers who study the context of their own schooling, and of their immediate communities, through the texts they use or are expected to use. Through this process of systematic textual examination and scrutiny, ELLs can also learn to uncover the underlying values that sustain the texts they read and produce. They may begin to decipher and, consequently, understand the conventions that make up various academic genres, a necessary condition to demonstrate genre expertise (Johns et al., 2006).

A second approach, a *socioliterate approach,* asks that those engaged in it begin by acquiring a better understanding of the community and culture in which texts are read and written, as well as an appreciation of the social influences of the context on discourses (Johns, 1997, p. 5). Following colleagues in the area of critical studies applied to L2 teaching and learning (e.g., Canagarajah, 2005; Kubota & Lehner, 2004; Pennycook, 2001), we need to add a *critical* perspective to our professional endeavors to ensure that we assist learners in becoming reflective/critical consumers of literacy practices, thus questioning and evaluating implicit ideologies found in the texts learners read and compose. Such an approach is compatible with Freire's perspective (cited in Gersten & Hudelson, 2005, p. 41) in that learners need "to use their developing literacy to read the world, that is, to examine their own lives, understand their own situation, realities, and problems, and use reading and writing to act on or resolve their problems." According to Johns (1997):

> Literacies are acquired principally through this exposure to discourses from a variety of social contexts. Through this exposure, individuals gradually develop theories of genre as they acquire and enhance their knowledge of the various genres. Those who can successfully produce and process texts within certain genres are members of communities. (p. 14)

Indeed, active participation in academic contexts can result in greater chances for ELLs to learn and acquire the protocol of the academic context. Consider, for example, the case of the discourse in science classes. As Gersten and Hudelson (2005) pointed out, "L2 learners learn the discourse of science as they ask their own questions, figure out ways to investigate these questions, collect and develop evidence, and construct their own theories" (p. 33). This approach, however, calls for teachers to identify and teach the language needed to communicate all this information. Thus, in their teaching role, teachers of ELLs truly become academic literacy brokers, which is both a linguistic and cultural practice. They are the mediators between the ELLs and the academic language that these learners must acquire. To accomplish this, teachers must feel comfortable helping ELLs learn and use the academic language needed to perform across subject areas. For this to be possible, teachers must have explicit knowledge of English to plan meaningful activities, select appropriate materials, and teach aspects of language students will need to successfully perform academically.

A third approach, one that complements the critical socioliterate approach, is a *systemic functional (SF) linguistics approach*. It is based on SF theory and can technically assist teachers and students to understand how language functions, especially in the academic context. It offers teachers the possibility to understand and, in turn, to help ELLs understand discursive practices in context (Hyland, 2007). It also provides teachers with the tools to understand the linguistic choices (e.g., lexico-grammatical, discourse organizational) writers make in the contexts in which they function, resulting in different types of texts that will be judged differently. This approach requires that teachers and students engage in functional analyses of language. In doing so, teachers may ask learners to address some basic questions as they encounter texts (Schleppegrell & Achugar, 2003): What is happening? What can one say about the participants and their roles as portrayed in the text? What is the point of view being presented? Are there converging or conflicting points of view in the text? How is information organized?

Systemic functional linguistics theory is not new. As Christie (1999) notes, its origins date back to the work of Michael Halliday and Ruqaiya Hasan in the early 1960s, and it has been sustained over time, probably best known in the British and Australian context. Yet because of recent attention to the academic development of ELLs, it has gained greater attention in the United States. Hallidan and Hasan were inspired by the work of Basil Bernstein in England, a sociolinguist interested in figuring out ways to help struggling working class children succeed in schools, and by the work of Malinowski who, in the early 1920s, had already suggested that language use was shaped by its situational context.

Why should teachers consider an SF linguistics approach? As we know, the use of language in the academic context has been typically described as "dense and abstract" (Schleppegrell & Achugar, 2003). When ELLs read academic texts in the content areas, not only are they learning content, but also "particular ways of representing events, enacting interpersonal relations, and organizing information" (Schleppegrell & Achugar, 2003). This information can then serve to guide their future composing practices as well as their abilities to comprehend academic texts. By explicitly teaching ELLs about what is implicated in the particular choices writers make in textual production, teachers are helping learners expand their repertoire of academic and linguistic choices they may want to consider as they encounter academic texts across the subject areas. In other words, teachers are providing ELLs with specific linguistic and rhetorical strategies to successfully function in the academic context in addition to supporting language development.

Thus, an SF linguistics approach sheds light on genre knowledge, characterized as knowledge that is abstract, schematic, complex, sociocognitive, systematic, conventional, dynamic, and typically acquired by its repetition in context. It is indeed a form of shared knowledge that we must explicitly teach, for not all ELLs will have acquired this specific type of knowledge. In providing ELLs with the opportunity to master the genres various writers use in society, teachers of ELLs are providing them with access to a number of communities of practice, with particular attention to the academic community. These professional endeavors offer ELLs the opportunity to acquire the knowledge necessary to successfully function in and, ideally, positively shape their discourse communities or communities of practice.

An Integrated Approach and Its Effect on Language Transfer

Adopting an integrated approach that includes at least the three approaches just introduced may significantly help teachers provide better cross-language support for their ELLs. When teachers consider cross-language links as they prepare to teach ELLs, the development of literacy in a second language is supported. This task asks that teachers teach for transfer and help ELLs learn to use the resources they bring from their L1 more effectively as they acquire an L2. Research has consistently shown that many L1-based influences are positive, but some may result in interference or in what some term "negative transfer." Even when the latter occurs, however, it provides evidence of active cognitive student engagement (Escamilla, 2000).

What does teaching for transfer involve? At minimum it calls for two basic elements. First, it requires that teachers understand the sociolinguistic differences that may affect their ELLs' literacy practices. Second, it asks that teachers become knowledgeable of their students and their previous linguistic/literacy experiences. The former is accomplished by learning about specific features of the languages involved; the latter is accomplished by researching our students' personal and educational backgrounds, by virtue of examining any available previous school records, talking to family members, and so on. Teachers need to begin with what learners know, build upon their background knowledge, add to what they need to have (through connections to past learning, previous experiences, etc.), and integrate new learning with old learning. Teachers must also convey to students the idea that what is learned at school is a means to expand what they learn at home (Fillmore, 2005).

Support for the idea of teaching for transfer comes from knowing that a rigid and complete separation of languages is unlikely to result in optimal transfer of cognitive, conceptual, and linguistic knowledge across languages. Consequently, in order to accelerate ELLs' acquisition of English, teachers need to actively and continuously encourage ELLs to explore not only the nature of the target language, but also their native language. For instance, as ELLs tap into their own L1 resources, they may realize that there is a lot more they know about English as they predict the meaning of words that can be cognates, that is, words that may look similar in two languages but may or may not mean the same. False cognates are words that look alike in two languages but are not the same because they are translated differently. For instance, the word in Spanish *embarazada* means "pregnant," but many language learners think it is the equivalent of *embarrassed* in English. Positive cognates, on the other hand, are words that look alike and can have equivalent translations, such as the word *coloquial* in Spanish that can be successfully translated into English as *colloquial*. As teachers work toward building ELLs' linguistic and metalinguistic awareness, they may thus also be attending to some affective factors that can work toward their academic success (Delpit, 1995). When ELLs discover that their L1 can be a resource that can support their acquisition of English, they gain self-confidence and make faster progress on the language learning continuum.

Instructional Recommendations

Listed below are seven instructional recommendations and accompanying teaching examples that are based on the integrated approach just described. These recommendations can assist teachers not only in learning to examine the language of schooling as evidenced across subject areas, but also in providing their adolescent ELLs with strategic ways of learning to access and to produce these types of texts.

1. Sensitize ELLs to the different ways in which writers compose texts according to the communicative situation and purpose. Teachers may do so easily by exposing ELLs to nonacademic discourses that relate to the contents discussed in classes in their academic textbooks and that illustrate the difference between academic and nonacademic discourses. Teachers and students can engage in a compare-and-contrast type of analysis.

Example: Have learners reflect on the home discourse or the discourses they encounter in their neighborhoods, and ask them to talk about the differences between them and the academic discourse they encounter in their school context across the various subject areas. Perhaps have them compare a community paper discussing a topic that is also presented in their school textbook, such as the subject of global warming. In this way, students can see the distinct differences in how language is used according to the communicative situation and purpose.

2. Provide ELLs with opportunities to discover how texts interact with other texts, thus introducing them to the concept of intertextuality. Emphasize to students that texts rarely stand alone. All texts refer to other texts in our environment, instances that are broadly defined as communicative occurrences (de Beaugrande & Dressler, 1981). Indeed, help ELLs understand that the "production and reception of a given text depends upon the participants' knowledge of other texts" (de Beaugrande & Dressler, 1981).

Example: Ask your students what notes, previous conversations, and experiences fed into the texts that they themselves have produced. For instance, teachers may ask students to examine a text studied in history their class, such as the Declaration of Independence, and to identify any allusions that are made to other texts.

3. Teach learners how linguistic choices in academic texts are tied to the context, such as the use of cohesive devices, conjunctions and clause-combining strategies, nominalization, and grammatical metaphors. Call attention to the metalanguage of academic texts, especially the use of metadiscourse elements, also known as linking devices, signaling words, or connecting words that imply logical relationships. *Metadiscourse* as defined by Crismore, Markkanen, and Steffensen (1993) refers to "the linguistic material in texts, whether spoken or written, that does not add anything to the propositional content but that is intended to help the listener or reader organize, interpret, and evaluate the information given" (p. 40). Through such activity, students can learn that writers convey ideas at two different levels. At one level, they write to communicate content. At another level, writers offer guidance as to how ideas are connected to one another. Words such as *furthermore, moreover,* and *in addition* ask readers to *add* ideas in their mind. Words like *similarly, likewise, differently,* and *unlike* call for readers to engage in mental operations that involve identifying similarities and differences between or among ideas in a text. Thus, writers purposefully guide readers as to how their texts need to be understood.

Example: Focus on the use of metadiscourse in social studies or, more specifically, history texts. History textbooks typically make use of chronology. Bring examples to the classroom and point at discourse markers that demonstrate the use of chronology (e.g., *first, second, third, at the beginning, later*). Then have students bring their own examples, highlighting when these or similar terms are used in the text they selected.

4. Help students understand the purposefulness of writing in that it entails decision making, which is also culturally mediated. After all, "all texts are organized in culturally accepted ways" (Lenski & Ehlers-Zavala, 2004, p. 46).

Example: Have students reflect on and discuss textbook organization or how different kinds of texts are presented to their readers. Provide learners with a set of questions that prompt ELLs to wonder why the text is laid out in a particular way. For instance, you may bring to the classroom different types of newspapers; ask students to talk about the differences in the use of lettering, pictures, and colors and have them predict the kinds of audiences by whom those newspapers are meant to be read. Also consider exploring how different texts are produced in different cultures. For example, you may direct students to online texts, where students can explore how obituaries are written in U.S. newspapers versus newspapers in other countries, perhaps their countries of origin or those of their relatives and friends.

5. Expose students to authentic academic texts that have been developed for native speakers and have not been simplified or abridged for nonnative speakers. Then guide learners in uncovering the ideologies those texts convey and recreate.

Example: Select texts that have not been altered in any way, but that are linguistically accessible to your ELL students. Ask students to think about what might have motivated the writing of a particular text by identifying textual features that support their perspectives. Are there any textual biases? What textual elements suggest a particular position versus another?

6. Expose students to the diversity of academic discourse within genres. Explicitly teach and introduce learners to some of the genres of schooling (e.g., personal, expository).

Example: Ask students to search for text samples, from online or traditional sources, that show the diversity of written discourse within a given genre in a particular content/subject area.

7. Guide students into understanding the responsive nature of texts.

Example: Ask them to predict what expectations readers may have when reading different types of texts or how prospective readers may interpret their texts in light of particular linguistic choices.

Accommodations to Consider for ELLs

Success in translating the series of instructional recommendations offered thus far into classroom practice depends on overall effective lesson planning and delivery that is sensitive to students' diverse needs. It will require that instructors shelter their instruction. For an in-depth understanding of what it means to shelter instruction, professionals should become well versed in the Sheltered Instruction Observation Protocol (SIOP) model. This approach to teaching ELLs is introduced and developed in *Making Content Comprehensible for English Learners* (Echevarria, Vogt, & Short, 2004), and recommendations highlighted here are derived from this research-based model:

1. As you prepare to motivate students and initiate classroom instruction, be sure to build background knowledge on what they know from their personal experiences or previous learning. Be sure to elicit previously taught vocabulary that pertains not only to content, but also, which is very important, to textual analysis.

2. Introduce and model the production of texts to scaffold learners' initiation into academic discursive practices. That is, begin by providing learners with instruction that requires that you model for them how you attend to factors involved in the production and comprehension of texts. You may do so following a think-aloud type of protocol in which you voice the active process you use to comprehend a particular piece. The well-known DR-TA (Directed Reading–Thinking Activity) strategy may be very useful for this purpose. Once you realize students understand what is expected of them, you may have them work in small groups prior to engaging them in independent practice.

3. Implement different types of grouping configurations for the activities suggested above. You may start by having students work in pairs, small groups, whole class, and then individually. Leave individual practice for the very end to allow ELLs plenty of opportunity to master the target task.

4. Bring realia, or real objects, into the classroom to appeal to and support different learning styles. ELLs also vary in modes of learning. For instance, some students are visually oriented, whereas others prefer kinesthetic ways of learning. When teachers bring real objects into the classroom, ELLs greatly benefit by having additional support to make sense of the language they hear and are expected to acquire.

5. Provide comprehensible input. Monitor your language and ensure that students receive clear explanations of what they are to accomplish. Provide explanations both orally and in writing to support language development and understanding.

6. Check for understanding. Always observe and informally assess students' level of understandings of academic tasks to determine if further support is necessary.

Conclusions

Two central ideas have been developed in this chapter. First, ELLs come equipped with a great deal of linguistic and sociocultural resources. Teachers who work with ELLs need to understand the nature of those resources and to help ELLs align their wealth of knowledge with the expectations of the classroom context. Second, teachers are the mediators of ELLs' academic success regardless of whether teacher certification programs prepared them to face this challenge. Successful teachers seek ways to further their knowledge regarding how best to work with ELLs and identify professional development opportunities that will make them better prepared to help diverse ELL students learn the target language necessary for academic success. This language becomes increasingly complex as students move from one grade level to the next in middle and secondary schools. This makes it necessary for teachers to acquire a meta-understanding of their own native language, the language(s) of their students, and the language of schooling. Only in this way will teachers be able to plan and implement meaningful instruction that will effectively accelerate their ELLs' language development for academic achievement and long-term success.

References

Adamson, H. D. (1993). *Academic competence: Theory and classroom practice: Preparing ESL students for content courses.* White Plains, NY: Longman.

Baca, L., & Escamilla, K. (2002). Educating teachers about language. In C. T. Adger, C. E. Snow, & D. Christian (Eds.), *What teachers need to know about language* (pp. 71–84). McHenry, IL: Delta Systems.

Bazerman, C. (1998). *Shaping written knowledge.* Madison, WI: University of Wisconsin Press.

Biber, D. (1995). *Dimensions of register variation.* New York: Cambridge University Press.

Brisk, M., & Harrington, M. (2007). *Literacy and bilingualism* (2nd ed.). Mahwah, NJ: Erlbaum.

Canagarajah, S. A. (2005). *Critical academic writing.* Ann Arbor: University of Michigan Press.

Christie, F. (1999). *Pedagogy and the shaping of consciousness.* New York: Continuum.

Crismore, A., Markkanen, R., & Steffensen, M. (1993). Metadiscourse in persuasive writing. *Written Communication, 10*(1), 39–71.

Cummins, J. (1979). Cognitive/academic language proficiency, linguistic interdependence, the optimum age question and some other matters. *Working Papers on Bilingualism, 19,* 121–129.

Cummins, J. (1991). Interdependence of first- and second-language proficiency in bilingual children. In E. Bialystok (Ed.), *Language processing in bilingual children* (pp. 70–89). New York: Cambridge University Press.

de Beugrande, R., & Dressler, W. (1981). *Introduction to text linguistics.* New York: Longman.

Delpit, L. (1995). *Other people's children: Cultural conflict in the classroom.* New York: New Press.

Delpit, L. (2002). No kinda sense. In L. Delpit & J. K. Dowdy (Eds.), *The skin that we speak* (pp. 31–48). New York: New York Press.

Echevarria, J., Vogt, M. E., & Short, D. (2004). *Making content comprehensible for English learners: The SIOP model.* New York: Pearson/Allyn & Bacon.

Escamilla, K. (2000, April). *Bilingual means two: Assessment issues, early literacy, and Spanish-speaking children.* Paper presented at the Research Symposium on High Standards in Reading for Students from Diverse Language Groups: Research, Practice, and Policy, Washington, DC.

Fillmore, L. W. (2005, January). *Changing times, changing schools: Articulating leadership choices in educating bilingual students.* Paper presented at the annual meeting of the National Association for Bilingual Education, San Antonio, TX.

Freeman, D., Freeman, Y., & Meyers, M. (2005, January). *Promoting the development of academic Spanish and English for teachers and students.* Paper presented at the annual meeting of the National Association for Bilingual Education, San Antonio, TX.

Freeman, Y., & Freeman, D. (2003). Struggling English language learners: Keys for academic success. *TESOL Journal, 12*(3), 18–23.

Freeman, Y., & Freeman, D. (2006). *Teaching reading and writing in Spanish and English in bilingual and dual language classrooms* (2nd ed.). Portsmouth, NH: Heinemann.

Genesse, F. (2005, January). *Literacy development in ELLs: What does the research say?* Paper presented at the annual meeting of the National Association for Bilingual Education, San Antonio, TX.

Gersten, B. F., & Hudelson, S. (2005). Developments in second language acquisition research and theory: From structuralism to social participation. In P. A. Richard-Amato & M. A. Snow (Eds.), *Academic success for English language learners* (pp. 22–46). White Plains, NY: Longman.

Hyland, K. (2007). *Disciplinary discourses: Social interactions in academic writing.* Ann Arbor: University of Michigan Press.

Johns, A. (1997). *Text, role, and context: Developing academic literacies.* New York: Cambridge University Press.

Johns, A. M., Bawarshi, A., Coe, R. M., Hyland, K., Paltridge, B., Reif, M. J., et al. (2006). Crossing the boundaries of genre studies: Commentaries by experts. *Journal of Second Language Writing, 15*(3), 234–249.

Kubota, R., & Lehner, A. (2004). Toward critical contrastive rhetoric. *Journal of Second Language Writing, 13*(1), 7–28.

Larsen-Freeman, D. (2000). *Techniques and principles in language teaching* (2nd ed.). New York: Oxford University Press.

Lenski, S. D., & Ehlers-Zavala, F. (2004). *Reading strategies for Spanish speakers.* Dubuque, IA: Kendall/Hunt.

Paltridge, B. (2005, July). *Genres in context: Extending the borders and crossing boundaries.* Paper presented at the 14th World Congress of Applied Linguistics, Madison, WI.

Pennycook, A. (2001). *Critical applied linguistics: A critical introduction.* Mahwah, NJ: Erlbaum.

Richard-Amato, P. A., & Snow, M. A. (2005). *Academic success for English language learners.* White Plains, NY: Longman.

Schleppegrell, M. (2004). *The language of schooling: A functional linguistics perspective.* Mahwah, NJ: Erlbaum.

Schleppegrell, M., & Achugar, M. (2003). Learning language and learning history: A functional linguistics approach. *TESOL Journal, 12*(2), 21–27.

Schleppegrell, M., Achugar, M., & Oteíza, T. (2004). The grammar of history: Enhancing content-based instruction through a functional focus on language. *TESOL Quarterly, 38*(1), 67–93.

Schleppegrell, M., & Colombi, C. (Eds.). (2002). *Developing advanced literacy in first and second languages*. Mahwah, NJ: Erlbaum.

PART II

Organizing Classroom Contexts That Promote Literacy

CHAPTER 5

The Role of Technology in Supporting Struggling Readers

Dana L. Grisham
Thomas DeVere Wolsey

Technology is changing the way human beings do things at an ever-increasing tempo. There is no longer any serious argument among educators about the importance of technology integration in schools, only worries about how this integration can occur in the quickest and most meaningful way. The *Encarta World English Dictionary* defines *technology* as "a method or methodology that applies technical knowledge or tools." The history of human communication can be traced by the application of technical knowledge to provide better, faster communication of people with each other. A system of writing, for example, is a technology developed by humans to communicate over time and distance. In this chapter we present the rationale, research, and examples of ways that modern technologies can assist secondary educators to accomplish a very important mission: to successfully reach and teach struggling adolescent readers to communicate through technologies such as reading, writing, and other media. Throughout this chapter we refer to the new technologies of mass communication as ICT (Information, Communication, and Technology).

The Case of Brenda

Brenda is an eighth grader at a suburban middle school in the Midwest. She is quiet, never makes trouble for her teachers, and she is failing in almost all her classes. A close observer would note that Brenda is having trouble reading the material that she is assigned. When pressed to read aloud, she reluctantly reads haltingly, one or two words at a time, and softly, so that no one can hear if she makes a mistake. If the teacher asks her questions about what she has read, she answers in generalizations, such as, "That was a really interesting story." Brenda never reads for pleasure and also avoids writing, turning in partial assignments and never asking for the teacher's help. Brenda is a loner at school, but outside school she participates avidly in IM (instant messaging) with her friends and has an active page with blog entries she updates regularly on *MySpace.com*—a popular social networking website.

What can teachers do to help students like Brenda and other struggling adolescent readers? How can we identify the strengths that Brenda brings to the classroom and the strategies we might use to build on those strengths?Brenda has access to technology—at least at home, perhaps at school. She has developed a substantial set of ICT skills, as evidenced by her presence on MySpace, the use of navigation and composition skills, the use of various emotions in her IM communications, and manipulation of visual images on MySpace (to highlight aspects of one's appearance and personality to create meaning). The competent social networking identity of the Brenda on MySpace contrasts starkly with her quiet and solitary school identity. Brenda is highly motivated by her out-of-school social networks that rely on technology and literacy.

Research on Technology and Struggling Readers

As Brenda's case illustrates, technology can play a crucial role in the academic literacy development of struggling adolescent readers. Four themes emerge from the research literature that can help teachers understand how technology can be used to help struggling readers: access, identity, motivation and engagement, and skills.

Access to Technology

Although Brenda has access to technology at home, this may not be true of other struggling readers who may have access to technology only at school. Further, many schools do not have technology available to their students, or the available technologies may not be used by students (Hoctor, 2005).

For all these students, the digital divide (see, e.g., Hoffman & Novak, 1999; U.S. Department of Commerce, 1999) represents the gulf between those who have access to technology, represented by electronic services such as the Internet, and those who do not. Learning to use ICT is critical to students' success in college and the world of work. All students, including struggling adolescent readers, need access to the most recent forms of technology that are available.

Bruce (2000) reminds us that access to tools such as computers and an Internet connection transcend mere availability. If students are to become adept at using technology for their learning and in their lives, schools must teach those technology skills and new literacies necessary for students to succeed regardless of students' access to technology outside the school. Alvermann (2004) describes these literacies as the "sociocultural, economic, and political struggles that come with reading the world, not just the word" (p. viii). This also requires a different view of "literacy" than many teachers espouse, as well as an approach to teaching that includes the use of technology as part of instruction, rather than an isolated skill-development perspective (Boling, 2005; Grisham & Wolsey, 2006b; Hoctor, 2005).

Schools and teachers must also take a long-term view. It will not be possible for transformation to occur quickly. Purposeful implementation with appropriate support and training opportunities are important. Such approaches must be flexible because the technology will change even as implementation occurs. Similarly, students' needs change from year to year and as they become increasingly proficient with current technologies. Indeed, a study in Australia suggested that students are now less motivated by the novelty of technology as an instructional tool simply because computers have come, in the students' minds, to be associated with school rather than with leisure (Woolcott Research Pty., Ltd., 2001).

Identity

Brenda has constructed an identity for herself as a nonreader and nonwriter in academic settings even though she uses many literacy skills in her life outside school. Adolescence is a time of identity building; often the identity built is a composite of many identities that adolescents "try on" as they navigate their academic and social worlds (Unrau, 2004). Indeed, Brenda is a literate individual who reads and writes in her world on social networking sites, but she just doesn't think about herself in those terms. In cyberspace, she uses literacy skills in manipulating symbol systems to create an identity without thinking of herself as literate. An adept teacher may help Brenda bridge the world of her online identity with the academic world where Brenda perceives that she has few, if any, competencies to bring to bear. A significant aspect of identity is the perceptions of others, such as a caring teacher, parents, and peer groups.

Often middle and high school students who struggle with reading do not think of the tasks they enjoy in cyberspace as literacy skills and may develop elaborate coping mechanisms to cover their perceived inadequacies (Brozo, 1990). Students who do not engage, or perhaps cannot engage, with complex texts at the secondary level may instead create identities as outsiders. Having created such identities, they seek out others with similar perceptions to categorize their mental constructions of the world (Chayko, 2002). In contrast to the outsider peer groups, struggling students may then categorize their peers who do engage with academic tasks as "schoolboys," "schoolgirls," or "geeks," thus letting themselves off the hook for further effort at engaging with texts or academic tasks. Technology, on the other hand, is appealing to students because it allows them to create identities that they view as positive and to create communities of individuals with similar views. Whether it has to do with gaming, creating a third space (see, e.g., Rowe & Leander, 2005) on MySpace, or downloading a massive collection of music, the identity that a student creates online can be a powerful bridge to a larger, more inclusive identity as a reader of many texts and sources of information.

For struggling adolescent readers, their self-perceptions as nonreaders are compounded daily by increasingly difficult literacy tasks and an increasing lack of engagement. Students who don't think of themselves as capable readers in academic classes that depend heavily on literacy skills for comprehension and learning are unlikely to work to close that gap. Technology, for many reasons, can help students view and identify themselves as literate individuals.

Motivation and Engagement

The findings of research on technology as a motivator for adolescent students are fairly positive (Grisham & Wolsey, 2006b; Leu, Kinzer, Coiro, & Cammack, 2004; O'Brien, 2001; Wolsey, 2004). For struggling adolescent readers, motivation to engage with reading is critically important because they have "failed" so often. Adolescents, in creating their identities as individuals, similarly seek to connect those identities with others. As Chayko (2002) states, "It is in groups and communities that our minds become structured in a manner similar to others" (p. 20). Technology makes such identity construction possible and at the same time allows the technically literate to connect with other people. We argue that the motivation to construct an identity and test it out is a powerfully motivating factor in the world beyond the classroom, and that it can be so in the classroom as well. If teachers learn to recognize the strengths students bring with them (Moje & Sutherland, 2003; Wiles & Bondi, 1986) in ways that don't, at first, appear to be academically useful, new connections and motivations to participate can occur.

Technology as motivator is more extensive and complex than Computer-Assisted Instruction (CAI)—whereby students learn basic skills from an endlessly patient and repetitive electronic teacher. In our research on the intersection of literature and technology, we found that boys identified themselves as better writers after participating in threaded discussions about literature conducted online. This was a statistically significant finding for both boys and girls, but the correlation for boys (.513) was much stronger, suggesting that boys' increased engagement in academic reading and writing tasks was linked with ICT (Grisham & Wolsey, 2006a).

Technology Skills

Literacy has traditionally been thought of as reading and writing; remedial programs tend to concentrate on skills that struggling readers lack, often going back to phonics and phonemic awareness levels to "fill in the gaps." However, literate individuals are now defined as those who are proficient in all forms of communication (Alvermann & Hagood, 2000; Bruce, 2004; O'Brien, 2001). As human beings, we are noted for our use of varied symbols and systems of symbols to communicate with one another. Reading and writing are only two of the many symbol systems that we use to communicate our thoughts and ideas. Any agreed-upon or culturally shared system of symbols that allows us to communicate with one another qualifies as communication.

Semiotics is the study of symbols, symbol systems, and meaning making from those symbols. From a social semiotic perspective (Gee, 2001), learners come to participate in "semiotic domains." A semiotic domain recruits one or more "modalities" to communicate distinctive types of messages. An example is "reading," in which communication takes place in highly specified ways. Readers must learn to participate in the domain according to a set of rules called a "design grammar." Readers must also belong to an "affinity group," which is formed through shared practices and common endeavors. Online gamers create a similar domain with rules for participation in the community that are complex and opaque to nonparticipants. An "insider–outsider" relationship exists for each domain, and Gee (2001) emphasizes that these are shared *practices*, not shared culture, gender, or ethnicity. The way that one becomes part of an affinity group, learns the design grammar, and ultimately becomes adept and a part of a semiotic domain is, in a nutshell, what learning is all about.

In reading, advantaged learners are those who have had some precursor domains to the new semiotic domain. A precursor domain, in this instance, could be 1,000 hours of "lap time," in which a young child interacts with an adult and a text, as in picture book sharing. This child is advantaged because he or she has already had exposure to and experience with the design grammar (taking turns, making shared meaning from a page, knowing letters, moving left to right, etc.). In contrast, disadvantaged learners have little experience in precursor domains and thus must pay a larger entry price to master a semiotic domain such as reading. For a learner to be willing to pay the entry price, there must be something in it for the learner (Cambourne, 1988) so that learners are willing and motivated to engage in extended practice in the domain in such a way that they take on and grow into a new socially situated identity—one that they can see as a fruitful extension of their core sense of who they are. If a learner cannot envision him- or herself as part of the semiotic domain (a reader), then that learner may not do the things necessary (pay the entry price) to learn the design grammar or become a part of the affinity group.

Social semiotics has a bearing on why struggling adolescent learners often decline to participate in learning activities that will enable them to make academic gains. They have opted out of the semiotic domain of reading and need to be convinced that there is something in it for them and that they are capable of being successful readers. Therefore, we believe that an important focus of reading instruction for struggling adolescents needs to support the struggling adolescent reader in joining the semiotic domain of reading. Technology competence can be an important and interrelated component of the means for joining the domain of academic readers (Goetze & Walker, 2004). Technology can potentially assist students to pay the entry price and join the ranks of the domain of readers for those students who have some affinity or proficiency with others who use technology in their lives. Similarly, some technologies have the potential, in the hands of a capable teacher, to reduce the entry price to become a reader.

A Rationale and Principles for Schoolwide Technology Integration

In order for technology integration to support all adolescent readers, not just struggling readers, important supports must be present in the school and classroom. One of the critical components is school and district support for technology. While there are many teachers who have grappled with integrating technology in their classrooms as solitary adventurers, when a school or a district makes the decision to use technology in a meaningful way, it supports the teachers' efforts. We argue that there should be an institutionalization of technology that will be consistent over time so as to exist after the possible exit of the technology pioneers.

Second, if teachers are to employ technology in the service of better education, and particularly in the service of those students least engaged with school, there are some considerations that must be given priority. Resources must be deployed in a way that makes them accessible. A typical school might have one or more computer labs and each teacher may have a computer on the teacher's desk. Although labs are useful in some ways, they do not perhaps provide the best way to deploy computers for student use (Wolsey, 2007; Zandvliet, 2006). Stewart (1999) suggests that businesses that make information accessible "just-in time" are likely to be more successful than businesses that have huge inventories of products or information "just-in-case." Imagine a business executive having to wait until his or her scheduled computer lab day to get work done. Students need access to computers and other ICTs whenever the need arises, not just on computer lab day. This means that a sufficient number of computers need to be in the classroom where the students work and learn every day, a view consistent with the National Academy of Engineering recommendations (Pearson & Young, 2002) and the Carnegie report *Writing Next* (Graham & Perin, 2007). This also means that teachers need to be comfortable in using these technologies and trusting that these policies on the deployment of resources will change over time.

Third, as technology emerges and changes, so must our teaching and learning practices. Bruce (2000) discusses technology using the metaphor of a digital river. In order to navigate the digital river, one must have a put-in point, a canoe, and the ability to paddle that canoe:

- Finding a canoe—the computer, the Internet link, data, and software,
- Being able to paddle—having the necessary tools so that factors like language and physical ability are no barrier,
- Finding an access point—having the network of social relationships and knowledge that make a journey possible.

Finally, the opportunity to engage meaningfully with texts and with other students using technology as a mediator has a strong influence on students' attitudes toward academics. Gardner (2000) challenges schools to do more with technology than "simply deliver the old lessons in more convenient and efficient formats" (p. 31). For that to happen, teachers, parents, and even students (Brozo, 2006) must be involved in a participatory and collaborative manner—the fourth principle. What technology will be used and how will it be implemented? In what ways can schools and school agencies support teachers? How might a teacher use technology to improve instruction rather than simply use it to accomplish the same old tasks with more expensive equipment (Means, Roschelle, Penuel, Sabelli, & Haertel, 2003)? Implied in this model is a further principle held by the school community regarding the contribution of technology to the educational infrastructure as one that is progressive, that the community continually explore how its needs may best be met through technology and at the same time continually reflect on the effectiveness of the tools already in place.

One example of effective technology integration is the Lemon Grove School District in California, a K–8 district that has focused its educational reform issues on technology innovation and integration over the past 10 years (Hoctor, 2006). In Lemon Grove's work, the five principles we have described can be observed. First, the district has marshaled and dedicated the necessary *resources* for the integration of technology into all its classrooms and for the professional development of all its teachers. Second, the reform effort has been *long-term*, beginning with a technology pioneer but sustained beyond this individual's efforts over a decade. Third, the technology program has proven *flexible*—able to adjust to new situations (for example, this district became a provider of technology to the city government) and new technologies (they adopted, and then adapted, a thin-client unit so that it could withstand students dropping them). Fourth, the process has been *collaborative*, in that the technology systems evolved to meet the needs of teachers, parents, and students, as well as the school administration. In addition, groups of teachers came to be leaders and mentors for other teachers as the reform unfolded. Fifth, the technology integration program was *progressive*: It included ever greater numbers of teachers using technology and increasingly complex uses of technology. For example, at the beginning a small group of willing teachers participated. As the years went by, increasing numbers of teachers became involved in a trainer-of-trainers model of professional development within the district, which began with PowerPoint® and later involved Internet searching for educational resources and individual webpages for classrooms. Finally, an intranet communications system called LemonLinks connected everyone in the district (for a full discussion, see Hoctor, 2006).

Professional development that is required for teachers to integrate technology meaningfully into their curricula and classrooms has been a recent focus in the professional literature (Gibson & Oberg, 2004; Kanaya, Light, & Culp, 2005; Meier, 2005). Gibson and Oberg (2004), however, identify three barriers to technology integration: limited infrastructure support, difficulties in infusing Internet use into existing curricula, and the lack of appropriate professional development for teachers. Schools in most states are now wired (or wireless) for Internet access, and hardware and common software (such as the Microsoft Office Suite components) are available for teacher and student use. For example, the California Technology Assistance Program (CTAP), in its 2003 report for *School Technology Survey Findings*, reported that the percentage of schools in California wired for Internet access grew from 58% in 2000 to 90% in 2003. Research also indicates, however, that many classroom computers are underutilized and

that hardware maintenance and technology support are often lacking and/
or take inordinate amounts of time to be furnished (California Technology
Assistance Program, 2003; Cuban, Kirkpatrick, & Peck, 2001). Some
teachers have reported that technology integration can be more trouble
than it is worth in view of the pressure to raise test scores "on the basics"
(Proctor, Dalton, & Grisham, 2007). Yet despite these barriers there are
many promising technological practices that support struggling readers in
secondary schools.

Practical Applications of Technology for Struggling Adolescent Readers

Researchers and scientists at CAST propose that as teachers work with students' diverse learning styles, those who struggle to learn in the traditional
school setting, and students with emotional, behavioral, linguistic, physical,
and sensory difficulties, they take an approach called the Universal Design
for Learning. This approach calls for the following:

- *Multiple means of representation,* to give learners various ways of acquiring
  information and knowledge,
- *Multiple means of expression,* to provide learners alternatives for demonstrating what they know,
- *Multiple means of engagement,* to tap into learners' interests, offer appropriate challenges, and increase motivation. (*www.cast.org/research/udl/
  index.html*)

Using this model as a framework for thinking about what struggling readers need, we examine several areas where technology may be of particular
help to teachers of struggling adolescent readers. They include meaningful
assessment, readability and engagement, and instruction that offers multiple ways of acquiring knowledge.

Meaningful Assessment

Technology facilitates assessment in powerful ways to assist teachers who
need to know why a particular student struggles with reading. It offers
learners alternatives for demonstrating what they know. Every struggling
reader is a unique amalgam of characteristics and only a teacher knowledgeable about the needs of struggling readers in general and the needs of a
specific student sitting in that teacher's classroom, can make any meaningful determination about ways to assess his or her students. Much pertinent
information can be gleaned from computer-based testing that effortlessly

tracks assessment results and supplements what a teacher gains from daily interaction with students, real reading situations, informal reading inventories, and knowing what interests and motivates the students in that class.

Computer-adaptive assessments such as those produced by the Northwest Evaluation Association (NWEA) (*www.nwea.org/assessments/*) allow teachers access to specific information about where students' skill-specific strengths and areas of need may be. Students evaluated with one assessment tool from NWEA are assigned an RIT (Rasch Unit) score, which can be used for refining instruction and grouping students. (See Figure 5.1.) The assessment components of Accelerated Reader® and Reading Counts!® (*www.teacher.scholastic.com/products/readingcounts/index.htm*) provide data on levels of comprehension as students read selected books

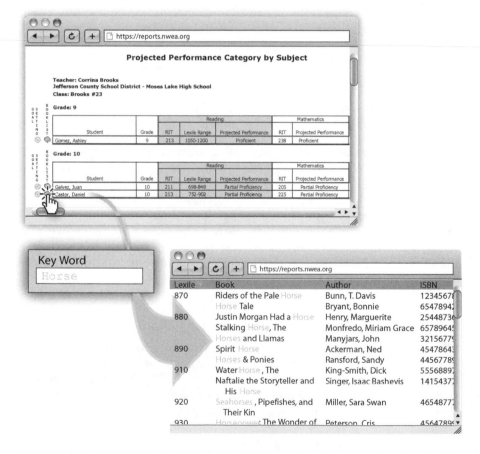

FIGURE 5.1. NWEA Rasch Unit and Lexile Report by classroom. Reprinted with permission from the Northwest Education Association.

and other texts. Nevertheless, there is a continuing dialogue as to whether the extrinsic motivators provided by such programs produce lasting improvement (Kohn, 1993; Krashen, 2005; Pavonetti, Brimmer, & Cipielweski, 2002).

Readability and Engagement

Technology can promote student engagement with text. Many struggling readers will not engage with texts that are too difficult to read (Allington, 2002). Often, texts and readers are matched on a sliding scale including independent reading, instruction-level reading, and frustration-level reading (see Table 5.1) (Betts, 1946; Ohlhausen & Jepsen, 1992; Tompkins, 2003), though this is more common in remedial programs, elementary schools, and to a lesser degree, middle schools. Teachers also need to keep in mind that comprehension scores for reading expository text may lag well behind those for reading narrative text (Moss & Hendershot, 2002). If teachers want to help students find books that they can read, then it is important to have some guidelines for selecting books. Readability formulas are helpful tools for finding texts that students should be able to read. Microsoft Word® is able to produce a readability summary using several different formulas. An example of the results for a draft of this chapter can be seen in Figure 5.2. An online resource for other readability formulas can be found on Kathy Schrock's discoveryschool.com website at *school.discovery.com/ schrockguide/fry/fry.html*.

The Lexile Framework is another tool that is able to match readers with texts. Online tools for educators include a book database where teachers can find the Lexile measure for various books, an online text analyzer that permits teachers to determine a Lexile measure for supplementary materials, and a Lexile calculator to determine expected comprehension. Click on the "Educator" link on the Lexile Framework® home page at *www.lexile.com*. Teachers who want students to engage with content-area reading tasks make use of information about their students' interests and abilities as well as data about the texts students will read. In addition to the information obtained from readability estimates, teachers should also consider specific content-area vocabulary and how sophisticated the concepts represented in the text are.

TABLE 5.1. Reading Levels

	Independent	Instruction	Frustration
Comprehension accuracy	90–100%	75–89%	Less than 75%
Word recognition accuracy	95–100%	90–94%	Less than 90%

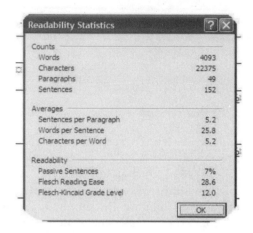

FIGURE 5.2. Readability statistics from Microsoft Word.

Instruction That Offers Multiple Ways of Acquiring Knowledge

A teacher knowledgeable about the needs of struggling readers in general, and the needs of a specific student in particular, can make meaningful determinations about how to address that student's instructional needs. Technology can be a useful tool for that teacher. Teachers should therefore consider their resources as they develop methods to help struggling middle and high school students become better readers.

What technologies and supports are available to the teacher? Does the teacher have access to computers? How many computers are available and at what times? What software programs does the school/district support? Can students (under the teacher's supervision) access the Internet? Gaining knowledge of available resources (and potential resources) is key to using technology for instruction. Even when only one computer is available to a teacher, there are numerous ways in which that computer may be used to enhance instruction for students (see, e.g., *www.kathyschrock.net/1computer/1computer.htm*). For a list of electronic resources and teacher-friendly and useful websites, see Appendix 5.1 at the end of this chapter.

CAI and Easily Replaceable Tasks

Many teachers are familiar with CAI. Most CAI consists of software programs bought to teach particular skills to students. Such programs are "infinitely patient" teachers, but they also focus on fairly low-level skills and provide needed repetition for some struggling readers, while providing "more of the same" to students who may become bored and disengaged with the software and the drills. Other software products such as the CAST e-Reader© can provide support for struggling readers by converting text to speech (for information, go to *www.cast.org/products/ereader/index.html*). A number of textbook publishers also provide an array of software programs for the classroom, but teachers need to be sure that such programs actually meet the needs of the students in their classes.

Teachers may start out with easily replaceable tasks that can be done more efficiently with technology. Begin with small steps that increase *transparency* with technology by enhancing instruction. Teachers may *replace* low-technology tasks, such as pencil and paper reports, by incorporation of technology such as PowerPoint® presentations. For example, in one class the researchers studied, groups of middle school students went online to investigate Civil War battles to produce reports about them in PowerPoint® slides that were combined to form a class museum exhibit. Figure 5.3, shows an example from that class project. In addition to learning about Native American tribes, students have learned to compare facts from pre-designated websites, work together to gather information, and to represent that information with technology.

Improve Low-Technology Tasks

Teachers can also improve low-technology tasks. One example is the use of graphic organizers for content instruction. A time line in social studies can be represented as easily using a computer as with a pencil and a ruler, but a timeline creation tool can generate a sophisticated and visually appealing product that will thrill students and their parents (see Figure 5.4). Tables,

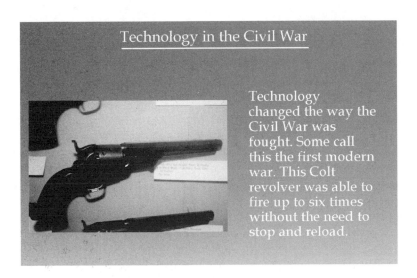

FIGURE 5.3. Museum PowerPoint slide.

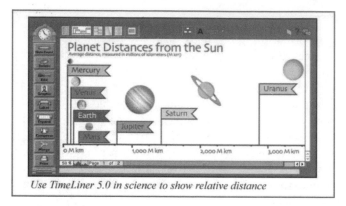

FIGURE 5.4. Example of TimeLiner 5.0 in science. Reprinted with permission from Tom Snyder Productions.

charts, and graphs can be represented in Microsoft Excel® in various formats. Converting a table to a pie chart, for example, can help students to see relationships that might elude them if only one representation is used.

Computer-Generated Visuals

Another example of improving instruction through technology is the use of computer-generated visuals and diagrams to demonstrate a range of concepts, such as vocabulary, structured chapter overviews, and organizing for prewriting; there are many other applications that can assist students to visualize content. Using "old" technologies, students can create clusters or diagrams with pencil and paper; today, they can use either Inspiration® or similar mind-mapping tools to create the diagrams, as shown in Figure 5.5 (a tree diagram). If such specialized software programs are not available, Microsoft Word's® drawing tools can be used for this purpose.

Include Projects of Greater Complexity

Although some technologies are useful for replacing tasks students could do with paper and pencil and others are useful enhancements for tasks that students can complete with traditional instructional tools, still other technologies make whole new realms of learning possible. One such technology is the asynchronous threaded discussion group. There are several ways to create threaded discussion groups (TDGs) using e-mail programs, commercial sites like Google Groups, nonprofit websites like Nicenet.org, or a bulletin board that can be included in a school or class webpage. A teacher of our acquaintance uses Moodle, a classroom management system, to upload student-created newspapers and then engage in dialogue about those artifacts.

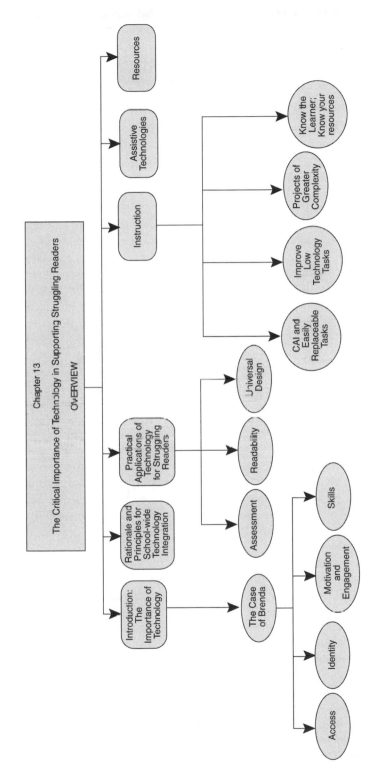

FIGURE 5.5. Overview using Inspiration software.

In threaded discussion, students post their thoughts about a topic, but they also respond to other students in the discussion. In this way, a TDG is like an ordinary conversation, but the comments are written down. However, TDGs are also asynchronous, which means, for example, that what Brenda wrote yesterday is still available for John to read today. Because of this time difference, John can stop and think about his reply, composing his thoughts in a more organized manner and with greater academic focus. TDGs do not occur in real time as chat rooms do. For this reason, we authors have not found many instructional uses of the chat room, which is a synchronous tool. It is only when students have time to consider what their peers have written and what they might write in response that critical thinking and increased motivation occurs. For readers who struggle because writing and reading tasks are of low importance, the TDG offers motivation; we found that peers often encouraged each other to keep reading, to keep up in the reading, and to engage in a social construction of a text's meaning by working thoughtfully with peers (Grisham & Wolsey, 2006a, 2006b; Wolsey, 2004).

The Use of Games

Games have the potential to help struggling readers in a variety of ways, too. Although games have been a pedagogical tool for millennia, a computer simulation can help a reader construct a complex understanding of an entire system that mechanical or two-dimensional models simply cannot. For example, students who play a U.S. Revolutionary War computer game may gain valuable background knowledge that can improve their reading about that period of history: place names, types of weapons, commanders and political figures, and geographical locations in relation to each other on a map. Complex principles of economics and politics may similarly be learned in advance of a reading assignment by playing interactive games designed for more than one student, like those from Tom Snyder Productions (*www.tomsnyder.com*). Search for other worthwhile simulations and demonstration downloads by typing "game demos" in the *About.com* reference tool. Students can gain valuable background knowledge needed to make sense of content-area texts through simulations like those at *www.froguts.com* before reading those texts. Once students become familiar with the visual representation and organization of the simulation, the reading on a given topic will be increasingly comprehensible for students who lack background knowledge for that topic. Of course, teachers must use such games and simulations judiciously, keeping instructional goals and standards in mind.

Students who may identify themselves less as readers or students and more as members of communities of online gaming or other cybercommunities may benefit from the bridge between the literacies needed to navigate such communities while doing what Alvermann and Heron (2001) call *literacy identity work*. Our students were interested in the popular game Halo (Microsoft Game Studios, 2003), then found and read books based on this game (Grisham & Wolsey, 2006a).

Student-Created Web Pages and Internet Searches

Student-created web pages (using tools such as DreamWeaver® and Blue Web'n) and blogs can be advantageous for students because they utilize both academic and new literacies like Hypertext and graphical user interfaces (GUI). Today's students tend to be savvy about multimedia and we should teach them to think of themselves as "literate" in these modalities as well as capitalizing on students' interests and strengths to learn more conventional literacies.

A new area of research interest and of interest to teachers working with struggling readers involves the practice of reading on the Internet. Hypertext Mark Up Language (HTML) provides text that may or may not be read in a linear manner. The study of how humans navigate websites is part of this interest. John McEneaney (2000) explored the idea of nonlinear reading through "nodes" of hypertext. Eagleton and Dobler (2007) take a more comprehensive look at strategies that teachers may use to teach Internet reading and searching in their book *Reading the Web: Strategies for Internet Inquiry*.

Assistive Technologies

As a result of the move toward inclusion, general education teachers face increasing diversity in their classrooms. Assistive technology is typically defined as any device that assists students to do tasks that their disabilities may otherwise have prevented. For example, a wheelchair is an assistive technology for a student who cannot walk. The range of assistive technology products continually changes because of new technological breakthroughs. By the time you read this, new products will have been invented, which did not exist at press time, to assist students in new ways, whether their disabilities are physical or cognitive in nature. Collaboration with other experts is crucial to the success of incorporating students using assistive technology into the classroom community.

Assistive technologies vary widely, according to the type of disability. There are high-incidence disabilities (most prevalent are the various *learning disabilities*). *Physical disabilities* are usually of low incidence—included in this category are auditory disorders (deaf and hard of hearing students) and visual disorders such as blindness. A final category that we recognize is the group of students with *multiple disabilities*. Currently, text messaging and instant messaging via cell telephones and other technologies, such as SideKick®, which were not available only a few years ago, provide deaf students access to communication with both deaf and hearing populations.

An excellent source of information on assistive technology is the IRIS Center for Faculty Enhancement, located at Vanderbilt University. Funded by the Office of Special Education Programs (OSEP), the IRIS site provides a comprehensive set of modules on various topics, including assistive technologies. The modules are based on anchored instruction for technology-based learning developed by the Cognition and Technology Group at Vanderbilt (CTGV) under the leadership of John Bransford (Cognition and Technology Group at Vanderbilt, 1993). The site contains—at this writing—14 modules and numerous other resources for teachers and may be accessed at *iris.peabody.vanderbilt.edu/index.html*.

Conclusions

New literacies permeate every aspect of our lives in the 21st century. Students should become proficient in navigating these media and making sense of them. Even though many students are familiar with today's technologies (Prensky, 2001, refers to them as digital natives) they are not necessarily proficient or critical users of the technologies they encounter. In addition to familiarity with hardware and software tools, access to technology includes knowing how to use them in productive ways. Teachers of struggling readers can use students' interests in technology as a bridge to increasing all aspects of students' literate lives, both traditional and new. Moreover, technology in the service of education may motivate students through the social worlds that technology enables in physical space and in cyberspace. For struggling readers, the value of any school activity is mediated in large part by the worth the reader attaches to the activity and how it contributes to the constructed identity of that student. A variety of assistive technologies improve the quality of educational life for students and teachers.

Ideally, computers need to be located where the students are, not off in some physically distant location like a computer lab. Teachers should familiarize themselves with what new and emerging technologies can do, even though they may not be proficient in using all of them. Teachers often consider themselves as digital immigrants, whereas their seemingly more proficient students are regarded as natives in the world of technology (Prensky, 2001), but it sometimes takes an *outsider* (Lankshear & Knobel, 2003) perspective to truly understand the implications of how an innovative tool may be used for instruction or what a new literacies perspective might entail. Schools and districts may enhance or impede the possibilities for effective employment of technology as a means to improve what students can do and what value they attach to literacy in the classroom and in their lives. Teachers can and should be the brokers who know their students well enough, who are willing to explore the potential of technology, and who take the necessary risks to assist struggling adolescent readers to build an identity as literate individuals.

References

Allington, R. L. (2002). You can't learn much from books you can't read. *Educational Leadership, 60*(3), 16–19.

Alvermann, D. E. (2004). Preface. In D. E. Alvermann (Ed.), *Adolescents and literacies in a digital world* (pp. vii–xi). New York: Peter Lang.

Alvermann, D. E., & Hagood, M. C. (2000). Critical media literacy: Research, theory, and practice in "new times." *Journal of Educational Research, 93*(3), 193–205.

Alvermann, D., & Heron, A. H. (2001). Literacy identity work: Playing to learn with popular media. *Journal of Adolescent and Adult Literacy, 45*, 118–122.

Betts, E. A. (1946). *Foundations of reading instruction with emphasis on differentiated guidance.* New York: American Book.

Boling, E. C. (2005, May). *Evaluating, selecting, and using technologies that support literacy instruction.* Paper presented at the 50th annual convention of the International Reading Association, San Antonio, TX.

Brozo, W. G. (1990). Hiding out in secondary content classrooms: Coping strategies of unsuccessful readers. *Journal of Reading, 33*(5), 324–328.

Brozo, W. G. (2006). Tales out of school: Accounting for adolescents in a literacy reform community. *Journal of Adolescent and Adult Literacy, 49*(5), 410–418.

Bruce, B. C. (2000, November). Access points on the digital river. *Journal of Adolescent and Adult Literacy, 44*(3). Available: *www.readingonline.org/electronic/elec_index.asp?HREF=/electronic/jaal/11-00_Column/index.html.*

Bruce, B. C. (2004). Diversity and critical social engagement: How changing technologies enable new modes of literacy in changing circumstances. In D. E. Alvermann (Ed.), *Adolescents and literacies in a digital world* (pp 1–18) New York: Peter Lang.

California Technology Assistance Program. (2003). *Summary of year 2003: School technology survey, California statewide report.* Sacramento: California Department of Education.

Cambourne, B. (1988). *The whole story: Natural learning and the acquisition of literacy in the classroom.* Auckland, NZ: Ashton Scholastic.

Chayko, M. (2002). *Connecting: How we form social bonds and communities in the Internet age.* New York: State University of New York Press.

Cognition and Technology Group at Vanderbilt. (1993). Anchored instruction and situated cognition revisited. *Educational Technology, 33*(3), 52–70.

Eagleton, M. B., & Dobler, E. (2007). *Reading the web: Strategies for Internet inquiry.* New York: Guilford Press.

Gardner, H. (2000). Technology remakes the schools. *Futurist, 34*(2), 30–32.

Gee, J. P. (2001). Reading as situated language: A socio-cognitive perspective. *Journal of Adolescent and Adult Literacy, 44*, 714–725.

Gibson, S., & Oberg, D. (2004). Visions and realities of Internet use: Canadian perspectives. *British Journal of Educational Technology, 35*(5), 569–585.

Goetze, S., & Walker, B. J. (2004). At-risk readers can construct complex meanings: Technology can help. *The Reading Teacher, 57*, 778–780.

Graham, S., & Perin, D. (2007). *Writing Next: Effective strategies to improve writing of adolescents in middle and high schools.* New York: Carnegie Corporation.

Grisham, D. L., & Wolsey, T. D. (2006a, April). *Adolescents and the new literacies:*

Access for achievement. Paper presented at the American Educational Research Association, San Francisco.

Grisham, D. L., & Wolsey, T. D. (2006b). Recentering the middle school classroom as a vibrant learning community. *Journal of Adult and Adolescent Literacy, 49*, 648–660.

Hoctor, M. (2005, May). *Collaborative technology training*. Paper presented at the 50th Annual Convention of the International Reading Association, San Antonio, TX.

Hoctor, M. (2006). *Investigating professional development in technology for literacy teachers*. Unpublished doctoral dissertation, San Diego State University and University of San Diego.

Hoffman, D. L., & Novak, T. P. (1999). *The evolution of the digital divide: Examining the relationship of race to Internet access and usage over time*. Retrieved June 26, 2005, from Vanderbilt University, Sloan Center for Internet Retailing website: *elab.vanderbilt.edu/*.

Kanaya, T., Light, D., & Culp, K. M. (2005). Factors influencing outcomes from a technology-focused professional development program. *Journal of Research on Technology and Education, 37*(3), 313–329.

Kohn, A. (1993). *Punished by rewards: The trouble with gold stars, incentive plans, A's, praise, and other bribes*. Boston: Houghton Mifflin.

Krashen, S. (2005). Accelerated Reader: Evidence still lacking. *Knowledge Quest, 33*(3), 48–49.

Lankshear, C., & Knobel, M. (2003). *New literacies: Changing knowledge and classroom learning*. Maidenhead, Berkshire, UK: Open University.

Leu, D. J., Jr., Kinzer, C. K., Coiro, J., & Cammack, D. W. (2004). Toward a theory of new literacies emerging from the Internet and other information and communication technologies. In R. B. Ruddell & N. Unrau (Eds.), *Theoretical models and processes of reading* (5th ed., pp. 1570–1613). Newark, DE: International Reading Association.

McEneaney, J. E. (2000, November). Ink to link: A hypertext history in 36 nodes. *Reading Online, 4*(5). Available: *www.readingonline.org/articles/art_index. asp?HREF=/articles/mceneaney2/index.html*.

Means, B., Roschelle, R., Penuel, W., Sabelli, N., & Haertel, G. (2003). Technology's contribution to teaching and policy: Efficiency, standardization, or transformation? *Review of Research in Education, 27*, 159–181.

Meier, E. B. (2005). Situating technology professional development in urban schools. *Journal of Educational Computing Research, 32*, 395–407.

Microsoft Game Studios. (2003). Halo® [Computer software]. Redmond, WA: Author. Information retrieved April 5, 2006, from *www.microsoft.com/games/ pc/halo.aspx*.

Moje, E. B., & Sutherland, L. M. (2003). The future of middle school education. *English Education, 35*(2), 149–164.

Moss, B., & Hendershot, J. (2002). Exploring sixth-graders' selection of non-fiction trade books. *Reading Teacher, 56*, 6–17.

O'Brien, D. (2001, June). "At-risk" adolescents: Redefining competence through the multiliteracies of intermediality, visual arts, and representation. *Reading Online, 4*(11). Available: *www.readingonline.org/newliteracies/lit_index.asp? HREF=/newliteracies/obrien/index.html*.

Ohlhausen, M. M., & Jepsen, M. (1992). Lessons from Goldilocks: Somebody's been choosing my books but I can make my own choices now! *New Advocate,* 5(1), 31–46.

Pavonetti, L. M., Brimmer, K. M., & Cipielweski, J. F. (2002). Accelerated Reader: What are the lasting effects on the habits of middle school students exposed to Accelerated Reader in elementary grades? *Journal of Adolescent and Adult Literacy, 46,* 300–311.

Pearson, G., & Young, A. T. (Eds.). (2002). *Technically speaking: Why all Americans need to know more about technology.* Washington, DC: National Academy Press.

Prensky, M. (2001). Digital natives, digital immigrants. *On the Horizon 9*(5) [Electronic version]. Retrieved April 20, 2006, from *www.marcprensky.com/ writing/Prensky%20–%20Digital%20Natives,%20Digital%20Immigrants%20– %20Part1.pdf.*

Proctor, P., Dalton, B., & Grisham, D. L. (2007). Scaffolding English Language Learners and struggling readers in a digital environment with embedded strategy instruction and vocabulary support. *Journal of Literacy Research, 39*(1), 71–93.

Rowe, D. W., & Leander, K. M. (2005). Analyzing the production of third space in classroom literacy events. In B. Maloch, J. V. Hoffman, D. L. Schallert, C. M. Fairbanks, & J. Worthy (Eds.), *54th yearbook of the National Reading Conference* (pp. 318–333). Oak Creek, WI: National Reading Conference.

Stewart, T. A. (1999). *Intellectual capital: The new wealth of organizations.* New York: Currency, Doubleday.

Tompkins, G. (2003). *Literacy for the twenty-first century* (3rd ed.). Upper Saddle River, NJ: Merrill Prentice-Hall.

Unrau, N. (2004). *Content area reading and writing: Fostering literacies in middle and high school cultures.* Upper Saddle River, NJ: Merrill Prentice-Hall.

U.S. Department of Commerce. (1999). *Falling through the net: Defining the digital divide.* Washington, DC: National Telecommunications and Information Administration. Available: *www.ntia.doc.gov/ntiahome/fttn99/.*

Wiles, J., & Bondi, J. (1986). *The essential middle school.* Columbus, OH: Merrill.

Wolsey, T. D. (2004, January/February). Literature discussion in cyberspace: Young adolescents using threaded discussion groups to talk about books. *Reading Online, 7*(4). Available: *www.readingonline.org/articles/art_index.asp?HREF= wolsey/index.html.*

Wolsey, T. D. (2007). Interface: Computers in the classroom. *The California Reader, 40*(3), 29–37.

Woolcott Research Pty., Ltd. (2001). *Young Australians reading: From keen to reluctant readers.* Retrieved June 14, 2006, from *www.slv.vic.gov.au/pdfs/ aboutus/publications/yar_report.pdf.*

Zandvliet, D. B. (2006). *Education is not rocket science: The case for deconstructing computer labs in schools.* Rotterdam, the Netherlands: Sense Publishers.

Appendix 5.1. Electronic Resources for Teachers

Organizations and Journals

1. *cnets.iste.org/currstands/* ISTE is the International Society for Technology in Education. Links to technology standards can be found on this site.
2. *reading.org* The International Reading Association (IRA). Included on the website are links to IRA's outstanding journals. The site has many resources for teachers.
3. *www.readingonline.org* The archives of IRA's online journal providing electronic texts that contain many resources for teachers of struggling readers and information on multiple literacies.
4. *llt.msu.edu/ Language Learning and Technology*, a refereed online journal for second and foreign language educators.
5. *www.cec.sped.org/* The Council for Exceptional Children provides guidelines and ideas for working with special populations.

Online Tools, References, and Resources

6. *scholar.google.com/* We entered *hypertext* and came up with a list of 202,000 entries. Talk about a surfeit of information!
7. *school.discovery.com/* Kathy Schrock's "Schrockguide" to evaluating websites is critical for all students to learn the differences in the value of the many varieties of websites on the Internet. The site also includes recommended websites for all content areas, free downloadable lesson plans, clip art, and helpful information on such things as "blogs."
8. *WebQuest.sdsu.edu/overview.htm* On this site find out about how the Web-Quest was invented, how to construct one, and several samples. The WebQuest is one of the most important learning tools a teacher may use to guide students in Internet inquiry.
9. *www.bestWebQuests.com/* This site, authored by Tom March, provides a compilation of WebQuests for all content areas—most submitted by teachers. If you want to author a WebQuest for yourself, you can submit it here.
10. *rubistar.4teachers.org/index.php* This website can help teachers create rubrics for projects based on templates that are designed as a basis for the various types of projects.
11. *www.bartleby.com/62/* Here is an online thesaurus (Roget's), plus dictionaries, that can provide students with alternative words for writing. Search by typing in a word, or through alphabetized word lists.
12. *owl.english.purdue.edu/workshops/hypertext/reportW/* Purdue University's sponsored online writing laboratory that helps students to get started writing a report, explains all of the sections of a report, and offers some general technical writing guidelines. There's more on the site (such as Internet searching guidelines).
13. *www.disciplinehelp.com/* This site, named "You Can Handle Them All," is sponsored by The Master Teacher and provides information about 117 different discipline problems.

Assistive Technologies, Accessibility, and Related Research

14. *iris.peabody.vanderbilt.edu/* The IRIS Center for Faculty Enhancement offers research-based modules on many topics essential to teachers working with struggling readers, including new modules on Response to Intervention (RTI).
15. *www.cast.org/research/udl/index.html* CAST's Universal Design for Learning and many other resources for working with struggling readers.
16. *www.edfacilities.org/rl/distance_learning.cfm* National Clearinghouse for Educational Facilities Distance Learning resource page. Includes links and resources for accessibility issues and using assistive technologies.
17. *www.edfacilities.org/rl/technologyII.cfm* Technology Integration resource page includes links and resources for teachers and facilities planners.

CHAPTER 6

Engaging Struggling Adolescent Readers in Conversations about Texts

INSTRUCTIONAL STRATEGIES FOR SUCCESSFUL EXPERIENCES

Kathleen Crawford-McKinney
Kattie Hogan

Getting struggling readers interested in books is a challenge for many middle and high school teachers. Struggling readers often do not choose to engage with texts on a personal level, which can hinder their reading growth. If literature in middle and secondary classrooms is authentic, contains rich language, and includes convincing stories about life, perhaps struggling readers will want to read. This is key for the maturing adolescent.

During adolescence, students develop a heightened awareness of themselves and begin to make conscious choices about how they will project themselves to others (Adamson & Lyxell, 1996). While students mature socially, they are also under a great deal of pressure to achieve academically. Teachers can use books to find ways to support students' social and academic growth. Characters in books provide role models for interactions and decision making, and learning about them can support an adolescent's increasing cognitive development. Through reading, students can examine different choices and the consequences of those choices, placing themselves in the shoes of the characters without having to face the dangers of the paths they take. Read-alouds and literature circles are excellent vehicles for such conversations in content classes. Teachers help students develop independence during adolescence, but "also help them feel some sense of unity or sameness" with others (Hammon & Hendricks, 2005, p. 73). Literary interactions allow students to view multiple perspectives of the world and to develop a sense of themselves in relation to the larger society. To attain such student responses to texts, teachers need to set up literacy-rich classrooms in a manner that allows students to explore their identities and make connections between themselves and society. Examining these texts should not be limited to language arts classrooms; teachers in math, science, social studies, and other content areas should find avenues that allow for such experiences. Gee (2001) notes, "Language demonstrates your ability 'to do' a particular identity, using that social language, or to be able to recognize such an identity, when we do not want to or cannot actively participate" (p. 718).

Through read-alouds and content-area literature circles students can become aware that language is a powerful force for conveying a message. According to Richardson (2000), "Learning becomes more relevant and exciting when fresh approaches such as read-alouds are infused into all content instructions" (p. 7).

All readers, and especially struggling readers, need strategies for selecting from the enormous variety of texts available. Struggling readers need opportunities to read a wide variety of materials, at different levels, and for multiple purposes. In this chapter the importance of encouraging struggling readers is examined through a consideration of read-alouds and content-area literature circles. Specific strategies, websites, and a book list are included so that teachers can increase their interactive literacy experiences with their students.

Read-Alouds

Although there is much discussion on the importance of reading aloud to students (Fisher & Fry, 2008; Serafini & Giorgis, 2003), this practice often disappears as students move to the upper grades, and especially during the adolescent years. "Most people associate read-alouds with bright-eyed preschoolers and elementary kids—not with struggling at-risk kids" (Blessing, 2005, p. 44). But the practice of reading stories aloud should not be relegated to only teachers of young children; it has value for older students as well. "Middle and high school students enjoy hearing read alouds, too. Yet we seldom think to include them in our instruction" (Richardson, 2000,

p. 3). The benefits that will be experienced by adolescent readers are similar to those gained by elementary students. According to Blessing (2005), "Students who are read to are more motivated to read themselves—increasing the likelihood that one day they will become independent, lifelong readers" (p. 44).

The ability to enjoy literature and become immersed in the language of stories is often lacking in struggling students, who may often disregard school because they feel it lacks relevance to their own lives. Teachers of adolescents often end the practice of reading aloud to students and, simultaneously, students lose interest in reading.

One approach to restoring interest in reading is to help adolescent students rediscover the love of language many children had when they were younger. Reading aloud is a literacy strategy that can provide an outlet for teachers to share their own love of language (Sanacore, 2000). When quality literature is read aloud, students can hear the beauty of language, increase their exposure to vocabulary in context, and become aware of text structure (Ivey, 2003). "Read alouds model enthusiastic reading, transmit the pleasure of reading, and invite listeners to be readers" (Richardson, 2000, p. 3). Read-alouds also allow students to become engaged in learning about language arts, math, science, social studies, and other curriculum areas.

Reading aloud gives struggling or reluctant readers a purpose for reading. Smith (1985) argues, "The most effective means of helping children of all ages who are in difficulty is to show them that reading is not a painful and pointless exercise and that learning to read is well within their grasp" (p. 148). Read-alouds create a low-risk environment where students can discover the joy of language without the pressure of failure (Allen, 2000). They allow struggling readers to be successful with literature and to hear texts they may not be able to read on their own. Read-alouds enhance a student's passion and knowledge of language in an English classroom and can also be utilized across the curriculum. "Read alouds in classrooms should show that reading really can expand horizons. Students will explore more about topics that are only mentioned in the classroom" (Richardson, 2000, p. 5). As students become more aware of the variety of genres, authors, and styles of writing available in books, they are more willing to take chances and connect with literature in a deeper and more meaningful way (Sanacore, 2000).

Creating a Positive Read-Aloud Experience

Prior to reading aloud to a group of students, teachers should read the material alone and become familiar with its language (Albright & Ariail, 2005). The classroom practice of reading aloud should not provide an experience like television watching, in which students sit back and passively listen to sound like background noise. It should also not be a marathon in which students are asked to continually participate, becoming exhausted and overwhelmed with the tediousness of the assignment. "We simply get out of the way of the text and let words work their magic" (Calkins, 1999, p. 25). Occasionally, students can be encouraged to make predictions, find connections, or ask questions about what is occurring in the text. This process opens up an arena for discussion. In addition to promoting literacy development, read-alouds also provide a framework for creating a safe and respectful community (Boomer & Boomer, 2001).

Used at the beginning or end of a class period, a read-aloud is powerful transition experience that allows students to get into the mind frame of that particular class (Blessing, 2005). Read-alouds should be used across the curriculum to expose students to a variety of texts and a variety of purposes for reading (Albright & Ariail, 2005). For example, in a secondary math classroom, the book *Flatland* (Abbott, 1994) was read to study geometry. This read-aloud examined properties of shapes and dimensions found in everyday life. The teacher chose to read this book at the beginning of her class session to help her students participate in the thinking process for these complex concepts.

To create a more relaxing environment, librarians or teachers may lower the lights or even play music. "Reading aloud allows us all to stay literally on the same page, to stop and think together as the horizon of the textual word shifts before us" (Boomer & Boomer, 2001, p. 71). When all students in a classroom have engaged in the same literacy experience, a classroom community begins to form. They have similar building blocks from which conversations, vocabulary, and further learning can develop.

As teachers use read-alouds in their classrooms, they can monitor struggling readers' reactions and guide students into thinking critically about the text. Students who have learned to sit back and passively count the minutes until class is dismissed are encouraged to read. They can then actively question and connect with the author. Read-alouds give teachers a time to share the content of their subjects as well as to model ways to critically think about the content areas. In one special education middle grade classroom, for example, the novel *The Girl Who Owned a City* (Nelson, 1977) was chosen for a read-aloud. This novel provided a reference point for discussing elements of a story and looking at the theme of survival. The students began that experience by sketching out their thoughts about the book and then writing about the connections they were making on a daily basis. As the teacher reached the end of the novel, she noticed students struggling to make real-life connections and to move beyond summarizing. The teacher then decided to extend the content of the novel and the students' thinking.

The students were asked to make a personal connection with the text by putting themselves in the situation of the main character, Lisa. The teacher asked, "What would it be like if everyone older than seventh grade died and you were the oldest ones alive?" The students talked with each other and then wrote down some ways their lives would be different. This writing experience started with one paragraph about sensory experiences of what it would be like to be the oldest people alive. As they explained one moment from the story, using their five senses, students began to visualize and think critically about the world. They then expanded their paragraphs into stories that connected with and extended the content of the novel. Students moved themselves out of the safe world of the classroom and into a creative world where young adolescents lived without adults. "If teachers can begin to slow down their thinking and notice what they do as expert readers of their content, they will know how to design effective strategy instruction" (Tovani, 2004, p. 26). Figure 6.1 includes a list of chapter books that can especially be interesting to adolescent struggling readers.

Anderson, L. H. (1999). *Speak.* New York: Farrar, Straus and Giroux.
Anderson, M. T. (2002). *Feed.* Cambridge, MA: Candlewick.
Avi. (1990). *The true confessions of Charlotte Doyle.* New York: Orchard.
Bauer, J. (2000). *Hope was here.* New York: Penguin.
Bloor, E. (1997). *Tangerine.* New York: Scholastic.
Creech, S. (1994). *Walk two moons.* New York: Harper Trophy.
Draper, S. M. (2006). *Copper sun.* New York: Atheneum.
Ellis, D. (2002). *Parvana's journey.* Toronto: Groundwood.
Enzensberger, H. M. (1998). *The number devil: A mathematical adventure.* New York: Henry Holt.
Flinn, A. (2001). *Breathing underwater.* New York: HarperCollins.
Hesse, K. (2001). *Witness.* New York: Scholastic
Hiaasen, C. (2002). *Hoot.* New York: Knopf.
Holm, J. L. (2006). *Penny from heaven.* New York: Random House.
Holt, K. W. (1999). *When Zachery Beaver came to town.* New York: Dell Yearling.
Koertge, R. (2003) *Shakespeare bats cleanup.* Cambridge, MA: Candlewick.
Lasky, K. (1994). *The librarian who measured the earth.* Boston: Little, Brown.
Lord, C. (2006). *Rules.* New York: Scholastic.
Lowry, L. (1993). *The giver.* New York: Houghton Mifflin.
Mazer, H. (2001). *A boy at war: A novel of Pearl Harbor.* New York: Simon & Schuster.
McCormick, P. (2000). *Cut.* New York: Front Street.
McDonald, J. (1997). *Swallowing stones.* New York: Random House.
Mikaelsen, B. (2001). *Touching spirit bear.* New York: HarperCollins.
Sones, S. (2001). *What my mother doesn't know.* New York: Simon Pulse.
Westerfeld, S. (2005). *Uglies.* New York: Scholastic.

FIGURE 6.1. Chapter books for struggling adolescent readers.

Read-Alouds and the Writing Process

Reading and writing skills are of the utmost importance because they are the foundations from which students will learn to think critically, comprehend, and express themselves (Coats & Taylor-Clark, 2001). Listening to teachers read aloud provides an opportunity for students to put most of their cognitive energies into understanding the story, rather than decoding words. They can see how language is used in different ways. "It's terribly important for children to listen to nonfiction texts read aloud. If children are going to comprehend and write news articles, essays, how-to texts, directions, arguments, and proclamations they need to develop an ear for the rhythms and structures used in these genres" (Calkins, 1999, p. 26). When teachers utilize a variety of texts, students have models, or mentor texts, from which to create their own writing. These allow students to hear and see the way writing can take shape and create informational text as well as stories. According to Morgan and Odom (2005), "Various authors are introduced to the classroom as the experts; their writing offers models of how to weave details through the text to make the message clear, to present it in a certain way, to evoke responses in readers" (p. 75). Authors such as Walter Dean Myers, Sandra Cisneros, Laurie Hals Anderson, Karen Hesse, and Jacqueline Woodson provide a variety of literary styles through their texts. When students are exposed to the writings of these authors through read-alouds, they may be able to see the possibilities for their own writing.

Content-Area Literature Circles

Learning occurs when teachers and students take time to collaborate and create a classroom community where learning is not an isolated event (Fisher & Fry, 2008). The conversations that occur among learners foster growth for all involved (Vygotsky, 1978). When content-area teachers provide opportunities for in-depth conversations, they model the importance of social as well as cognitive development. A content-area literature circle is one curricular component that allows for this type of development.

Content-area literature circles are student-led, small-group discussions built around a particular concept or theme (Johnson & Freedman, 2005). They offer opportunities for readers to become literate through critical analysis of texts and in-depth interactions within groups. Learners construct knowledge by bringing meaning *to* as well as taking meaning *from* a text (Rosenblatt, 1978). The books chosen for literature circles are those that evoke a response or leave readers with more questions than answers.

Unlike most literature circles in the lower grades, literature circles for adolescents do not need to be highly structured. Adolescent readers usually do not need assigned roles or preset lists of questions. These readers are at a stage where they are forging new relationships. They want to engage in authentic dialogue that is important to their social and cultural development. From the analysis of a recent research study on effective literacy instruction with middle school students (Johnson, Freedman, Thomas, & Crawford, 2006), a majority of the students interviewed stated that they did not like literature circles as they were implemented in their classrooms. The middle school student participants, who represented diverse ethnic, socioeconomic, and geographic populations, thought that literature circles were not effectively used in their classrooms because students did not have choice or voice in their learning. The teachers of these students had implemented literature circles based on a cooperative model, wherein the students responded to a teacher-provided list of questions. Literature discussion tasks and roles, such as discussion leader, summarizer, question finder, vocabulary finder, were assigned by the teacher and divided among the group members. These clearly defined roles made students feel shut down, with no choice about their discussion topics. The way literature circles were implemented in these classrooms hindered communication and natural discussions about texts.

In literature circles where teachers embrace a *collaborative* approach, learners are encouraged to be active participants in the learning process and to change their thinking about the texts they read. This approach allows all students opportunities to freely discuss and investigate texts on multiple levels. The circle dialogue leads students to form new perspectives about themselves as learners, about the literature itself, and about other participants in the group (Short, Harste, & Burke, 1996). Students' ideas change because of interactions and discussions among peers. When students collaborate, they listen carefully and push each other to new meanings and deeper understandings instead of addressing specific prompts from worksheets (Crawford et al., 1998; Short et al., 1996; Smith, 1990; Wilson, 2004).

The following discussion addresses types of content-area literature circles, text selection, and management of this curricular component. It highlights the importance of supporting adolescent readers as they make choices, voice their opinions, and question authors.

Types of Content-Area Literature Circles

Content-area literature circles do not look the same in all classrooms. They utilize different settings such as large groups, partners, and small groups. The strategies chosen for each of these settings should be deliberate and purposeful. The *large group* provides a vehicle for multiple voices in the learning community to be heard. A text can either be read to or by the entire class. Conversations about a book can be initiated by any class member and can offer useful ideas for stimulating future critical discussions. Struggling adolescents have an opportunity to observe other members utilize specific strategies and to listen to others' multiple perspectives from the books. Through this initial large-group experience, students learn how to talk about books. Strategies modeled during the whole-group discussions include webbing, brainstorming, and journaling.

A popular strategy used with whole-class content-area literature circles is to write journals, also referred to as literature logs. This involves writing personal responses to literature that can be shared with the class. Journaling helps students remember specific parts of the text, personal reflections, and connections, as they reflect on issues, questions, or concerns they encounter during the readings, which can provide a springboard for classroom discussions.

In one instance, sixth-grade students were asked to share their insights after reading *Journey of the Sparrows* (Buss, 1991), a fictional book that examines immigration. Sadie, a Mexican American girl, came to the whole-class circle prepared to share a journal entry from her literature log (see Figure 6.2). She made personal connections to the characters in the book and shared her own reaction of illegal immigration into the United States from Mexico. Illegal immigration was a topic currently being addressed in the social studies class, as well as within her neighborhood community. The content-area literature circle provided Sadie space to voice her ideas; the text and current events in her community served as sources to help her form opinions. Other class members responded to her log, and thus a critical conversation emerged. The students in this class were allowed to view multiple perspectives of immigration to better understand themselves as citizens.

The next type of circle, *partner discussions*, can be utilized to facilitate the transition to small-group content-area literature circles. Partner circles continue to provide opportunities for students to engage in critical conversations. In these circles two people discuss the literature with each other. As students learn how to actively participate by both listening and speaking to one another, topics that are too personal to share in whole-group conversations can be revealed. *Written conversation* and *Sketch-to-Stretch* are two strategies that can be utilized to enhance partner discussions.

In written conversations, learners are encouraged to consider the reactions of each other and to defend their own points of view. As students read the responses of their partners, they have an opportunity to examine their own positions and see texts through another person's eyes. These exchanges help students find commonalities in their thinking as well as understand that every reader gains something different from a text. To begin the conversation, partners write for 5 minutes on their initial reactions to the text. The students trade papers, read them, and respond to the partner's writing. The writing should continue for several rounds, allowing

Journey of the sparows   Sadie Bulowski

I think it was unfair tha people were getting killed just because they were metican. I also think that the people who helped mexico people are good people and they should keep that way. They don't just think about there self they think about other people. I think it made a difference because the african american woman helped Maria and Teresa not get caught because she put the sign on the door of the restroom some people also M.A.D. because they gave the familys food.

FIGURE 6.2. Sadie, journal reflection.

each partner several opportunities to question the other and, if necessary, fine-tune his or her own thinking. This strategy works well with issues that are complex because it provides an outlet for students to hear from a peer. In addition, in content-area classes, such as math, science, or social studies, written conversations can help clarify misconceptions involving complex concepts.

A similar type of social response is the strategy Sketch-to-Stretch (Short et al., 1996). While reading multiple texts for a social studies unit on "Cultural Encounters," two students, Brooke and Thea, read *Less than Half, More than Whole* (Lacapa & Lacapa, 1994). The book explores issues of diverse backgrounds and the feelings of a child of mixed ethnicity. Using Sketch-to-Stretch, Brooke and Thea created a drawing that expanded their meaning of the book. The two students in this classroom were culturally different because of their race and socioeconomic status, yet lived only blocks apart in their neighborhood. They did not socialize with each other outside the classroom, but after discussing issues from the book and drawing upon their personal experiences, they created a sketch that shows them working toward an understanding and making personal connections to their own lives (see Figure 6.3). Their interpretation was, "We used to fight all the time, but we're learning to accept each other." Through positive interactions during this partner content-area literature circle, these two students saw each other in a new light and were able to understand their differences with a new level of social acceptance.

As students become more comfortable in participating in content-area literature circles in large and partner groups, they develop the discussion tools necessary to move toward the more independent setting of small groups, consisting of four to five students. When time is spent practicing reading strategies in whole or partner groups, students can then transfer these skills to more in-depth discussions of particular content. Students

FIGURE 6.3. Thea and Brooke, Sketch-to-Stretch.

begin by choosing the specific strategies they will use to guide their discussions in small groups. They negotiate with one another by reviewing the strategies they have learned in class and deciding how those strategies will be utilized with the text they are reading.

The teacher's role is to help students listen and discuss alternative perspectives in small-group settings. Content-area literature circles provide an avenue for students to become more active in understanding concepts that are common to content-area learning such as discovery, relationships, matter, cycles, and changes. Students gain multiple perspectives from the exchange of differing experiences in content-area literature circles and built a deeper understanding of the basic concept.

Selecting Texts for Content-Area Literature Circles

When teachers select texts for content-area literature circles, knowing their students including their interests, is vital. Teachers also need to have a vast knowledge of books in order to find just the right selection for each student. In addition, they must think about the curriculum; district, state, and federal requirements; and the availability of books for the specific content, inasmuch as the goals of literature circles are guided by curricular content and "should complement the variety of instructional strategies used in math, science, social studies, language arts and the related arts to promote content knowledge and conceptual understandings" (Johnson & Freedman, 2005, p. 7).

Once the goals of a literature circle are determined and texts have been identified, it is time to look for books that provide students with opportunities to engage in critical conversations. The books should include issues worthy of discussion. They should also strike a chord in readers, make them think, wonder, and question, so as to promote genuine conversations.

Literature circles can be utilized in the curriculum to introduce key concepts in a particular subject area and to generate talk about students' understandings (or misunderstandings) about these concepts. Such experiences provides students "a framework in which to place additional information that helps them understand the material in a more comprehensive way" (Johnson & Freedman, 2005, p. 71). Further, this framework can help struggling readers with comprehending more difficult types of texts, as it can be used as a backdrop for discussions of how and why texts are presented in particular ways.

Content-area literature circles are an excellent means of meeting social and academic challenges. Academically, they provide students with opportunities to integrate content information they have been reading and address curricular needs while, socially, also offering choices to students and promoting discussion. Both narrative and expository texts can be used. There are several resources that can help in the selection of appropriate

- Mystery Writers of America: *www. mysterywriters.org*
- What Is Nonfiction: *falcon.jmu.edu/~ramseyil/nonfic.htm*
- Orbis Pictus: *www.ncte.org/elem/awards/orbispictus*
- Young Adult Literature: *falcon.jum.edu/~ramseyil/yalit.htm*
- Graphic Novels: *eprentice.sdsu.edu/F034/rvasquez/teacher_wip.html*
- American Library Association (award-winning books): *www.ala.org/*
- National Council of Teachers of English: *www.ncte.org/*
- International Reading Association: *www.ira.org/*
- Children's Literature Assembly Notable Books: *www.childrensliteratureassembly.org*

FIGURE 6.4. Websites about adolescent literature: Fiction and nonfiction.

books for content-area literature circles, including websites, book lists, and professional references. Figure 6.4 lists websites that provide excellent information about adolescent fiction and nonfiction.

Management of Content-Area Literature Circles

This section provides a summary of how teachers can manage content-area literature circles. Effective teacher management can help students with book selection and preparation and organization of meetings.

Engaging Students in Literature Circles

Because students will be choosing the books to read for literature circles the teacher should give a brief talk on the books available and allow students an opportunity to view them for readability and content. Students can list individual preferences, then the teacher can create the circles using these preferences as a starting point. When organizing groups, teachers must also consider such issues as male:female ratio, stronger/struggling students, and individual dynamics. Students should also have a voice with both book and group member selection.

A typical discussion group includes four or five students. With fewer members, the possibility of students being absent makes a group too small for multiple perspectives to be shared. If groups are much larger, voices that are dominant or silenced may not be detected easily. In smaller groups of four or five this dynamic becomes more obvious and can be addressed more easily at the beginning of the time spent together before it becomes an issue.

Coming Prepared

After the groups are organized and the texts distributed, students read on their own. Students can use such writing formats as logs, blogs, or journals to record their initial reactions to the text before coming to the content-area literature circles. Initially, all circles can meet simultaneously because they are simply the stepping-stones for all groups to learn to negotiate conversations. Generally, though, most teachers find that having two or three groups meet at a time is best, as it allows teachers to navigate and guide discussions, providing support and additional questioning as needed. As the circles become more focused, teachers should guide individual groups through the process of examining critical issues at a deeper level.

Organization of Meetings

Students are continually negotiating their places in the circle. They learn how to move in and out of discussions through strategies that support their listening and speaking skills, such as "Save the last word for me," a strategy whereby all members are asked to write on a piece of paper a segment from the text that caught their attention. On the other side of the paper, students write their reflections on that segment; they then read their segments to the group so that group members can react to the selections. At the end of each discussion, the student who chose the segment "has the last word" and offers the final remarks based on both the discussion and the reflections originally written on the back side of the paper. This negotiation of ideas helps to move the discussion forward. One nonnegotiable aspect, however, is that all students are expected to come prepared for discussion at each meeting and to provide written reflections or other types of representations that provide evidence of their understandings and transactions with the text. These should help to support their thinking and can allow for teacher assessment. One should keep in mind that literature circles do not necessarily have a beginning or an end. They are simply a means for students to engage in critical thinking about a text with their peers, in which the text serves as a basis for conversation. The guidelines below illustrate literature discussions as a recursive process from which students and teachers can deviate as they become more comfortable with literature circles.

- *Recording initial insights.* Each member is given an opportunity to share his or her individual journals, logs, or blogs and to document questions, concerns, and insights that may have arisen during the reading. This brainstorming environment allows a space where all answers are acceptable and briefly explored. Each group records responses on a web or chart.
- *Organizing combined thoughts.* Students work together to organize their responses by analyzing the chart and finding common themes, issues, or concepts from the initial brainstormed list. The list is expanded during continued elaboration and discussion of items on the list.
- *Discussing each issue.* Students choose issues that are of greatest interest to the group to begin their "critical conversations." References

from the book and personal experiences are included to support students' thinking. From these discussions, students negotiate and move toward a shared understanding of the concepts central to the curricular content. The teacher's role then becomes monitoring and observing these discussions to assure the content objectives come to the forefront of the discussions that guide students' conversations.

  • *Sharing what we learned.* Students prepare a formal or informal presentation to the class and/or teacher. These presentations should allow all of the group members a time to practice social communications, demonstrate their knowledge of the text, and, most important, describe how their insights into the curricular concepts evolved.

  • *Creating future inquiries.* Students share collaborative understandings and begin investigations that further enhance concepts derived from the content area. Their findings can push their thinking to a deeper level, allowing their own interests to emerge through personal inquiries.

It is important to recognize that the teacher is not a spectator during these discussions, but rather a facilitator who circulates through the classroom and monitors interactions. Teachers guide the students through the process of carefully developing their own ideas without interfering in the natural flow of conversation.

At the end of each meeting, students should take time to write reflections about what occurred in the literature circles by answering questions such as:

1. What did your circle accomplish today?
2. What new aspects of the book(s) did your circle talk about?
3. What did you decide to talk about next time your circle meets?
4. How will you prepare for that discussion?

Writing responses to these questions helps students to become accountable for the day's discussion and provides an organizational strategy to help prepare them for future discussions. These written responses also assist teachers with assessing students' progress and identifying individual and group needs.

Cautions about Book Selection

Not all books are appropriate for content-area literature circles. Series books, simplified texts, and those that sensationalize for the purpose of getting the attention of the reader are not appropriate because they usually fail to have enough critical plot moments and engaging dialogue. Further, they may not address the teacher's curricular objectives. As teachers work to meet these objectives, they may encounter books that are controversial. In order to prevent contentious situations during a unit study, a list of books can be sent to parents and the administration in advance to let them know what books students might read and why these particular books have been chosen. The teacher should emphasize that the selections will guide students through multiple perspectives on an issue or topic being discussed.

For example, one middle school teacher's social studies class explored the theme "Discovery," with many sensitive books chosen for particular purposes. Parents/caregivers were invited to visit the classroom to examine the reading materials. One parent, who previously had censored many texts her children's teachers had selected, came to the class to give her opinions on the materials for a discovery theme. By communicating why each book was selected and what was hoped students would discuss in terms of multiple perspectives, the teacher was able to address the parent's concerns. In this case the parent had particular religious concerns about three of the sets of books, and by knowing she could ask her son to choose from only four of the seven sets that were remaining in this social studies literature selection, the parent left the meeting feeling that she, as well as her son, had choice in curricular decisions.

Conclusions

The age-appropriate reading list included in this chapter provides a starting point for teachers to move away from their comfort zone, using traditional instructional strategies, and use new strategies to enliven the classroom learning experience. Read-alouds and content-area literature circles provide a socially relevant forum for enhancing learning about content-specific material. As teachers implement new learning strategies and give students opportunities to self-select literature, they may find that their students are more motivated to read, write, and discuss texts on a deeper level. "Ongoing everyday reading is so important if we are going to grow as readers" (Boomer & Boomer, 2001, p. 67).

The goals for educational programs should include developing students who know the importance of reading, writing, and sharing their ideas. These goals should be carried across multiple content areas. When teachers value the voices of all students, including those who struggle, a creative and supportive classroom community emerges and opportunities for ongoing discussions in which all students are engaged can occur. Schools should provide a diverse selection of materials for teachers so that students can identify themselves in literature. The reading materials should also provide a depth to various subject areas as they explore math, science, social students, and other content areas.

When students become better readers, they are better able to implement their skills in an authentic manner both inside and outside the classroom. Students can then become engaged, critical thinkers (Allington, 2006). Read-alouds and content-area literature circles provide a variety of avenues for teachers to begin classroom discussions, helping to bridge the gap between those who find reading natural and easy and those who may have more difficulty.

References

Abbott, E. (1994). *Flatland: A romance of many dimensions*. New York: Harper-Collins.

Adamson, L., & Lyxell, B. (1996). Self-concept and questions of life: Identity development during late adolescence. *Journal of Adolescence, 19*, 569–582.

Albright, L. K., & Ariail, M. (2005). Trapping the potential of teacher-read-alouds in middle schools. *Journal of Adolescent and Adult Literacy, 48*, 582–592.

Allen, J. (2000). *Yellow brick roads: Shared and guided paths to independent reading 4–12*. Portland, ME: Stenhouse.

Allington, R. L. (2006). *What really matters for struggling readers: Designing research-based programs* (2nd ed). Boston: Allyn & Bacon.

Blessing, C. (2005). Reading to kids who are old enough to shave. *School Library Journal, 51*(4), 44–45.

Boomer, R., & Boomer, K. (2001). *For a better world reading and writing for social justice*. Portsmouth, NH: Heinemann

Buss, F. L. (1991). *Journey of the sparrows*. New York: Lodestar.

Calkins, L. (1999). Let the words work their magic. *Instructor, 110*(3), 25–28.

Coats, L. T., & Taylor-Clark, P. (2001). Finding a niche for reading: A key to improving underachievers' reading skills. *Reading Improvement, 38*(2), 70–73.

Crawford, K., Ferguson, M., Kauffman, G., Laird, J., Schroeder, J., & Short, K. (1998). Examining children's historical and multicultural understandings: The dialectical nature of collaborative research. In T. Shanahan & F. Rodriguez-Brown (Eds.), *47th yearbook of the National Reading Conference* (pp. 323–333). Chicago: National Reading Conference.

Fisher, D., & Fry, N. (2008). *Improving adolescent literacy: Content area strategies at work*. Columbus, OH: Merrill Prentice-Hall.

Gee, J. P. (2001). Reading as situated language: A sociocognitive perspective. *Journal of Adult and Adolescent Literacy, 44*, 714–725.

Hammon, D., & Hendricks, C. B. (2005). The role of generation in identity formation: Ericson speaks to teachers of adolescents. *Clearing House, 79*(2), 72–75.

Ivey, G. (2003). The intermediate grades: "The teacher makes it more explainable" and other reasons to read aloud in the intermediate grades. *Reading Teacher, 56*(8), 812–814.

Johnson, H., & Freedman, L. (2005). *Content area literature circles: Using discussion for learning across the curriculum*. Norwood, MA: Christopher-Gordon.

Johnson, H., Freedman, L., Thomas, K., & Crawford, K. (2006, November). *Actions that create, actions that destroy: Middle school students' thoughts on reading self-efficacy and in-school practices*. Paper presented at the 56th annual meeting of the National Reading Conference, Los Angeles.

Lacapa, K., & Lacapa, M. (1994). *Less than half, more than whole.* Flagstaff, AZ: Northland.

Morgan, B., & Odom, D. (2005). *Writing through the tween years.* Portland, ME: Steinhouse.

Nelson, O. (1977). *The girl who owned a city.* New York: Laurel Leaf.

Richardson, J. S. (2000). *Read it aloud using literature in the secondary content classroom.* Newark, DE: International Reading Association.

Rosenblatt, L. (1978). *The reader, the text, the poem: The transactional theory of the literary work.* Carbondale: Southern Illinois University.

Sanacore, J. (2000). Promoting the lifetime reading habit in middle school students. *Clearing House, 73*(3), 157–161.

Serafini, F., & Giorgis, C. (2003). *Reading aloud and beyond: Fostering the intellectual life with older readers.* Portsmouth, NH: Heinemann.

Short, K., Harste, J., & Burke, C. (1996). *Creating classrooms for authors and inquirers.* Portsmouth, NH: Heinemann.

Smith, F. (1985). *Reading without nonsense.* New York: Teachers College Press.

Smith, K. (1990). Entertaining a text: A reciprocal process. In K. Short & K. M. Pierce (Eds.), *Talking about books: Creating literate communities* (pp. 17–31). Portsmouth, NH: Heinemann.

Tovani, C. (2004). *Do I really have to teach reading?* Portland, ME: Stenhouse.

Vygotsky, L. (1978). *Mind in society: The development of higher psychological processes.* Cambridge, MA: Harvard University Press.

Wilson, J. (2004). *Talking beyond the text: Identifying and fostering critical talk in a middle school classroom.* Unpublished doctoral dissertation, University of Missouri, Columbia.

CHAPTER 7

Making Time
for Independent Reading

Susan Lenski
Ercxenia Lanier

$\mathbf{M}$any students, even good students, have difficulty reading in middle and high school and can be termed "struggling readers." Data from the National Assessment of Educational Progress (NAEP), a national test given to students in grades 4, 8, and 12, indicate that 27% of the eighth- and twelfth-grade students tested could not read at even the basic level (Center on Education Policy, 2006). Several factors influence adolescent reading progress, including the amount that students actually read. Approximately half of the eighth-grade readers reported on the 1996 NAEP survey that they read 10 or fewer pages each day at school (Donahue, Voelkl, Campbell, & Mazzeo, 1999). According to Krashen and McQuillan (1996), students also do not read at home. Theorizing that the amount of reading makes a difference, adolescent literacy initiatives are beginning to institute independent reading as part of comprehensive literacy programs (Brozo & Hargis, 2003; Ivey & Fisher, 2006). This chapter builds on the existing momentum by examining the research on independent reading, developing a rationale for implementing independent reading in middle and high schools, and introducing new ways of using independent reading in 21st-century classrooms.

The Growth of Independent Reading

Independent reading was instituted as a part of reading instruction in the 1970s. At that time, reading instruction was primarily delivered with leveled basal (core) reading programs. Students were typically divided into three or four ability groups. Teachers delivered skills instruction in small groups and listened to students read orally. Students, however, read very little silently. As teachers came to recognize the importance of silent reading, however, they began to actively look for ways to supplement their reading programs (Smith, 1986).

Independent reading, in the form of Sustained Silent Reading (SSR), was one of the means teachers used to increase the amount of time students spent reading silently. The purpose of SSR was to develop students' ability to read silently for long periods of time without interruption and to provide time for students to "practice" reading (McCracken, 1971). According to Hunt (1967), the original SSR conceptualization was developed around six principles:

1. Students read self-selected books silently.
2. The teacher models reading silently with the students.
3. Students select one book, magazine, or newspaper to read for the entire time period.
4. A timer is set for a prescribed, uninterrupted time period.
5. No reports or records are kept.
6. The whole class, department, or school participates in SSR.

SSR began to catch on as a way for students who were in skills-based instructional settings to make decisions about which books to read and to read connected texts for a substantial period of time. As teachers experimented with SSR, they made slight revisions and renamed it with a variety of creative acronyms such as Drop Everything and Read (DEAR), Free Reading Every Day (FRED), Reading Is Our Thing (RIOT), and Students and Faculty All Reading Independently (SAFARI) (Johns & Lenski, 2005). These first innovations were based on the original SSR principles and did not deviate significantly from them.

As SSR became more popular, teachers began to modify it in a variety of ways. For example, many teachers decided not to read with students, and some teachers began to incorporate reading conferences to evaluate students' comprehension (Krashen, 1993). Other teachers found that their students did not have enough access to books to make good choices about reading, and, as a result, some students did not use SSR time to read. Teachers began building classroom libraries and developing ways to teach students about books. By the end of the 20th century, therefore, SSR retained distinct characteristics such as providing time for students to read, but teachers began to assume more active leadership in its implementation.

By the end of the 20th century, many teachers were emphasizing access to books and other components of the social environment as important features of SSR. Teachers also began incorporating follow-up activities in some instances. The characteristics of SSR had changed in several important ways, but most writers about SSR were still opposed to any type of accountability. In 2000, Pilgreen published the *Sustained Silent Reading Handbook*, in which she introduced eight features that she thought were critical for successful SSR programs:

- Access
- Appeal
- Conducive environment
- Encouragement
- Nonaccountability
- Follow-up activities
- Time to read

Independent Reading in the 21st Century

The popularity of independent reading continued to increase into the beginning of the 21st century. Block and Mangieri (2002) conducted a study of 549 elementary teachers in three states about their knowledge of reading and literature. They found that teachers in 2001 were more knowledgeable than teachers in 1981 about children's literature and about ways to incorporate it into independent reading. Teachers were also incorporating other types of reading activities, in which students read connected texts, such as using novels as core texts. Other types of reading activities that required considerable silent reading, such as literature circles (Daniels, 2002) and book clubs (McMahon & Raphael, 1997), became popular. Silent reading and independent reading were becoming an integral feature of reading instruction in the United States. The publication of the influential National Reading Panel (2000) report, however, reversed this trend.

Influence of the National Reading Panel Report

The National Reading Panel was charged by the Department of Education to report on the status of reading research in the United States. The panel decided to review research in five areas in which there was a substantial body of experimental research: phonemic awareness, phonics, fluency, comprehension, and vocabulary. In its review of the extant research on reading, the panel found hundreds of correlational studies indicating that the more students read, the more quickly they grew as readers. Correlational studies, however, do not imply causation, so the panel examined the 14 experimental studies that investigated whether independent reading *without teacher guidance* had an impact on fluency, vocabulary development, or reading comprehension. After reviewing this body of research, the panel concluded that it was "unable to find a positive relationship between programs and instruction that encourage large amounts of independent reading and improvements in reading achievement, including fluency" (pp. 12–13). These findings caused many teachers to reevaluate their use of independent reading, inasmuch as the National Reading Panel did not seem to endorse its use in the classroom.

Rationale for Independent Reading

Despite the lack of support for independent reading from the National Reading Panel, many educators believe that all students, especially struggling adolescent readers, need to have time in their school day to read books of their own choosing. Stephen Krashen (2001), one of the most outspoken proponents of independent reading, suggests that making generalizations about independent reading based on the National Reading Panel is flawed. In fact, the panel wrote, "The available data do suggest that independent silent reading is not an effective practice *when used as the only type of reading instruction to develop fluency and other reading skills,* particularly with students who have not yet developed critical alphabetic and word reading skills" (p. 13, emphasis added). Independent reading is not intended to be a complete reading program that meets the needs of all adolescent readers. A strong case can be made, however, for incorporating independent reading as one part of a comprehensive reading program for students of all levels. Part of the rationale for continuing with independent reading within a larger reading program includes the research on volume of reading, student motivation, differentiation of instruction, and the opinions of students themselves.

Volume of Reading

According to Allington (2001), evidence suggests that reading volume, or the number of pages and books students read, should be a central component of all reading programs. Allington argues that the volume of students' reading can have an effect on their overall reading ability and that some of the reading improvements are difficult to substantiate with experimental research. The belief that reading volume can make a difference in reading achievement is often attributed to Stanovich's (1986) seminal research on literacy development. Stanovich found that students who read more pages of books exponentially increased their ability to read, a phenomenon he termed "the Matthew effect," after the Bible verse stating that the rich get richer and the poor get poorer. Stanovich's study and argument are compelling; when students increase the volume of reading, they become better readers.

Other researchers have supported and built on this idea. For example, Taylor, Frye, and Maruyama (1990) investigated the in-school and out-of-school reading done by 195 fifth- and sixth-grade students. The results of this study indicated that time spent reading in school significantly supported students' reading growth. Lewis and Samuels (2003) conducted a meta-analysis of the studies of independent reading that included correlational studies. Their analysis included 10 reviews on time spent reading and 97 studies about the effect of independent reading. From this study, the researchers found that there is a moderate, positive effect between reading exposure and reading outcomes.

Motivating Students to Read

Despite a robust research base on reading engagement, teachers continue to have difficulty motivating students to read (Wood, Edwards, Hill-Miller, & Vintinner, 2006). According to surveys associated with the NAEP, virtually all kindergartners come to school wanting to read, but by the time those students reach their senior year of high school, only 25% of them are likely to enjoy reading (Donahue et al., 1999). By the time students progress through high school, their motivation changes and, in many cases, declines (Eccles & Midgley, 1989). According to Guthrie and Davis (2003), adolescent readers tend to lose much of their intrinsic motivation to read, possibly because of instructional practices that do not match their interests (Dembo & Eaton, 2000).

Research indicates that reading motivation includes self-efficacy, purposes and goals, and social aspects (Wigfield & Guthrie, 1997). Unfortunately, struggling readers, who often have little motivation to read, tend to lack self-efficacy, or the personal belief that they can succeed; few reading goals; and no opportunities to discuss books with others in their social groups. In contrast, good readers are able to get immersed in academic activities. According to Csikszentmihalyi (1991), this "state of flow" is common to people who are engaged in any task that is enjoyable to them. When students are in the state of "flow," hours pass without their realizing it. This characteristic can be acquired when teachers make a concerted effort to help struggling readers become interested in books (Smith & Wilhelm, 2006).

Independent reading can increase the reading engagement of many students. Fisher (2004) investigated the results of independent reading in a high school and found that many students became more engaged in reading and had improved academic achievement. When students are given opportunities to read during school, they are able to learn about topics of interest to them and they learn that reading is a useful life skill (Gardiner, 2005a).

Student Opinions

Adolescents often have strong opinions about their learning. Researchers who interviewed students found that students enjoy having time to read in school. Ivey and Broaddus (2001) surveyed sixth graders in 23 schools and learned that a majority of students in their study said independent reading was one of their favorite activities in language arts classes. Two studies that surveyed the opinions of high school students found that secondary students believed that independent reading in school improved their motivation to read (Stewart, Paradis, Ross, & Lewis, 1996; Worthy & McKool, 1996). According to Beers (2003), struggling middle and high school students become more motivated to read when they have an opportunity to select books that fit their interests and reading levels. She writes, "Students like to read when we let them read what they like" (p. 284).

Differentiating Instruction in Secondary Schools

Instruction in secondary schools has typically used a "stand and deliver" model: The teacher stands in front of the class and gives lectures while students listen. With the recent focus on the achievement gap, however, secondary teachers have become more sensitive about students who have difficulty in learning their subject material, and they are urged to differentiate instruction. Differentiating instruction is of paramount importance for struggling readers inasmuch as struggling readers often have difficulty in academic classes.

Teachers who differentiate instruction accept the premise that they will adjust student assignments on the basis of students' achievement, progress, and ability. The prevailing thought in education today, based on the work of Vygotsky (1978), is that students learn best when they encounter moderately challenging material. If learning is too easy, students become disengaged; if learning is too difficult, they become frustrated. According to Vygotsky, learning occurs most rapidly when it is within the zone of proximal development, that is, when the learning stretches students but doesn't pull them apart.

Teachers who differentiate instruction also accept the premise that all students bring different sets of abilities and tools to the learning environment, and they work toward creating situations in which all students can learn. Carol Tomlinson (1999) explains, "The teacher in a differentiated classroom understands that she does not show respect for students by ignoring their learning differences. . . . She shows respect for learners by honoring both their commonalities and differences, not by treating them alike" (p. 12). Tomlinson suggests that differentiation can be made by making changes to the content of instruction, the process, and the products expected of students within the context of students' actual abilities and interests. This blueprint for differentiation works nicely with independent reading. Independent reading can indeed be used to differentiate instruction for struggling readers.

Independent Reading as Differentiation

Independent reading is one part of a larger differentiation plan that teachers can use as they design lessons and programs to meet the needs of struggling readers. When students are able to select their own materials to read, along with teacher guidance, teachers can tailor reading instruction according to students' interests and abilities. As teachers look at the needs of their struggling readers, they can orchestrate experiences so that students progress through reading in ways that promote optimal progress. Struggling readers, for example, may need to spend more or less time reading independently than students for whom reading is not a challenge. Samuels (2006) has suggested that teachers differentiate the amount of time students spend reading and that teachers work to match the time allotments with students' reading abilities. When teachers use students as the centerpiece of program design, they can modify independent program requirements based on students' actual needs.

As teachers differentiate independent reading instruction, they need to work on guiding students toward books that are challenging but not frustrating. According to Primeaux (2000), struggling readers need an opportunity to read texts that are within their reach, as well as texts that match their ability. Locating materials for struggling readers can be difficult. Many secondary teachers complain that there are not sufficient books available that have mature content and offer easy reading. A number of publishers, however, sell high-interest books and short stories written at low reading levels. Content-area books that are written at intermediate reading levels and adapted classics are also available. Further, some fictional and nonfiction materials are written in graphic novel formats, which students find easily accessible. A supply of books at different levels of difficulty is critical for differentiating instruction using independent reading. Figure 7.1 contains a list of websites of resources for high-interest, low-level materials that can help you locate books to use with struggling readers.

www.capstonepress.com/
Resources for struggling and ELL readers.

www.tealeafpress.com/
Books of high interest for struggling readers.

www.ala.org/ala/booklist/speciallists/speciallistsfeat/Top10GraphicNovels.htm/
Lists of top graphic novels.

agsglobe.com
A wide range of adapted classics.

www.orcabook.com/
Publisher of high-quality award-winning books for kids and teens.

www.mnstate.edu/cmc/Bibliographies/HighLowBooks.htm
Book lists of titles for struggling readers. Reading levels and interest levels are provided.

www.seemore.mi.org/booklists/fiction.html#Readers
Books that appeal to struggling adolescent readers.

www.kidsinbetween.com/high_interest_-_low_vocabulary.htm
Various high-interest, low-vocabulary books that are available for purchase.

mgrn.evansville.edu/5fall2005.htm
List of book titles of high interest for reading levels third through fifth grade.

sec.evso.com/wc.dll?wieser~&sess=2291415&page=branch&tree=1000001814
Resources and novels available to appeal to various interests and reading levels.

www.sandralreading.com/struggling_readers_grades_3-adult_3.htm
Reading materials available to meet various reading and interest levels.

www.hip-books.com/
Novels published for middle and high school students that are of lower reading levels but of high interest.

www.lexile.com/EntrancePageFlash.html
Lexile website to help find books for students at various reading levels.

www.glencoe.com/gln/jamestown/index.php4
Supplementary materials to help struggling readers.

FIGURE 7.1. Resources for high-interest, low-readability materials.

Implementing Independent Reading in New Ways

Teachers who want their students to become more motivated to read and who believe that struggling readers can benefit from time to read books of their own choosing in schools have modified SSR in many ways. As mentioned earlier, many teachers no longer implement SSR in the way it was originally developed. Instead, they have retained the central idea behind SSR and have developed a variety of adaptations. A popular trend is implementation of an independent reading program based on page counts. Another change is to incorporate informal assessment as a way of gathering data on student progress. A third idea that we describe is adding instructional conversations to independent reading. The final idea we present is incorporating independent reading in content-area classes.

Racing to Read: The Indy 500 Approach

Many teachers have developed independent reading programs that are based on page counts. A page count program requires students to keep track of how many books or pages they have read in a specific amount of time. Some page count programs offer rewards for reading (one of the most common is pizza), and often these programs rely solely on extrinsic rewards. Other programs, such as Indy 500 (Lanier & Lenski, 2008), are based on page counts but include teacher guidance and instruction. Indy 500 is a classroom-tested program that includes several features that make it successful: matching students with books, a strong motivational component, documenting student reading, teacher instruction, and informal assessment.

Indy 500 hooks students into reading by having them participate in an individual and group "race." Students are asked to read 500 pages from fictional or informational texts during each grading period. Some students read three books to meet the 500-page requirement, whereas other students may only read one book to meet this goal. Additional modifications can be made for struggling readers by lowering their page requirements when necessary.

Page counts are documented using assessment tools such as story maps, character analysis papers, journals, and responses to reading. The assessment tools used to document the individual books can vary, depending on the text and the focus of instruction. The teacher can use the documentation in evaluating students' comprehension as part of a grade. If teachers assign grades for independent reading time, they can calculate the number of pages a student has read and give a grade for the percentage of pages they have completed. (For example, if a student read and documented 400 pages, that student would earn an 80% for his or her Indy 500 grade.)

The amount of time teachers allow for independent reading depends on their schedules. Most commonly, teachers devote one class period (or a part of one class period) each week to independent reading. Other teachers may provide students with 20 minutes two times per week, or 30 minutes three times a month. Some teachers in teams might share the independent reading time. For example, a team of middle school teachers decided that students would read independently for 30 minutes each week, but they would rotate the classes in which students read: language arts twice a month, social studies and science once a month each.

Indy 500 is not a program that merely gives students time to read books of their own choosing. Teachers need to make sure that they understand their students as readers and are aware of their students' interests. Acquiring this information about their students through interest inventories and/or one-on-one conversations is one step toward promoting their students' success with an independent reading program. Taking time to learn about students' reading abilities is another important part of a successful reading program. This information can come from a variety of resources and/or strategies. The use of standardized test scores, informal assessments, and student observations help the teacher to find books that students can read. Once these two factors are in place, teachers also need to be knowledgeable of the texts that will interest their students and to encourage them to read books that are neither too frustrating nor too challenging.

Indy 500 works for all students and has been especially successful with struggling readers. Teachers who have used the Indy 500 program have adapted it in the following ways:

- Modifying the number of pages that are needed to complete Indy.
- Allowing students to use books on tape if they are following along (reading) with the audio.
- Making sure that every book that students read is at an appropriate reading level for their ability.
- Allowing English language learners (ELLs) to read books in their home languages.
- Counting books that teachers read aloud in resource classes.
- Working on group-created story maps for students reading the same title.

Indy 500 has been used for 15 years, and it has met the needs of all students in a classroom. Even the most reluctant readers have made comments such as this:

> "I notice that I read a lot more than I used too. I used to find reading very boring and I couldn't find a lot of books that interested me. But now I find it easy to find books that I like. I used to be a lot slower as

a reader but the more I read the better I get. I have met all of the reading goals I set for myself. I am also reading a lot more than I expected. My reading goals for my next book are to finish it faster and to get a better understanding of what it is I'm reading."

Assessing Independent Reading

Another trend in independent reading is the addition of an assessment component to the program. At the time that SSR was introduced, the prevailing belief was that students should have opportunities to read without any type of assessment. Much has changed in the past four decades. Many teachers who have implemented independent reading programs have found some accountability measure necessary. For example, Marshall (2002) found that some students were not reading during independent reading time, which she attributed to the lack of accountability. She writes, "Some followers of SSR programs will argue that there should not be any accountability; that it takes the fun out of reading for students. I believe that my students needed the accountability piece (they actually asked for it) and it worked for us" (p. 58).

Marshall is just one of the educators who now incorporate some type of assessment in their independent reading programs. Lanier and Lenski (2008) also believe that assessment is an important component of an independent reading program. They suggest that students' reading can be assessed in three primary ways: through reading logs, anecdotal records, and student conferences.

Reading Logs

One of the most widely used means of assessment of independent reading is a reading log. A reading log is a list of books that a student has read. The list can record the books, the number of pages, the genre, the reading level, or a combination of these components. It is not an assessment, however, unless the teacher uses the information as part of a grade and/or to draw conclusions about the reader.

Michael, for example, may be classified as a struggling reader. He is in ninth grade, but he is most comfortable reading books written at a fourth- or fifth-grade level. When Michael began reading books in an independent reading program, he selected books that were too difficult for him, books that were at grade level. Even though Michael tried hard to make sense of the books he had chosen, he was unable to comprehend much of the text. His reading log revealed this trend. The reading log also showed his teacher the kinds of books that interested him. From the reading record, the teacher was able to identify several themes that appealed to Michael and was able to make suggestions about books that would pique his interest and would

Student Name: Michael

1st Quarter

Title	Author	Pages
The Body of Christopher Creed	Carol Plum-Ucci	331
Tangerine	Edward Bloor	324
Heart of a Champion	Carl Deuker	208
Twilight	Stephanie Meyer	488

2nd Quarter

Stormbreaker	Anthony Horowitz	264
Point Blank	Anthony Horowitz	304
Forensic Science: Evidence, Clues, and Investigation	Andrea Campbell	80
Fingerprints and Talking Bones: How Real-Life Crimes Are Solved	Charlotte Foltz Jones	144

FIGURE 7.2. Michael's reading log.

also be more readable for him. (See Figure 7.2 for an example of Michael's reading record in the fall and one from later in the year.)

Anecdotal Notes

Because secondary teachers typically have class loads of 60–180 students per day, they may not think about recording information about their students' reading progress. Teachers, however, are continually observing, analyzing, and drawing conclusions about their students; they actually record anecdotal records in their minds. The conclusions teachers draw about their students from this undocumented approach may not be completely accurate, so a variety of informal methods to record observational data have been developed, one of which is the production of anecdotal notes.

Anecdotal notes are the short comments teachers write as they observe student behavior. They are typically factual observations collected over time. Many teachers find that identifying one or two students to observe for a few moments at the beginning, middle, and end of a class works best. Teachers who systematically observe and record a student's behavior are often surprised by what they learn.

Teachers can be creative about the method they use for anecdotal note taking. Some teachers write on sticky notes and transfer these to a larger sheet with the student's name on it; others write in notebooks, devoting two or three pages to each of their struggling readers. They can also observe the students during reading time and record behaviors they notice.

Teachers with access to handheld computers can use this new technology to easily record notes about students. These anecdotal notes are valuable as teachers try to meet the needs of struggling readers, as in the case of Michael, the student presented in the previous section.

Michael, for example, is a resistant reader who lacks self-confidence. During independent reading time, he wastes as much time as he can—slowly getting his book out, slowly turning the pages, slowly looking down at his book. His slow-motion actions signal to the teacher that he doesn't want to read. In addition, Michael tries to distract students sitting near him by whispering, poking, and trying to send text messages. Watching Michael during independent reading time is revealing. Matching Michael with books that are at his own reading level may not inspire him to read. The teacher needs more information in order to find ways to encourage him to read.

Independent reading was scheduled during a 30-minute homeroom period at Michael's school that was used for increasing reading achievement. The teacher in charge of independent reading also had Michael in science class. In science, the teacher noticed that Michael was seriously engaged in the class, often volunteering answers to difficult problems. Michael enjoyed the inquiry projects and the experiments, but did not use his textbook as a resource for learning. These observations led the teacher to take a few minutes to talk with Michael about his interest in science and his lack of interest in books. As the teacher jotted down anecdotal notes from the two classes over several days, enough information surfaced for some preliminary conclusions that shed light on Michael's reading identity. From the notes, the teacher concluded that easy-reading science material that matched his science interests should be available for Michael to read during independent reading time. An example of anecdotal notes on Michael's behavior can be found in Figure 7.3.

Conferencing with Students

Learning about students' needs and interests is critical for teachers who want to connect struggling readers with books. One way to learn about students is to talk with them about their ideas and interests. Some teachers spend a few minutes during every independent reading class to conference with students about their reading choices. The purpose of this type of conference is for teachers to learn about the students and for the students to express their ideas, concerns, and interests to the teacher. Some teachers use an interest interview as a framework during their conferences, such as the example in Figure 7.4.

Some teachers use conferencing time for additional instructional purposes. Conferences can be used to discuss students' reading records, for example, or to talk with students about the books they are reading.

Student Name: Michael

1st Quarter

Observations: Taking time to get out a book, not having his book open, why is he choosing a different book—reading level too high? He went to the library 8 times this quarter and each time came back with a different book. Many times doesn't come to class with his book and has to go back to his locker to get it. He looks for ways to get others' attention by either whispering or poking other students.

Notes to self: After these observations, I am going to recommend to Michael some books that he would be more successful reading. From what I can see of the titles he has chosen, he may like books with strong male characters. The areas of interest may be sports, mystery, and adventure. He may not have thought about books with a science theme. He is always on task in science class. For the next quarter, I will help him with his book selection, offering him titles that may be of interest to him as well as being at his reading level.

2nd Quarter

Observations: Went to library twice to get books. Has his book with him on a daily basis.

Notes to self: I suggested the *Stormbreaker* series to Michael. He is enjoying this series. The main character is a young boy who loves action, adventure, and sports. I also thought starting with a series would be a good way to ease him into wanting to read. This book was also turned into a movie. From our conversations, I knew that he had seen the movie and he might want to read the book. This would then help him get into the series. This book is at his reading level. After helping Michael find a series that helps him feel more successful as a reader, I am going to begin to introduce some nonfiction that ties into this theme. Maybe a James Bond picture book? Something about inventions, sports? I know that he enjoys science so maybe a few books on forensic science, etc. This would tie into the mysteries as well.

FIGURE 7.3. Teacher anecdotal notes.

1. What do you do after school?
2. What kinds of television programs or movies do you like to watch?
3. Who is your favorite author?
4. What kinds of books do you prefer to read?
5. Do you play sports? If so, which ones?
6. What is your favorite type of vacation?
7. Whom do you admire most?
8. What magazines or journals do you read?
9. What newspapers do you read?
10. Do you live near a bookstore or public library? If so, do you go there regularly?

FIGURE 7.4. Questions for reading conferences.

Teachers can review instructional ideas as well, such as reminding students to look for the theme of a fictional book or showing students how to use an index for an informational book. Conferencing is a time for teachers to learn about students' reading and to generate ideas about ways to improve struggling readers' motivation to read and reading development.

Adding Instructional Conversations to Independent Reading

One of the ideas that has been incorporated into independent reading in the past decade is that reading does not need to be silent. Teachers are finding that some students respond better to independent reading programs in which discussions about books are a core feature of the program (DeBenedictis, 2007). Students who enjoy reading want to share their books with others, and giving students time to talk about their books in small groups or with the entire class can inspire even reluctant readers. Kelley and Clausen-Grace (2006) called this type of discussion "rap" in their adapted SSR program. They restructured SSR to R5 (read, relax, reflect, respond, and rap) in which the rap (discussion) portion is prominently featured.

Another type of instructional conversation that Parr and Maguiness (2005) have used involves asking reluctant readers to talk about their resistance to reading. A student who resists reading in an independent reading program may have developed an identity as a nonparticipant. According to Moje, Young, Readance, and Moore (2000), employing talk about the topic can help students situate themselves differently and change their place in the community of readers. Teachers can either talk with students as an entire class or discuss reading with small groups of students. The point is not to *tell* students that they should be readers, but to *discuss* with students how they use reading in their lives, to let them know how to find books that are interesting, and to talk about books that made a difference in the students' lives. These conversations should occur throughout the year, giving struggling readers opportunities to give voice to their experiences as readers. Parr and Maguiness found that their independent reading program was revitalized and reluctant readers showed more interest in reading once the teachers realized the importance of instructional conversations.

Content-Area Independent Reading

Independent reading is typically thought of as occurring during a reading or English class, or even during a common homeroom period. Some schools allocate 20 or 30 minutes of their schedule solely for the purpose of having an independent reading time. This framework works for many students; however, struggling readers often have great difficulty reading textbooks in disciplines such as social studies and science. As a result, students are not taking advantage of one of the tools for learning content-area material. This doesn't mean that struggling readers do not want to read about a content subject. According to Moss and Hendershot (2002), most students like reading informational books to learn. The problem is that many content classrooms do not have books that are accessible for students who are unable to read middle and high school materials.

Ivey and Broaddus (2003), who have a strong belief in the value of independent reading, addressed this problem by incorporating independent reading in a science class, allowing students to read materials of their own choosing for 20 minutes at the beginning of the period, including science trade books. The classroom library had 150–200 books that spanned a variety of difficulty levels, content, and types of books. All of the students, except one, chose to read books about science during the independent reading time.

This example illustrates the potential of independent reading in content-area classrooms. Students who struggle with reading can learn about instructional content through reading books that are written at a level that they can read. If students are given time and if teachers make books available to students, the likelihood of struggling readers learning from text increases (Gardiner, 2005b). Teachers, though, need to be able to locate content-area books that struggling readers can use. A number of resources for content-area trade books are shown in Figure 7.5.

Conclusions

Should middle and high school teachers carve out time from their schedules for students to read books or other texts of their own choosing? Our knowledge of adolescents and schooling lead us to conclude, absolutely

www.promo.net/pg/
Site for free e-books and texts on various topics to use in your classroom.

www.ala.org/ala/yalsa/booklistsawards/quickpicks/quickpicksreluctant.htm
Quick pick of books for reluctant readers. Books are listed by nonfiction and fiction.

www.reading.org/resources/tools/choices.html
Contains annually published book lists chosen by teachers, children, and young adults.

www.socialstudies.org/resources/notable/
Contains a comprehensive list of social studies literature resources for young people.

www.carolhurst.com/subjects/curriculum.html
Provides links, ideas, and book titles for using literature in teaching various subject areas.

www.nsta.org/ostbc/
Features outstanding science trade books chosen by the National Science Teachers Association.

www.csusm.edu/csb/intro_eng.html
Contains a searchable database of more than 6,000 Spanish-language books.

FIGURE 7.5. Resources for content area independent reading books.

yes! Struggling readers have little opportunity during the school day for providing input into the curriculum and for following their unique interests. Because reading progress is closely tied to motivation and interest in reading, giving students an opportunity for independent reading can help them learn that reading is a tool for increasing their knowledge about topics that they find interesting. Worthy, Broaddus, and Ivey (2001) write, "Struggling learners need instructional approaches that focus on enhancing motivation and providing reading and writing practice" (p. 258). Making time for independent reading can be one way to provide this essential reading practice.

References

Allington, R. L. (2001). *What really matters for struggling readers: Designing research-based programs.* New York: Longman.

Beers, K. (2003). *When kids can't read: What teachers can do.* Portsmouth, NH: Heinemann.

Block, C. C., & Mangieri, J. (2002). Recreational reading: 20 years later. *Reading Teacher, 55*(6), 572–580.

Brozo, W. G., & Hargis, C. H. (2003). Taking seriously the idea of reform: One high school's efforts to make reading more responsive to all students. *Journal of Adolescent and Adult Literacy, 47,* 14–23.

Center on Education Policy. (2006). *A public education primer.* Washington, DC: Author.

Csikszentmihalyi, M. (1991). *Flow: The psychology of optimal experience.* New York: Harper & Row.

Daniels, H. (2002). *Literature circles: Voice and choice in book clubs and reading groups* (2nd ed.). Portland, ME: Stenhouse.

DeBenedictis, D. (2007). Sustained Silent Reading: Making adaptations. *Voices from the Middle, 14*(3), 29–37.

Dembo, M. H., & Eaton, M. J. (2000). Self-regulation of academic learning in middle-level schools. *The Elementary School Journal, 100*(5), 473–490.

Donahue, P. L., Voelkl, K. E., Campbell, J. R., & Mazzeo, J. (1999). *NAEP 1998 reading report card for the nation and states* (NCES 1999500). Washington, DC: National Center for Educational Statistics, U.S. Department of Education.

Eccles, J. S., & Midgley, C. (1989). Stage–environment fit: Developmentally appropriate classrooms for young adolescents. In C. Ames & R. Ames (Eds.), *Research on motivation in education* (pp. 139–186). New York: Academic Press.

Fisher, D. (2004). Setting the "opportunity to read" standard: Resuscitating the SSR program in an urban high school. *Journal of Adolescent and Adult Literacy, 48,* 138–151.

Gardiner, S. (2005a). A skill for life. *Educational Leadership, 63*(2), 67–70.

Gardiner, S. (2005b). *Building student literacy through Sustained Silent Reading.* Alexandria, VA: Association for Supervision and Curriculum Development.

Guthrie, J. T., & Davis, M. H. (2003). Motivating struggling readers in middle school through an engagement model of classroom practice. *Reading and Writing Quarterly, 19,* 59–85.

Hunt, L. (1967). Evaluation through teacher–pupil conferences. In T. C. Barrett (Ed.), *The evaluation of children's reading achievement* (pp. 111–126). Newark, DE: International Reading Association.

Ivey, G., & Broaddus, K. (2001). "Just plain reading": A survey of what makes students want to read in middle school classrooms. *Reading Research Quarterly, 36,* 350–377.

Ivey, G., & Broaddus, K. (2003, December). *"It's good to read if you can read it": What matters to middle school students in content area independent reading.* Paper presented at the National Reading Conference, Scottsdale, AZ.

Ivey, G., & Fisher, D. (2006). *Creating literacy-rich schools for adolescents.* Alexandria, VA: Association for Supervision and Curriculum Development.

Johns, J. L., & Lenski, S. L. (2005). *Improving reading: Strategies and resources* (4th ed.). Dubuque, IA: Kendall/Hunt.

Kelley, M., & Clausen-Grace, N. (2006). R5: The Sustained Silent Reading makeover that transformed readers. *Reading Teacher, 60,* 148–156.

Krashen, S. (1993). *The power of reading: Insights from the research.* Englewood, CO: Libraries Unlimited.

Krashen, S. (2001). More smoke and mirrors: A critique of the National Reading Panel report on fluency. *Phi Delta Kappan, 83*, 119–123.

Krashen, S., & McQuillan, J. (1996). *The case for late intervention: Once a good reader always a good reader.* Culver City, CA: Language Education Associates.

Lanier, E., & Lenski, S. D. (2008). *Developing an independent reading program: Grades 4–12.* Norwood, MA: Christopher-Gordon.

Lewis, M., & Samuels, S. J. (2003). *Read more—read better? A meta-analysis of the literature on the relationship between exposure to reading and reading achievement.* Unpublished manuscript.

Marshall, J. C. (2002). *Are they really reading? Expanding SSR in the middle grades.* Portland, ME: Stenhouse.

McCracken, R. (1971). Initiating Sustained Silent Reading. *Journal of Reading, 14*, 521–524, 582–583.

McMahon, S. I., & Raphael, T. E. (Eds.). (1997). *The book club connection: Literacy learning and classroom talk.* Newark, DE: International Reading Association.

Moje, E. B., Young, J. P., Readance, J. E., & Moore, D. W. (2000). Reinventing adolescent literacy for new times: Perennial and millennial issues. *Journal of Adolescent and Adult Literacy, 43*, 400–410.

Moss, B., & Hendershot, J. (2002). Exploring sixth graders' selection of nonfiction trade books. *Reading Teacher, 56*, 6–17.

National Reading Panel. (2000). *Teaching children to read: An evidence-based assessment of the scientific research literature on reading and its implications for reading instruction.* Washington, DC: National Institute of Child Health and Human Development.

Parr, J. M., & Maguiness, C. (2005). Removing the silent from SSR: Voluntary reading as social practice. *Journal of Adolescent and Adult Literacy, 49*, 98–107.

Pilgreen, J. L. (2000). *The SSR handbook: How to organize and manage a Sustained Silent Reading program.* Portsmouth, NH: Boynton/Cook.

Primeaux, J. (2000). Shifting perspectives on struggling readers. *Language Arts, 77*, 537–542.

Samuels, S. J. (2006). Toward a model of reading fluency. In J. S. Samuels & A. E. Farstrup (Eds.), *What research has to say about fluency instruction* (pp. 24–46). Newark, DE: International Reading Association.

Smith, M. W., & Wilhelm, J. D. (2006). *Going with the flow: How to engage boys (and girls) in their literacy learning.* Portsmouth, NH: Heinemann.

Smith, N. B. (1986). *American reading instruction.* Newark, DE: International Reading Association.

Stanovich, K. (1986). Mathew effects in reading? Some consequences of individual differences in the acquisition of literacy. *Reading Research Quarterly, 21*, 360–407.

Stewart, R. A., Paradis, E. E., Ross, B., & Lewis, M. J. (1996). Student voices: What works best in literature-based developmental reading. *Journal of Adolescent and Adult Literacy, 39*, 468–478.

Taylor, B. M., Frye, B. J., & Maruyama, G. M. (1990). Time spent reading and reading growth. *American Educational Research Journal, 27*, 351–362.

Tomlinson, C. A. (1999). *The differentiated classroom: Responding to the needs of all learners.* Alexandria, VA: Association for Supervision and Curriculum Development.

Vygotsky, L. (1978). *Mind in society: The development of higher psychological processes.* Cambridge, MA: Harvard University Press.

Wigfield, A., & Guthrie, J. T. (1997). Relations of children's motivation for reading to the amount and breadth of their reading. *Journal of Educational Psychology, 89,* 420–432.

Wood, K. D., Edwards, A. T., Hill-Miller, P., & Vintinner, J. (2006). Motivation, self-efficacy, and the engaged reader. *Middle School Journal, 37,* 55–61.

Worthy, J., Broaddus, K., & Ivey, G. (2001). *Pathways to independence: Reading, writing, and learning in grades 3–8.* New York: Guilford Press.

Worthy, J., & McKool, S. (1996). Students who say they hate to read: The importance of opportunity, choice, and access. In D. J. Leu, C. K. Kinzer, & K. A. Hinchman (Eds.), *Literacies for the 21st century: Research and practice. 45th yearbook of the National Reading Conference* (pp. 245–256). Chicago: National Reading Conference.

PART III

Implementing Classroom Instruction for Struggling Adolescent Readers

CHAPTER 8

Fluency Strategies for Struggling Adolescent Readers

Gay Fawcett
Timothy Rasinski

For middle and high school teachers, content knowledge is central to their instruction—and rightly so. Teachers want students to learn the content of their disciplines. Academic content, however, is frequently imparted through the written word; thus literacy, the ability to read and write, is a critical vehicle for achieving content learning. Middle and high school teachers, then, have come to the realization that the use of reading and learning strategies can improve students' knowledge of academic content.

With the support of professional development, more and more content-area teachers are incorporating literacy strategies into their content instruction to help all students, but especially struggling readers. Comprehension strategies that were once the realm of elementary teachers now show up regularly in secondary classrooms—What I Know, What I Want to Know, What I Learned (KWL); anticipation guides; three-level guides; and Directed Reading–Thinking Activities. We celebrate the progress students can make with such a change in instruction. However, we also hope the focus on literacy embraced by an increasing number of content teachers can now be broadened to include a focus on reading fluency for struggling adolescent readers.

Professional development and university courses that focus on content-area reading typically omit fluency instruction for adolescent readers.

Recently, we reviewed a number of the widely read professional books and college textbooks devoted to instruction in middle and high school classrooms. The list of comprehension skills addressed in those books is long: visualizing, inferring, vocabulary knowledge, story grammar, schemas, main idea and details, retelling, questioning, prereading strategies, study strategies, writing to learn, and more. We found little evidence, however, of fluency instruction being addressed. For years reading fluency has been a neglected area of reading instruction at all grade levels, and it has been all but nonexistent at the secondary level (Allington, 1983; Rasinski & Zutell, 1996). In this chapter, therefore, we make the case for instruction in reading fluency for struggling middle and high school students.

What Is Reading Fluency?

Reading fluency refers to the ability of readers to read quickly, effortlessly, and efficiently with appropriate, meaningful expression or prosody (Rasinski, 2003). Fluent reading is accurate, smooth, not too slow, but also not too fast. Fluent readers automatically recognize words in the passages they read and "chunk" words into phrases so that a passage makes sense. They know where to pause, where to place emphasis, and how to use intonation.

Fluent reading allows readers to reserve their limited cognitive resources for the more important task in reading, which is comprehension (LaBerge & Samuels, 1974). Duke, Pressley, and Hilden (2004) estimate that 75–90% of students with significant comprehension difficulties have reading fluency problems that, in turn, can be a major cause of comprehension difficulties. Students struggle with comprehension, not because they cannot understand the concepts in the text, but rather because their laborious, word-by-word reading renders the information all but incomprehensible.

Traditionally, fluency has been associated with reading aloud, a practice more common in elementary classrooms than in secondary classrooms. Because fluency requires basic skills such as decoding, word recognition, and expression, it seems logical that fluency should be mastered in the early grades. Indeed, the development of instructional frameworks for reading has been at the elementary level. Jeanne Chall's (1996) stage model of reading development, for example, puts reading fluency as a goal for the primary grades. Stahl and Heubach (2005) developed an effective model of fluency instruction that was implemented exclusively in the second grade. Similarly, the Fluency Development Lesson (Rasinski, Padak, Linek, & Sturtevant, 1994) was initially used with second graders. Rasinski and Stevenson (2005) implemented an effective home-based fluency and decoding program for beginning first-grade students.

In like manner, state standards, courses of study, and curriculum guides place fluency instruction at the elementary level, mainly in the primary grades. Further, until recently, the preponderance of fluency research focused on the early elementary grades (i.e., Kuhn & Stahl, 2000; Rasinski et al., 1994). However, evidence and interest are building about the importance of fluency instruction for upper-grade students as well (Rasinski et al., 2005; Rasinski & Fawcett, in press; Rasinski & Padak, 2005a).

Research on Reading Fluency

It has only been in recent years that the literacy community has taken notice of the importance of reading fluency, thanks in large part to the widely publicized report of the National Reading Panel (2000). The panel identified fluency as one of five instructional factors, supported by empirical research, to be critical to students' overall reading development. Members of the panel looked at research across grades K–12 and found that fluency instruction has an impact on the reading ability of all readers at least through fourth grade, as well as students with reading problems throughout high school. The panel concluded that attention to fluency is appropriate for all ages.

A study sponsored by the U.S. Department of Education (Pinnell et al., 1995) found that fluency, whether measured in terms of word recognition automaticity or expression (prosody), was strongly associated with silent reading comprehension for fourth-grade students. Because nearly half of the sample of more than 1,000 fourth graders in this study lacked even a minimal level of fluency, the findings warrant serious consideration. A recent replication of the study (Dane, Campbell, Grigg, Goodman, & Oranje, 2005) found much the same results; reading fluency is significantly related to overall reading achievement for students beyond the primary grades and a significant number of these students lack even basic reading fluency skills.

Rasinski and Padak (1998) found that, among struggling elementary students in grades one through five referred for Title I supplementary reading instruction by their regular classroom teachers, the lack of reading fluency appeared to be the area of greatest need. In Kent State University's reading clinic, difficulties in reading fluency are manifested in a majority of second- through eighth-grade students who are referred for reading intervention. Although comprehension difficulties is the primary reason cited for most referrals, especially among intermediate- and middle-grade students, problems with fluency invariably accompany the difficulties in comprehension.

A recent study (Rasinski et al., 2005b) examined fluency among a large group of ninth-grade students in an urban school. Students in this district have historically performed poorly on the Ohio Graduation Test, which is given in tenth grade. Although word recognition accuracy was strong for most students (average decoding accuracy was 97.4%), more than 60% of students in the sample read below the 25th percentile on fluency norms developed for eighth graders (as established by Johns & Berglund, 2002). More than 12% of the students assessed read fewer than 100 words per minute, a rate normally associated with primary-grade readers. It is likely that the poor scores on the test were a result of disfluent reading, which drained cognitive resources away from where they were needed most—comprehension of content.

More recently, working with school personnel from a large urban school district, Rasinski and Padak (1998) examined the results of informal reading inventories (IRIs) administered in the fall to 76 ninth-grade students who were enrolled in schools identified as low performing. Again, although accuracy in word recognition was strong (94.5%), fluency as measured by words read correctly per minute (109) was, on average, poor. Students were reading at a rate that would be expected of second and third graders (using norms from Hasbrouck & Tindal, 1992). The students were also measured for prosody or intonation, using a 4-point scale developed by Pinnell and her colleagues (1995) in their study of fourth-grade students. Of the 76 students assessed, 58% received scores of 1 or 2 on the 4-point scale, indicating that they were not able to read with a minimal level of expression that reflected meaning making in their reading.

In addition to the aforementioned studies that demonstrated a relationship between reading achievement and fluency, another study confirmed that such correlations decline very little as students move beyond the primary and intermediate grades into the middle grades. Rasinski, Johnston, and Rikli (2007) measured the fluency of approximately 400 students in each of grades 3, 5, and 7. The correlations of fluency with scores on a standardized test of silent reading comprehension were $r = .64$, $r = .657$, and $r = .571$, respectively. One of the conclusions drawn from this study was that fluency is as important for adolescent readers as it is for elementary students. If students do not develop fluency in their reading in the elementary grades, is there any reason to expect that they will enter the middle grades and beyond as fluent readers?

Although studies that demonstrate a correlation between fluency and comprehension do not prove causation, these studies along with others hold the promise that gains in fluency may account for significant gains in comprehension. We cannot say conclusively that disfluent reading causes poor comprehension; there are certainly other contributing factors such as inadequate background knowledge, insufficient vocabulary, or lack of reading strategies. However, helping struggling readers to become more fluent can certainly benefit these students. Adolescent readers who read at a rate less than half of the expected norm are at a significant disadvantage.

At the very least, reading assignments take twice as long for students who lack fluency than for students reading at a more normal rate. Thus, if nothing else, struggling readers who are given fluency instruction may be better able to keep up with homework and in-class reading assignments because their reading rate can be more consistent with that of their more fluent classmates.

The Importance of Fluency for Adolescent Readers

"Young people do more reading and writing today—on paper and online—than ever before. This means their literacy development is just as important, and requires just as much attention, as that of beginning readers" (Focus on Adolescent Literacy, 2006, p. 1, Retrieved May 1, 2007, from *www.reading.org/resources/issues/focus_adolescent.htm*). Students need explicit instruction in all those comprehension skills found in the professional books and college textbooks: visualizing, inferring, vocabulary knowledge, story grammar, schemas, main idea and details, retelling, questioning, prereading strategies, study strategies, and writing to learn. But they also need instruction in fluency. Willingham (2007) argues that although instruction in reading comprehension strategies is important and worthwhile, such instruction may not be as effective if students are not sufficiently fluent readers.

The message from the research cited earlier is clear: Disfluent reading hinders reading achievement. Students who read at an excessively slow pace, even without its impacting comprehension, are at a disadvantage as compared with their classmates who read at a more normal rate. When faced with an in-class reading assignment, these students find they are only partway through the reading when the teacher and their more proficient peers are ready for the discussion that follows. Hence, they are "left behind," not ready to participate in the discussion and unable to benefit from what others have to say. In addition, homework takes as much as twice the time it should. Clearly, such levels of reading performance can easily lead to frustration, lack of efficacy, avoidance of reading, and, ultimately, school failure.

Fluency and Testing

Students can be further disadvantaged when it comes to testing. High-stakes testing seems to be here to stay for the near future. Nearly all state tests currently include extended reading passages, regardless of the subject, for which students must provide short or extended responses. Disfluent students are at a distinct disadvantage when taking high-stakes tests of this type. For one thing, such tests are often timed, and a slower reading rate puts these students at an obvious and practical disadvantage for completing the test. In addition, the cognitive connection between disfluent reading and comprehension prevents some students from demonstrating what they understand about the subject because they employ their limited cognitive resources for reading the text, not understanding the passage.

Finally, we note that although some struggling adolescent readers obtain a degree of fluency in the primary grades, they flounder when the nature and difficulty of the texts they encounter in the middle and high school grades present new challenges. In our own work with students at a variety of grade levels, for example, we find that students are often less fluent when reading expository, poetic, and rhetorical texts than they are with narrative or story materials that are of the same readability. They read such texts more slowly, and with less expression appropriate for the passage, than they read narratives.

Practical Applications
for Improving Adolescents' Reading Fluency

A complicating factor for students who lack fluency as they enter middle school and high school is that they are less likely to find the instructional support they need to remedy the situation. There are a number of possible reasons for this. First, fluency has not been part of preservice or inservice training for secondary teachers. Second, teachers have so much content they must teach that they see teaching reading strategies as a hindrance to completing their curricula. Third, students themselves can lessen the chance of getting help because they learn to hide their inadequacies in reading by not volunteering in class or pretending not to care about doing well in school. Although the solution to the problem is not easy, there are things that can be done that are not difficult for teachers to learn or implement.

Independent Reading

Students of all ages need many opportunities to read for their own purposes as well as for school-assigned purposes (Biancarosa & Snow, 2004; National Reading Panel, 2000). However, like fluency instruction, time set aside for independent reading, such as Sustained Silent Reading (SSR) or Drop Everything and Read (DEAR) has traditionally been relegated to the elementary school. It doesn't have to be that way, as illustrated by the example that follows:

Every morning at 9:25 a.m., a bell rings at Montevallo High School that makes students stop in their tracks. No matter what class they are in—science, math, even P.E.—they must find something to read for the next 15 minutes. Some students choose novels; others pick newspapers or magazines. What they choose to read is up to them, but having to read it is not. The reading time is part of the Alabama Reading Initiative (ARI). (Leech, 2006, p. 1, Retrieved October 12, 2006, from *www.al.com/news/birminghamnews/index.ssf?/base/ news/11606446104380.xml&coll=2&thispage=1#continue*)

High school and middle school staff members who think they do not have time for SSR should consider that since Montevallo High School started using ARI, test scores have increased not only in reading, but in all subjects. Montevallo High is one of 18 schools using it now, and the Alabama Department of Education is making a push toward taking ARI to more high schools. Independent reading serves more purposes than fluency development, of course, but it does provide a very effective context for fluency development.

Teacher Modeling

Teacher modeling is a powerful way for students to gain an internal sense of fluency. This can be done in the context of the subject matter a teacher wishes students to learn. For example, when assigning a section of a textbook to be read for homework, the teacher can read the first paragraph or so, using appropriate expression and rate. Then, in addition to strategies such as asking students to predict what the assignment will be about or discussing what students already know about the topic, the teacher can have a conversation with the students about fluency, pointing out the volume, voice modulation, and phrasing or chunking that were used. The teacher can ask students if they noted times when the reading slowed down or sped up, and ask what the teacher was attempting to convey (e.g., a sense of urgency, elation, or despondence). The conversation can conclude with instructions to the students to apply the same strategies to the homework and be prepared to discuss their fluent reading strategies the next day, along with the content of the assignment.

Teacher modeling can also take place as teachers supplement their content-area textbooks by reading aloud from quality adolescent literature. In recent years there has been a torrent of good books, both fiction and nonfiction, published for adolescents. Many of these books have beautiful illustrations that can capture even the most reluctant readers. A simple Google search using the term *Adolescent Literature* can help one to locate books to supplement just about any topic being studied. Websites for the National Council of Teachers of English (*www.ncte.org*) and the International Reading Association (*www.reading.org*) provide reliable book lists.

Middle school and high school teachers can also adopt a successful elementary grades strategy called "twin texts." The teacher selects a fiction and a nonfiction text on a topic currently being studied and shares those books with students. Again, the teacher models good fluent reading and then engages students in conversation about what fluent reading sounds like, as well as about the content.

Explicit Fluency Instruction

Fluency can be directly taught to students by a variety of methods including repeated reading, assisted reading, coaching, and word study. Not every middle and high school teacher needs to use all of the strategies discussed in this section, but teachers should find the strategies that fit best in their academic disciplines. For example, English teachers may benefit from having students read texts more than once by using repeated reading, and science teachers may find assisted reading more beneficial. The important point we want to emphasize is that all middle and high school teachers should incorporate the explicit instruction of fluency in their classes.

Repeated Reading

Independent reading and teacher modeling, in and of themselves, can do much to improve reading fluency in secondary schools. However, when combined with explicit and regular teaching of fluency strategies, these practices can be powerful. A strategy that has proven effective is *repeated reading* (Rasinski & Hoffman, 2003; Samuels, 1979), a strategy well established in the research literature and endorsed by the National Reading Panel (2000).

In repeated reading students are asked to read short passages several times until they achieve a level of fluent reading. Research has demonstrated, and common sense tells us, that when students engage in repeated readings they improve on the passage they have practiced. An exciting finding, however, is that students also improve on passages they have not previously read (Rasinski & Hoffman, 2003; Rasinski et al., 1994; Samuels, 1979; Stahl & Heubach, 2005). In other words, repeated reading instruction leads to improvements in fluency, not only on passages practiced but also on new passages never read before.

The problem we face with repeated reading in middle school and high school is motivating students to read a text multiple times. A solution to that dilemma is to tie a repeated reading to a performance; no one wants to appear incompetent or foolish in front of peers. Students should not be required to memorize the text for the performance, but simply be prepared to read it aloud.

Material that lends itself well to repeated reading includes poetry, plays (including readers' theater scripts), song lyrics, rhetoric, letters, diary entries, monologues, and dialogues. An added benefit is that such performances can extend the reading material of a classroom into genres that have not been explored in the past. A class might have its own "coffee house poetry slam" on a regular basis, complete with refreshments, a bar stool, and an audience. Not only would fluency develop, but students may also gain a new appreciation for poetry.

Music teachers and social studies teachers can join forces to integrate their subjects with songs from time periods or cultures being studied. Speeches of historical significance can be performed for special occasions such as Martin Luther King Jr. Day, Veterans Day, or Women's History Month. Speeches by famous people, such as John F. Kennedy, Susan B. Anthony, or Abraham Lincoln, can be recited in conjunction with studies of their lives.

The materials for such performances are readily available, often at no cost. For example, the website *www.americanrhetoric.com* provides teachers and students with the texts (and audio recordings) of some of the most famous speeches from American history. Once students become familiar with this strategy, they can write, practice, and perform their own poetry, plays, and rhetoric. Their pieces can either be originals or modified from magazines, literature, or textbooks.

Assisted Reading

Assisted reading involves students reading a text while simultaneously hearing it read to them by more fluent readers. The integration of seeing a text while simultaneously hearing it can have a profound impact on students' ability to recognize the words accurately and fluently in text (Rasinski & Hoffman, 2003). A common and effective form of assisted reading is choral reading. Choral reading, whether as whole-group choral reading, antiphonal choral reading (parts are read by different groups), or echo reading, allows the more fluent readers in a group to provide support for their less fluent classmates. It is a wonderful way to build group spirit and cohesion. Many texts, such as poems, song lyrics, school and class cheers, calls and responses, and quotations lend themselves to choral reading. The key to choral reading, as with any form of fluency activity, is to ensure that the students have access to the written text and are prompted to actually read the text, even if they already have it memorized.

Paired reading, another form of assisted reading, is reading done by two readers. It involves pairing a struggling reader with a more skilled reader, who then read a text aloud together. When reading and simultaneously listening to a fluent oral rendering of the same text, struggling readers gain in fluency and comprehension (Rasinski & Hoffman, 2003; Topping, 1987, 1995). Struggling readers can take over reading independently those sections that they feel confident reading. This strategy can be employed as students do repeated readings in preparation for performances. With each reading, the struggling reader should be able to take over more sections of the reading. The more fluent partner for the less fluent readers may be a teacher, parent, classroom aide, older student, or classmate.

Audio-assisted reading employs the use of technology to provide assistance for less fluent readers. A student reads a passage while listening to a prerecorded rendering of the text (Opitz & Rasinski, 1998). The student reads and listens to the assigned passage repeatedly until he or she is able to read it fluently without the assistance of the recording. Support for the use of audio-assisted reading with struggling readers comes from several lines of research (Carbo, 1978a, 1978b; Chomsky, 1976; Pluck, 1995; Rasinski & Hoffman, 2003).

In their need to cover required content, middle and secondary teachers sometimes resort to reading the textbook to students. Teachers can turn such an activity into an assisted-reading event by requiring students to open their own textbooks to the assigned pages and read along silently while the teacher reads the text aloud.

Coaching

Explicit fluency instruction includes providing individual feedback to students regarding their reading. This can be done as classroom assignments or answers to essay questions are read aloud, or it can be done as students do repeated readings in preparation for presentations. Teachers should point out places where students need to practice more, to read with greater emphasis, or to slow down or speed up. Such suggestions should be made one-on-one rather than in a group setting so as not to embarrass a student. Of course, acknowledgement of good fluent reading can be given publicly as genuine and deserved praise to students, which can also serve to make fluency strategies visible to all students.

Teachers may also use explicit and visible fluency rubrics (Rasinski, 2003) to rate students' oral reading and guide their discussion on the expressive quality of their reading of particular texts. Such rubrics can be used by students to judge the expressive quality of their own reading of passages.

Word Study

A large part of reading fluency involves the automatic recognition of the words in text. Automaticity in word recognition is a must for fluent reading. Various word study strategies such as the use of word banks, word sorts, and word games provide needed practice in developing word recognition automaticity.

Many secondary teachers have successfully adopted another elementary strategy to build students' vocabularies—the development of a *Word Wall*. Selected and key words encountered in the content of the course are posted on a chart on the classroom wall, usually in alphabetical order, so that students and teachers can refer to them when reading, discussing, or writing. Word Walls can be read chorally on a daily basis by students in a matter of minutes as a class warmup. We have personally seen Word Walls used successfully in high school physics, economics, and English classes, and in middle school math, social studies, language arts, and science classes.

Parent Support for Adolescents' Fluent Reading

Parental involvement in schools typically tapers off when students reach middle school. However, there are still many parents of adolescents, especially those of struggling learners, who are baffled by their children's school problems and really desire to help. No doubt, in parent conferences these parents have heard that their children have trouble with the subject matter because they are poor readers. But it is highly unlikely that any teacher has talked to them about reading fluency. It is not a difficult concept for a parent to understand and not a difficult one for a parent to work on at home.

Modeling fluent reading can also be a part of home support. Few adolescents want bedtime stories, but there are other ways to incorporate fluency in daily activities. We know one family that goes to the public library (parent and children together) and checks out books on tape anytime the family has a long drive coming up. Even a casual, "Hey, listen to this!" when the parent is reading a newspaper and comes upon something that would interest an adolescent can be a valuable modeling of fluency.

Paired reading was initially developed for elementary-age children and their parents. Keith Topping (1987) reported remarkable results in his work with parents using paired reading. It works with older students too, and during parent conferences teachers can demonstrate the procedure and ask parents to spend 10–15 minutes nightly helping their children read homework assignments in this way.

Middle school and high school teachers do have a great deal of content to cover, thus limiting the time they can devote to fluency instruction. Enlisting parents to help at home can be of great benefit. Most parents welcome something concrete and simple that they can do to help their child.

A Note to Language Arts Teachers

In this chapter we have presented the need for fluency instruction in *all* classrooms. We recognize that for content-area teachers this may seem to be something added onto what they have traditionally done. For language arts teachers, fluency should be an essential component of the curriculum, including explicit instruction in fluency every day. The strategies mentioned earlier also work well with literature.

As you assess reading skills, include a regular assessment of fluency. *Three-Minute Reading Assessments* (Rasinski & Padak, 2005b) contains leveled passages to help teachers quickly assess the word recognition, fluency, and comprehension of students in grades 5–8. Rubrics and grade-level norms make interpreting the data simple and easy, and record-keeping forms allow teachers to document and monitor students' performance. Essentially, the Three-Minute Reading Assessment provides much the same information as most informal reading inventories, but actually takes a matter of minutes per child. It is an excellent assessment tool for screening students for more intense diagnoses of reading problems and for monitoring all students' progress in reading. A similar assessment for students in grades 9–12 is available at the Ohio Literacy Alliance website (*www.ohioliteracy-alliance.org/fluency/fluency.htm*).

The need for and effects of practice are strong reasons for considering a reading workshop approach (Atwell, 1998), where students are allowed plenty of reading time every day. If there is not a time set aside in your school for everyone to do SSR, be sure to include it in your classroom. One key to SSR is to make students accountable for the time spent in silent reading. Have them keep an SSR journal in which they log in the titles, summaries, and personal responses to their daily reading.

Encourage SSR in yourself and among your colleagues. Consider using Indy 500 (Lenski & Lanier, Chapter 7, this volume) as described in this book. Read some professional books on reading fluency (Rasinski, 2003; Rasinski, Blachowicz, & Lems, 2005a; Samuels & Farstrup, 2006). Better yet, start a book study with some colleagues. As the literacy expert in your school, be an advocate of fluency for adolescents.

A Note to Intervention Specialists

No doubt all, or nearly all, of your students are struggling readers. Is fluency included in their Individual Education Plan (IEP) goals? Can you help the IEP team understand that an increase in fluency can result in increased school performance overall? The strategies presented in this chapter can easily be implemented if you have a pull-out program. If you are in an inclusion setting, you can work with small groups in the classroom. Share what you know about fluency with your inclusion team members.

Your students are probably reading significantly below grade level. One way to practice fluency without embarrassing your students is to have them develop listening libraries for younger students. They can practice and then tape-record picture books that are frequently found in elementary libraries. Your students, more than any others, need fluency. Make it a part of your daily instructional repertoire.

Conclusion

Evidence is mounting that attention to fluency in the middle school and high school can pay dividends in student achievement across all subject areas. More research is needed. However, there are many things a teacher can do now to improve students' reading skills. Clearly, teaching fluency in the middle school and high school requires a commitment of time and means additional work for the teacher. But if we want students to learn the content, we have to help them read the content. It is time well invested. Every teacher can incorporate literacy instruction into classroom teaching, and that includes instruction in fluency.

References

Allington, R. L. (1983). Fluency: The neglected goal of the reading program. *Reading Teacher, 36,* 556–561.

Atwell, N. (1998). *In the middle: New understanding about writing, reading, and learning.* Portsmouth, NH: Boynton/Cook.

Biancarosa, G., & Snow, C. (2004). *Reading Next: A vision for action and research in middle and high school literacy.* Washington, DC: Alliance for Excellent Education.

Carbo, M. (1978a). Teaching reading with talking books. *Reading Teacher, 32,* 267–273.

Carbo, M. (1978b). A word imprinting technique for children with severe memory disorders. *Teaching Exceptional Children, 11,* 3–5.

Chall, J. S. (1996). *Stages of reading development* (2nd ed.). Fort Worth: TX: Harcourt Brace.

Chomsky, C. (1976). After decoding: What? *Language Arts, 53,* 288–296.

Dane, M. C., Campbell, J. R., Grigg, W. S., Goodman, M. J., & Oranje, A. (2005). *Fourth-grade students reading aloud: NAEP 2002 special study of oral reading.* Washington, DC: U.S. Department of Education, Institute of Education Sciences.

Duke, N., Pressley, M., & Hilden, K. (2004). Difficulties with reading comprehension. In C. A. Stone, E. R. Silliman, B. J. Ehren, & K. Apel (Eds.), *Handbook of language and literacy: Development and disorders* (pp. 501–520). New York: Guilford Press.

Focus on adolescent literacy: IRA programs and resources. (2006). International Reading Association [Online]. Available: *www.reading.org/resources/issues/focus_adolescent.htm.*

Hasbrouck, J. E., & Tindal, G. (1992). Curriculum-based oral reading fluency norms for students in grades 2 through 5. *Teaching Exceptional Children, 24,* 41–44.

Johns, J., & Berglund, R. (2002). *Fluency: Questions, answers, evidence-based strategies.* Dubuque, IA: Kendall/Hunt.

Kuhn, M. R., & Stahl, S. A. (2000). *Fluency: A review of developmental and remedial practices* (CIERA Rep. No. 2-008). Ann Arbor, MI: Center for the Improvement of Early Reading Achievement.

LaBerge, D., & Samuels, S. A. (1974). Toward a theory of automatic information processing in reading. *Cognitive Psychology, 6,* 293–323.

Leech, M. (2006, October 12). State reading initiative may spread: State education department wants program in more high schools. *Birmingham News* [Online]. Available: *www.al.com/news/birminghamnews/index.ssf?/base/news/11606446104380.xml&coll=2&thispage=1#continue.*

National Reading Panel. (2000). *Report of the National Reading Panel: Teaching children to read: Report of the subgroups.* Washington, DC: U.S. Department of Health and Human Services, National Institutes of Health.

Opitz, M. F., & Rasinski, T. V. (1998). *Good-bye round robin: 25 effective oral reading strategies.* Portsmouth, NH: Heinemann.

Pinnell, G. S., Pikulski, J. J., Wixson, K. K., Campbell, J. R., Gough, P. B., & Beatty, A. S. (1995). *Listening to children read aloud.* Washington, DC: U.S. Department of Education, Office of Educational Research and Improvement.

Pluck, M. (1995). Rainbow Reading Programme: Using taped stories. *Reading Forum, 1,* 25–29.

Rasinski, T. V. (2003). *The fluent reader: Oral reading strategies for building word recognition, fluency, and comprehension.* New York: Scholastic.

Rasinski, T. V., Blachowicz, C., & Lems, K. (2005a). *Fluency instruction: Research-based best practices.* New York: Guilford Press.

Rasinski, T. V., & Fawcett, G. (in press). Fluency for adolescent readers: The research we have, the research we need. In M. Conley (Ed.), *Adolescent reading: The research we have, the research we need.* New York: Guilford Press.

Rasinski, T. V., & Hoffman, J. V. (2003). Theory and research into practice: Oral reading in the school literacy curriculum. *Reading Research Quarterly, 38,* 510–522.

Rasinski, T. V., Johnston, S., & Rikli, A. (2007). *Analysis of fluency and reading comprehension scores among third, fifth, and seventh grade students.* Unpublished manuscript.

Rasinski, T. V., & Padak, N. D. (1998). How elementary students referred for compensatory reading instruction perform on school-based measures of word recognition, fluency, and comprehension. *Reading Psychology, 19,* 185–216.

Rasinski, T. V., & Padak, N. D. (2005a). Fluency beyond the primary grades: Helping adolescent readers. *Voices from the Middle, 13,* 34–41.

Rasinski, T. V., & Padak, N. D. (2005b). *Three Minute Reading Assessments: Word* recognition, fluency, and comprehension for grades 5–8. New York: Scholastic.

Rasinski, T. V., Padak, N. D., Linek, W. L., & Sturtevant, E. (1994). Effects of fluency development on urban second-grade readers. *Journal of Educational Research, 87,* 158–165.

Rasinski, T. V., Padak, N. D., McKeon, C., Krug-Wilfong, L., Friedauer, J., & Heim, P. (2005). Is reading fluency a key for successful high school reading? *Journal of Adolescent and Adult Literature, 49,* 22–27.

Rasinski, T. V., & Stevenson, B. (2005). The effects of Fast Start Reading: A fluency based home involvement reading program, on the reading achievement of beginning readers. *Reading Psychology, 26,* 109–125.

Rasinski, T. V., & Zutell, J. B. (1996). Is fluency yet a goal of the reading curriculum? In E. Sturtevant & W. Linek (Eds.), *Growing literacy: The eighteenth yearbook of the College Reading Association* (pp. 237–246). Harrisonburg, VA: College Reading Association.

Samuels, S. J. (1979). The method of repeated readings. *Reading Teacher, 32,* 403–408.

Samuels, S. J., & Farstrup, A. (2006). *What research has to say about reading instruction.* Newark, DE: International Reading Association.

Stahl, S., & Heubach, K. (2005). Fluency-oriented reading instruction. *Journal of Literacy Research, 37,* 25–60.

Topping, K. (1987). Paired reading. A powerful technique for parent use. *Reading Teacher, 40,* 604–614.

Topping, K. (1995). *Paired reading, spelling, and writing.* New York: Cassell.

Willingham, D. (2007). The usefulness of brief instruction in reading comprehension strategies. *American Educator, 30,* 39–50.

CHAPTER 9

Comprehension Strategies That Make a Difference for Struggling Readers

Micki M. Caskey

Comprehension is a requisite cognitive process for successful reading in academic settings and life-long learning that eludes many adolescents. Recent and highly visible reports attest to a crisis in adolescent literacy (Biancarosa & Snow, 2004, 2006; Kamil, 2003; National Association of State Boards of Education, 2005; National Governors Association, 2005). Data from a national representative assessment, the National Assessment of Educational Progress (NAEP), indicate that 71% of eighth-grade students in public schools are less than proficient readers—with 42% at basic and 29% below basic levels (Perie, Grigg, & Donahue, 2005). When considered together, these reports and assessment data suggest that many middle and high school students struggle to comprehend texts.

Struggling readers often do not comprehend the materials that they are expected to read in school. Comprehension of informational text is particularly difficult. Among the reasons that explain why middle and high school students experience comprehension problems are (1) lack of motivation and engagement (Guthrie, 2004; Guthrie & Wigfield, 2000), (2) text difficulty (Allington, 2003, 2006, 2007; Armbruster, 1984), and (3) insufficient or ineffective strategies instruction and use (Pressley, 2002). This chapter reviews the salient research literature, addresses the significance of comprehension, identifies effective comprehension practices, and concludes with a set of recommendations for improving the comprehension of struggling adolescent readers.

Research on Reading Comprehension

This review of the research begins with descriptions of struggling readers and reading comprehension. Next, it addresses research on reading comprehension, motivation and engagement, and text difficulty. Then, the review examines research findings related to comprehension instruction that emphasize explicit teaching and strategy instruction.

Defining Struggling Readers and Reading Comprehension

Who are struggling readers? In simple terms, they are students who grapple unsuccessfully with written text. Hall (2007) lists other labels for these readers, including poor readers, remedial readers, and at-risk readers. The term *struggling readers* is also used to reference youth with reading disabilities, English language learners (ELLs), at-risk readers, striving readers, and those who are unmotivated, disenchanted, or unsuccessful in school-related reading (Brozo & Simpson, 2007; Strickland & Alvermann, 2004). Typically, struggling readers are defined as low-achieving students who experience cognitive difficulties when reading (Vacca & Vacca, 2006); yet this definition is not inclusive of marginalized readers (Moje, Young, Readance, & Moore, 2000). In this chapter, the expression *struggling readers* is widened to include students who are disengaged from school-related literacy.

Literacy theorists, researchers, and educators agree that reading is an active process and offer comparable definitions of reading comprehension, such as "the process of constructing meaning from written text" (Gambrell & Koskinen, 2002, p. 303), "the ability to understand and construct meaning from what one reads" (Almasi, 2003, p. 74), "the process of constructing a supportable understanding of a text" (Neufeld, 2006, p. 302), and "the process of simultaneously extracting and constructing meaning through interaction and involvement with written language" (RAND Reading Study Group, 2002, p. xiii). Similarly, there is general agreement that reading entails interaction between the reader, the text, and a context-specific activity.

Theorists examine reading comprehension from multiple perspectives, including schema theory and transactional reader–response theory. Schema theory emphasizes the importance of background knowledge. This theoretical stance views comprehension as an interactive–compensatory process that links new information from the text with existing information, or prior knowledge (Almasi, 2003). Another perspective, the transactional reader–response theory, posits that comprehension results from a transaction between the reader, the text, and the context (Rosenblatt, 1978). Almasi (2003) considers the integration of the schema and transaction theories and suggests, "If a reader is able to select an appropriate schema and make a connection between it and the message of the text, with a context, then comprehension occurs" (p. 79). She further reasons that problems with schema availability, schema selection, and schema maintenance can impair or inhibit reading comprehension.

Underpinning reading comprehension is the sociocultural theory of language and literacy, which hypothesizes that individuals acquire language and literacy through social interactions with more expert peers and adults (Vygotsky, 1978). With guidance and scaffolding from teachers or knowledgeable peers, readers can learn to comprehend text that is slightly beyond their independent knowledge and ability levels. As readers internalize the instructional principles and learn independently, the supports are withdrawn. From a sociocultural perspective, instructional processes, including the social interactions that contextualize the learning experience, and the content are most important (RAND Reading Study Group, 2002). The aforementioned theories—schema theory, transactional reader–response theory, and sociocultural theory—emphasize the complexity of reading comprehension and the reading comprehension instruction.

Though considerably more reading comprehension research has been conducted in the elementary grades than in middle school or high school, the findings contribute to the comprehension knowledge base and are useful when considering how to address the needs of struggling adolescent readers. In his detailed synthesis of reading comprehension research, Pressley (2000) reported, "Text comprehension begins with decoding of words, processing of those words in relation to one another to understand the many small ideas in the text, and then, both unconsciously and consciously, operating on the ideas in the text to construct the overall meaning encoded in the text" (p. 551). Pressley recommended a broad approach to reading comprehension improvement that included teaching decoding skills, encouraging the development of sight words, teaching students to use semantic context cues to evaluate whether decodings are accurate, teaching vocabulary meanings, encouraging extensive reading, encouraging students to ask themselves why the ideas related in a text make sense, and teaching self-regulated use of comprehension strategies. Further, researchers across grade levels found that effective comprehension entails teaching readers multiple strategies to allow them to construct meaning from text (Alfassi, 2004; Pressley, 2000).

In its analysis of reading comprehension research, the RAND Reading Study Group (2002) reported that comprehension instruction is content and context specific. It noted, "Specific reading comprehension tasks must be mastered in the context of specific subject matter" (p. 6). It recommended simultaneously teaching discipline-specific vocabulary words, text structures, and approaches for acquiring content knowledge and reading skills. The RAND Reading Study Group asserted that high-quality instruction was the most powerful means to develop reading comprehension and prevent reading comprehension problems. However, it also acknowledged the effects that contextual factors (e.g., socioeconomic status, ethnicity, economic resources, school and community culture, as well as the classroom environment) have on the development of reading comprehension ability.

Motivation, Engagement, and Adolescents' Reading Comprehension

Motivation and engagement play a principal role in students' ability to comprehend text (Alvermann, 2001; Biancarosa & Snow, 2004; Kamil, 2003; Wigfield, 2004). Researchers find motivation and engagement to be interrelated and view motivation as a precursor to engagement (Meltzer & Hamann, 2004). The basic premise is that when students are motivated to read, they are more likely to engage in reading tasks and construct meaning from text. For struggling readers, the motivation to engage in text, and expend effort to comprehend text, declines as they transition to higher grades (Guthrie & Davis, 2003; Guthrie & Knowles, 2001; Guthrie & Wigfield, 2000).

Guthrie and Wigfield (2000) define reading motivation as an individual's personal beliefs, values, and goals about the topics, processes, and outcomes of reading. Wigfield (2004) further articulates that reading motivation includes self-efficacy, intrinsic and extrinsic motivation, valuing of reading, and goal orientation. Self-efficacy is viewed as individuals' judgment of their own abilities and their belief that they can perform a task (Bandura, 1997). Adolescents who struggle with reading often believe that they are not capable and that their efforts will not result in successful reading comprehension. Researchers suggest that intrinsic motivation (coming from within the individual), rather than extrinsic motivation (coming from external sources), results in long-term engagement and deeper learning (Guthrie & Knowles, 2001; Wigfield, 2004). In addition, Wigfield (2004) notes that intrinsic or extrinsic motivation relates to goal orientation. Individuals with a learning (mastery) orientation focus on improving skills and developing competence, whereas those with a performance orientation are more concerned with rewards. Other factors that affect reading motivation are instructional processes (e.g., real-world experiences, interesting texts), student choice, and collaboration among students (Guthrie & Wigfield, 2000).

A recent study by Pitcher and colleagues (2007) exploring adolescents' motivation to read warrants attention. The research team surveyed 384 adolescents across the United States using the *Adolescent Motivation to Read Profile*, which it adapted from the *Motivation to Read Profile* (Gambrell, Palmer, Codling, & Mazzoni, 1996). Survey results showed gender-specific differences regarding how adolescents perceive themselves as readers and how they value reading—with females scoring higher than males. The researchers conducted conversational interviews with nearly 100 adolescents to gain a better understanding of adolescents' reading experiences and motivations. Interview data revealed students' significant use of multiliteracies (e.g., magazines, newspapers, e-mail, instant message, Internet resources), preferred learning modes (e.g., literature circles), and the importance of choice. Findings led the researchers to conclude, "Using adolescents' preferred reading materials and modes of instruction will lead to increased motivation" (p. 378). Increasing adolescents' motivation to read is essential for all adolescents because it ties directly to reading engagement.

Long-term engagement with reading leads to literacy development and improved comprehension (Meltzer & Hamann, 2004). *Reading engagement* refers to students' actual involvement with reading, which includes the construction of meaning and metacognitive processes. Guthrie (2004) characterizes engaged readers as cognitively competent, self-motivated, knowledge-driven, and socially interactive during learning. In contrast, he finds that disengaged readers do not possess the cognitive strategies to read independently nor do they exhibit curiosity, confidence, or a desire to learn concepts in books. Guthrie asserts, "Engaged reading is the primary pathway toward the competencies and expertise needed for achievement" (p. 4). Because of the strong connection between engagement and reading achievement, literacy instruction must address issues of motivation and engagement (Alvermann, 2001).

Text Difficulty and Reading Comprehension in Middle Grades and High School

Texts in middle school and high school are more complex and challenging than those in the elementary grades (Lenski, Wham, Johns, & Caskey, 2007). For example, the emphasis tends to shift from narrative text to informational text by the middle grades. The syntax of these informational texts is more demanding, the vocabulary is more specialized and technical, and concepts are more abstract. The amount students are required to read textbooks also increases with the move to separate, discipline-based settings (content-area classrooms). Textbooks are typically more formal and formidable (Guthrie & Davis, 2003), more comprehensive and encyclopedic in nature (Vacca & Vacca, 2005), and "foster a limited understanding of a wide range of topics" (Allington, 2006, p. 55). Textbooks also are "inconsiderate" of readers because they do not provide adequate background information, consistent structure, or vocabulary support, nor do they make sufficient connections between concepts (Armbruster, 1984). Often, the reading levels of content-area textbooks are even higher than students' assigned grade levels (Allington, 2003; Mastropieri, Scruggs, & Graetz, 2003). Though text difficulty is an issue for all students, for struggling readers text difficulty becomes a major barrier to comprehension.

Text difficulty also has an effect on instructional practice and student learning. To make the textbook content accessible, content-area teachers have students listen to texts that teachers read aloud (Nist & Simpson, 2000). Teachers often opt to teach content without expecting students to read their textbooks, thus avoiding the issue of text difficulty (Shanahan, 2004). Content-area teachers do not typically teach their students the strategies needed to use textbooks (National Institute of Child Health and Human Development [NICHHD], 2000), yet they view textbooks as essential tools for student learning. Readability and the length of texts affect how readers approach and understand the content of the texts (Almasi, 2003). Allington (2006) notes that using texts that are too difficult yields little or no benefit for students. Hall (2004) identifies the possible consequences of text difficulty for students, which "can include: (a) not learning the required content, (b) failing to pass high-stakes tests, (c) low self-efficacy, and (d) behavior problems" (p. 77). Text difficulty has serious implications for both struggling readers and their teachers.

Research on Explicit Comprehension Instruction

Research reveals a number of excellent approaches for improving comprehension instruction, including comprehension strategies, comprehension monitoring and metacognition instruction, teacher modeling, scaffolded instruction, and apprenticeship models (Biancarosa & Snow, 2006). To advance comprehension across all grades, Pressley (2002) reasserts the importance of extensive reading, tapping prior knowledge, and teaching vocabulary meanings. "Vocabulary development is both an outcome of comprehension and a precursor to it with word meanings making up as much as 70–80 percent of comprehension" (Bromley, 2007, p. 528). Researchers identify other methods for comprehension instruction such as process-based comprehension instruction, (Block, Schaller, Joy, & Gaine, 2002), self-directed comprehension instruction (Brown, 2002), and the use of learning strategies and content enhancement approaches (Fisher, Schumaker, & Deshler, 2002). Successful comprehension instruction depends on the thoughtful selection and adaptation of approaches to fit the context (Duffy, 2002). Although there are many effective ways to teach comprehension, this chapter focuses on explicit instruction and comprehension strategies. Duffy contends, "Explicit teaching rose out of a concern for struggling readers. Because struggling readers do not pick up on the relatively subtle cues and prompts provided by other activities, research was conducted on a number of instructional techniques designed to provide more explicit information about how reading works" (p. 30). He distinguishes explicit teaching from other reading comprehension approaches. In explicit teaching, a strategy is a learner-controlled technique—rather than a teacher-controlled technique—that readers use to better comprehend text. He continues, "Explicit teaching is intentional and direct about teaching individual strategies on the assumption that clear and unambivalent information about how strategies work will put struggling students in a better position to control their own comprehension" (pp. 30–31). Explicit teaching requires direct explanation of the strategy, immediate application of the strategy to text, and explicit teacher talk to develop students' metacognitive awareness.

Comprehension strategies are the conscious plans or steps that readers use to make sense of text (Harris & Hodges, 1995). They are specific, learned procedures that foster active, proficient, self-regulated, and intentional reading (Trabasso & Bouchard, 2002). Teaching students to use comprehension strategies—comprehension strategy instruction—is explicit. Comprehension strategy instruction consists of teachers' direct instruction, scaffolding through teacher modeling (think aloud), guided practice, and application to text (Guthrie & Wigfield, 2000; Harris & Hodges, 1995; Walker, 2005). Comprehension strategy instruction needs to occur "within a context where students use the strategies to read and learn from the actual text they are expected to read" (Neufeld, 2006, p. 308). The goal of comprehension strategy instruction is students' independent use of strategies when reading.

There is considerable consensus in the research literature regarding the importance of teaching comprehension strategies. The National Reading Panel identifies the following strategies as scientifically sound: comprehension monitoring, using graphic organizers, question answering, question generation, story structure, and summarization (NICHHD, 2000). Pressley (2002) reports that strategies that were "validated as effective in improving comprehension" include relating text to prior knowledge, mental imagery (constructing mental pictures), questioning, and summarizing (p. 16). On the basis of an analysis of more than 200 experimental studies, Trabasso and Bouchard (2002) identify 12 types of strategies for comprehension instruction: comprehension monitoring, graphic organizers, listening actively while reading, mental imagery, mnemonics, prior knowledge, question answering, question generation, story structure, summarization, vocabulary, and multiple-strategy instruction. They illustrate multiple-strategy instruction by describing reciprocal teaching (Palincsar & Brown, 1984), which incorporates four critical strategies: questioning, clarifying, predicting, and summarizing. Trabasso and Bouchard (2002) conclude:

There is very strong empirical, scientific evidence that the instruction of more than one strategy in a natural context leads to the acquisition and use of reading comprehension strategies and transfer to standardized comprehension tests. Multiple strategy instruction facilitates comprehension as evidenced by performance on tasks that involve memory, summarizing, and identification of main ideas. (p. 184)

Knowing how to apply comprehension strategies makes a difference for both good and struggling readers.

Compelling evidence supports the teaching of comprehension strategies. Pressley (2002) finds that students who have had comprehension strategy instruction (1) are more willing to try challenging reading, (2) are more active while reading, (3) interact more effectively with peers, (4) are better able to interpret text, and (5) outperform peers on standardized tests. The RAND Reading Study Group (2002) also reports that comprehension strategies are effective in targeted interventions settings and experimental settings. "In summary, there is quite a bit of evidence that elementary, middle and secondary students benefit from instruction in the use of a small repertoire of reading comprehension strategies" (Pressley, 2002, p. 21).

Importance of Reading Comprehension

Reading comprehension as an integral facet of literacy is critically important for adolescent learners. "Literacy—the ability to read, write, speak, listen, and think effectively— enables adolescents to learn and to communicate clearly about what they know and what they want to know"(Meltzer, 2002, p. 6). In order to become contributing members of society, adolescents must comprehend text. Highlighting the significance of adolescent literacy is the International Reading Association's position statement:

Adolescents entering the adult world in the 21st century will read and write more than at any other time in human history. They will need advanced levels of literacy to perform their jobs, run their households, act as citizens, and conduct their personal lives. They will need literacy to cope with the flood of information they will find everywhere they turn. They will need literacy to feed their imaginations so they can create the world of the future. (Moore, Bean, Birdyshaw, & Rycik, 1999, p. 3)

Adolescents require both the knowledge and skills to succeed in higher education and/or a postsecondary job market (RAND, 2005).

Too many students lack adequate literacy skills, as evidenced by the more than eight million struggling readers in grades 4–12 in schools across our nation (National Center for Education Statistics [NCES], 2005). Though efforts to improve the early literacy ability of children appear to be working, comparable results are not visible in middle and high school students' reading scores (Biancarosa & Snow, 2004). In the United States, nearly 50% of incoming ninth graders in public high schools cannot comprehend their assigned texts (Strickland & Alvermann, 2004). Young and older adolescents alike who experience reading difficulties are at risk of academic failure and of losing interest in school (Smith & Wilhelm, 2006). Leakage in the education pipeline is due to some extent to the large numbers of youth entering high school without the ability to read with sufficient fluency and comprehension to do serious academic work (RAND, 2005). "Even those who manage to stay in school often have a history of reading difficulties that prevent them from acquiring the requisite background knowledge, skills, and specialized vocabulary needed for learning in the subject area" (Strickland & Alvermann, 2004, p. 3). Not only are struggling readers are at risk of failure in academic settings, they are also vulnerable in the future. Poor literacy skills follow adolescents into adulthood and limit their employment options.

The significance of the adolescent literacy issue is also discernable in the range and volume of publications on the subject across the past decade. Professional organizations articulate positions and offer practical guides for improving adolescent literacy (Moore et al., 1999; National Association of Secondary School Principals, 2005; National Council of Teachers of English, 2006). Policy groups, which develop and influence public policy in response to public challenges, disseminate print and downloadable versions of their policies concerning adolescent literacy (Biancarosa & Snow, 2004, 2006; Kamil, 2003; National Association of State Boards of Education, 2005; National Governors Association, 2005) and struggling readers (Buly & Valencia, 2002; Education Trust, 2005). Educational laboratories and others provide instructional guides for improving adolescent literacy proficiency (Peterson, Caverly, Nicholson, O'Neal, & Cusenbary, 2000; Torgesen et al., 2007). Together these publications represent a critical focus on adolescent literacy and signify a call to action for improvement.

Effective Comprehension Practices

The intensive attention to adolescent literacy suggests changes in secondary education, specifically instructional practice. Owing to the complexity of the issue, schools must create literacy-rich environments that supply students with informational texts at wide-ranging levels (Ivey & Fisher, 2006). Teachers have the distinct opportunity to respond instructionally to help adolescents acquire the skills and disposition necessary to read informational text (Lenski et al., 2007). Teachers also have the inherent responsibility to regard struggling readers positively, inasmuch as deficit views erect barriers for struggling readers (Nierstheimer, Hopkins, Dillon, & Schmitt, 2000). This section identifies effective comprehension strategies that align well with explicit teaching, motivation, and active engagement. It ends with practical suggestions for dealing with text difficulty.

Explicit Teaching

Content-area teachers can make a difference for struggling readers by incorporating reading comprehension strategies in their teaching—without being teachers of reading (Fisher & Ivey, 2006). To begin, teachers explicitly state the goal of a strategy to help students become more strategic readers and foster a culture of literacy (Langer, 2001, 2002; Lenski et al., 2007; National Association of Secondary School Principals, 2005). Next, content-area teachers explicitly teach the strategy by modeling how to execute the strategy, guiding students' use of the strategy, and providing multiple opportunities for students to apply the strategy. Through this type of explicit and scaffolded instruction, teachers steer struggling readers' journeys to become confident, competent, and independent users of strategies.

Content-area teachers can further improve struggling readers' comprehension of text by teaching multiple strategies and orchestrating their use before, during, and after reading. For example, a teacher can use an *Antici pation/Reaction Guide* (Herber, 1978) to build students' interest in a topic before they begin to read. An Anticipation/Reaction Guide is a set of statements that a teacher drafts to probe students' opinions or beliefs about a topic. While students are reading, the teacher can guide students' comprehension with a strategy such as *Inquiry Questions* (Unrau, 2004). Inquiry Questions includes a series of questions based on the cognitive levels of Bloom's (1956) taxonomy, which students ask themselves as they read. Following the reading, students respond to the statements of the Anticipation/ Reaction Guide (Herber, 1978).

Content-area teachers can also implement an integrated strategies approach, such as *Reciprocal Teaching* (Palincsar & Brown, 1984), *K-W-L* (Ogle, 1986), or *Collaborative Strategic Reading* (Klingner & Vaughn, 1998) to engage struggling readers throughout the reading process. Reciprocal Teaching is an interactive activity between the teacher and students (or between students) that incorporates four strategies: summarizing, question generating, clarifying, and predicting. K-W-L is another integrated strategy that asks students what they <u>K</u>now about a topic, what they <u>W</u>ant to learn about the topic, and what they have <u>L</u>earned about the topic. The third approach, Collaborative Strategic Reading, is composed of four strategies—*Preview, Click and Clunk, Get the Gist,* and *Wrap Up*—that students use before, during, and after reading. Using multiple strategies or an integrated strategies approach, teachers cultivate interest, promote active engagement, and advance comprehension.

Motivation

Teachers and instructional practice play a central role in students' motivation to read (Edmunds & Bauserman, 2006; Pitcher et al., 2007). Specific actions that teachers can employ to increase readers motivation include (1) encouraging self-selection of books, (2) increasing exposure to informational and literary books, (3) identifying personal interests, using interest inventories or conversations, (4) increasing access to books in classroom, school, and neighborhood libraries, and (5) encouraging active involvement with adult and peer readers (Edmunds & Bauserman, 2006). Teachers' use of cognitive hooks (e.g., analogies or personal anecdotes) helps to foster interest and bridge connections between a topic and readers (Vacca, 2006). Similarly, teachers can use artifacts, primary sources, and online resources to motivate students to read text. For example, content-area teachers can build interest in the American experience by using the *American Memory* (n.d.), a collection of digitized historical documents, photographs, moving pictures, sound recordings, maps, prints, and other resources, which is freely available via the Internet. By capitalizing on adolescents' preference for multiliteracies (Pitcher et al., 2007), teachers capture their attention and interest.

Strategies are great vehicles for kindling struggling readers' curiosity in a topic and building excitement before reading (Vacca, 2006). To activate prior knowledge and interest, teachers can employ strategies that tap students' input into strategies, such as an Anticipation/Reaction Guide (Herber, 1978) and K-W-L (Ogle, 1986), which were previously described, as well as *Problematic Perspectives* (Vacca & Vacca, 2005) and *ReQuest* (Manzo, 1969). Problematic Perspectives is a strategy that requires students to think critically about an issue before reading, and ReQuest is a strategy that compels students to ask themselves questions. Teachers may also select strategies that promote interaction among students, such as *People Search* (Hemmrich, Lim, & Neel, 1994), and *Tea Party* (Beers, 2003). The People Search strategy has students interviewing one another in search of answers to 10–20 teacher-prepared statements or questions about a topic. The Tea Party strategy creates a situation where students share teacher-selected excerpts of text in order to become acquainted with a topic. Teachers can find that providing opportunities for student voice and social interaction is especially motivating for adolescents.

Active Engagement

Teachers can use strategies to activate readers' engagement with a text and improve reading comprehension. To help readers make sense of text, teachers need to teach and promote students' use of questioning strategies such as *Questioning the Author* (Beck, McKeown, Hamilton, & Kucan, 1997),

Inquiry Questions (Unrau, 2004), and *DRAW* (Draw, Read, Attend, Write; Agnew, 2000). Another questioning strategy, *Question Answer Relationship* (QAR; Raphael, 1982), guides students to see how answers relate to types of questions posed. To make the process of comprehension monitoring visible to students, teachers can model *Think Aloud* (Davey, 1983), Reciprocal Teaching (Palincsar & Brown, 1984), and the *Paraphrasing Strategy* (Shumaker, Denton, & Deshler, 1984). A number of comprehension strategies require symbolic and written interaction with the text, including *Graphic Organizers* (Burke, 2002), *GIST* (Generating Interactions between Schemata and Text; Cunningham, 1982), and *Biopoem* (Gere, 1985). Likewise, note-taking strategies advance comprehension by helping students to monitor their understanding of the text. Specific examples include *Cornell Note-Taking* (Pauk, 1974), *Double Entry Diaries* (Tovani, 2000), and *Power Notes* (Santa, Havens, & Maycumber, 1996). In summary, comprehension strategies by design promote struggling readers' active engagement with text.

Dealing with Text Difficulty

To tackle the issue of text difficulty, teachers need to provide students with appropriate texts and strategies. Struggling readers need books they can read (Allington, 2006), which requires teachers to gather texts at wide range of levels. To do so, teachers can work with librarians to collect books and other print material and collaborate with reading specialists to determine the difficulty level of various texts. Once struggling readers have appropriate texts, teachers can guide them to navigate their texts using specific strategies. For example, *SCAN and RUN* (Survey, Capture, Attack, Note and Read, Use, Note; Salembier, 1999) is an effective strategy for helping struggling students comprehend informational text. Using a set of cues, students learn to monitor their comprehension before, during, and after reading the text. As students' reading ability improves, they can be taught to use a textbook survey, textbook scavenger hunt, or *THIEVES* (Title, Heading, Introduction, Every paragraph, Visuals and vocabulary, End-of-Chapter Questions, Survey; Manz, 2002) to develop a schema for the text. Combining strategies with suitable texts can mitigate text difficulty for struggling readers.

Concluding Thoughts

The number of students who struggle to comprehend text warrants sustained attention and action. To build confidence and competence among struggling adolescent readers, their teachers need to design instruction that supplies suitable and sufficient challenge, expansive opportunities for learning, and successful academic experiences. Teachers must explicitly teach and prompt the use of multiple strategies in specific contexts so that adolescents can learn from text (Ogle, 2007). Further, struggling readers need their teachers to use whole-class, small-peer-group (cooperative learning), and individual forms of instruction (Allington, 2007). To provide appropriate and adequate educational experiences that support all learners, schools need to develop and implement a coherent literacy program—one with both horizontal (across subjects) and vertical (across grades) alignment.

Struggling readers' impressions of themselves, judgments about what they can do, and reading motivation are important considerations. Teachers need to build students' sense of competence so that they can acquire enough positive reading experiences to internalize comprehension strategies (Vacca, 2006). Without this sense of competence, struggling readers may become resistant readers (Lenters, 2006). Cognizant of the connection between motivation and engagement, teachers must continually consider what motivates their students. Students who are motivated to read spend more time reading, which positively influences their comprehension (Edmunds & Bauserman, 2006).

Just as all adolescents deserve access to reading material that they can and want to read (Moore et al., 1999), struggling readers warrant texts that they can and want to read (Allington, 2006, 2007). Rather than backpacks, lockers, and classrooms filled with books these students cannot read (Allington, 2007), schools need to ensure that struggling readers have access to an abundance of interesting texts that are also high-quality, readable texts (Fisher & Ivey, 2006). In addition, teachers need to recognize adolescents' affinity for multiple literacies (i.e., those typically used outside school) and new literacies (i.e., electronic environments), and so must find ways to integrate these into their instructional practice (Coiro, 2003; Coiro & Dobler, 2007; Leu, Kinzer, Coiro, & Cammack, 2004; Luke & Elkins, 2000).

Initial and continuing teacher education is fundamental for improving reading comprehension at the middle school and high school levels. Despite the fact that preservice teacher education programs introduce comprehension strategies, teachers may not implement them in their classrooms (Nourie & Lenski, 1998). Consequently, teacher education programs need to provide educative experiences for preservice teachers to learn, and then apply, comprehension strategies in authentic contexts. Because many in-service secondary teachers know too little about the teaching of literacy, schools must invest in teachers' knowledge through ongoing professional development (Shanahan, 2004).

Understandably, additional research regarding struggling readers and reading comprehension is necessary. Among the topics for research are (1) how struggling readers approach and comprehend text, (2) how increased access to informational text affects comprehension, (3) the role of motivation among struggling readers, (4) the relationship between text difficulty and strategy effectiveness, (5) the outcome of multiple strategy implementation, (6) the consequence of balanced adolescent literacy programs, (7) how students comprehend online text, and (8) the effect of new literacies on comprehension. Furthermore, longitudinal studies are necessary to determine the sustained effectiveness of literacy interventions.

To move from rhetoric to reality—to borrow a phrase from middle school curriculum reform (Beane, 1993)—requires content-area teachers to provide comprehension strategy instruction for struggling readers within the context of their own classrooms. The use of strategy instruction can make a difference in the comprehension of struggling adolescent readers.

References

Agnew, M. L. (2000). DRAW: A motivational reading comprehension strategy for disaffected readers. *Journal of Adolescent and Adult Literacy, 43*(6), 574–576.

Alfassi, M. (2004). Reading to learn: Effects of combined strategy instruction on high school students. *Journal of Educational Research, 97*(4), 171–184.

Allington, R. L. (2003). You can't learn much from books you can't read. *Educational Leadership, 60*(3), 22–25.

Allington, R. L. (2006). *What really matters for struggling readers: Designing research-based programs* (2nd ed.). Boston: Pearson Allyn & Bacon.

Allington, R. L. (2007). Intervention all day long: New hope for struggling readers. *Voices from the Middle, 14*(4), 7–14.

Almasi, J. (2003). *Teaching strategic processes in reading.* New York: Guilford Press.

Alvermann, D. (2001). Reading adolescents' reading identities: Looking back to see ahead. *Journal of Adolescent and Adult Literacy, 44*(8), 676–690.

American Memory. (n.d.). Retrieved January 22, 2007, from *www.memory.loc.gov.*

Armbruster, B. B. (1984). The problem of inconsiderate text. In G. Duffy, L. Roehler, & J. Mason (Eds.), *Comprehension instruction* (pp. 128–143). New York: Longman.

Bandura, A. (1997). *Self-efficacy: The exercise of control.* New York: Freeman.

Beane, J. A. (1993). *The middle school curriculum: From rhetoric to reality* (2nd ed.). Columbus, OH: National Middle School Association.

Beck, I. L., McKeown, M. G., Hamilton, R. L., & Kucan, L. (1997). *Questioning the author: An approach for enhancing student engagement with text.* Newark, DE: International Reading Association.

Beers, K. (2003). *When kids can't read, what teachers can do: A guide for teachers, 6–12.* Portsmouth, NH: Heinemann.

Biancarosa, G., & Snow, C. E. (2004). *Reading Next—A vision for action and research in middle school and high school literacy: A report to Carnegie Corporation of New York.* Washington, DC: Alliance for Excellent Education.

Biancarosa, G., & Snow, C. E. (2006). *Reading Next—A vision for action and research in middle and high school literacy: A report to Carnegie Corporation of New York* (2nd ed.).Washington, DC: Alliance for Excellent Education.

Block, C. C., Schaller, J. L., Joy, J. A., & Gaine, P. (2002). Process-based comprehension instruction: Perspectives of four reading educators. In C. C. Block &
M. Pressley (Eds.), *Comprehension instruction: Research-based best practices*
(pp. 42–61). New York: Guilford Press.

Bloom, B. S. (Ed.). (1956). *Taxonomy of educational objectives: Handbook I. Cognitive domain.* New York: David McKay.

Bromley, K. (2007). Nine things every teacher should know about words and
vocabulary instruction. *Journal of Adolescent and Adult Literacy, 50*(7), 528–
537.

Brown, R. (2002). Straddling two worlds: Self-directed comprehension instruction
for middle schoolers. In C. C. Block & M. Pressley (Eds.), *Comprehension instruction: Research-based best practices* (pp. 337–350). New York: Guilford
Press.

Brozo, W. G., & Simpson, M. L. (2007). *Content literacy for today's adolescents:
Honoring diversity and building competence.* Upper Saddle River, NJ: Merrill
Prentice-Hall.

Buly, M. R., & Valencia, S. W. (2002). Below the bar: Profiles of students who fail
state reading assessments. *Educational Evaluation and Policy Analysis, 24*(3),
219–239.

Burke, J. (2002). *Tools for thought: Graphic organizers for your classroom.*
Portsmouth, NH: Heinemann.

Coiro, J. (2003). Reading comprehension on the Internet: Expanding our understanding of reading comprehension to encompass new literacies. *Reading
Teacher, 56*(6), 458–464.

Coiro, J., & Dobler, E. (2007). Exploring the online reading comprehension strategies used by sixth-grade skilled readers to search for and locate information on
the Internet. *Reading Research Quarterly, 42*(2), 214–257.

Cunningham, J. W. (1982). Generating interactions between schemata and text. In
J. A. Niles & L. A. Harris (Eds.), *New inquiries in reading research and instruction: Thirty-First yearbook of the National Reading Conference* (pp. 42–
47). Rochester, NY: National Reading Conference.

Davey, B. (1983). Think aloud: Modeling the cognitive processes of reading comprehension. *Journal of Reading, 27*(1), 44–47.

Duffy, G. G. (2002). The case for direct explanation of strategies. In C. C. Block &
M. Pressley (Eds.), *Comprehension instruction: Research-based best practices*
(pp. 28–41). New York: Guilford Press.

Edmunds, K. M., & Bauserman, K. L. (2006). What teachers can learn about reading motivation through conversations with children. *Reading Teacher, 59*(5),
414–424.

Education Trust. (2005). *Stalled in secondary.* Washington, DC: Author.

Fisher, D., & Ivey, G. (2006). Evaluating the interventions for struggling adolescent
readers. *Journal of Adolescent and Adult Literacy, 50*(3), 180–189.

Fisher, J. B., Schumaker, J. B., & Deshler, D. D. (2002). Improving the reading comprehension of at-risk adolescents. In C. C. Block & M. Pressley (Eds.), *Comprehension instruction: Research-based best practices* (pp. 351–364). New
York: Guilford Press.

Gambrell, L. B., & Koskinen, P. S. (2002). Imagery: A strategy for enhancing comprehension. In C. C. Block & M. Pressley (Eds.), *Comprehension instruction: Research-based best practices* (pp. 305–318). New York: Guilford Press.

Gambrell, L. B., Palmer, B. M., Codling, R. M., & Mazzoni, S. A. (1996). Assessing motivation to read. *Reading Teacher, 49*(7), 518–533.

Gere, A. R. (Ed.). (1985). *Roots in the sawdust: Writing to learn across the disciplines.* Urbana, IL: National Council of Teachers of English.

Guthrie, J. T. (2004). Classroom contexts for engaged reading: An overview. In J. T. Guthrie, A. Wigfield, & K. C. Perencevich (Eds.), *Motivating reading comprehension: Concept-oriented reading instruction* (pp. 1–24). Mahwah, NJ: Erlbaum.

Guthrie, J. T., & Davis, M. H. (2003). Motivating struggling readers in middle school through an engagement model of classroom practice. *Reading and Writing Quarterly, 19,* 59–85.

Guthrie, J. T., & Knowles, K. T. (2001). Promoting reading motivation. In L. Verhoeven & C. Snow (Eds.), *Literacy and motivation: Reading engagement in individuals and groups* (pp. 159–176). Mahwah, NJ: Erlbaum.

Guthrie, J. T., & Wigfield, A. (2000). Engagement and motivation in reading. In M. L. Kamil, P. B. Mosenthal, P. D. Pearson, & R. Barr (Eds.), *Handbook of reading research* (Vol. 3, pp. 403–422). Mahwah, NJ: Erlbaum.

Hall, L. A. (2004). Comprehending expository text: Promising strategies for struggling readers and students with reading disabilities? *Reading Research and Instruction, 44*(2), 75–95.

Hall, L. A. (2007). Understanding the silence: Struggling readers discuss decisions about reading expository text. *Journal of Educational Research, 100*(3), 132–141.

Harris, T. L., & Hodges, R. E. (Eds.). (1995). *The literacy dictionary: The vocabulary of reading and writing.* Newark, DE: International Reading Association.

Hemmrich, H., Lim, W., & Neel, K. (1994). *Primetime!* Portsmouth, NH: Heinemann.

Herber, H. L. (1978). *Teaching reading in content areas* (2nd ed.). Englewood Cliffs, NJ: Prentice-Hall.

Ivey, G., & Fisher, D. (2006). *Creating literacy-rich schools for adolescents.* Alexandria, VA: Association for Supervision and Curriculum Development.

Kamil, M. L. (2003). *Adolescents and literacy: Reading for the 21st century.* Washington, DC: Alliance for Excellent Education.

Klingner, J. K., & Vaughn, S. (1998). Collaborative strategic reading. *Teaching Exceptional Children, 30*(6), 32–37.

Langer, J. A. (2001). Beating the odds: Teaching middle and high school students to read and write well. *American Educational Research Journal, 38*(4), 837–880.

Langer, J. A. (2002). *Effective literacy instruction: Building successful reading and writing programs.* Urbana, IL: National Council of Teachers of English.

Lenski, S. D., Wham, M. A., Johns, J. L., & Caskey, M. M. (2007). *Reading and learning strategies: Middle grades through high school* (3rd ed.). Dubuque, IA: Kendall/Hunt.

Lenters, K. (2006). Resistance, struggle, and the adolescent reader. *Journal of Adolescent and Adult Literacy, 50*(2), 136–146.

Leu, D. J., Jr., Kinzer, C. K, Coiro, J., & Cammack, D. W. (2004). Toward a theory of new literacies emerging from the Internet and other information and communication technologies. In R. B. Ruddell & N. Unrau (Eds.), *Theoretical models and processes of reading* (5th ed., pp. 1570–1613). Newark, DE: International Reading Association. Retrieved May 15, 2007, from *www.readingonline. org/newliteracies/lit_index.asp?HREF=/newliteracies/leu.*

Luke, A., & Elkins, J. (2000). Re/mediating adolescent literacies. *Journal of Adolescent and Adult Literacy, 43*(5), 396–398.

Manz, S. L. (2002). A strategy for previewing textbooks: Teaching readers to become THIEVES. *Reading Teacher, 55*(5), 34–435.

Manzo, A. V. (1969). The ReQuest procedure. *Journal of Reading, 13,* 123–126, 163.

Mastropieri, M. A., Scruggs,T. E., & Graetz, J. E. (2003). Reading comprehension instruction for secondary students: Challenges for struggling students and teachers. *Learning Disability Quarterly, 26*(2), 103–116.

Meltzer, J., & Hamann, E. T. (2004). *Meeting the literacy development needs of adolescent English language learners through content area learning: I. Focus on motivation and engagement.* Providence, RI: Education Alliance at Brown University.

Meltzer, J., with Smith, N., & Clark, H. (2002). *Adolescent literacy resources: Linking research and practice.* Providence, RI: Northeast and Islands Regional Educational Laboratory at Brown University.

Moje, E. B., Young, J. P., Readance, J. E., & Moore, D. W. (2000). Reinventing adolescent literacy for new times: Perennial and millennial issues. *Journal of Adolescent and Adult Literacy, 43*(5), 400–410.

Moore, D. W., Bean, T. W., Birdyshaw, D., & Rycik, J. A. (1999). *Adolescent literacy: A position statement for the Commission on Adolescent Literacy of the International Reading Association.* Newark, DE: International Reading Association.

National Association of Secondary Schools Principals. (2005). *Creating a culture of literacy: A guide for middle and high schools principals.* Reston, VA: Author.

National Association of State Boards of Education. (2005). *Reading at risk: How states can respond to the crisis in adolescent literacy.* Alexandria, VA: Author.

National Center for Education Statistics. (2005). *The condition of education.* Washington, DC: U.S. Government Printing Office.

National Council of Teachers of English. (2006). *NCTE principles of adolescent literacy reform: A policy research brief.* Urbana, IL: Author.

National Governors Association. (2005). *Reading to achieve: A governor's guide to adolescent literacy.* Washington, DC: National Governors Association, Center for Best Practices.

National Institute of Child Health and Human Development. (2000). *Report of the National Reading Panel. Teaching children to read: An evidence-based assessment of the scientific research literature on reading and its implications for reading instruction* (NIH Publication No. 00-4769). Washington, DC: U.S. Government Printing Office.

Neufeld, P. (2006). Comprehension instruction in content area classes. *Reading Teacher, 59*(4), 302–310.

Nierstheimer, S. L., Hopkins, C. J., Dillon, D. R., & Schmitt, M. C. (2000).

Preservice teachers' shifting beliefs about struggling literacy learners. *Reading Research and Instruction, 40*(1), 1–16.

Nist, S. L., & Simpson, M. L. (2000). College studying. In M. L. Kamil, P. B. Mosenthal, P. D. Pearson, & R. Barr (Eds.), *Handbook of reading research* (Vol. 3, pp. 645–666). Mahwah, NJ: Erlbaum.

Nourie, B. L., & Lenski, S. D. (1998). The (in)effectiveness of content area literacy instruction for secondary preservice teachers. *Clearing House, 71*(6), 372–374.

Ogle, D. (1986). K-W-L: A teaching model that develops active reading of expository text. *Reading Teacher, 39*, 564–570.

Ogle, D., with Lang, L. (2007). Best practices in adolescent literacy instruction. In L. B. Gambrell, L. M. Morrow, & M. Pressley (Eds.), *Best practices in literacy instruction* (pp. 127–156). New York: Guilford Press.

Palincsar, A. S., & Brown, A. (1984). The reciprocal teaching of comprehension-fostering and comprehension-monitoring activities. *Cognition and Instruction, 1*, 117–175.

Pauk, W. (1974). *How to study in college.* Boston: Houghton Mifflin.

Perie, M., Grigg, W., & Donahue, P. (2005). *The Nation's Report Card: Reading 2005* (NCES 2006-451). U.S. Department of Education, National Center for Education Statistics. Washington, DC: U.S. Government Printing Office.

Peterson, C. L., Caverly, D. C., Nicholson, S. A., O'Neal, S., & Cusenbary, S. (2000). *Building reading proficiency at the secondary school level: A guide to resources.* San Marcos, TX: Southwestern Texas State University and the Southwest Educational Development Laboratory.

Pitcher, S. M., Albright, L. K., DeLancy, C. J., Walker, N. T., Seunarinesingh, S. M., Headley, K. N., et al. (2007). Assessing adolescents' motivation to read. *Journal of Adolescent and Adult Literacy, 50*(5), 378–396.

Pressley, M. (2000).What should comprehension instruction be the instruction of? In M. L. Kamil, P. B. Mosenthal, P. D. Pearson, & R. Barr (Eds.), *Handbook of reading research* (Vol. 3, pp. 545–561). Mahwah, NJ: Erlbaum.

Pressley, M. (2002). Comprehension strategies instruction: A turn-of-the-century status report. In C. C. Block & M. Pressley (Eds.), *Comprehension instruction: Research-based best practices* (pp. 11–27). New York: Guilford Press.

RAND. (2005). *Achieving state and national literacy goals: A long uphill road: A report to Carnegie Corporation of New York.* Santa Monica, CA: Author.

RAND Reading Study Group. (2002). *Reading for understanding: Toward an R&D program in reading comprehension.* Santa Monica, CA: RAND. Retrieved February 12, 2007, from *www.rand.org/pubs/monograph_reports/2005/MR1465.pdf.*

Raphael, T. E. (1982). Questioning-answering strategies for children. *Reading Teacher, 36*, 186–191.

Rosenblatt, L. M. (1978). *The reader, the text, the poem: The transactional theory of the literacy work.* Carbondale, IL: Southern Illinois University Press.

Salembier, G. B. (1999). SCAN and RUN: A reading comprehension strategy that works. *Journal of Adolescent and Adult Literacy, 42*(5), 386–394.

Santa, C. M., Havens, L. T., & Maycumber, E. M. (1996). *Creating independence through student-owned strategies* (2nd ed.). Dubuque, IA: Kendall/Hunt.

Shanahan, T. (2004). Improving reading achievement in secondary schools: Struc-
    tures and reforms. In D. S. Strickland & D. E. Alvermann (Eds.), *Bridging the
    literacy achievement gap, grades 4–12* (pp. 43–55). New York: Teachers Col-
    lege Press.
Shumaker, J. B., Denton, P. H., & Deshler, D. D. (1984). *The paraphrasing strategy.*
    Lawrence: University of Kansas Press.
Smith, M. W., & Wilhelm, J. D. (2006). *Going with the flow: How to engage boys
    (and girls) in their literacy learning.* Portsmouth, NH: Heinemann.
Strickland, D. S., & Alvermann, D. E. (Eds.). (2004). *Bridging the literacy achieve-
    ment gap, grades 4–12.* New York: Teachers College Press.
Torgesen, J. K., Houston, D. D., Rissman, L. M., Decker, S. M., Roberts, G.,
    Vaughn, S., et al. (2007). *Academic literacy instruction for adolescents: A
    guidance document from the Center on Instruction.* Portsmouth, NH: RMC
    Research Corporation, Center on Instruction.
Tovani, C. (2000). *I read it, but I don't get it: Comprehension strategies for adoles-
    cent readers.* Portland, ME: Stenhouse.
Trabasso, T., & Bouchard, E. (2002). Teaching readers how to comprehend text
    strategically. In C. C. Block & M. Pressley (Eds.), *Comprehension instruction:
    Research-based best practices* (pp. 176–200). New York: Guilford Press.
Unrau, N. (2004). *Content area reading and writing: Fostering literacies in middle
    and high school cultures.* Upper Saddle River, NJ: Merrill Prentice-Hall.
Vacca, R. T. (2006). They can because they think they can. *Educational Leadership,
    63*(5), 56–59.
Vacca, R. T., & Vacca, J. L. (2005). *Content area reading: Literacy and learning
    across the curriculum.* Boston: Pearson Allyn & Bacon.
Vygotsky, L. S. (1978). *Mind in society: The development of higher psychological
    processes.* Cambridge, MA: Harvard University Press.
Walker, B. J. (2005). Thinking aloud: Struggling readers often require more than a
    model. *Reading Teacher, 58*(7), 688–692.
Wigfield, A. (2004). Motivation for reading during early adolescent and adolescent
    years. In D. S. Strickland & D. E. Alvermann (Eds.), *Bridging the literacy
    achievement gap, grades 4–12* (pp. 86–105). New York: Teachers College.

CHAPTER 10

Vocabulary Strategies for Struggling Readers

Margaret Ann Richek
Becky McTague

Vocabulary is uniquely important to reading and to school achievement. Unfortunately, word learning is an area often regarded as difficult to teach and tedious to learn. Approached in the right way, though, vocabulary instruction can be engaging and enjoyable. In the first part of this chapter, we discuss the importance of knowing word meanings, the research on vocabulary learning in general, and the findings for struggling adolescent readers in particular. We also address the kinds of word learnings that are necessary for struggling secondary students and give principles to guide this instruction. The second part of the chapter is devoted to effective and motivating strategies to teach a subject that infuses every area of learning.

Research Insights into Vocabulary Instruction

Research going back almost a century has established that vocabulary is the best single predictor of reading comprehension (Daneman, 1991). In fact, the correlations between the two are in the .85–.95 range (Stahl & Nagy, 2006). Carver (1992) has even argued that, from a measurement point of view, the two can be considered identical. In short, vocabulary knowledge is critical to school achievement. Studies over the past decades have provided many insights into vocabulary learning.

Defining the Vocabulary Learning Task

The task of vocabulary instruction is a large one. Our best estimates indicate that students learn, on average, 2,000–3,000 words per year (Stahl & Nagy, 2006). These words are learned both through exposure to language during adolescence and through direct and conscious instruction (Baumann, Kame'enui, & Ash, 2003).

Adolescents need to know several different types of words. Beck, McKeown, and Kucan (2002) divide vocabulary into three categories. The first, Tier I words, are the common words we all use in conversation, such as *run, look*. Almost all of our students know these core words, yet they may still be challenging to some, especially English language learners (ELLs). The second category consists of Tier II words, "educated," but nontechnical words, such as *scamper* and *scrutinize*. A third class, Tier III words, is composed of the technical vocabulary generally used in content areas, words like *onomatopoeia, igneous,* and *blastosphere*.

Students typically learn Tier II and III words in different ways. Tier II words, those used in nontechnical, but educated language, are generally learned from exposure to words, especially in written language—the language of books. This is because written materials have many more varied and difficult vocabulary words than the spoken language of even very highly educated people (Cunningham & Stanovich, 1991, 1998). Studies have shown that reading is an important, perhaps even a primary, method of learning vocabulary (Anderson, 1996; Graves, 2000; Sternberg, 1987). As people read, they simply pick up word meanings—often unconsciously. Thus, wide reading is an important component of learning Tier II words. It is estimated that there is a 15 percent chance of picking up the meaning of an unknown word during reading (Swanborn & de Glopper, 1999). Although this may not sound impressive, over a year it adds up to the learning of hundreds, if not thousands of words.

In contrast to Tier II words, Tier III words often require direct instruction by content-area teachers in order for students to learn them. This is because Tier III words tend not to be met in general reading. In addition, a high percentage of these words introduce new concepts and require precise understandings that are critical to subject-area learning.

Challenges for Struggling Adolescent Readers

Vocabulary knowledge is often problematic for struggling adolescents. Lags in the mastery of word meanings develop early in life and widen as students progress throughout the grades (Baker, Simmons, & Kame'enui, 1995).

When struggling students reach their secondary years, therefore, they are typically far behind their peers. Becker (1977) identifies limited vocabulary as a critical factor that constrains the achievement of disadvantaged students through the high school years.

Blachowicz and Fisher (2000) define some of the specific difficulties for struggling readers in mastering vocabulary. The students we teach are more likely than their peers to be assigned material that is above their reading level and contains large quantities of unknown words. Because struggling students often experience difficulties in decoding assigned material, they have little energy to spare for learning word meanings from context.

Struggling readers also read less than their peers, and this further limits their vocabulary development. The students we teach read slowly and often have difficulty in completing their reading assignments. Low achieving adolescents (as well as teenagers in general) are typically not enthusiastic leisure readers, a factor that severely inhibits the learning of Tier II words. An important challenge, then, is to keep struggling secondary students conversant with the language of books. To the extent that teaching professionals can encourage students to do leisure reading, it is invaluable not only to vocabulary growth, but also to students' world knowledge.

Another way to expose students to the language of books is to read written works to them. This activity fosters vocabulary growth in students who find reading difficult. At least one study found that students pick up words from listening at about the same rate as they learn them from reading (Stahl, Richek, & Vandevier, 1991). Here, struggling middle school readers, as well as their peers, learned word meanings as effectively from listening to a passage as it was estimated they would have learned them from reading that passage.

Struggling students, for whom subject learning is often difficult, find Tier III vocabulary a special challenge. Such words are important, not only because they occur in the academic disciplines, but also because they embody concepts that are essential to content-area study. Learning such words requires substantial conscious effort and fine, clearly reasoned distinctions. These are the words that are most worthy of direct instruction by teachers.

Research on Effective Vocabulary Learning

What vocabulary strategies work for struggling readers? Though limited in number, recent studies in direct vocabulary instruction support a variety of approaches. There is some evidence for including personal choice, making associations, and fostering conceptual connections between words. Ruddell and Shearer (2002) found that middle school low-achieving readers effectively learned words that they selected themselves and practiced intensively. Consistent with this finding, Hopkins and Bean (1989/1998) found that secondary students on a Cheyenne Reservation were successful at learning vocabulary if definitional cards also included a personal association and picture. Bos and Anders (1990), working with middle school learning-disabled students, found that exploring relationships between words (semantic feature analysis and semantic mapping) resulted in improved learning of science vocabulary, as compared with the learning of students who simply studied definitions. Fawcett and Nicholson (1991), however, were unable to duplicate these findings with reading-disabled students, ages 11–14.

Four studies support direct instruction of vocabulary. Lee (2003) and Lee and Muncie (2006) found that direct instruction of words helped secondary ELLs to incorporate new words in their writing. Hughes and Fredrick (2006) experienced success with three middle school inclusion students, as well as the larger class, using peer tutoring of word cards with definitions under systematic time delay conditions. Finally, the *Keyword* strategy of association received validation in one study. In this strategy, an easy word that sounds like a hard word is chosen as a mnemonic device (e.g., *truck* for *truculent*), and then students make an association between the two words (e.g., an angry person driving a truck). Terrill, Scruggs, and Mastropieri (2004) demonstrated that tenth-grade special education students learned effectively with the *Keyword* method.

Despite the existence of studies demonstrating success, struggling readers generally have more difficulty with vocabulary instruction than their normally achieving peers. Strategies that have proven effective for normally achieving readers may not demonstrate effects for those with difficulties. In a meta-analysis (an analysis of several existing studies) of 15 research projects with "poor readers," Marmolejo (1990) found that direct teaching of vocabulary seemed to be an effective approach only when combined with deep processing and manipulation of words (a semantic-based approach). Teaching definitions, as well as definitions supported by context clues, was less effective. Results of this study are consistent with those of the subsequent studies by Ruddell and Shearer (2002), Hopkins and Bean (1989/1998), and Bos and Anders (1990), all cited above.

It also appears that there are no special principles or programs that are unique to teaching struggling readers. The approaches that work for students, in general, seem also to be most productive for struggling readers (Blachowicz & Fisher, 2000). The results of several studies cited above, for example, support an analysis of Stahl and Fairbanks (1986), indicating that deep processing of words contributed to the best vocabulary learning. Teachers of struggling adolescents, therefore, are well advised to use the strategies that have been found to be most effective for vocabulary development. They should also remember, however, that their students may have to work harder to achieve effective word learning.

Research-Based Instruction on Independent Vocabulary Learning Strategies

The vast number of words adolescents need to learn suggests that they need strategies that help them to learn vocabulary independently. Three strategies often used in instruction are morphological analysis (the use of prefixes, suffixes, and roots), learning from context, and learning from dictionary (or glossary) definitions (Nagy, 2007).

Morphological Analysis

The analysis of words into their parts is a time-honored way of teaching new words. Student use of prefixes, roots, and suffixes can facilitate vocabulary learning (Baumann et al., 2003; Carlisle, 2007).

Suffixes that form plurals, possessives, comparatives, and verb tenses are generally mastered in primary grades. A significant number of suffixes also change parts of speech. These *derivational* suffixes may be seen for such words as *nation,* which can form *national, nationalize,* and *nationalization.* Understanding the relationship of these words is an excellent vehicle for multiplying word learning. In fact, at least one study has found that a significant proportion of word learning between grades 3 and 8 may be accounted for through these types of word changes (Nagy, Diakidoy, & Anderson, 1993). We have often found that struggling adolescent readers do not know how they may multiply their vocabularies by looking for these derivatives.

Focusing on derivational suffixes, therefore, is an excellent strategy to expand student vocabulary. If teachers present these suffixes primarily as changing parts of speech rather than as affecting meaning, struggling adolescents can better understand them. For example, when showing how *stagnate* and *stagnation* are related, teachers should explain and demonstrate how *-tion* changes the noun to a verb, rather than giving a meaning (such as "a state") for *-tion.*

When they teach derivational suffixes, teachers are also helping students to recognize root words, another important skill. A student who can identify root words has a firm basis for understanding how one word can be changed to another. Root words and derivational suffixes work hand in hand. One of us (M.A.R.) recently worked in a language arts class with a struggling middle school ELL who could not determine a meaning for *desperation.* When he was asked to look for the root word *desperate,* though, he could infer what the derived word meant.

In addition, a large number of roots that come from ancient Greek and Latin can help students to infer word meanings. In modern English, these roots are generally incorporated into words and do not stand alone. Examples are *gen* (birth, beginning) and *fac* (make, do). Such word roots are useful for clustering related vocabulary and for building conceptual thinking. Bromley (2007) suggests that the most useful root words to teach are *tract* (pull), *spect* (look), *port* (carry), *dict* (say), *rupt* (break), *scrib* (write), *cred* (believe), *vid* (see), and *aud* (hear). Science teachers may foster word learning and conceptual connections by helping students to collect words that come from roots commonly found in biology, chemistry, and so on. Such word roots include *gen* (birth, life), *tele-* (far) and *dyn* (power). Although students can profitably collect and discuss words that share roots, remember that at times a root may provide only a weak clue to word meaning. For example, although the root, *tract* (pull) appears in many words, it provides relatively weak clues to such words as *detract, distraught, entreaty,* and *tract.*

Instruction in a few prefixes yields much benefit. The ones that should be taught are those that are reliable indicators of meaning and occur frequently in English. White, Power, and White (1989) found that 20 prefixes account for 97% of all prefixes that attach to free standing words in English These are *un-, re- in- (im-)* (with the meaning of "not"), *dis-, en- (em-), in- (im-)* (with the meaning of "in"), *over, mis, sub, pre, inter, fore, de-trans, super, semi, anti, mid-,* and *under-*. In addition, number prefixes, such as in *uni*cycle, *bi*cycle, *tri*cycle, and *deci*mal, are commonly encountered in mathematics, as well as in general language.

Context Clues

The strategy of using known text around an unknown word to infer its meaning is also important to students. In fact, the unconscious use of context during reading is an important source of word learning. Analyses of research also suggest that teaching students, including those at the secondary level, how to derive word meanings from context is worthwhile (Fukkink & de Glopper, 1998). This effort, however, has not always yielded results for struggling students (Marmolejo, 1990). It has been our experience that struggling secondary students have difficulty using context and are at times extremely averse to the risk taking inherent in employing this strategy. Suggestions for instruction in using context clues are given later in this chapter.

Dictionary Use

The dictionary, which is a rich repository of information about words, might seem to be the answer to independent word learning. Unfortunately, the dictionary is an ineffective word learning tool for struggling secondary students. Research indicates that students rarely can learn words, unassisted, from a dictionary, even one designed for their grade level (McKeown, 1993; Miller & Gildea, 1987). Dictionary definitions often use arcane language that is harder than the word being defined. The format of definitions is also difficult for students to access. Further, struggling adolescents often cannot choose a definition appropriate to the context of their reading. A seventh grader we worked with copied the definition of *magazine* as *a periodical publication*, yet the sentence from the novel he was reading was, *The gunpowder was found in the magazine*. Not surprisingly, when students produce sentences from definitions, they generally reflect this incomplete understanding (Miller & Gildea, 1987). One of our at-risk adolescents defined *soberly* as *seriously* and composed the sentence, *She flunked the test soberly*. Such examples serve to illustrate the limitations of this valuable resource.

Principles to Guide Vocabulary Instruction

The preceding discussion of vocabulary learning for struggling adolescent readers suggests several principles to guide instruction:

1. *A vocabulary program needs to include several facets of word learning.* Wide exposure to written texts (in reading or listening mode) can foster the learning of Tier II words. In addition, content-area teachers need to focus on direct instruction of selected words, generally Tier III words, to facilitate learning in chemistry, American history, language arts, and other subjects. A third component is the learning and use of vocabulary strategies. Strategic focus on the use of context and morphology is productive for our students. In contrast, a dictionary may easily be overused. In a departmentalized setting, it may be difficult for any one teacher to implement a complete vocabulary program, but each instructor can make a worthwhile contribution.

2. *Direct instruction works best if the number of words is controlled and students practice them extensively.* Struggling adolescents experience difficulties in learning words. Because Tier III vocabulary for content areas are often dense in new concepts, teachers should limit the number of difficult words they teach. A few words mastered well are more effective than several half-learned words (Bromley, 2007). Research has established that words are learned gradually (Nagy & Scott, 2000), as students go from hazy knowledge to more specific and delineated understanding. Extensive practice is particularly important if students are to understand words with precision and use them in writing. Review, therefore, is a critical piece of any vocabulary program. Similarly, word learning strategies need to be practiced until students can use them independently.

3. *Words to be learned should be actively approached in many different ways.* To most effectively learn words, struggling secondary readers need to be actively engaged in formulating definitions, reading words in

context, writing contexts for words, categorizing words, connecting words, and playing games with them. Because vocabulary is used to communicate, working with peers on vocabulary can also help students to build their vocabulary knowledge. Analyses of vocabulary learning studies in general (Stahl & Fairbanks, 1986) and of those of struggling readers (Marmolejo, 1990) found that learning words is most effective when several methods are combined into active and deep instruction.

4. *Vocabulary learning should be comfortable and fun.* Struggling secondary students who enjoy vocabulary learning tend to practice words. Several seemingly small steps help increase student comfort with vocabulary.

First, if students ask the meaning of a word, teachers should avoid instructing them to look it up in the dictionary. This procedure is time-consuming, even with electronic and online dictionaries, and, as mentioned previously, students often come away with inappropriate definitions. Instead, we *give students the meaning of the word*, and then *thank them for asking*. Over time, this approach encourages students to learn even more words. We have even made lists of such words and displayed them. Students are delighted to find "their" words publicly recorded.

Second, when introducing words, especially difficult or high-concept words, try formulating initial definitions for struggling students and discussing these definitions. We often have students think of examples and associations to refine our initial definitions, and then use the jointly formulated definitions. We also try to give them examples of these words used in sentences. Such procedures remove stress from the word-learning process and thus foster deeper learning of words.

Finally, recognize the difficulty of learning words. If students forget a word, *gently* remind them of its meaning. In this way, students are encouraged to use the word again, rather than discouraged from trying. Although it is tempting for a teacher to express frustration, it is also unproductive.

Strategies for Vocabulary Success

In the first part of this chapter we outlined vocabulary research, principles, and instructional implications. In this section, we offer several strategies that we have used successfully with struggling adolescent readers. Based on suggestions from research, they include several aspects of the vocabulary-learning process.

Strategies for Learning Specific Words

Two strategies, *Brain Power* and *Word Expert Cards*, help struggling adolescents to actively engage in learning content-area words. Both involve students in practicing strategies and in interacting with their peers. They may be used for any subject area in which a body of words needs to be learned by students.

Brain Power Words

Students become engaged in learning vocabulary when they participate in choosing words. Brain Power, developed by Caldwell (Richek, Caldwell, Jennings, & Lerner, 2001), has helped our students to anticipate difficult words in content materials and to decide which ones are most important. We have found it particularly helpful in history and other social science classes.

To use this strategy, ask small groups of students to preview different sections of a text (such as one on American history) and to identify words that are difficult, but seem essential to understanding the subject. If a chapter is lengthy, teachers can assign various sections to different groups of students. Students should identify unknown words that seem key to understanding the text and place Post-it™ notes next to these words within the text. We ask students to choose no more than five words that are specific to the subject area. We also try to focus their choices on words that are repeated, italicized, bolded, or listed as words to learn in the text.

After choosing these words, students should look back at the text and try to establish what the words mean by using the context in which they appear. Three guidelines can be offered for "hypothesizing" the word meaning from context:

- Clues of substitution: A known word would actually make sense in the context, and is probably a pretty good definition.
- Clues of definition: The word is actually defined in context. Textbooks often highlight such words and provide definitions after them, within the context.
- Clues of opposition: Words like *not*, *unlike*, and so forth, often give excellent clues to what a word is *not*, and thus help define the word.

When using these clues, we also warn students that they may have to put together several parts of the text to formulate a satisfactory meaning.

After students formulate a list of Brain Power words and try to define them, they check with the teacher. Often students can give fairly accurate definitions. Because the words chosen tend to be dense in new concepts, though, the teacher may have to help students redefine some of the words. At this point, students may consult a dictionary. Finally, each group lists its words and definitions, and these are duplicated and presented to other groups. This is an excellent and empowering way to learn Tier III words, the content-specific, high-concept words found in almost every textbook. The teacher should feel free to add some words that students have overlooked.

Word Expert Cards

In another strategy (Lansdown, 1991; Richek, 2005) each student in a class takes responsibility for thoroughly learning a few words—and then teaching them to peers. Word Expert Cards are suitable for any novel or unit of study that involves many technical new vocabulary words; thus, it is excellent for teaching Tier III words. The procedure also gives hands-on experience in using reference sources.

Before the class begins studying a unit or chapter, the teacher makes a list of important words and concepts. The teacher then divides these words among the students, with each student receiving a few words (generally between two and five). Each "word expert" is responsible for both knowing and teaching the words assigned to him or her. To foster this learning, the word expert constructs a card for each of the words. The cards are made from card stock, folded once. Each student develops a rough draft, which must be approved by the teacher before it can be put on a card. Cards include a sentence copied from the text, definition, part(s) of speech, the student's original sentence, and an illustration. (Directions can be found in Figure 10.1.) We suggest that, before constructing the cards, each student be given a page number where each word can be found in a sentence context. An example of a card from a biology class, made by a struggling secondary reader, is shown in Figure 10.2.

- Use the page number to locate the word in the story.
- Copy the sentence containing the word inside the card.
- Use a dictionary to look up the definition for each word; you may discuss it with others.
- On scratch paper, write the part of speech and the definition in your own words that matches the use of the word in the story.
- On scratch paper, write your own sentence using the word.
- Get the definition and sentence approved for accuracy by the teacher.
- Copy onto the inside of your card the approved definition, part of speech, and sentence.
- Write the vocabulary word on the front outside of the card in big bold letters.
- On the front of the card, illustrate the vocabulary word neatly and creatively. Get your illustration approved.
- Write your name, word, and class period on the back side of the card.
- Completed cards must be turned in by (date).

FIGURE 10.1. Directions for Word Expert Cards. From Richek (2005). Courtesy of Susan Ali.

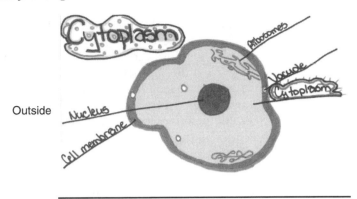

Outside

Inside

FIGURE 10.2. Word Expert Card for unit on cellular structure: Card outside shown on top; card inside on bottom.

The card-making process fosters several important learnings. First, students learn to consult a dictionary (or glossary) to reference word meaning. Teacher assistance is usually needed, and thus students get expert guidance in using reference tools. Second, struggling adolescents come to feel comfortable with those words for which they are "experts." Knowing a few words well builds students' confidence and gives them a firm basis for learning other words. As they work through their assigned words, students come to understand the subtleties in meaning. Finally, students demonstrate creativity and develop personal associations to words. In addition to working with the teacher, they may also consult their classmates in interpreting definitions, composing sentences, and creating illustrations.

Of course, students must learn *all* of the important words in their chapters, not just the few for which they make cards. To do this, students are paired or assigned to small groups. Each student teaches his or her words to peers, using the cards. First, covering the illustration of a word, the expert simply pronounces this word and asks what it means. If the others do not know (and usually they do not), the word expert gives a further hint by uncovering the illustration. Then the expert reads the inside of the card. After one expert is finished with his or her word card(s), another student presents his or her *Word Expert Card* words. The students then rotate. Student engagement in this activity is extremely high. We usually do it for 10–15 minutes for several days, beginning when the students start to study the content-area topic or novel. Typically, word learning is also extremely effective (Landsdown, 1991). Students also quickly learn who is the expert for any given word and then consult that person when they have a question.

Efficient, Effective, and Motivating Word Review

A vocabulary program for struggling adolescents should include frequent review, because students typically learn words gradually and forget them easily. Review is particularly important for Tier III words. The activities we use are short and game-like. Most can be done as a whole class, in small groups, or even individually, and within a time period of about 10 minutes. At times, especially when we start such activities, struggling readers have difficulty in individually responding to words; if this happens, we ask students to work in pairs.

Sentence Starters

Students forming sentences with words is a time-honored way of practicing vocabulary, but it can be difficult. Because these sentences form records of word use for students, it is important to maximize the chances of success. One way to support students is to work from stems. In these stems, students are presented with incomplete sentences containing target words and are asked to finish them. Examples of sentence starters follow:

> I *invariably* have difficulty _____.
> If I were a *philanthropist*, _____.

Supported by this type of context, struggling readers generally produce well-formed sentences that help them to learn new words. We have also found that when students compare their responses, they are delighted by each other's creativity. In short, this exercise is as amusing as it is productive.

Two in One

Once students have a bit more practice with a group of words, they can compose their own sentences—with a twist. In *Two in One*, students are challenged to work in small groups putting *two* words from a list into a sentence. The small-group work helps students to support each other, discuss the words, and approach the task enthusiastically. As students work together, the teacher should monitor their work, providing input and refining word meanings when necessary.

We find it wise to check their sentences before they are given publicly. At times, our at-risk students have even taken lists home and tried to do more. One 10th-grade teacher, Sean Rochester (2006), used this strategy in a novel study with the tenth grade literature class containing many struggling readers. An example of a student-composed Two in One sentence of Sean Rochester was: It is hard to feel empathy for people who are alien to you.

Teacher input into another sentence showed the students how context could be enriched. The original sentence read, "Adam *lingered passively*." The teacher put the sentence on an overhead and helped the group to revise it until it read, *Adam lingered passively in Germany although he knew that the Nazis would come for him.*" As these sentences also illustrate, the Two in One activity also gives students opportunities to use different forms of a base word, thus helping them to develop morphological strategic learning. Thus *protrude*, in the original list, became *protruding*, and *passive* was used as *passively*

Enthusiastic students often try to cram as many as five words into one sentence. Although an occasional judicious use of a third word may be allowed, try not to allow students to use too many vocabulary words together.

Connect Two

The *Connect Two* activity, first published by Blachowicz and Lee (1991), is excellent for reviewing words because it challenges students to deepen and refine concepts by forming connections between words. In this game, two lists of words are put on a blackboard or overhead projector. Students are asked to make a connection between a word on the first list and a word on the second list. In the most valuable part of the activity, they must explain the reason for the connection that they made.

The following is an example from a health class:

antibodies	leukemia
leukocytes	hemorrhage
sickle cell anemia	plasma
fibrin	coagulation
hemoglobin	red blood cells

Among the connections students made were the following:

Leukemia and *sickle cell anemia* are diseases.

Leukocytes and *red blood cells* are types of blood cells.

Fibrin aids in the *coagulation* of blood.

Anything Goes

To learn words, students must be able to use them quickly, easily, and flexibly. They should be able to formulate derivatives and think of contexts for words. A word that is used only with hesitation has not been fully assimilated. *Anything Goes* is a quick review of words that will move students from hesitation to rapid use (Richek, 2005).

To implement this game, present students with a list of words. Generally, we write them on the board or overhead, or post them on a Word Wall. Students are then asked to respond to teacher questions. The teacher may point to a word or, when indicated, ask students to find words. The following are examples of questions to ask:

What part of speech is _____?

What is the definition of _____?

Give another form (derivative or inflected form) of _____.

Spell (a derivative or inflected form) of _____.

Use _____ in a sentence.

Use _____ and _____ in a sentence.

What do _____ and _____ have in common?

Find two words that have to do with _____.

Find a (the) root (or prefix, suffix) in _____.

An example of this game in action serves to illustrate the many things it can teach. The words and questions listed in a biology class for Anything Goes are shown in Figure 10.3.

Find That Word

One way for students to review words is to notice them in their environments, and to use them. The *Find That Word* strategy (Richek, 2005) is an adaptation for middle and high school students of Beck et al.'s (2002) *Word Wizard*. In Find That Word, students are asked to record words they are studying when they encounter them in reading and speech. This enables students to see the words in different contexts and thus deepen their vocabulary knowledge.

Words and phrases to learn:

Intertidal
Organism
Bacteria
Open ocean
Adaptations
Sulfides
Near-shore
Kelp
Plume
Salt marsh
Hydrothermal

Questions and activities for students:
Give one example of an *organism*.
Find a word that contains the ancient Greek root for *water*.
What is the difference between *open ocean* and *near-shore*?
Spell the singular form of *bacteria*.
Give the verb form of *adaptations*.

FIGURE 10.3. Anything Goes: Biology example.

To begin, students are given a list of target words and are asked to look for them. Every time a student sees or hears a word, he or she is asked to write *the sentence* in which the word appears. We sometimes give students small strips of paper for this purpose. To add interest, we may count the sentences to see how many a class can collect. Some classes have collected more than 1,000!

A few minutes each week should be devoted to reading the sentences. When used with struggling secondary students, the game may start slowly. Then, however, the word collection can accelerate, and there will probably not be enough time to read all of the sentences. Whether or not students read the sentences, we generally post them in the classroom. Teachers who wish to emphasize editing skills may include the additional rule, that the sentence must be correctly spelled and punctuated before it is read or counted for the class.

Using this strategy, students can also be encouraged to use new words in speech and writing. A group of middle school classes, composed of students who spoke English as a second language, decided to share words across classes. Each class suggested 3 words for a joint pool of 12 words every week. The complete list for the week was then given to each grade level. Students set to work, and the sentences they found were posted in the hallway, according to the following categories:

- 1 point—A student saw or heard the word in print, speech, or in the media.
- 2 points—A student used the word in speech. (This had to be written down by a peer.)
- 5 points—A student used the word in writing.

This activity resulted in a dramatic surge in the use of new words in writing. When posted, the 1-point sentences were put on 1-inch-high strips, 2-point sentences were put on 2-inch-high strips, and 5-point sentences were put on 5-inch-high strips. The strips were displayed in the hallway so that other students could see them. Examples of the sentences given by these students are shown in Figure 10.4.

The Find That Word review strategy takes a minimum of instructional time, yet it encourages struggling secondary students to notice and use new vocabulary words. We do have some special rules. First, we do not allow Internet "hits" for searching for a word on the Internet, because that activity requires students to make little effort. Second, a word *and a derivative* of that word (e.g., *humid, humidity*) count equally.

Word Up!

The research cited above indicates that vocabulary is often learned simply through reading, because written text is rich in difficult words. Struggling adolescent students who cannot read easily may be exposed to such vocabulary when teachers read to them. Novels, short stories, news articles, and excerpts from classics are excellent materials. Attention may be specifically focused on words with the use of the *Word Up!* strategy (Richek, 2004). For this strategy, we simply take difficult words from the selected material and write them on cards. We then distribute one or two cards to each student, making sure that the student can read the given word(s).

---

1 point (noticed in adult speech, met in print, or in the media)
    Ms. Khan (the teacher) said, "Do you think it's *overwhelming*
        to have spelling every week?"
    Hygrometrics measure *humidity.*
    Why was it so *concise*?
2 points (used by students in speech)
    Sergio, you have an *authentic* jersey today.
    The class did a *fabulous* job with the words.
5 points (used by students in writing)
    Engaging in sports is great for your health.
    They went to the China Buffet and the food was *delectable.*

FIGURE 10.4. Find That Word: Sentence examples.

Next, we read the selection, and each student holds up the appropriate word card each time a targeted word is read. If the selection is short, it can be reread. When doing a second reading, we often stop every time a "student" word comes up to see if the students can predict which word will be read next. Or, to have the students more consciously utilize context clues, we may reread the sentences containing "their" words and ask each student to provide a definition for his or her word. We may follow up by making a list of these words and posting them. The use of Word Up! is a non-threatening way to encourage students to engage in the learning of Tier II words as well as to become more comfortable with the literary style of language and the use of context clues.

We may use difficult material intentionally for this strategy. Working with a class of high school struggling readers, we read Edgar Allen Poe's "Cask of Amontillado" and excerpts from *A Christmas Carol* by Charles Dickens. Although usually reading such literature would have been met with dismay, the game-like nature of the Word Up! task delighted students. They were intrigued by the archaic words and enjoyed guessing what they might once have meant.

Word Up! can also be adapted for use with Tier III words. Internet searches easily uncover articles on science and social studies topics that contain many of the words students find in content-area textbooks. Teachers can read such articles, using word cards that contain vocabulary students must learn, as well as related words relevant to the topics they are studying. This activity helps students realize that the seemingly arcane topics in their content areas are important to today's world.

Learning Vocabulary: A Challenge for Engagement

The learning of vocabulary is an enormous task, yet our struggling secondary students can engage in it with joy and creativity. As students listen and read, they can notice words and be supported in adding them to their Tier II vocabulary. Participatory introduction and practice that focuses on empowerment, group activity, and games can help students enjoy mastering the Tier III words they need for school success. Motivating strategies encourage students to maximize learning, because they willingly focus on vocabulary and treat unknown words as "opportunities" rather than "problems."

Struggling secondary readers can, and do, enjoy learning vocabulary, as much as Maria, an ELL junior. Engrossed in teaching and learning Expert Word Cards, she was startled when the bell rang. "I guess I was working *diligently*," she said.

References

Anderson, R. C. (1996). Research foundations to support wide reading. In V. Greaney (Ed.), *Promoting reading in developing countries* (pp. 55–77). Newark, DE: International Reading Association.

Baker S. K., Simmons, D. C., & Kame'enui, E. J. (1995). *Vocabulary acquisition: Synthesis of the research* (Technical report No. 13). Eugene: National Center to Improve the Tools of Educators, University of Oregon.

Baumann, J. F., Kame'enui, E. J., & Ash, G. E. (2003). Research on vocabulary instruction: Voltaire redux. In J. Flood, D. Lapp, J. R. Squire, & J. M. Jensen (Eds.), *Handbook of research on the teaching of the English language arts* (2nd ed., pp. 752–785). Mahwah, NJ: Erlbaum.

Beck, I. L., McKeown, M. G., & Kucan, L. (2002). *Bringing words to life: Robust vocabulary instruction.* New York: Guilford Press.

Becker, W. C. (1977). Teaching reading and language to the disadvantaged: What we have learned from field research. *Harvard Educational Review, 47,* 518–542.

Blachowicz, C. L. Z., & Fisher, P. (2000). Vocabulary instruction. In M. L. Kamil, P. Mosenthal, P. D. Pearson, & R. Barr (Eds.), *Handbook of reading research* (Vol. 3, pp. 503–523). Mahwah, NJ: Erlbaum.

Blachowicz, C. L. Z., & Lee, J. (1991). Vocabulary development in the whole literacy classroom. *Reading Teacher, 45,* 188–195.

Bos, C. S., & Anders, P. L. (1990). Effects of interactive vocabulary instruction on the vocabulary learning and reading comprehension of junior-high learning disabled students. *Learning Disability Quarterly, 13,* 31–42.

Bromley, K. (2007). Nine things every teacher should know about words and vocabulary instruction. *Journal of Adolescent and Adult Literacy, 50,* 528–536.

Carlisle, J. F. (2007). Fostering morphological processing, vocabulary development, and reading comprehension. In R. K. Wagner, A. E. Mise, & K. R. Tannenbaum (Eds.), *Vocabulary acquisition: Implications for reading comprehension* (pp. 78–103). New York: Guilford Press.

Carver, R. P. (1992). What do standardized tests of reading comprehension measure in terms of efficiency, accuracy, and rate? *Reading Research Quarterly, 27,* 346–359.

Cunningham, A. E., & Stanovich, K. E. (1991). Tracking the unique effects of print exposure in children: Associations with vocabulary, general knowledge, and spelling. *Journal of Educational Psychology, 83,* 264–274.

Cunningham, A. E., & Stanovich, K. E. (1998). What reading does for the mind. *American Educator, 22,* 66–73.

Daneman, M. (1991). Individual differences in reading skills. In R. Barr, M. L. Kamil, P. Mosenthal, & P. D. Pearson (Eds.), *Handbook of reading research* (Vol 2, pp. 512–538). White Plains, NY: Longman.

Fawcett, A. J., & Nicolson, R. I. (1991). Vocabulary training for children with dyslexia. *Journal of Learning Disabilities, 24,* 379–383.

Fukkink, R. G., & de Glopper, K. (1998). Effects of instruction in deriving word meaning from context: A meta-analysis. *Review of Educational Research, 68,* 450–469.

Graves, M. (2000). A vocabulary program to complement and bolster a middle-grade comprehension program. In B. Taylor, M. Graves, & P. van den Broek (Eds.), *Reading for meaning: Fostering comprehension in the middle grades* (pp. 116–135). Newark, DE: International Reading Association.

Hopkins, G., & Bean, T. W. (1989/1998). Vocabulary learning with the verbal–visual word association strategy in a Native American community. *Journal of Adolescent and Adult Literacy, 42,* 274–281.

Hughes, T. A., & Fredrick, L. D. (2006). Teaching vocabulary with students with learning disabilities using classwide peer tutoring and constant time delay. *Journal of Behavioral Education, 15,* 1–23.

Lansdown, S. (1991). Increasing vocabulary knowledge using direct instruction, cooperative grouping, and reading in junior high school. *Illinois Reading Council Journal, 19,* 15–21.

Lee, S. H. (2003). ESL learners' vocabulary use in writing and the effects of explicit vocabulary instruction. *System, 31,* 537–562.

Lee, S. H., & Muncie, J. (2006). From receptive to productive: Improving ESL learners' use of vocabulary in a postreading composition task. *TESOL Quarterly, 40,* 295–320.

Marmolejo, A. (1990). *The effects of vocabulary instruction with poor readers: A meta-analysis.* New York: Teachers College, Columbia University. (AAT 9021296 Proquest Digital Dissertations).

McKeown, M. (1993). Creating definitions for young word learners. *Reading Research Quarterly, 28,* 16–33.

Miller, G., & Gildea, P. (1987). How children learn words. *Scientific American, 257,* 94–99.

Nagy, W. (2007). Metalinguistic awareness and the vocabulary–comprehension connection. In R. L. Wagner, A. E. Muse, & K. R. Tannenbaum (Eds.), *Vocabulary acquisition: Implications for reading comprehension* (pp. 52–77). New York: Guilford Press.

Nagy, W. E., Diakidoy, I. N., & Anderson, R. C. (1993). The acquisition of morphology: Learning the contribution of suffixes to the meaning of derivatives. *Journal of Reading Behavior, 25,* 155–170.

Nagy, W. E., & Scott, J. A. (2000). Vocabulary processes. In M. L. Kamil, P. Mosenthal, P. D. Pearson, & R. Barr (Eds.), *Handbook of reading research* (Vol. 3, pp. 269–284). Mahwah, NJ: Erlbaum.

Richek, M. A. (2004). Have fun: Increasing vocabulary for at-risk learners. *Perspectives* (Newsletter of the International Dyslexia Association), *30,* 17–23.

Richek, M. A. (2005). Words are wonderful: Interactive, time-efficient strategies to teach meaning vocabulary. *Reading Teacher, 58,* 414–423.

Richek, M. A., Caldwell, J. S., Jennings, J. H., & Lerner, J. W. (2001). *Reading problems: Assessment and teaching strategies* (4th ed.). Boston: Allyn & Bacon.

Rochester, S. (2006, May). *Consolidating learning through creative review.* Paper presented at the International Reading Association annual convention, Chicago.

Ruddell, M. R., & Shearer, B. A. (2002). "Extraordinary," "tremendous," "exhilarating," "magnificent": Middle school at-risk students become avid word learners with the Vocabulary Self-Collection Strategy (VSS). *Journal of Adolescent and Adult Literacy, 45,* 352–353.

Stahl, S., & Fairbanks, M. (1986). The effects of vocabulary instruction: A model-based meta-analysis. *Review of Educational Research, 56,* 72–110.

Stahl, S. A., & Nagy, W. E. (2006). *Teaching word meanings.* Mahwah, NJ: Erlbaum.

Stahl, S. A., Richek, M. G., & Vandevier, R. (1991). Learning word meanings through listening: A sixth grade replication. In J. Zutell & S. McCormick (Eds.), *Learning factors/teacher factors: Issues in literacy research. Fortieth yearbook of the National Reading Conference* (pp. 185–192). Chicago: National Reading Conference.

Sternberg, R. B. (1987). Most vocabulary is learned from context. In M. G. McKeown & M. E. Curtis (Eds.), *The nature of vocabulary acquisition* (pp. 89–105). Mahwah, NJ: Erlbaum.

Swanborn, M. S. L., & de Glopper, K. (1999). Incidental word learning while reading: A meta-analysis. *Review of Educational Research, 69,* 261–285.

Terrill, M. C., Scruggs, T. E., & Mastropieri, M. A. (2004). SAT vocabulary instruction for high school students with learning disabilities. *Interventions in School and Clinic, 39,* 288–294.

White, T., Power, M., & White, S. (1989). Morphological analysis: Implications for teaching and understanding vocabulary growth. *Reading Research Quarterly, 24,* 283–304.

CHAPTER 11

Classroom Instruction for Struggling Writers

Leif Fearn
Nancy Farnan

In September, seventh grade Flora wrote about the best room in her house, as follows, shown with no editorial adjustment.

I ting that I my sleep the rome doing hapy. Baby site and I lik that I the fel happy becas I with my bat and I fel very hapy. And somitg I fee sad.

In April, Flora wrote about her vacation, also shown with no editorial adjustment by the teacher.

On my vaction I wall go to see my ant and I wall go to See Ward to. An I will pray in my church. That is all. Of curse were goinge to my prants beccais that is her brthey.

Struggling writers is a redundant term. Writers who do not struggle are either Isaac Asimovs or oblivious to just what hard work and struggle feel like. In this chapter, we begin by defining *struggling* in the context of writing; but the struggle itself is not the center of our work. This chapter is about Flora. It is about what she does and does not know about writing, what she thinks and feels, why she struggles in her special way, and what teachers can do about it. The chapter explains who Flora is as a writer whose struggles are directly related to her experience in school. We lay out a plan for helping Flora that comes from a perspective on what the literature says about struggling writers. We then respond to the patterns we find when we teach middle and high school writers.

Meet Flora

The struggle in writing is intense for Flora. It will not go away easily or quickly. It may never go away, but we can help Flora become basically literate at the keyboard or with a pencil in her hand. This chapter discusses the knowledge base that informs our practice and the tools we can use in our practice to help Flora become an increasingly better writer.

Flora struggles with writing, as much in April as in September, but she is better in April than in September because of intentional writing instruction (Fearn & Farnan, 2001), some of which is described in this chapter. Had we started with the intervention when she was in the third grade, Flora could have been a much better writer by the seventh grade because she would have been better in the fourth, fifth, and sixth grades. Had her writing improved as much between September and April in the third, fourth, fifth, and sixth grades, perhaps she would not be a struggling writer in eighth grade. Or perhaps Flora would remain a more or less struggling writer forever. We don't know. However, our responsibility is to ensure that Flora, now in the seventh grade, writes increasingly better, whether or not she struggles with writing, so that she can write sufficiently well to live a literate life.

A lot of people struggle with writing. It isn't so much the struggle that is the problem. Far more problematic is the active avoidance that accompanies a sense of incompetence. Flora may always struggle; she may always be a reluctant writer and avoid writing. But because there will be times when Flora cannot avoid writing, when she needs to be able to communicate effectively in writing, we owe it to her and to the Floras of the world to ensure that they can write comprehensible text by the time they leave our classrooms.

Defining the Struggling Writer

What would it mean were Flora to struggle forever as a writer? What does it mean to be a struggling writer? What characterizes Flora as a struggling writer? First, just because Flora is a struggling reader in seventh grade does not necessarily mean that Flora does not write well. She doesn't, even though she is better in April than in September, but that alone is not what makes her a struggling writer. Flora struggles in writing because she knows she isn't very good at it. She avoids writing, so she rarely practices, and she has little or no idea about what to do when faced with a writing demand. She is like everyone else who struggles with writing in school.

- When faced with writing, she doesn't know what to do.
- When faced with writing, and she knows what to do, she doesn't know how.
- When faced with writing and she knows what to do, even after being shown how, she simply doesn't want to.

Flora isn't a management problem. She is smart. Smart people engage in what they feel competent doing, and they avoid what they do not do well. Flora avoids writing because she doesn't want to display what she does not do well. Are there readers of this page who, left to their own devices, gravitate toward what they do not do well? Neither does Flora.

Flora's struggle is like that of others, including accomplished authors. The "struggling" writer is a reflection of the struggle of writing itself. To quote Mike Rose (1985), "No one writes effortlessly." Anne Dillard (1989) opened her autobiography discussing the difficulty of writing. She wrote, "When you write, you lay out a line of words. The line of words is a miner's pick, a woodcarver's gouge, a surgeon's probe. You wield it, and it digs a path you follow. Soon you find yourself deep in new territory. Is it a dead end, or have you located the real subject? You will know tomorrow, or this time next year" (p. 3). Dillard continues by further describing the journey and the tools, especially the tools—hammers, courage, communication systems. "The line of words is a hammer. You hammer against the walls of your house. You tap the walls, lightly, everywhere. After giving many years' attention to these things, you know what to listen for" (p. 4).

Writers use the line of words to hammer against a sense that the thing can be revealed better, the image can be more vivid, the idea clearer. Flora does not have a very good hammer. Is it any wonder why students like Flora experience writing as a struggle? She needs tools.

Rose (1985) describes the nature of the struggle to write. One element of the struggle is that thoughts don't come. Struggling writers cannot think of what to write. It isn't that they do not have a prompt or a topic. Prompting doesn't help. They cannot think of what comes next after they write the first sentence or the first idea. There is no next idea or next sentence, because the attentional demand of the moment is thoroughly consuming for struggling writers.

As a consequence, those inevitable pauses when writing stops become longer and longer. There are pauses in every writer's writing event. The pauses are natural. But with struggling writers, the pauses have a life of their own. Struggling writers do not pause to catch their breath or allow a phrase to percolate, as the rest of us do; they pause because they are out of words and ideas and their capacity to persevere is replaced with the terrifying notion that there may not be another word or idea in their lives, and if one should happen along, they will capture it incorrectly, if at all.

Rose also notes that inner conflicts are revealed in jumbled syntax and word selections and word uses that are unclear. Struggling writers have so much energy invested in their battle against avoidance and their sense of incompetence that even when there is an idea, so much of their energy is committed elsewhere that they do not use the idea as well as they can. They know they are not expressing themselves as they would like when they see the writing coming out of the end of the pencil, which confirms what they know perfectly well about themselves as writers. They feel inadequate.

For struggling writers, conventions of genre interfere with rather than guide their writing. In other words, they do not focus on purposes for writing and elements of a particular genre that could help them fulfill their purposes. Struggling writers are so close to the edge of disaster that in order to avoid going over, they are counting sentences and paragraphs, filling in boxes, adhering to this or that formula as though the formula were the point of the writing.

Likewise, formal writing processes that contain narrow assumptions and procedures for writing interfere with a writer's natural flow. Struggling writers in school go to their teachers for something to grab hold of, a raft in the swirling pools of avoidance and fear of being wrong. The teacher gives them metaphors and posters, worksheets and task cards. Struggling writers grab hold, and often their writing comes back at them from the paper looking like worksheets and hamburgers, and they know they have done it wrong again.

There is a pattern building here. Flora is not very skilled, and she knows it. She often does not know what to do, she usually does not know how, and she invariably avoids the task. Ideas are hard to come by for Flora. It is painful to watch her work, for she fights against relentless avoidance. She has so much energy tied up in the battle against avoidance that what skills she has do not come out in her writing. She writes directly to the prompt or direction and asks over and over if "this" is okay and what to do next. For Flora, writing is a struggle from the first moment she faces the blank sheet of paper until the moment the bell rings, signaling a blessed end to the struggle for today. That is what "not doing well" means. That is what makes writing a struggle.

What Research Says about Struggling Writers

Collins (1998) takes a closer look at struggling writers. They are more comfortable talking their ideas than writing their ideas. Struggling writers are not necessarily ideationally barren; they are more comfortable expressing themselves orally. They have better control over oral language. They understand talk. The conventions of talk, equally complex though they are, are automatic, so although struggling writers' ideas are derailed by writing, they remain on track when they talk.

Collins's description of struggling writers indicates that they tend more to knowledge telling when they write, and knowledge construction when they talk (see Berieter & Scardamalia, 1987, for a detailed description of the distinction between knowledge-telling and knowledge-transforming). In other words, they take the more comfortable of the two roads. They retell the story, they paraphrase the caption under the illustration in the social studies book, and they write about when the character was born and died in the biography. Rather than communicating meaning through their own thinking, they simplify by merely telling the information. Young writers who have experienced their own competence are more likely than Flora to write what they noticed from the reading and what it reminded them of (i.e., to integrate their own meaning constructions into the writing). They are more likely to explain the illustration and connect it to the topic it is intended to reveal in the text, and they tend, more than Flora, to tell the biographical subject's story. Struggling writers may be as capable as anyone else of using language to construct meaning, but they are more likely to elaborate on the biographical subject's story in talk than in writing. Aren't we all? If our distress zone were scribal, we all would more likely simply retell the biography in writing and use our oral skills to take others through the subject's life.

In addition to relying on information-telling, rather than knowledge-construction, in their writing, struggling writers "write short," according to Collins (1998), not because they write sufficiently well to compose with brevity and precision, but because short gets them out more quickly. And struggling writers' writing is mechanically nonconventional. It is difficult to read because the boundaries and connections between and among sentences are unclear, paragraphs begin on one point and end on another, sentences and paragraphs are out of order, capitalization and punctuation are not used effectively to enhance meaning, the writing shows motion but little if any movement, and readers end the reading wondering what the piece is about, if anything.

There seems to be more evidence associated with Collins's (1998) observations—about struggling writers—coming out of higher education than out of K–12 schools. An example is the work of Musgrove (2006) with community college students. He asked why students make errors in organization and mechanics when they write. Struggling writers seem not to arrange their thoughts logically so that readers can follow the writer's meaning. The struggle is revealed in the quality and organization of young writers' thinking when they write, and in the quality of the writing itself. Error rate is an attribute of quality in writing; the lower the rate, the better the writing, all other things being equal. So why the disorganization, the high error rate, the seemingly rudimentary thinking on paper?

Musgrove found three primary reasons for these errors of writers:

1. They don't care.
2. They don't know how to think on paper, organize thoughts, and reduce the error rate.
3. They don't see (read "sense" or "notice") the problems.

Of these three reasons, Musgrove observed, the first and third are the more frequent causes of error. He found that, in fact, most community college students *know how*, in the sense that they can write sentences and paragraphs and address most of the mechanical demands in what they write. The instructional tasks, then, are to help them care about the quality of their thinking and writing and to help them to manage their writing time so they can compose properly, which includes "seeing" their errors.

Struggling writers, faced with the writing demand, tend to operate on the basis that they will do what they must but no more than the least they can get away with. And they seem to have little interest in writing because they have had few or no satisfying experiences with a pencil in hand or at a keyboard.

Furthermore, few struggling writers experience authentic consequences for writing poorly, because their teachers often accept nearly anything and let the students off with a poor grade (Musgrove, 2006).

The following questions emerge from the patterns Musgrove describes. As you consider the questions, consider whether the struggling writers we see in the middle grades and high school fit into Musgrove's patterns and, if so, what that means for writing instruction.

- Are the ideas thin and poorly organized?
- Does the writing itself appear unorganized?
- Is the error rate, at both the draft and edited level, higher than appropriate for the student's age?
- Does it appear the students are writing as little and as infrequently as they can get away with?
- Do struggling writers appear not to know how to approach the writing task and to make it work?
- Do they appear not to care, or claim not to care?
- Do struggling writers experience school as a place where the only consequence of writing poorly is a poor grade?
- If asked, would struggling writers say that they rarely, if ever, experience satisfaction when they write and/or with what they have written?

Writing and Self-Concept

Research related to student motivation suggests that if students who struggle in writing (or mathematics, reading, violin playing, or free-throw shooting) feel better about themselves as writers (or readers or free-throw shooters), they will write (or read) better. Such a line of inquiry enjoys a fair amount of evidence, and it goes back a while. Purkey's (1970) conclusion after his analysis of the interaction between self-concept and academic achievement indicates that there is "a persistent and significant relationship between the self-concept and academic achievement" (p. 23). Purkey refers to the relationship as "reciprocal" and suggests there is reason to believe that enhancing self- concept can influence academic achievement. Among the investigations on the basis of which Purkey drew his conclusions, three showed a correlation between self-concept and academic achievement: in primary grade reading, Lamy (1965) and Wattenberg and Clifford (1962); and in seventh grade test taking, Gibby and Gibby (1967). All were correlation studies, though the Gibby and Gibby investigation posited, although not unambiguously, that self-concept was responsible for higher test scores.

Research that shows noncausative relationships between self-concept and school achievement are interesting, but teachers are in the business of making change happen; therefore, teachers need evidence that if they do X kinds of things with Y kinds of students, Z kinds of things are likely to occur. Data of this kind are very difficult to find, for the variables (language of instruction, use of instructional aids, social and academic background, grade level, gender, perception of subject matter, student–teacher relationships, and so forth) confound researchers' ability to isolate effects clearly (Kulubya and Glencross, 1997). Furthermore, achievement itself can have varying definitions, and even "attitude" is not uniformly defined.

Basically, there are three models of the interaction between self-concept and academic achievement. In the self-enhancement model, self-concept of ability tends to influence academic achievement, so people who perceive themselves as more able tend to commit greater effort and persevere (Schiefele & Csikszentmihalyi, 1995). In a skills development model, a history of achievement produces a sense of potency (self-concept of ability) in that area (Helmke & vanAken, 1995). And then there is a reciprocal model in which achievement and self-concept of ability tend to be described as interactive, but the evidence does not show that one causes the other (Purkey, 1970).

Although there clearly is a relationship between self-concept of ability and academic performance, the evidence is far too ambiguous to generalize that one causes the other. With regard to struggling writers, therefore, it may be appealing to bring self-concept of ability into the change mix by emphasizing struggling writers' feelings about their writing ability, but the

1. How writers craft the language (writers' craft)
   - Organization of ideas and images in sentences and paragraphs
   - Lowering of error rate (increasingly effective use of meaning markers and other conventions such as spelling)
   - Responsibility for writing better
2. How writers approach and perform writing: ideation, monitoring, and assuming responsibility for quality
3. How writers experience the writing and its aftermath
   - Learning how to persevere
   - Experiencing satisfaction related to writing

FIGURE 11.1. Instructional categories for writing.

evidence favors a skills model in which instruction helps struggling writers to write better (Collins, 1998).

So What Can Teachers Do?

To help struggling writers write better, it is important to know who they are and what the struggle means. Let's go back to Flora. Our first responsibility is to give her the tools she needs to write better. Among those tools is how to know what effective writing entails. The second responsibility is to help Flora get ideas on paper and notice what she is doing. And the third responsibility is to teach in a way that ensures that Flora will experience a degree of satisfaction associated with the writing. In April, when we laid Flora's September and April papers side by side on her desk, she glowed. She knew the progress she had made. She knew she was better. With a few more such experiences, she might begin to think she can control being a better writer. She may not fall in love with writing—most people do not, not even professional writers, if their self-reports can be believed. But she can write better and experience the writing with a degree of satisfaction, even if she is not in love with the process. Our responsibility is Flora's writing skill and her ability to use it. A sense of satisfaction, and perhaps even a love affair, will take care of itself. On the basis of Musgrove's (2006) patterns, we pose three instructional categories that subsume five subcategories: how writers craft the language, how writers approach and perform writing, and how writers experience the writing and its aftermath. (See Figure 11.1.)

The Writer's Craft

Most people would agree that it is not possible to make music at the keyboard of a piano without striking the right keys. To know the keys, the right ones for the purpose, which fingers to use, and how hard and for how long to strike the keys are all fundamental to making music with a piano. Making meaning in writing is not the same as making music with a piano, but the analogy is sufficiently useful to establish the importance of teaching the writers' craft if part of the instructional purpose is to help struggling writers to write better.

For our purposes, *craft* is winnowed down to three categories of skills and responsibilities that emerge from the patterns we have described: organizing ideas and images into sentences and paragraphs, lowering error rate (more effective use of meaning markers such as capital letters and punctuation marks and other conventions such as spelling), and assuming responsibility for writing better.

Writing Sentences

Writers organize ideas and images in sentences and paragraphs. People who speak English have the capacity to think in and write a sentence in English; people who cannot, cannot. English is arranged in sentences. Everything that follows is a variation on the theme. Every sentence contains ideas, and possibly details. A paragraph contains a main idea and details. Both a chapter in a history book and a scene in short fiction contain a main idea and details. It is all about main idea and details, in one, two, or three sentences or more; one or more paragraphs; and whole pieces of writing. What are main ideas and details? They are the big ideas (This is what the book is about) and images (trees, characters, and joy). We help Flora write better by teaching her to handle ideas and images better in better sentences and paragraphs.

Teachers may say that they have been teaching that all along, and still Flora doesn't understand. She still doesn't write sentences and paragraphs. When we teach sentences as subject and predicate, "complete" thought, and where to put the big letters and dots, Flora doesn't get it. She can get sentences and big letters and dots; she just doesn't get the notion of "complete" thought. And no one else does, either. Thoughts do not occur incomplete. "Under the table" is a complete thought. It refers to an object, and where that something is located, but it is not a sentence. If we want Flora to write sentences, we should talk to her about sentences in a way that she can understand, not about the magnitude of thoughts, which tells her nothing about sentences. When we teach "complete" thought in seventh grade, after teaching it in the six previous grades, teaching it again merely reinforces for Flora that she is missing something, and she knows perfectly well that it is her fault because, after all, she just doesn't get it.

Let us begin with something other than what Flora has been taught and knows but has never understood. In our plan we can teach sentences to Flora without reference to subject and predicate, the size of ideas, and big

letters and dots, none of which accurately capture the sentence (i.e., introductory clauses contain a subject and predicate, and they are "complete"
thoughts; and although big letters and dots make sentence boundaries for
readers, they tell writers nothing about writing, for they aren't there until
writers put them in).

So we say, "Flora, think of a sentence that contains the name of a character in the book. No, you don't need a pencil. Think about it. Write the
sentence in your mind."

We invite you, our reader, in your mind, to sit at your keyboard. You
are writing: tap-tap-tap-tap-tap-tap-tap-tap-tap-tap-tap-donk-tap-tap-tap-
tap-tap-tap-tap-donk-tap-tap. . . . The taps are letter keys, and the donks
are periods. Ignore the fact that the sentences are painfully short. You get
the idea. How do you know when to hit the donks? You don't calibrate the
relative completeness of your thoughts, and you aren't keeping track of
subjects and predicates. How do you know where the period goes? In fact,
you know the period is coming well before you get there. How do you
know? If Flora is ever to become skilled in the craft of writing, she has to
know that too. Flora has a right to what we know, and we have a responsibility to teach it to her.

The kind of instruction Flora needs isn't about audience or voice or
descriptive adjectives. It is about the sentence, without which the rest of
what we teach about writing is irrelevant. Ask Flora what a sentence is. She
will fire off the definition like a well-memorized line from a script:
"IT HAS A SUBJECT AND PREDICATE, AND IT'S A COMPLETE
THOUGHT." Look again at her writing from September of her seventh-
grade year. There are three strings of words that masquerade as sentences.
The first doesn't work even if the spelling were closer to correct. Neither
does the second. The third is a sentence. But Flora knows the mantra of
subject, predicate, and complete thought. She is a whizbang at that.

So ask her instead to think of that sentence with the book's character
in it. Then ask her, "Read your sentence to me, Flora." Flora reads from
her mind. "Max is bigger than all the other children."

"Write that sentence on the paper, Flora. But first, read your sentence
to me again before you write it on your paper." Flora reads. "Good, Flora.
Write the sentence on your paper exactly as you hear it in your mind."
Flora writes: *Max iz bigr then all the uthr childr.*

We just learned something about Flora's struggle. She can think in a
simple sentence about her book, *Max the Mighty* (Philbrick, 1998), but she
cannot spell the words. Can she think in two related sentences about Max,
that is, two sentences that are cohesive? We ask her. "Flora, think of two
sentences about Max in the book. Make your idea about Max two sentences long. In your mind, Flora; write the two sentences in your mind."
Flora thinks, then reads from her mind. "Max is bigger than the other children. Sometimes he thinks he's weird." Good. Flora can make two sen-

tences cohere on the same topic. Now all we have to do is help her make automatic what she has shown she can do. And we have to teach her to spell the words.

What about the capital letters and periods? What we have found is that if she can hear the beginnings and ends of sentences, she will use the capital letters and periods properly, just as we all do. But she has to spell, capitalize, and punctuate automatically first, and that means Flora has to write about 1,500 single and double sentence pieces this seventh-grade year. That works out to about 8 per day in a 180-day year, more like 10 a day because she will miss some days. That works out to 5 per day in class and 5 per night for homework. She can write 1 in each of her five periods during the day and 1 for each of the five periods for homework. The homework will take her 5 minutes because she can write 1 sentence in about 35–45 seconds. Her sentence in each of her five periods can be single or double sentence pieces that tell what she thinks she learned during that period. She and the other students read many of their sentences aloud, filling the room with the sounds of sentences. Why is this important? It's important, perhaps even necessary, because language, all language, is learned in the ear; and Flora and her classmates need the sounds of sentences in their ears.

Writing Paragraphs

To help Flora and her struggling peers think in and write paragraphs is not much different from helping her think in and write sentences. First, we stop referring to numbers and kinds of sentences, geometric shapes, architectural designs, metronomic ditties, and fast food charts. If asked, Flora will tell us that a paragraph has five sentences and looks like a hamburger. In fact, it has as many sentences as it needs, and not one more, and it looks like lines on a page, just like all other text. But it has a "sense," for us a sound, and if Flora does not have a sense of paragraph, she will never use paragraphs as a way to organize her sentences into larger chunks of meaning, no matter how fast she answers a question about numbers of sentences in a paragraph.

First, paragraphs are organized, and Flora must learn about that type of organization. "Flora, which of these two sentences from our social studies this morning comes first? *He was born in 1746. Benjamin Rush was a doctor in early American history.* If she says the second comes first, we ask why. She will say because if it started with the "*He*" sentence, we wouldn't know who *he* is. If she says they are in the right order, we ask how we would know who *he* is in the first sentence. Most of the world's Floras say the sentences should be reversed. "What do you think might be the main idea if this were the beginning of a paragraph?" She will say it is about Benjamin Rush. "Where does this sentence go? *His father died when he was five years old.*" She will say it comes next. "Could it come second?"

Most of the time she will say it is the third sentence, and when we ask why, she will say it just seems like it is third. "How about this sentence? Where does this one go? *He studied in Scotland to become a doctor.*" We engage Flora in a conversation about organization. The fourth sentence could come third or fourth. "Now, what is the paragraph about? What is its main idea? Is the paragraph finished? If not, how many more sentences does it need to complete the main idea?"

That is the conversation about paragraphs. Writers think in paragraphs for organizing their writing. Paragraphs are clusters of sentences about the same main idea. The conversation with struggling writers about paragraphs should engage their minds. Their struggle is with writing, not thinking. They need a lot of thinking and talking, listening and talking, about the sense of paragraph.

They also need practice thinking in and writing paragraphs. However, just about everything they bring to the class about paragraph writing they learned in the years before they came to our class, and still they struggle. It makes no sense to just give them more of it, slower, louder, and in smaller groups. (See Figure 11.2 for Flora's example.)

We say to Flora, "There are six sentences in the paragraph. The first one is finished. What do you think might be the main idea of the paragraph?" Most of the world's Floras say that Omar lost something and then he found it. "Well, then, you write the paragraph by finishing the five sentences that are not finished. Then you can read the paragraph aloud, and we can talk about its main idea" (Fearn & Farnan, 2001). If facing Flora with the five is too much for her, take it one sentence at a time, on the board or overhead screen so everyone can participate in the thinking. "If the main idea is that Omar lost something and then found it, how do you think the second sentence will read?" Then the third, fourth, fifth, and sixth. Each time a student dictates a sentence, write it on the board and ask someone to read the paragraph aloud so far, and ask about the main idea again. When the sixth sentence is on the board, the paragraph is finished, because it has a main idea, and there are details that elaborate on the main idea. "What do you think could be the main idea of the next paragraph?" Always ask about the next paragraph. The students do not have to write it, but they do have to think about it. Every time. That's how writers write extended discourse.

Omar searched all around. He looked under.   .   .   . He went outside
and looked.   .   .   . Down the street.   .   .   . Then he saw.   .   .   .
Omar was so happy .   .   .

FIGURE 11.2. Paragraph completion.

There is one more thing. Flora and her friends must write (copy) every paragraph they collaboratively write on the board. And the teacher must tell them that they have written a paragraph that works. Remember, they are struggling because so little of what they have ever written works. Now something works every day. They have to know it, because increased self-confidence occurs through knowing it.

Lowering Error Rate

The vast preponderance of struggling writers' errors are in spelling and punctuation. How to avoid and/or correct those errors is taught by second-, third-, and fourth-grade teachers and has been learned by many second, third, and fourth graders, but not Flora. She knows this, and she would like very much to do better.

Begin with spelling. There are three parts to spelling well: word study, self-concept of spelling ability, and spelling conscience or sense of responsibility. Spelling instruction, where it occurs, is limited to word study, and teachers do that very well. But people spell well not only because they know how (word study), but because they know they can (self-concept of ability). And they spell well when they write, not only because they know how and know they can, but because they know they should (spelling conscience). We can develop self-concept of spelling ability when we organize instruction so our students attend to the words, they attend to the right cues in the right modality, and our expectations do not exceed their capacity to remember.

Regarding punctuation (and capitalization), we need to consider what young writers need to know. There are more than 100 conventions for capitalizing and punctuating English, and most of them have at least one variation. There are scores of manuals for capitalization and punctuation, and at least as many books of black-line masters for editing practice. Flora has been through several of them, and still the comma is a mystery.

Flora will use capital letters and punctuation marks more precisely when she knows which ones go where, and she practices thinking in and writing sentences that contain them, over and over, as we described earlier. Consider the complex sentence, the one that starts with an introductory clause and becomes a sentence with the addition of an independent clause. Flora has heard the term *clause*, but she probably does not know what it means; and even if she did, she wouldn't necessarily write complex sentences more frequently.

Complex sentences begin with words such as *although, since, because, though, as, while*, and so forth. Go ahead, think of a sentence that begins with *because*. Immediately, you hear a soft break down the line followed by an independent clause. Literate people start sentences with *because* and lie in wait for the comma that makes the break between the two clauses, not because literate people know about clauses, but because they can hear the break in a sentence that starts with *because*. We have to teach Flora what more literate people know.

Ask her to think of a sentence that begins with *although*. If she responds, *Although it was raining*, ask her to listen as you "read" all of her sentence: *Although it was raining, I went to the game anyway.* "Read" your sentence aloud several times, and ask her to listen to the two sounds in the sentence (introductory clause and independent clause). Don't trouble her with the terminology right now; just read the sentence several times so she can hear its sound. Then ask her to think of a sentence in which the first word is *as*. About seven times out of ten she will share a sentence that reads something like this: *As I was walking down the street, a girl passed me.* Then you read/repeat her sentence twice and ask her to notice the two parts. Next, ask her to think of a sentence in which the first word is *while*. Flora needs to think in and write a lot of complex sentences before we tell her that there is a comma between the two parts. Thereafter, Flora needs to use at least one complex sentence in every piece she writes.

Why is this important? As Flora grows and develops, her thinking will become increasingly complex, which means that she will need increasingly complex structures so she can communicate her thoughts in writing. Learning to write complex sentences is not just an academic exercise we teach because it will appear on tests. It is important for Flora so that she can become increasingly adroit at what writers do, that is, communicate her thinking effectively in writing.

We teach compound sentences the same way, and compound/complex sentences. Every sentence has a sound, and every literate writer knows what it is. Flora will never write compound sentences, complex sentences, and compound/complex sentences adroitly and automatically until she knows what we know, that there are sounds in sentences. Once she becomes automatic, we can teach her all we know about clauses and phrases. She can learn those things to explain what she can do; she will not learn to write the sentences because she knows those things.

How Writers Approach Writing:
Writing Processes

The term, *writing processes*, and the action, are plural. There are writing processes typically idiosyncratic to the writer, often to the genre, sometimes to the day. The processes are neither linear nor stage-bound in any manner whatsoever—not even *recursive*, which is linear and stage-bound—just forward and backward rather than forward alone. Furthermore, writing processes do not teach well. They are much better learned than taught. Rather, they are iterative (Fearn & Farnan, 2001), which means they occur again and again throughout a writing experience.

One way to begin to teach the writing process is to use *Power Writing* (Fearn & Farnan, 2001, pp. 167–169). Ask students to write as much as they can as well as they can for three rounds of 1 minute, perhaps in biology class (e.g., "Write as much as you can as well as you can about either *mitosis* or *osmosis*"). Then ask them to think about their second or third round of writing. "Did any of you know what you were going to write before you began? Lisa, did you know?" If she says she knew, ask how many sentences she wrote. Then ask if she knew, before she began, what her second sentence would say. Lisa may say she didn't. "When did you find out what to write in your second sentence?" She may say that she thought of it when she wrote the first sentence. "Do you mean that while you were writing the first sentence, you started to think about what to write in the second sentence? So we can think about our ideas and how to write them even while we are writing our draft?"

Most of the students will say they didn't know before they started, that they figured it out as they went. Some will say they did know, and they wrote it just as they had it figured out before they started. There are several conclusions we can draw on the basis of what the young writers self report.

1. Prewriting can take seconds.
2. Prewriting need not involve making lists.
3. Writers can draft and think of ideas at the same time.
4. Everyone writes in his or her own way.
5. Everyone can write, by which is meant get a lot of text in a short time limit.
6. Most writers begin writing without knowing what will come next.
7. It is okay to write without knowing what will come next.

Given the nature of writing processes and the various ways they can be experienced, the focus of instruction should be to help young writers come to understand what they do when they write (awareness) and to help them master a variety of ways to start, to persevere, and to finish. The task is to empower young writers, to help them know they are in control.

Try another way to engage your students. Ask them to make an image. The prompt sounds something like this: "Think of a hawk seeming to float high in the air. Get a picture in your mind. Listen. Watch. What colors do you see, what sounds do you hear? What details do you see when you look at the hawk? What do you think is happening? See the image in your mind. Make the picture. Now write the image. Write as much as you can as well as you can, in 2 minutes."

We ask Justin to read his piece. *It's flying really high. It's gray and black. The wings aren't flapping. He's looking for a mouse to eat. The sky is blue. There isn't any sounds. He has really good eyes so he can see a mouse on the ground from really far away. It's like a lot of stress for the hawk and the mouse.*

"Joyce, what do you see? What kind of image does Justin's piece make for you?" *I see a mouse that's going to be dead pretty soon because this hawk is going to swoop down and get him.* "What else, Joyce? What else do you see?" *The hawk is hungry. It's hot, like maybe in the afternoon. Maybe the hawk has babies in a nest, and it's going to give the dead mouse to the babies to eat.*

"Justin, what do you think? Did Joyce get your image about right? Is that about what your picture looked like when you saw it in your mind?" *I didn't see any nest and babies.*

"Is it okay that Joyce did?" *Sure.*

That is a *Process Piece* (Fearn, 1985; Fearn & Farnan, 2001). It requires that students make an image, write the image, and receive feedback on their writing from a peer audience. Young writers develop ideas, draft the ideas, publish (i.e., in this case, share orally), receive feedback, and think about revising on the basis of audience feedback. It takes about 6 minutes per round (draft, share, and receive feedback from three peers). One round (one draft) and four read-alouds, plus feedback, take about 12–15 minutes. Do that each of 5 days, and 20 students can receive feedback on their writing. In addition, each "write" involves ideation, drafting, publishing, feedback, and the possibility of revising. That means five experiences with writing processes per week. And it takes only 12–15 minutes a day. In addition, when the teacher regularly engages students in conversations about where their ideas came from, when they knew what they would write next, and changes that occurred during the writing (i.e., adding, deleting, rethinking an idea, erasing and changing a word or phrase), students learn about the iterative nature of writing processes and the role *they* play in moving a writing forward.

The key to empowerment relative to writing processes is the number of times young writers use whole writing processes, as opposed to writing longer pieces in which they use writing processes only once. Young writers need many experiences with starts. They have to start many pieces of writing, and they have to push many pieces of writing through to completion. They need many experiences with starting and finishing. That means they have to write short, and they have to focus on the writing. Struggling writers focus on the struggle. Process Pieces and Power Writing (explained earlier) as well as other *Short Cues* (Fearn & Farnan, 2001), such as writing directions, *Word Limiters*, and summaries, are short-writes from which struggling writers can gain numerous experiences of starting and finishing and of using their writing processes effectively, thus increasing the probability of having satisfying experiences with writing.

Struggling Writers: Teaching How to Persevere

As mentioned earlier, writing itself is a struggle for nearly everyone. The point is to help struggling writers gain the tools and experiences that effective writers use to bear up under the burden. Struggling writers need satisfying experiences with writing, even as they struggle. They need to understand that we all sometimes feel we have nothing to write; some people know they will find something, and some people fear they will not. We need to help struggling writers experience finding something so their confidence that they can increases.

Teachers need to recognize that it is not so much the students' attitude that we need to change; what we need to change is their belief that they can't do it, a belief backed by extensive experience to prove it.

Flora isn't less intelligent than others whom we don't call "struggling" writers. She is bright enough to have learned from her experience that writing is a special struggle for her. Part of what she struggles with is the delusion of uniqueness (Klenbort, 1978). She thinks she is the only one. She isn't, and the weight of her burden will decrease when she realizes that.

Conclusion

We know from our work with struggling young writers that Flora will not write better merely because she realizes that she has a lot of company in the struggle. She will write better as she knows more about how. She comes to know more about how to write through intentional instruction. This chapter does not describe everything there is to know about teaching writing. What we have attempted to do is define the concept of the "struggling writer" and in doing so to clarify the experiences of students like Flora and provide some instructional insights gleaned from our experiences with struggling writers. Although the instructional insights are far from comprehensive, they may allow readers to gain a better understanding of how to help struggling writers in the classroom tomorrow morning.

References

Bereiter, C., & Scardamalia, M. (1987). *The psychology of written composition.* Hillsdale, NJ: Erlbaum.

Collins, J. (1998). *Strategies for struggling writers.* New York: Guilford Press.

Dillard, A. (1989). *The writing life.* New York: Harper & Row.

Fearn, L. (1985). *Process pieces.* San Diego: Kabyn Books.

Fearn, L., & Farnan, N. (2001). *Interactions: Teaching writing and the language arts.* Boston: Houghton Mifflin.

Gibby, R. G., Sr., & Gibby, R. G., Jr. (1967). The effects of stress resulting from academic failure. *Journal of Clinical Psychology, 23*, 35–37.

Helmke, A., & vanAken, M. A. G. (1995). The causal ordering of academic achievement and self-concept of ability during elementary school: A longitudinal study. *Journal of Educational Psychology, 87*(4), 624–637.

Klenbort, I. (1978). Another look at Sullivan's concept of individuality. *Contemporary Psychoanalysis, 14*, 125–135.

Kulubya, M. M., & Glencross, M. J. (1997). Mathematics achievement and attitudes of senior secondary students in Transkel, South Africa. *Psychological Reports, 80*, 915–919.

Lamy, M. W. (1965). Relationship of self-concept of early primary children to achievement in reading. In I. J. Gordon (Ed.), *Human development: Readings in research* (p. 251). Chicago: Scott Foresman.

Musgrove. L. (2006). *The real reasons students can't write.* Retrieved April 28, 2006, from *www.insidehighered.com.*

Philbrick, R. (1998). *Max the mighty.* New York: Scholastic.

Purkey, W. (1970). *Self-concept and school achievement.* Englewood Cliffs, NJ: Prentice-Hall.

Rose, M. (1985). *When a writer can't write: Studies in writer's block and other composing process problems.* New York: Guilford Press.

Schiefele, U., & Csikszentmihalyi, M. (1995). Motivation and ability as factors in mathematics experience and achievement. *Journal of Research in Mathematics Education, 26*(2), 163–181.

Wattenberg, W. W., & Clifford, C. (1962). *Relationship of self-concept to beginning achievement in reading* (U.S. Office of Education, Cooperative Research Project No. 377). Detroit: Wayne State University Press.

CHAPTER 12

Teaching from a Critical Literacy Perspective and Encouraging Social Action

Susan Lenski

One of the hallmarks of childhood is egocentricity; children typically view the world from only their perspectives. As children develop into young adolescents, however, they begin to form a sociocentric point of view and become concerned with issues of relevance, social justice, and the meaning of life (George & Lawrence, 1982). Some adolescents become idealistic, expecting life to be fair and just. Others become cynical and suspicious. Young teens also begin to establish their identities and to look for ways that they fit into the larger society. During this time of growth, middle and high school students want teachers to initiate conversations about the questions they have about life and society. At the same time, literacy programs tend to emphasize the functional aspects of language learning rather than challenging students to think deeply, question texts, and become involved in their communities (Edelsky, 2006). Teachers, however, can capitalize on students' newly developed sociocentric attitudes by helping them read and think about texts from a critical literacy perspective.

Critical literacy is viewed as a way to read, analyze, and evaluate texts within a sociocultural framework. According to Wood, Soares, and Watson (2006), "the goal of critical literacy is to raise students' critical and social consciousness" (p. 56). Critical literacy is different from the kinds of skills

227

and strategies taught under the name of critical reading. Critical reading strategies, such as distinguishing facts from opinions, were popular in the 1980s (Unrau, 1997). By the end of the 20th century, however, theorists redefined critical reading to correspond to a larger educational movement called critical pedagogy, which evolved into what we know now as critical literacy (Siegel & Fernandez, 2000). Critical literacy theory was also shaped by the views of the Frankfurt School of Critical Social Theory, which posits that society can change the world by analyzing the ways dominant groups hold power (Kellner, 1989). Critical literacy, therefore, is set of recently developed theories that hold real promise for incorporation into adolescent literacy programs.

Although critical literacy is a relatively new field, its central theme has been endorsed by two large professional literacy associations, the International Reading Association and the National Council of Teachers of English. One of the standards from the national *Standards for the English Language Arts* states that students need to "question assumptions, explore perspectives, and critique underlying social and political values or stances" (International Reading Association and National Council of Teachers of English, 1996, p. 71). More recently adolescent literacy experts identified eight principles for practice, one of which includes a call for increased critical literacy in classrooms (Sturtevant et al., 2006). According to Sturtevant and her colleagues, "adolescents need opportunities to develop critical perspectives toward what they read, view, and hear" (p. 125). This chapter, therefore, describes critical literacy theory, gives a rationale for including critical literacy in the instruction of struggling readers, and gives practical applications for classroom instruction.

The Development of Critical Literacy

Many people believe that critical literacy is an outgrowth of Freire's (1985) belief that readers should read texts by engaging in a critical analysis of society and texts and using that knowledge to become agents for social justice. Reading from a critical stance requires not only constructing meaning from the text but also "reading the world," or looking for the cultural implications of texts (Freire, 1970). Reading from a critical perspective also means that readers acknowledge the text's complexity, raise questions, and look for alternative answers. Critical literacy suggests that texts are not only products of words but are also the results of authors' social worldviews. Authors make choices about content and language in their writing, all of which are products of the authors' sociocultural backgrounds and beliefs.

Critical literacy, therefore, is a developing set of beliefs about reading that focus on examining a text's social and cultural implications. Previous popular reading theories examined how readers construct meanings of texts through a transaction between a reader's personal knowledge and experiences and what is learned from the texts (Rosenblatt, 1978). Critical literacy, however, goes beyond reading to construct meaning. It encourages readers to develop a critical awareness of the notion that texts are not neutral and that texts represent particular points of view while omitting others (Luke & Freebody, 1997).

In order for each to teach students to read critically, students first need to believe that meaning resides in themselves as readers. Students must recognize that a text represents an author's views of reality that are based on the author's social, cultural, and political beliefs. Students who read critically also understand that they frame their interpretations using their own sociocultural beliefs and acknowledge that they bring their own biases to every reading situation. Reading from a critical literacy perspective, therefore, is more than constructing meaning; it suggests that readers use their reading of texts to understand the social realities of the world.

Using a Critical Literacy Perspective with Struggling Readers

Critical literacy appeals to adolescents, and it also helps give purpose to their reading. According to Franzak (2006), "the importance of purpose in literacy learning cannot be understated; the remaining question is how to help marginalized readers find authentic purpose in school literacy learning—something that experience may have taught them is improbable" (p. 227). Langer (2002, 2004) found the same thing to be true in her research. Langer investigated the differences in instruction between schools that were in the same neighborhoods but had drastically different achievement results. She found, among other things, that schools that "beat the odds" included instructional content that connected students to authentic and interesting central concepts that gave purpose to their reading. When struggling readers are able to connect learning to larger concepts using a critical framework, their interest in learning increases (Hobbs, 2007).

One example of using critical literacy for real purposes is helping students think about their roles in democracies. Bean and Harper (2006) investigated how students reading young adult literature can use critical literacy. The students studied the characters by analyzing how they were depicted, how the novel fostered or disrupted the status quo, and how freedom and democracy were represented. Another example for a social studies class may be teaching students to understand the roots of poverty in Mexico rather than just studying about the North American Free Trade Agreement (NAFTA; Bigelow, 2006). When students learn how to think about governmental policies from a larger perspective, rather than just learning the content, they become more interested in what they are learning.

Teaching Students to Think Critically

Struggling readers may have had few experiences thinking critically in schools. Many struggling readers have been disengaged from school learning, and those who have been in special reading classes most likely have spent more time in learning skills than in thinking broadly (Edelsky, 2006). English language learners (ELLs) may be at a more pronounced disadvantage. ELL classes typically focus on developing the new language through vocabulary development and translating words, sentences, and texts. Examining texts from a critical perspective, however, can help ELLs understand that "their cultural perspectives and primary languages are valued in mainstream American society even when these differ from those of the majority culture" (Daniel & Lenski, 2007, p. 33). Because one of the tenets of critical literacy is to explore minority cultural constructions of texts (Comber, 1992), students who come from nonmainstream cultures can enrich classroom discussions when they are given an opportunity to discuss texts from a critical literacy perspective.

Practical Suggestions for Incorporating Critical Literacy in Classroom Instruction

Just because struggling readers cannot read grade-level material does not mean that they are unable to think about texts from a critical perspective. Reading or even examining texts and ideas from a critical stance requires not only constructing meaning from the text but also "reading the world," or understanding the text's wider implications (Freire, 1970). Teachers, therefore, may need to help students develop the ability to think critically through incremental steps by teaching some of the underlying principles of critical literacy before expecting students to apply more abstract critical literacy skills.

Teaching from a critical literacy perspective may include the following areas:

- Examining meanings within texts
- Considering the purposes of the text
- Thinking about the author's motives
- Understanding that texts represent particular worldviews
- Questioning and challenging the ways in which the texts have been constructed

- Analyzing the power of language in the texts and in society
- Emphasizing multiple readings of texts
- Encouraging students to take a stand on issues presented in texts
- Providing students with opportunities to consider and clarify their own positions
- Providing students with opportunities to take social action

The following discussion elaborates on several of these broad areas of critical literacy and provides ideas and strategies that help students think from a critical literacy perspective by identifying alternate views, researching language choices, responding critically, interrogating texts, and reacting critically to media.

Identifying Alternate Views

Identifying alternate views is especially important for today's students, who are constantly flooded with information from print and nonprint sources. Students who read critically understand that a particular text represents the view of the author(s) at the time it was written. The text, therefore, presents one view of reality at one period of time. In order for students to go beyond this small slice of thinking, they need to consider alternate views, or views that are not stated in the text. Students should not simply believe what they read; they need to develop a mindset that identifies the view presented and then look beyond that content for assumptions, reasons, justifications, and implications that underlie the ideas (Paul, 1993).

Struggling adolescent readers need to learn how to identify alternate views for yet another reason. During reading instruction in elementary schools, students have been taught to access prior knowledge and use background experiences to construct meaning from texts. Although this strategy is useful in many reading situations, it can cause real problems when students are presented with counterintuitive concepts. Many students resist learning new ideas that do not fit with already established schema (Stahl, Hynd, Glynn, & Carr, 1996). Students who are able to identify alternate views, a critical literacy process, are also able to let go of their preconceived ideas and embrace new learning. Because some students bring misconceptions to learning, they need to keep their minds open, understand other points of view, and be prepared to change their opinions.

Discussion Charts

There are several strategies that help students think of alternate views while they read. The use of a *Discussion Chart* is a strategy that prompts students to think of alternate views by having them learn what their classmates are thinking about an idea. To use a Discussion Chart, the teacher develops a number of ideas or concepts that are important for students to consider and then lists them on a chart. Each student writes down his or her own views and asks two classmates for their opinions. After the students have each completed a Discussion Chart, the teacher can use the information to discover the opinions of the students and to adapt class discussion accordingly. A sample Discussion Chart from a social studies class that is learning about federal, state, and individual rights is shown in Figure 12.1.

Researching Language Choices

Students who are learning how to think from a critical literacy perspective know that authors choose language to evoke emotion, set a tone, persuade, and/or influence readers (Comber, 2001). Students can understand the language choices that authors make by learning that authors consciously or subconsciously select words that establish social identity and power relationships (Luke, O'Brien, & Comber, 2001).

Concept or idea	Student's opinion	Opinion #2	Opinion #3
Mountain climbers should be required to carry some type of global positioning system (GPS) device.	Yes, they will be easier to rescue.	No, GPS can give climbers a false sense of security.	No, the government shouldn't interfere with personal rights.
Motorcyclists should be required to wear helmets in every state.	Yes, injuries not only hurt individuals, they drive up health costs.	No, the decision should be made by each state.	No, motorcyclists should be allowed to make their own decisions.
Smoking should not be allowed within 20 feet of a doorway to a public building.	Yes, smoke near a doorway can hurt others who don't want to breathe the air.	Yes, smoking near a doorway interferes with other people's rights.	No, smoking outside a public building should not be regulated.
Immigrants without legal documentation should be provided with free health care.	Yes, everyone needs health care.	No, they do not have legal status.	No, it's up to each person to pay for medical care.

FIGURE 12.1. Discussion chart.

An example of looking at language from a critical perspective can be found in the article, "Lies My Spanish Textbooks Tell" (Shedivy, 2007). Shedivy reviewed a variety of Spanish textbooks to determine how Latin Americans were represented in the texts and in the pictures in books. She found that there were many false representations and blatant overgeneralizations. The language used by the authors of these textbooks portrayed Spanish-speaking people from a certain viewpoint. This example illustrates the ways in which authors, editors, and publishers embed cultural views in texts. Having students look at textbooks with the same critical eye can help them to discover the author's perspectives and to determine whether they believe the authors were fair in their portrayals.

Developing Critical Responses

Students are very familiar with responding to their readings through journal writing and other response strategies. Critical response, however, draws on reader response theory by having students respond to the text through a critical lens. This thinking process helps students imagine how to reconstruct or redesign the text using more socially just and equitable messages (Vasquez, 2003). To have students develop a critical response, teachers identify a fictional or informational text, either print or nonprint, that they want students to read from a critical perspective. Then they prepare questions, similar to the following, for students to consider.

- Why do you think people should or should not read this text?
- What surprised you about this text?
- What questions would you like to ask the author?
- What experiences have you had that connect with the theme of this text?
- What worldview is expressed?
- What worldview is not represented?

Students should discuss potential answers to the questions in small groups before they respond individually. After students have completed a critical response, they can discuss their ideas in class, focusing on how the text represents a particular worldview. An example using the text *Americans Who Tell the Truth* (Shetterly, 2005) is shown in Figure 12.2.

Reciprocal Teaching Plus

Many struggling adolescent readers still need support in reading comprehension strategies as well as in learning how to think and read critically. *Reciprocal Teaching Plus* (Ash, 2005) is a strategy that adds a critical literacy response component to the well-researched Reciprocal Teaching strat-

Why do you think people should or should not read this book?	What questions would you like to ask the author of this book?
I don't think this book should be widely read. Although the illustrations are intriguing, the book is very predictable and bland.	How did you select the title? How did you select the people to be in the book? What is your definition of truth?
What surprised you about this book?	**Write an experience from your own life that connects with this book.**
I was surprised that I didn't know about many of the people who were included in this book. I thought I was pretty knowledgeable about famous Americans, but this author found quite a few that were new to me.	I admire many of the people described in this book. Once I even created a list of people I admire. Our lists overlapped in a few cases.
What worldview is expressed?	**What worldview is not represented?**
Americans who live in the United States are noble, generous, and brave. They fight for the good of humanity, no matter the cost.	Truth can also hurt.

FIGURE 12.2. Critical response.

egy (Brown & Palincsar, 1984). In Reciprocal Teaching Plus students use five thinking strategies as they read: questioning, clarifying, summarizing, predicting, and critiquing.

To use Reciprocal Teaching Plus, a teacher selects a text that is not familiar to the students but is within their reading ability. *The Best Book of Volcanoes* (Adams, 2001) is rich in content knowledge about volcanoes and is written using a text format and vocabulary that is accessible to the majority of struggling adolescent readers. In the first step of the strategy, students make predictions about the content of the book. After the students have made predictions, they read a section of the book, monitoring their predictions and looking for confusing ideas. The students list confusing ideas in the column labeled "Clarifying." The students then form groups to discuss the content of the text, to make sense of the confusing issues, and to develop questions that focus on textual content. They take turns leading the group and asking questions they have developed about the text. At this point, some students may ask for more clarification about an item. After questions have been successfully answered, the group members generate a summary of what they have learned. The students should have a reasonable grasp of the content after these steps in the strategy. At that point, Ash

(2005) suggests, the students should think critically and respond to one or more of the following questions:

- Whose story is being told? What is the perspective of the author or narrator?
- Does the author believe certain things about the world? How can you tell? Does the author tell us the perspective from which the story is being told?
- Whose story is not told in this text selection? Why or why not?
- Do you agree or disagree with the ideas the author is presenting? Why or why not?

The students can discuss their answers to these questions in small groups or with the entire class. As students become proficient in the thinking strategies used in Reciprocal Teaching Plus, they can learn more detailed ways of critically thinking about texts. An example of Reciprocal Teaching Plus is shown in Figure 12.3.

Predicting	Clarifying	Questioning	Summarizing	Critiquing
The major types of volcanoes in the world will be discussed.	Relationship between tectonic plates and Ring of Fire.	How does the movement of the Pacific Plate form volcanoes?	The movement of a tectonic plate called the Pacific Plate caused mountains to form in the Pacific, a formation that is called the Ring of Fire.	The illustration does not seem to show the proportion of active volcanoes in Asia. The areas of Japan and Indonesia are near the crease of the book and the words are hard to read.
Famous volcanic eruptions will be described.	Mt. Pinatubo, 1991	What was the largest volcanic eruption in the second part of the 20th century?	Mt. Pinatubo, in the Philippines, erupted in 1991, and this was one of the most significant volcanic eruptions in history.	More print was given to the eruption of Mount St. Helens than to the other major eruptions, possibly because this book is written for U.S. readers.

FIGURE 12.3. Reciprocal Teaching Plus.

Interrogating Texts

As students read critically, they need to think of the author as separate from the text and as someone who has made deliberate choices about the content and language of the text. As they read with the author in mind, the students should acknowledge the "power of the text on the reader as well as an understanding of *why* the text exercises that power" (Soter, 1999, p. 114). Readers can keep these issues in mind by asking questions of the text as they read, or interrogating the text.

Interrogating the text is a useful strategy for readers in all content areas, and especially for struggling adolescent readers. As students ask questions during reading, they automatically think about the meanings represented by the text, which is a valuable metacomprehension tool. Readers need to monitor comprehension during reading as they ask questions. Further, as students read, they enter the domain of sociocentric thinking by asking questions that move beyond the text, the author, and themselves.

Developing Textual Questions

The kinds of questions that teachers want students to ask before, during, and after reading depend on the subject they are teaching and the purpose for having the students read the text. For example, a mathematics teacher can have students discuss how mathematics is culturally situated by having students question how their textbook approaches mathematical problems. The teacher can also ask immigrant students if they have learned different ways to approach mathematics. Through this experience, students can learn that mathematics texts express views that are valued in the United States, but that there are other ways of thinking mathematically.

Language arts or reading teachers who require students to write in personal journals can have students read the book *My Diary from Here to There* (Pérez, 2002). This story shows how a young immigrant used a diary to reflect on leaving her home and family members to come to the United States. Students can discuss how diaries or journals can help writers process new experiences in addition to learning about the often painful process of leaving one's home for a new country.

Social studies teachers have many opportunities to apply critical literacy perspectives in their classrooms. An interesting perspective is presented in Bigelow's (2006) book about border issues, *The Line between Us*. In this book, Bigelow suggests that social studies teachers help students understand the historical implications of boundaries and borders. As students read about the development of borders, they begin to understand that the distinction between "us" and "them" becomes an artifact of time. As students approach history from this critical perspective, they can discuss the ways in which historical events have influenced their lives.

The questions listed in Figure 12.4 can help teachers think about the kinds of critical questions students should be asking about texts in their disciplines. Many teachers try to focus on one or two areas for several lessons before moving to additional categories.

The questions listed in Figure 12.4 can be used by ELL teachers. However, Daniel (2006) recommends that teachers who have ELLs in their classrooms also consider incorporating the following questions as the teachers interrogate texts:

- How will deconstructing this text help my ELLs better understand the world in which they live?
- What stereotypical behaviors are promoted by the author of this text?
- Will reading this text give power and voice to my learners and facilitate adaptation to American society?
- Might the topic of this book serve as a source of dinnertime conversation for my ELLs with their parents?

Having teachers ask these questions of the texts they use will serve as both employing a critical literacy perspective and will help ELLs learn about their new country and culture.

Critically Viewing Media

The world of most adolescents today is permeated by media to a greater degree than ever before, which O'Brien (2001) has termed the "mediasphere." According to the Committee on Public Education (2001), adolescents spend more than 6 hours every day listening to or watching some sort of media messages. The kinds of media they are exposed to vary; their experiences include listening to music, watching television, surfing the Internet, e-mailing, and text messaging. Members of the current generation are often referred to as "digital natives" because they have been exposed to technology for their entire lives.

Even though adolescents have spent their lives listening to and viewing various media, they may not be critically evaluating the messages they receive from those media. The messages that students get from media are biased or slanted, even those that have been reviewed and edited. According to critical literacy theory, no text is neutral, and the aim of all media is to persuade listeners or viewers to believe their messages. Some messages are obvious—a television commercial for shampoo, for instance. Other messages are more subtle, as in the example of a poster for a school play. Not all media messages, however, are negative; some messages students read or view are positive and helpful. The point of critical media literacy is not to motivate students to resist every message they encounter. Instead,

Purpose of text
What is the text about? How do we know?
What is the purpose of the text?
Who would be most likely to read or view this text?
Why are we reading or viewing this text?
What does the author want us to learn or know?
How does the author try to convince readers to accept his or her premise?

Textual structures and features
What are the structures and features of the text?
In what genre would this text be included?
What do the images or illustrations suggest?
What kind of language is used in the text?

Construction of groups and characters
How are children, adolescents, and adults represented?
Why has the author represented the characters this way?
How does the author represent different groups in the text?
How are meanings assigned to certain figures?

Gaps and silences
Are there gaps or missing pieces in the text?
Who is not present in the text?
What has been left out?
What questions about itself does the text raise and not raise?
How might we rewrite this text to deal with the gaps and silences?

Power and interest
Whose interests are served by the dissemination of this text? Whose interests
    are not served?
In whose interest is the text written?
Who benefits from the text?
In what ways does the text seem to be fair?
What knowledge does the reader need to bring to the text?
Which positions, voices, and interests are central to the text?
Who is the reader, in relation to the author?
How does the text depict age, gender, and/or cultural groups?
Whose views are excluded or privileged in the text?

View of reality
What view of the world is put forth by the ideas in this text? What views are not?
What are other possible constructions of the world?
What does this text tell us about our understanding of different cultures?
What kinds of social realities does the text portray?
How does the text construct a version of reality?
How would the text be different if it were told in another time or place?

Interrogating the author
Why did you include this example in the text?
What do you mean here?
What background do you have in this area?
Do you have any contact with readers my age?
Why didn't you write with more common vocabulary?

Multiple meanings
What different interpretations of the text are possible?
How do contextual factors influence how the text is interpreted?
How else could the messages of the text be conveyed?

FIGURE 12.4. Interrogating Texts

critical media encourages readers to think for themselves before responding to the messages of the media.

Incorporating critical media into a curriculum may have a secondary benefit. In a study of English teachers who developed classes using critical media literacy as a central tenet, Hobbs (2007) found that students improved in reading comprehension and other academic skills. It is essential, therefore, that adolescents learn how to listen to and view media critically—from television commercials to Internet ads.

Media Log Prompts

A strategy for helping students think deeply about media is the use of a *media log* or journal in which students can record the kinds of media to which they are exposed (Lenski, Wham, Johns, & Caskey, 2007). As students record the various media, they critically analyze the media's messages and their responses to them. Students do not need to answer each of the questions; part of being a critical reader is to determine which questions to ask. For example, a reader who sees a pop-up Internet ad for new software needs to think about the reasons the business has for advertising on the Web, the appeal of new software for using the Internet, the ease of linking to new products, and how the ad could be resisted. Additional questions that prompt students to think about media, developed by Lenski et al. (2007), follow:

- How is this message presented?
- What message is conveyed by the media?
- Do you personally agree or disagree with the media's message? Why?
- How is language used to present the message?
- How could you resist the message if you wanted to do so?
- What is implied by the media?
- What is missing from the presentation?
- How is the text situated culturally and historically?
- How does this text position you as a viewer or listener?

The Importance of Taking Social Action

As teachers include critical literacy in their classrooms, some students can begin to view the world from a critical perspective. Although this is the purpose of incorporating critical literacy strategies, some students may begin to form an overnegative attitude. It is important, therefore, to take critical literacy to the next level and introduce ways in which students may recapture hope in their lives (Christensen, 2000). Fleming and Boulton

(2006) write, "Social action is a community development theory based on the simple premise that *change is possible*" (p. 87). When critical literacy is coupled with social action, some students may begin to look at the world through the lens of a champion for social justice (Singer & Shagoury, 2005/ 2006). This change in perspective opens the door for hope.

According to Lewison, Flint, and Van Sluys (2002), critical literacy instruction in schools should include four components:

- Disrupting the commonplace
- Interrogating multiple viewpoints
- Focusing on sociopolitical issues
- Taking action and promoting social justice

A growing number of teachers agree that taking social action is a part of critical literacy and have become interested in teaching students to read about social issues and to discuss them in the classroom (Damico & Riddle, 2004). Many middle and high school students, especially struggling readers, are concerned about issues of fairness, equality, and justice. Teachers can interest adolescents in reading and writing by introducing topics that deal with social justice or human rights that are culturally relevant for their students (Ciardiello, 2004). One of the reasons that social injustices persist is that we fail to "ask why things are the way they are, who benefits from these conditions, and how can we make them more equitable" (Shannon, 1995, p. 123). When students ask these questions, they find new hope and power in their own lives. And hope may be linked in some way to achievement. A study measuring student achievement in schools that focused on autonomy, belongingness, and connectedness found that students were more hopeful. They were also more engaged in learning, and reading achievement began to improve (Newell & Van Ryzin, 2007).

An example of the kinds of life-transforming experiences that can occur when students learn how to take social action is that of Craig Keilburger. When Craig was a young teen, he learned about child labor in Pakistan. Craig became a passionate voice against child labor by organizing a movement called Kids Can Free the Children. Free the Children, begun in 1995, was made up of adolescents who wanted to work to end child labor. Free the Children has since grown to more than 100,000 members in 30 countries. Craig coauthored a book, titled *Free the Children: A Young Man's Personal Crusade against Child Labor* (Keilburger & Major, 1998), about this issue. In the past decade, Craig and his brother, Marc, have expanded their vision of social justice to other issues and have recently coauthored a book titled *Me to We: Finding Meaning in a Material World* (Keilburger & Keilburger, 2006) that promotes the personal responsibility of social action.

The example of the Keilburger brothers may be atypical, but it illustrates how reading about a topic can inspire action. Topics for units about social justice issues can be taken from students' lives or from readings about social issues. Students of all ages have local issues that may be used for these units. As students become more adept at thinking from a critical perspective, however, it is important that themes outside students' experiences also become topics of study. Students who have little experience with poverty, for example, might read about the reasons for homelessness, and, conversely, students who live in poverty can read about the very different problems of the rich. As students learn about social issues outside their own experiences, they become more aware of the complexities of society and learn how to think about issues of social justice (Singer, 2006).

Service Learning

Service learning is another way for students to learn to think from a critical perspective and to find meaning in learning. Service learning is an idea that stemmed from Dewey's work on active, real-world learning (Dewey, 1954). All service-learning projects incorporate two main components: an activity that provides a needed service to the school, community, or agency, and learning about the project. There are varying degrees of involvement in service-learning projects. Service-learning projects are typically divided into three categories: community service, community exploration, and community action (Terry & Bohnenberger, 2007). Community service projects typically are opportunities for students to learn about their communities and to perform voluntary services. Examples of community service projects include collecting litter from a school yard, cleaning up graffiti, tutoring younger students, and reading to senior citizens. Community exploration projects involve a deeper commitment to a project by more extensive learning before beginning the service. For example, the students who investigated the mining of Black Mountain needed to learn more details about the community before they met with city officials to discuss their views about strip mining (Powell, Cantrell, & Adams, 2001). The final type of service-learning activity is community action. According to Terry and Bohnenberger (2007), community action "results in students becoming aware of a need in the community and providing a service, but it can also lead to students becoming so engrossed in and committed to the need area that they go beyond just supplying a service" (p. 59).

Students at one school, for example, were concerned about the nutritional content of the food banks that supplied the community's homeless population. When the school conducted its can drive, during which students brought canned goods to replenish the food bank, a group of students used the canned food to host a luncheon—for the teachers! Then the students identified the nutritional content of the luncheon's foods and displayed the information on graphs. They found that the food had a very high percentage of sodium and fat but not many nutrients. The students continued researching the nutritional needs of different age groups and then instituted a nutritional can drive for the local food bank, with lists of recommended nutritional canned foods. Some of the students volunteered at the food bank and distributed information about nutrition with the food. This project exemplifies the critical reading of food labels, providing a service to the community, and taking social action.

Conclusions

Critical literacy is a way of thinking about texts that goes beyond comprehension. Although most struggling adolescent readers need to be supported in basic reading skills and strategies, they should also learn how to read and think about texts from a critical literacy perspective. Critical literacy instruction can provide adolescents with the kinds of thinking they need in order to address larger societal issues and to become functioning citizens in a democratic nation. In addition, critical literacy can help students think beyond schooling and apply critical thinking strategies to media that they experience on a daily basis. Finally, by moving from critical literacy to social action, students who may be disengaged from school and learning can find hope and recapture their natural optimism about life. When students learn how to move from thinking critically to taking social action, they learn how to make sense of the complexity of the world around them, through involvement in the kinds of actions that benefit not only themselves, but also the larger world.

References

Adams, S. (2001). *The best book of volcanoes*. Boston: Houghton Mifflin.

Ash, G. E. (2005). What did Abigail mean? *Educational Leadership*, *63*(20), 36–41.

Bean, T. W., & Harper, H. J. (2006). Exploring notions of freedom in and through young adult literature. *Journal of Adolescent and Adult Literacy*, *50*, 96–104.

Bigelow, B. (2006). *The line between us: Teaching about the border and Mexican immigration*. Milwaukee, WI: Rethinking Schools.

Brown, A. L., & Palinscar, A. S. (1984). Reciprocal teaching of comprehension: Fostering and monitoring activities. *Cognition and Instruction*, *1*, 117–175.

Christensen, L. (2000). *Reading, writing, and rising up: Teaching about social justice and the power of the written word*. Milwaukee, WI: Rethinking Schools.

Ciardiello, A. V. (2004). Democracy's young heroes: An instructional model of crucial literacy practices. *Reading Teacher*, *58*(2), 138–147.

Comber, B. (1992). Critical literacy: A selective review and discussion of recent literature. *South Australian Educational Leader, 3*(1), 1–11.

Comber, B. (2001). Classroom explorations in critical literacy. In H. Fehring & P. Green (Eds.), *Critical literacy: A collection of articles from the Australian Literacy Educators' Association* (pp. 90–102). Newark, DE, and South Australia, Australia: International Reading Association and Australian Literacy Educators' Association.

Committee on Public Education. (2001). Children, adolescents, and television. *Pediatrics, 107*(2), 423–426.

Damico, J., & Riddle, R. L. (2004). From answers to questions: A beginning teacher learns to teach for social justice. *Language Arts, 82,* 36–46.

Daniel, M. (2006). *Taking all children to the head of the class: Bilingual learners explore cultural nuances in text.* Paper presented at the National Association of Bilingual Education annual conference, Phoenix, AZ.

Daniel, M., & Lenski, S. D. (2007). The importance of critical literacy for English Language Learners. *Illinois Reading Council Journal, 35*(2), 32–36.

Dewey, J. (1954). *The public and its problems.* Athens, OH: Swallow Press.

Edelsky, C. (2006). *With literacy and justice for all: Rethinking the social in language and education.* Mahwah: NJ: Erlbaum.

Fleming, J., & Boulton, I. (2006). Principles for practice: What is social action? In K. Berdan, I. Boulton, E. Eidman-Aadahl, J. Fleming, L. Garner, I. Rogers, et al. (Eds.), *Writing for change: Boosting literacy and learning through social action* (pp. 87–96). San Francisco: Jossey-Bass.

Franzak, J. K. (2006). Zoom: A review of the literature on marginalized adolescent readers, literacy theory, and policy implications. *Review of Educational Research, 76*(2), 209–248.

Freire, P. (1970). *Pedagogy of the oppressed.* New York: Herder and Herder.

Freire, P. (1985). *The politics of education: Culture, power, and liberation.* New York: Bergin & Garvey.

George, P., & Lawrence, G. (1982). *Handbook for middle school teaching.* Glenview, IL: Scott, Foresman.

Hobbs, R. (2007). *Reading the media: Media literacy in high school English.* New York: Teachers College Press.

International Reading Association and National Council of Teachers of English. (1996). *Standards for the English language arts.* Newark, DE, and Urbana, IL: Author.

Kielburger, C., & Kielburger, M. (2006). *Me to we: Finding meaning in a material world.* New York: Simon & Schuster.

Kielburger, C., & Major, K. (1998). *Free the children: A young man's personal crusade against child labor.* New York: HarperCollins.

Kellner, D. (1989). *Critical theory, Marxism, and modernity.* Baltimore, MD: Johns Hopkins University Press.

Langer, J. (2002). *Effective literacy instruction.* Urbana, IL: National Council of Teachers of English.

Langer, J. (2004). *Getting to excellent: How to create better schools.* New York: Teachers College Press.

Lenski, S. D., Wham, M. A., Johns, J. L., & Caskey, M. (2007). *Reading and learn-*

ing strategies: Middle grades through high school (3rd ed.). Dubuque, IA: Kendall/Hunt.

Lewison, M., Flint, A. S., & Van Sluys, K. (2002). Taking on critical literacy: The journey of newcomers and novices. *Language Arts, 79,* 382–392.

Luke, A., & Freebody, P. (1997). Shaping the social practices of reading. In S. Muspratt, A. Luke, & P. Freebody (Eds.), *Constructing critical literacies: Teaching and learning textual practice* (pp. 185–225). Cresskill, NJ: Hampton Press.

Luke, A., O'Brien, J., & Comber, B. (2001). Making community texts objects of study. In H. Fehring & P. Green (Eds.), *Critical literacy: A collection of articles from the Australian Literacy Educators' Association* (pp. 112–123). Newark, DE, and South Australia, Australia: International Reading Association and Australian Literacy Educators' Association.

Newell, R. J., & Van Ryzin, M. J. (2007). Growing hope as a determinant of school effectiveness. *Phi Delta Kappan, 88,* 465–471.

O'Brien, D. G. (2001). "At risk" adolescents: Redefining competence through the mulitliteracies of intermediality, visual arts, and representation. *Reading Online, 4*(11). Available at *www.readingonline.org/newliteracies.*

Paul, R. W. (1993). *Critical thinking: How to prepare students for a rapidly changing world.* Santa Rosa, CA: Foundation for Critical Thinking.

Pérez, A. I. (2002). *Mi diario de aquí hasta allá: My diary from here to there.* San Francisco: Children's Book Press.

Powell, R., Cantrell, S. C., & Adams, S. (2001). Saving Black Mountain: The promise of critical literacy in a multicultural democracy. *Reading Teacher, 54,* 772–781.

Rosenblatt, L. (1978). *The reader, the text, the poem: The transactional theory of the literary work.* Carbondale, IL: Southern Illinois University Press.

Shannon, P. (1995). *Text, lies, and videotape: Stories about life, literacy, and learning.* Portsmouth, NH: Heinemann.

Shedivy, S. (2007). Lies my Spanish textbooks tell. *Rethinking Schools, 21*(3), 49–50.

Shetterly, R. (2005). *Americans who tell the truth.* New York: Dutton Children's Books.

Siegel, M., & Fernandez, S. L. (2000). Critical approaches. In M. L. Kamil, R. Barr, P. D. Pearson, & P. Mosenthal (Eds.), *Handbook of reading research* (Vol. 3, pp. 141–151). Mahwah, NJ: Erlbaum.

Singer, J. (2006). *Stirring up justice.* Portsmouth, NH: Heinemann.

Singer, J., & Shagoury, R. (2005/2006). Stirring up justice: Adolescents reading, writing, and changing the world. *Journal of Adolescent and Adult Literacy, 49,* 318–339.

Soter, A. O. (1999). *Young adult literature and the new literary theories: Developing critical readers in middle school.* New York: Teachers College Press.

Stahl, S. A., Hynd, C. R., Glynn, S. M., & Carr, M. (1996). Beyond reading to learn: Developing content and disciplinary knowledge through texts. In L. Baker, P. Afflerbach, & D. Reinking (Eds.), *Developing engaged readers in school and home communities* (pp. 139–163). Mahwah, NJ: Erlbaum.

Sturtevant, E. G., Boyd, F. B., Brozo, W. G., Hinchman, K. A., Moore, D. A., &

Alvermann, D. E. (2006). *Principled practices for adolescent literacy: A framework for adolescent literacy.* Mahwah, NJ: Erlbaum.

Terry, A., & Bohnenberger, J. (2007). *Service learning . . . by degrees: How adolescents can make a difference in the real world.* Portsmouth, NH: Hcinemann.

Unrau, N. J. (1997). *Thoughtful teachers, thoughtful learners: A guide to helping adolescents think critically.* Scarborough, ON: Pippin.

Vasquez, V. (2003). *Getting beyond "I like the book": Creating space for critical literacy in K–6 classrooms.* Newark, DE: International Reading Association.

Wood, K., Soares, L., & Watson, P. (2006). Empowering adolescents through critical literacy. *Middle School Journal, 37*(3), 55–59.

PART IV

Developing Schoolwide Contexts to Support Achievement

CHAPTER 13

Meaningful Assessment
of Struggling Adolescent Readers

Peter Afflerbach

The most difficult job I've ever had was teaching remedial reading and writing in a junior high school. I worked with students in seventh, eighth, and ninth grade, all of whom were experiencing difficulties with reading. The needs of these students were consistently framed in relation to cognitive reading skills and strategies—skills and strategies that were not working to expectation. The students needed to practice their reading so that skills and strategies would improve and become automatic. They needed to master comprehension strategies. Many of the students did not want to be in school. They often skipped class, arrived late, disrupted their classmates, or slept. Brusque and confrontational students were actually quite fragile when it came to reading: They avoided public performances and the accompanying demonstrations of being struggling readers at all costs. As I reflect on this teaching assignment, I appreciate the difficulties that the students faced.

In retrospect, I realize that my attention was directed mainly at the students' need to "get better" at skilled reading. I knew that the majority of students lacked motivation and that some of them had lost it long ago. The risk to self-esteem, the reinforcement of poor self-concept, and the continuing message that "you are not reading to expectation" were part of a powerful undercurrent in my classroom, yet I failed to assess the students in relation to these important aspects of their reading. My students also brought with them diverse experiences and histories as individuals, but I did not use assessments to focus on these prior experiences, to know the details of my students' lives, and to understand what mattered to them. Thus, I believe I may have missed opportunities to best connect my reading instruction to the things that the students knew and cared about.

My experiences with struggling adolescent readers taught me that students need considerable help with cognitive skills and strategies. Just as important, struggling readers need to believe that reading is something worthwhile, that it is rewarding, and that it can be done without threat to their egos. I believe that many students face the challenges that my students faced. I also believe that we have at our disposal considerable research and theory that helps us conceptualize and address students' needs in reading.

Reading assessment is key in helping struggling readers learn to read well, and learn to want to read. Therefore, this chapter focuses on the diverse factors that can influence reading achievement and proposes that formative and summative assessments, used across the school year, are needed to help teachers best meet the needs of struggling adolescent readers.

Characteristics of Struggling Adolescent Readers

It is of utmost importance that we accurately characterize struggling adolescent readers, and we have three distinct and interrelated areas of research that should inform this work. I refer to these as the cognitive, the affective, and the experiential. The cognitive aspects of reading are well researched, from the need to develop accurate sound–symbol correspondences to the need for strategies in the complex construction of meaning. We know that successful readers must develop phonemic awareness, learn and use phonics skills, read fluently, build vocabulary, and possess comprehension strategies (National Institute of Child Health and Human Development [NICHD], 2000; Snow, 2002). Moreover, as readers develop they must learn and apply critical reading strategies (Pressley & Afflerbach, 1995), they must be increasingly metacognitive (Veenman, 2005), and they must successfully apply what it is they learn from reading in relevant tasks in school and out (National Center for Education Statistics [NCES], 2005). This research base suggests that struggling adolescent readers may have challenges related to cognitive skill and strategy acquisition and use (Afflerbach, Pearson, & Paris, in press).

Readers' cognitive processes do not operate in a vacuum. Rather, they can be influenced by affective factors that include the reader's self-esteem, self-concept, motivation, attitude, and attributions for failure or success. Although skills and strategies allow students to process printed information and construct meaning, readers need reasons and motivation to do so in the first place (Guthrie & Wigfield, 1997). Successful school reading represents positive motivation combined with appropriate skills and strategies: Students are engaged with the texts they read and related tasks, and they have positive attitudes toward reading (McKenna & Kear, 1990). Students' reading is also influenced by how they perceive themselves (Dweck, 1999) and how they conceptualize their ability to read. Low self-esteem, a common characteristic of struggling readers, can lead students to try to avoid reading. Poor self-concept leads students to question why they should even begin a reading task, let alone finish it (Chapman & Tunmer, 1995).

A third critical aspect of success or failure in reading relates to students' prior knowledge and experiential background. Home and community culture can have varying influences in preparing (or not preparing) students for success in school (Heath, 1983). Socioeconomic factors also influence students' preparedness for school and achievement (Hart & Risley, 1995), as particular aspects of daily home life can provide extensions of learning, practice of things learned, and enrichment. In contrast, lack of preparedness may contribute to missed opportunities for learning and enrichment. School, home, and community cultures may have common ground in classrooms, or home and community experience may not be reflected in the content and process of the school day. Gonzalez, Moll, and Amanti (2004) describe funds of knowledge—accumulations of learning and practice—that are particular to communities and individuals within those communities. For example, a rich tradition of narrative storytelling, or of working in an agricultural or urbanized trade in a particular community, may be connected to different parts of the students' school day, such as English/language arts, economics, and history. Teachers' ability to know these aspects of students' lives and to connect them with curriculum and the goals of schooling can help them create motivating learning environments.

Although research demonstrates that cognition, affect, and experience can exert a significant influence on student learning, it is critical to note that there are also interactions between the three. These interactions can have a powerful effect on adolescent readers. For example, a seventh-grade student who is fortunate enough to have a personal computer at home may be adept at surfing the Internet. This part of the student's experiential background contributes to the ability to expertly use search engines and critically appraise the contents of websites (Coiro & Dobler, 2007). This developing expertise allows the student to efficiently find information related to favorite school subjects and hobbies. In turn, it fuels the student's interest and contributes to an overall positive motivation for combining a skill learned at home (critical Internet use) with school tasks (finding enriching information for class projects). The three components—cognitive, affective, and experiential—interact to effect a good outcome.

Consider next a student without a personal computer and home access to the Internet. This student may lack this positive set of experiences and connections to the classroom and school. Skills and strategies related to the effective use of the computer and the Internet as learning tools are yet to develop. Motivation emanating from successful learning experiences with computers may also be lacking. The connection between home life and school, in relation to computers, is, at best, tenuous. We must acknowledge, therefore, the importance of cognition, affect, and experience to student success in school.

In 1986, Keith Stanovich proposed the "Matthew effect." Its premise is that readers who experience success have great possibilities for continuing their growth, because success builds on success, or, as in the biblical passage from Matthew, "the rich get richer." We see this across many students' school careers: reading works for these students, it is considered a valuable or necessary tool, and it finds its way into the daily lives of the students. Reading progresses because students have and use repeated opportunities to practice skills and strategies, situated in an environment of positive affect and motivation. I propose that the suggested benefits of the Matthew effect have a counterpart that is present in many struggling adolescent readers, one that I call the reverse Matthew effect. Consider that while some students read, encounter success, and grow cognitively and affectively in their ability to read and desire to read, there are others whose experiences take them in a different direction. Here, assessment may not only document the outcomes of negative experiences for struggling adolescent readers, it may also be a negative experience itself. For all the readers who progress and then get caught up in the success cycle described by Stanovich (1986), there are readers who are moving away from the possibility of successful experiences with reading. Failure in reading contributes to low self-esteem and poor self-concept, which lead to decreased motivation, which leads to avoidance of reading, which leads to fewer opportunities for students to practice their reading, or to make the determination that some forms of reading are good.

Struggling adolescent readers, in effect, must unlearn some of the lessons of their prior schooling: that reading is boring, is an exercise in futility, is failure ridden, is threatening, is useless, is never worth the effort. They must unlearn that although many of their prior efforts to read were not rewarded, this state of affairs is not necessarily permanent. They must unlearn their attributions to low ability, bad luck, or task difficulty for explaining why they do not read well. And they must unlearn their low self-esteem and low self-concepts as readers.

Our research-based understandings of struggling adolescent readers describe a complex and multilayered set of concerns. We need assessment materials and procedures that map well onto this complex construct, describe it in detail, and provide us with the means to successfully address our students' needs.

Research on Assessment

Current practice in the assessment of struggling readers is marked by both promise and challenge (Afflerbach, 2007). We increasingly understand the complex demands of helping these readers, and we have assessments that describe students' growth over time in relation to cognition, affect, and experience. Yet within our schools is an overemphasis on summative, high-stakes tests of cognitive skills and strategies. This represents a severe skewing of our allocation of assessment resources, one that limits the potential success of our efforts to foster reading development in struggling adolescent readers.

Reading assessment results, most typically standardized test scores, are a frequent outcome measure for reading research. The comparison of test scores prior to and following research interventions yields the dependent variable of a test score. Even though reading assessment outcomes have a long history of playing a central role in signifying program quality, we do not have much research that demonstrates the optimal forms and foci of reading assessment. Thus, we commonly use summative assessment to describe school success, but we do not pay nearly as much attention to formative, classroom-based assessment that can influence daily student success. The extant research does suggest the potential power of particular assessments for helping struggling adolescent readers, along with the challenges of developing and using effective reading assessment materials and procedures.

Crooks's (1988) research synthesis focuses on the interactions of teachers and students in regard to evaluation. Crooks found that many of these interactions are the result of particular assessments, such as teacher questioning, and that the direct and indirect impacts of assessment can be positive or negative. Crooks identified the need for considerable research on the nature and outcomes of classroom assessment, with a goal of best understanding this assessment potential. Stiggins and Conklin (1992) provide a detailed account of the general assessment competencies of classroom teachers. The researchers found large discrepancies in teachers' ability to accurately assess students, which, in turn, reflects discrepancies in how teachers are trained to "do" assessment. Because teachers may have limited professional training in how to assess students, high-stakes tests assume the default role of *the* reliable and valid reading assessment. Many states' teacher certification requirements address teacher assessment ability as more an afterthought than a focus, and a not surprising result is that many teachers do not feel comfortable in conducting classroom-based assessments.

Black and William (1998) describe classroom assessment as a seeming "black box." By this they mean that for many students assessment is a puzzling unknown, something someone else does to their work that yields a score or grade. When assessment is a mystery to students, an opportunity is lost to help them understand the nature and importance of assessment. Also lost is the possibility that students might learn about assessment and eventually develop the ability to conduct self-assessment independently and benefit from the agency and control that self-assessment can provide. The attention given classroom assessment is small when compared with the attention given high-stakes tests. This is unfortunate, because high-stakes tests are summative assessments that have little or no ability to shape daily instruction. An imbalance in the types of assessment we conduct leads to a situation in which struggling adolescent readers and their teachers can fairly anticipate many tests, whereas the daily work of assessment that best helps students and teachers meet instructional goals may be ignored.

Characteristics of a Useful Reading Assessment Program

I propose that we need to develop a comprehensive approach to the assessment of struggling adolescent readers. We must have a detailed understanding of students' reading and their lives as they enter our classrooms, we must come to know them well through the school year, and we must be able to provide summary accounts of what they achieve and accomplish. To this end, an assessment program must be an apt combination of formative and summative materials and procedures. In addition, our assessments must inform us about student characteristics, which can help us provide the most appropriate reading instruction and experiences. We can conceptualize students' individual differences in relation to their cognitive skills and strategies, and most assessment in school does exactly this. In addition to their skills and strategies, we must know about students' motivations, attitudes, and experiential backgrounds—their prior knowledge and their lives outside school. These three related constructs represent important and powerful aspects of student learning, and they must be addressed if we are to have any hope of meeting struggling adolescent readers' needs.

How can a comprehensive assessment program provide us with information that is central to addressing our teaching goals and our struggling students' needs? Useful reading assessment programs share a number of characteristics: a balance in the amount of formative and summative assessments, systematic approaches to gathering and using assessment information, and a broad sampling of student characteristics. Effective reading assessment is always beholden to the idea that we assess to help our students become better readers.

A comprehensive approach to reading assessment that benefits struggling adolescent readers seeks information about these students' cognitive, affective, and experiential lives. Such an approach to assessment provides us with information so we can act in students' best interests. To do so, assessment must provide information about students as they begin a reading program, as they progress through the program, and as they complete the program. A useful, comprehensive assessment program provides information about students at all points of their work in school. We need to determine, therefore, what assessments help us best know students as they arrive in our classrooms, as they progress through the school year, and as they complete work in school semesters, marking periods, and years. Each time period has special and shared foci for assessment and each demands our attention.

Assessments at the Beginning of Instruction

The assessment information we use as students begin the year serves several critical purposes. It provides a baseline against which future progress can be measured. It describes, in detail, the essence of the student reader: cognitive skills and strategies, affective characteristics, and prior knowledge and experiences. The assessments we conduct and use early in the school year help us identify impediments and supports for individual students' learning. This information is critical to our understanding of students in relation to the different curricula that need to be learned across the school year, and to our tailoring of instruction to meet students when they encounter the obstacles that contribute to their struggling adolescent reader status.

At the beginning of the school year, or at the beginning of a student's entry into a specific reading program, we need formative assessment information that helps us understand the current level of student capability and student need. This information must be detailed, so that we can make initial decisions related to matching students with texts and related reading tasks of appropriate difficulty and content. We must have confidence that the "read" of the student that the assessment provides is accurate. This accuracy in assessment helps to ensure that our critical, initial work is well guided. Given the prior school experiences of many struggling adolescent readers, we must gather information on our students' attitudes and motivations. These data help us determine the challenges that students may interpret as possible, to overcome, and those activities that will evoke negative student response. We should also strive, at the beginning of the school year, to learn about our students as individuals. What do they do when not in school? What are their hobbies, or how do they spend time? What expertise do they possess? The answer to this question can figure largely in how we determine texts and reading tasks that place our struggling student readers in the best possible position to succeed.

Assessments during Instruction

Assessment conducted during the school year serves related and critical purposes. A primary use of this type of assessment is to help us define teachable moments—as students progress in their reading in general and as it applies to different content areas. Such teachable moments depend on the teacher's ability to identify the appropriate learning challenges for students, perhaps their understanding and using a critical reading strategy, or developing the ability to determine the meaning of unfamiliar vocabulary words. Assessment conducted during learning should focus, in part, on the students' zones of proximal development (Vygotsky, 1978). Attention to teachable moments and zones of proximal development represents our commitment to assessments that provide fine-grained details of students' progress. Assessment during the school year should also focus on students' progress in relation to curricular benchmarks. We need to know how a student is developing as a reader and how the reader is meeting grade-level goals for content-area learning.

Formative assessment can help us understand the details of students' learning, growth, and challenges throughout the year. We want this assessment to provide information related to students' reading level and the content-area learning covered, so we can refine both our understanding of the students and the appropriate instruction to provide them. Complementing our regular formative assessment are the quizzes and tests that describe student attainment of standards and learning goals in the content areas, including science, social studies, and language arts. At the start of the school year, we attended to students' affective and experiential lives, and our continued attention to these critical factors allows us to measure change or stasis in how struggling readers approach reading tasks, conceptualize themselves as readers, and take the initiative to read.

Assessments at the End of Instruction

Reading assessment conducted at the conclusion of the school year is, of course, the most dominant form of assessment. The focus on summative statements of what students can and cannot do is important as we seek to certify levels of accomplishment and to provide this type of evidence to demonstrate accountability. As noted earlier, schools in the United States share a strong focus on such summative assessments, with less attention given to the formative assessment that is necessary to help struggling adolescent readers meet daily, regular learning challenges and to provide their teachers with the means to do so. Given the argument for conceptualizing student readers broadly, we can appreciate the need to determine how students have changed affectively. A student who begins the school year as a timid and withdrawn reader and then finishes the year as an enthusiastic reader has changed, and this change represents important teaching and learning outcomes.

Our year-end (or program-end) assessments tilt toward the summative, as we seek to describe adequate yearly progress and how well we have performed as teachers at meeting the perennial challenge of helping struggling students succeed. We must also help them pick up the pace of learning in an effort to rejoin their classmates at some level of shared achievement. Summative assessments offer approximate measures of how much students have grown as readers, in terms of a grade-level equivalent score, a percentile ranking, or stanine. This information is essential for stakeholders such as parents, legislators, and taxpayers.

In summary, a comprehensive assessment program that is geared to helping struggling adolescent readers provides consistent and coordinated information throughout the school year. The program begins, at the start of the school year, with collecting baseline data on students' cognitive, affective, and experiential status. Initial information is collected and used to inform instruction, and formative assessment is conducted across the school year to consistently update teachers' mental models of their individual students' needs and accomplishments. This process contributes to accuracy in identifying and teaching to students' zones of proximal development and addressing students' affective needs. Finally, year-end assessment offers an opportunity to examine the sum of teacher and student achievements, in terms of reading development, content-area learning, and affect.

Portrait of a Struggling Adolescent Reader and a Suitable Assessment Program

This section provides a detailed example of assessment in the case of Tim, an eighth-grade reader, and his teacher, Liza. Tim is best characterized as a struggling and extremely reluctant reader. He can read with fluency and comprehension when texts are easy, typically in a range 3–4 years below his current grade. Unfortunately, the reading Tim must do for content-area classes is not adjusted to this level. Tim's reluctance to engage in reading makes it extremely difficult to envision a means for him to "get to grade level" in reading: Reading is a struggle and time to practice is nonexistent. Tim does manage to read high-interest, lower-reading-level books and can read with fluency when the text is simple enough. He can make inferences and his literal comprehension is satisfactory when the text content is familiar, but his comprehension is hindered by a distinct lack of reading comprehension strategies. Tim struggles to construct meaning from many of the content-area texts that he must read across the school year. He is far from being a critical reader in school, because he lacks reading strategies and prior knowledge that would allow him to question the text or render critical judgments about the quality of text. On the basis of his experience with reading and assessment, Tim is strategic in trying to figure out what a teacher might include on a quiz or test. When he can understand the assigned texts in school, he reads with "passing the test" as his sole goal.

A history of failure and struggle creates in Tim an avoidance of reading. His self-concept as a reader is in some respects accurate: He believes himself to be a poor reader, and this belief is regularly reinforced by the reality that he earns low grades and low test scores, that he cannot read many of the books his classmates read, and that he is shut out of conversations about books, magazines, and Internet texts that he cannot or will not read. Tim attributes his poor reading internally. He thinks of himself as a reader who will always struggle, because he thinks that he is, if not just slower then his classmates, stupid. These affective components are wound tightly within Tim, leading him to avoid required reading in school whenever possible and to ignore reading outside school, except when he finds accessible texts related to basketball and automobile racing.

How might an assessment program best provide Tim's teachers with information that can help them understand the exact nature of his needs, the powerful negative influence of his past failures in reading, and the possibility that his life interests represent for enhancing his reading? Figure 13.1 outlines the assessment approach taken by Tim's teacher, Liza. Figure 13.1 helps illustrate that Liza requires assessments that focus on cognitive skills and strategies, content-area learning, affective learner characteristics, and prior knowledge and experiences. In addition, Liza believes that a truly effective assessment system operates from the first to the last day of the school year. Critical information is gathered as the school year begins, as the weeks, units, months, and marking periods unfold, and as the school year is completed.

As the School Year Begins

What characterizes Tim as a struggling adolescent reader as the school year begins? There is a vast collection of possible influences on reading and reading achievement, and it is of utmost importance that we are able to determine, with specificity, these influences. An effective reading assessment program, therefore, includes materials and processes that help us situate the student in relation to our instructional goals, his or her current level of reading achievement, and factors that may influence this interface. Moreover, what we choose to assess prior to (or at the beginning of) instruction sets us up for follow-through assessments during and after our in-

	As student begins instruction	During instruction	As instruction is completed
Cognitive skills and strategies	Oral reading, retelling, and answering questions; information from prior school years	Teacher observation; questions; oral reading, retelling, and answering questions	Year-end reading test; year-end content-area tests
Content-area learning	Questions related to content to be learned	Questions; quizzes and unit tests; performance assessments	Unit, marking period, and semester comprehensive tests
Affective characteristics	Self-concept, attitude toward reading, and reading motivation questionnaires; information from prior school years	Teacher observation; discussions with student	Self-concept, attitude toward reading, and motivation to read questionnaires
Prior knowledge and experiences	Interest inventory; discussion with student, teacher observation; information from prior school years	Ongoing observations of student	Interest inventory

FIGURE 13.1. Assessment of struggling adolescent readers across the school year and across reader characteristics.

struction. Liza consults Tim's academic record, noting the insights of previous years' teachers. This initial information is then complemented by information gained from a reading inventory conducted in the first few weeks of school. The inventory provides data on Tim's text processing, his comprehension ability, and his sight-word vocabulary. Each of these is useful for Liza as she prepares her reading instruction.

Liza's observations of Tim at the beginning of the year help to triangulate her first impressions. For example, Tim's hesitancy to read in front of anyone is noted early on, and information from the *Reading Self-Concept Scale* (Chapman & Tunmer, 1995) provides further information about why Tim is so hesitant. An additional source of assessment information, the *Motivation to Read Profile* (Gambrell, Palmer, Codling & Mazzoni, 1996) identifies Tim as a student with generally low motivation to read, in school and out. Liza uses a reading interest inventory (Hildebrandt, 2001) to determine Tim's interests and to consider texts that might hold Tim's attention as he learns to be a better reader.

During the School Year

Liza regards her initial information about Tim as a first impression, always revisable on the basis of a high-quality formative assessment. As Tim progresses through the year, it is imperative that Liza continues to gather formative assessment information. Such assessments help Liza to identify and define teachable moments, tailor instruction to Tim's needs, and keep an ongoing record of Tim's reading profile. For example, Liza's close attention to Tim's oral reading of an article about NASCAR helps her identify Tim's need to develop metacognitive strategies: He reads through sentence boundaries and rarely understands that he has made a miscue. Liza combines the assessment information gained from listening to Tim read with the information provided by the interest inventory to identify both the need and the context in which she and Tim might work successfully toward his learning metacognitive strategies. This reflects the approach she takes throughout the school year—using assessment information to address immediate needs in the most conducive environment. Liza knows that accountability is measured by a single high stakes test on a single day, but it is accomplished by high-quality assessment that is conducted regularly throughout the school year. Adequate yearly progress is indicated by a test score, but it is achieved through expert assessment and teaching across the school year.

Throughout the school year, Liza strives to connect Tim's interest in automobile racing and basketball to lessons that focus on reading skills and strategies. She is a keen observer of the changes in Tim's motivation, and she notes that ongoing successes with particular skills and strategies fuel a shift in Tim's motivation. His experiences of success are cumulatively building his strategic reading repertoire and his positive motivation to read. The unit tests and quizzes that Tim must take in content-area courses also demonstrate the ongoing transformation of Tim as a reader. These summary statements of how well Tim learned the content of a unit on ecosystems, or how well he understands the concepts of the words *kingdom, revolution,* and *democracy,* indicate that progress in reading is influencing content-area learning. As Tim reads across the semester, Liza's attention is focused on different and related aspects of reading. These include near and far progress toward individual reading and curricular goals and attention to the cognitive and affective characteristics of becoming a better reader.

As the School Year Ends

Summative assessment serves several important purposes for Tim and Liza. Test results demonstrate that Tim is understanding, remembering, and using important information in science, social studies, math, and English.

The high-stakes test that is used to measure Tim's adequate yearly progress provides an opportunity to compare his reading achievement level at the end of seventh grade with his achievement level at the end of eighth grade. The important information provided by these summative assessments is complemented by assessment that documents the changes in Tim's motivation and engagement. Tim's self-concept as a reader and his motivation to read have changed, and in a positive direction. Moreover, it is clear that Tim's attributions for success and failure are undergoing a change—he has always been willing to take responsibility for learning (or not learning) in school. Now, however, he is attributing his reading outcomes to the amount of effort he puts into his work. This is an infinitely more positive attribution for Tim to make, as compared with the prior attributions for failure to lack of "smarts."

Liza works in a school in which district and administrative support for her comprehensive approach to reading assessment is evident. This support is critical as Liza and her colleagues plan assessment that is logical and connected. For example, Liza's use of reading inventories at the beginning of the year demands school resources. The school and district make decisions that are based on their support for such initial, detailed reading assessment.

Additional Challenges to the Meaningful Assessment of Struggling Adolescent Readers

Given our focus on assessment in school, it would be heartening if our assessment efforts resulted in a comprehensive and fine-grained account of how students are doing. Unfortunately, these efforts may not yield such comprehensive information. We can trace the possible shortcomings of assessment to several factors; many are related to the very structure of secondary schooling in the United States. First, teachers of adolescents typically work with large numbers of students on a daily basis. It is extremely difficult for a teacher to understand through assessment how each of 50, 100, or 150 students is developing in relation to cognitive skills and strategies, affect, and experience. Thus, as struggling students benefit from our detailed understanding of their reading, class size and time constraints may not make this possible.

The compartmentalization of curriculum across middle school and high school results in much assessment that is disconnected. Assessment in social studies, science, English language arts, or mathematics is frequently compartmentalized by content domain. This prevents the development of comprehensive accounts of students and their core needs, and such within-domain sets of assessment do not add up to a greater understanding of students' overall reading accomplishments or challenges.

As discussed elsewhere, there is a near total allocation of our assessment resources to summative assessments of cognitive skills and strategies. This creates a situation in which opportunities for developing effective programs that provide both formative and summative assessment information related to students' cognitive, affective, and experiential lives must compete with assessment systems that are mandated by federal law and require high levels of funding. Finally, the lion's share of assessment is focused on high-stakes testing (Afflerbach, 2002, 2005), for the main purposes of demonstrating annual yearly progress, certifying that a minimum has been learned, or making retention decisions.

Conclusions

In teaching struggling adolescent readers, there is no task more important than helping them to build ability and confidence in reading. Effective assessment plays a central role in providing information to teachers that helps them determine struggling readers' initial baseline performance levels and characteristics, define teachable moments and teachable content, and certify progress and accountability. Many teachers use assessment to gauge students' learning of the cognitive skills and strategies of reading. We must continue our focus on the cognitive aspects of reading, for without this we cannot help our students attain reading proficiency or plan for the meaningful inclusion of reading in their future lives. Within these efforts in assessment, we must incorporate attention to readers' affective and experiential lives.

The work of Tim and Liza illustrates that developing and using a comprehensive reading assessment program is a considerable challenge. This program must describe students' cognitive skills and strategies, their affective characteristics, and their prior knowledge and experience. It must also provide useful information as students begin each school year and each reading program, as they progress through school years and programs, and as they complete them. I cannot overstate the importance of helping struggling adolescent readers. A comprehensive and thoughtful assessment program provides us an opportunity to know our struggling readers. We can use this knowledge to address these students' needs and interests and help make reading, finally, a central and powerful force in their lives.

References

Afflerbach, P. (2002). The road to folly and redemption: Perspectives on the legitimacy of high stakes testing. *Reading Research Quarterly, 37*, 348–360.

Afflerbach, P. (2005). High stakes testing and reading assessment. *Journal of Literacy Research, 37*, 1–12.

Afflerbach, P. (2007). *Understanding and using reading assessment, K–12.* Newark, DE: International Reading Association.

Afflerbach, P., Pearson, P., & Paris, S. (in press). Clarifying differences between reading skills and reading strategies. *Reading Teacher.*

Black, P., & William, D. (1998). Inside the black box. *Phi Delta Kappan, 79*, 139–148.

Chapman, J., & Tunmer, W. (1995). Development of young children's reading self-concepts: An examination of emerging subcomponents and their relationship with reading achievement. *Journal of Educational Psychology, 87*, 154–167.

Coiro, J., & Dobler, B. (2007). Exploring the online comprehension strategies used by sixth-grade skilled readers to search for and locate information on the Internet. *Reading Research Quarterly, 42*, 214–257.

Crooks, T. (1988). The impact of classroom evaluation on students. *Review of Educational Research, 58*, 438–481.

Dweck, C. (1999). *Self theories: Their role in motivation, personality and development.* Philadelphia: Psychology Press.

Gambrell, L., Palmer, B., Codling, R., & Mazzoni, S. (1996). *Motivation to read profile (MRP).* Athens, GA: National Reading Research Center.

Gonzalez, N., Moll, L., & Amanti, C. (2004). *Funds of knowledge: Theorizing practices in households and classrooms.* Mahwah, NJ: Erlbaum.

Guthrie, J., & Wigfield, A. (1997). *Reading engagement: Motivating readers through integrated instruction.* Newark, DE: International Reading Association.

Hart, B., & Risley, T. (1995). *Meaningful differences in the everyday experiences of young American children.* Baltimore: Brookes.

Heath, S. (1983). *Ways with words: Language, life and work in communities and classrooms.* New York: Cambridge University Press.

Hildebrandt, D. (2001, Fall). But there's nothing good to read (in the library media center). *Media Spectrum: The Journal for Library Media Specialists in Michigan*, 34–37.

McKenna, M., & Kear, D. (1990). Measuring attitude towards reading: A new tool for teachers. *Reading Teacher, 43*, 626–639.

National Center for Education Statistics. (2005). *2009 NAEP reading framework.* Washington, DC: Author.

National Institute of Child Health and Human Development. (2000). *Report of the National Reading Panel: Teaching children to read: An evidence-based assessment of the scientific research literature on reading and its implications for reading instruction.* Washington, DC: U.S. Government Printing Office.

Pressley, M., & Afflerbach, P. (1995). *Verbal reports of reading: The nature of constructively responsive reading.* Hillsdale, NJ: Erlbaum.

Snow, C. (2002). *Reading for understanding: Toward an R&D program in reading comprehension.* Washington, DC: Rand Corporation.

Stanovich, K. (1986). Matthew effects in reading: Some consequences of individual differences in the acquisition of literacy. *Reading Research Quarterly, 21*, 360–407.

Stiggins, R., & Conklin, N. (1992). *In teachers' hands: Investigating the practice of classroom assessment.* Albany: State University of New York Press.

Veenman, M. (2005). The assessment of metacognitive skills: What can be learned from multi-method designs? In C. Artelt & B. Moschner (Eds.), *Learning strategies and metacognition: Implications for research and practice* (pp. 75–97). Berlin: Waxman.

Vygotsky, L. (1978). *Mind in society: The development of higher psychological processes.* Cambridge, MA: Harvard University Press.

CHAPTER 14

Literacy Coaching at the Middle School/High School Levels

Rita Bean

U ntil recently, efforts to improve the reading achievement of adolescents were focused primarily on those students who were struggling with basic reading skills and required instruction from a reading specialist. Although the need for remedial programs of this type may still exist at the middle and high school levels, educators have begun to realize that a different type of intervention is warranted: specifically, instruction in content-area classrooms that helps struggling readers understand subject-area material. Instruction in these disciplines requires all teachers to have a sense of how they can most effectively engage students, using instructional techniques related to how students' interact with print, electronic, and visual media. Toward this end, literacy coaching has become an integral part of professional development efforts in middle and high schools.

Content teachers, such as teachers of English, science, social studies, and mathematics, must have the knowledge and the understanding that enable them to both address specific content demands and to "teach literacy in their disciplines as an essential way of learning" (National Council of Teachers of English [NCTE], 2004). This includes being able to:

Provide materials that meet the needs and interests of students;
Recognize when students are experiencing difficulty and provide strategic instruction;

Facilitate conversations about text; and

Develop environments that allow students to engage in discussions of texts in which they critically examine what they are reading (NCTE, 2004).

In order to help middle and high school teachers meet these demands, many schools are hiring literacy coaches to work collaboratively with content teachers to improve instruction for all students, and especially those who struggle with reading.

Content-area instructors are experts in their respective fields; however, many do not have a background in or knowledge of literacy instruction. Traditionally, preservice teachers seeking certification in a content field have been required to take one course that addresses reading across the content areas as part of their preservice program. Too often these content experts do not realize that by providing instruction that facilitates reading and writing, they enable students to better grasp the contents of their disciplines (Readance, Bean, & Baldwin, 2004). After all, shouldn't students have learned to read in the primary grades? Or isn't there a reading specialist who can handle students with "reading problems"?

Fortunately, there is increasing recognition that helping students to effectively use the textbook of a discipline as a means of learning *is* a responsibility of content-area teachers (Biancarosa & Snow, 2004). Indeed, students need certain literacy skills to comprehend content effectively and to become independent learners—hence, the literacy coach. Findings from the field of professional development provide evidence that the best form of ongoing education for teachers is that which is job embedded (American Educational Research Association [AERA], 2005; National Staff Development Council [NSDC], 2001). Teachers appreciate and value that which is related to their work and to the students they teach. Joyce and Showers (2002), in fact, talk about four activities important in any professional development program. First, with any new educational initiative or innovation, teachers must be introduced to the theory that supports the initiative so that they understand the rationale for implementation. They also need to be shown how such an innovation works (e.g., to see a demonstration). Often such a demonstration is done with peers, using a video, or with a small group. Further, teachers benefit when they practice on their own. Finally, as Joyce and Showers (2002) note, it is coaching with feedback that produces the desired effect—transfer to classroom practice. The work of Joyce and Showers and subsequent efforts of various researchers and evaluators (Coggins, Stoddard, & Cutler, 2003; Feldman & Tung, 2002; Neufeld & Roper, 2003; Poglinco et al., 2003) have led to various initiatives or projects in which literacy coaches are serving as a primary means of improving the classroom practices of teachers.

This chapter focuses on several features of literacy coaching at the middle/secondary school level, including what coaches might be responsible for doing and how their responsibilities differ from those at the elementary level. Several middle and high school coaching initiatives are described to illustrate models that are being implemented, along with a vignette of a daily schedule of a literacy coach. Guidelines are also suggested for those who find themselves in a coaching position at those levels.

Defining Literacy Coaching at the Middle/Secondary School Levels

It is not difficult for individuals thinking about school personnel to visualize the role of a teacher, a principal, or a guidance counselor; however, the role of "literacy coach" is somewhat more difficult to describe. In *The Literacy Coach's Handbook*, Walpole and McKenna (2004) describe a literacy coach as "a learner, a grant writer, a planner, a researcher, and a teacher who directs continual school improvement work at the state, district and school levels" (p. 20). Costa and Garmston (2002) address coaching more broadly and explain that the purpose of coaching is "to convey a valued colleague from where he or she is to where he or she wants to be" (p. 21). Toll (2005) has a similar definition, suggesting that a literacy coach is "one who helps teachers to recognize what they know and can do, assists teachers as they strengthen their ability to make more effective use of what they know and do, and supports teachers as they learn more and do more." (p. 4). A review of the literature and research supports the following assumptions about literacy coaching:

1. *Literacy coaching is a form of professional development that is job embedded, ongoing, and related to specific needs of teachers and their students.* This view of literacy coaching requires coaches to build relationships with teachers and to personalize efforts in terms of content pedagogy and process. For example, coaches may work with teachers on such instructional content as vocabulary (how to introduce new words or provide rich experiences) or questioning skills (using high-level questioning). At the same time, coaches can differentiate how they work with teachers. With one teacher, a coach may co-plan and co-teach; with another, the coach may observe classroom practices and provide feedback. Coaching can be either one-to-one or group oriented. A literacy coach may meet with teachers from a specific discipline or content area to develop awareness of specific strategies especially useful for them, such as meeting with social studies teachers interested in learning how to help their students learn to use maps, globes, and other graphic tools. Or they may meet with teachers

across disciplines to discuss strategies useful to all, such as reinforcing vocabulary instruction so that students build a deep understanding of words important to specific content learning. Coaches may also meet with all teachers at a grade level to talk about the achievement test results of students at that level and how those results should influence classroom instruction. Figure 14.1 identifies and defines the possible activities that a literacy coach might use in working with teachers.

2. *Literacy coaching is an interactive process, or a form of inquiry, that occurs between a coach and an individual or between a coach and a group of individuals.* Conversations are an important element of coaching. It is essential for coaches to understand how to communicate effectively. The coach must be a good listener who is able to question and respond to questions appropriately. Likewise, the coach must be able to "frame" suggestions or comments in a collegial, nonthreatening manner. Although some teachers appreciate direct suggestions about how to improve instruction, others may resent such directness from the coach and may value a more collaborative, problem-solving approach to discussions about instruction.

3. *Literacy coaching occurs in a cultural context, and there are various features that must be in place if coaching is to be successful.* Specifically, coaches must have the support of the principal in the school. Likewise, that administrator must have an understanding of what the coach should and should not be asked to do. For instance, coaching will not be effective if administrators misuse the coach, relying on the coach to cover classes or study halls or to handle administrative tasks. Further, coaching will not be effective if administrators dismiss the work of a coach as "irrelevant" or unneeded. The research on educational leadership highlights the importance of the principal in setting the tone for school improvement (Spillane & Louis, 2002). In effective schools, all personnel see the need for making instructional improvements and value the support that comes from coaching (Fullan, 2001; Taylor, Pearson, Peterson, & Rodriguez, 2005).

4. *Literacy coaching is an effort to build school capacity and to promote school change.* The literacy coach's role is to support teachers and administrators, all of whom are attempting to improve instruction and, ultimately, student learning in the school. As part of building school capacity, coaches support teacher learning that results in improved classroom practices. At the same time, they encourage and support teacher leadership. Successful coaches recognize that much can be learned from the teachers with whom they work. These coaches work collaboratively with teachers in analyzing data, problem solving, and deciding on the next steps for helping students learn. In order for coaches to serve as change agents, they must work with all teachers in the school, from those who may need specific assistance for improving instruction to those who should be recognized for the excellent work they are doing.

Co-planning. Meeting with a teacher to plan a lesson that could be taught by that teacher or with the coach.

Co-teaching. Coach teaches a group along with the classroom teacher. This activity is undertaken primarily to enhance teachers' knowledge of specific approaches or strategies, but can also assist teachers in differentiating instruction for students. (Example: Teacher and coach co-teach a lesson introducing vocabulary of a new history unit; teacher introduces the unit, using a concept map. Coach then talks about the key vocabulary words, asks a student to self-assess how familiar he or she is with the word by completing a self-awareness check sheet. This sheet is used again at the end of the unit.)

Meetings with groups. Leading or participating in meetings. Includes curriculum meetings, study groups, and so forth. (Example: Coach may meet with grade-level teachers to discuss assessment data and how the results should be used to modify instruction.)

Modeling/demonstrating. Demonstrating specific strategies or procedures to help teachers better understand how to use them in the classroom. (Example: Coach models how to do a jigsaw activity for the psychology teacher, who wants students to discuss a specific article they have read.)

Planning and organizing. Preparing a model lesson, co-teaching, or organizing/obtaining materials for a specific teacher or teachers. (Example: Coach locates materials for the foreign language teacher, who wants to have students read a novel about the culture of a country in which Spanish is the native language.)

Assessing students. Coach assesses students, as a means of helping the teacher better understand students' strengths and needs. (Example: Coach does an informal reading inventory with a ninth grader, new to the school, who seems to be having much difficulty with reading in several classes).

Instructing students. Coach teaches a group of students, to provide the reading instruction they need (often for a short-term period). This can occur in the classroom or on a pull-out basis. The focus is on providing specific instruction for students. (Example: Coach is responsible for teaching a group of students identified as those who would have difficulty with the state assessment scheduled for the following month. Coach works with students on test-taking strategies during their study hall period.)

Outreach work. Coaches often work with outside agencies or with efforts to involve parents in various school activities. (Examples: Coach meets with student teachers from a nearby university to help them understand the literacy

(continued)

FIGURE 14.1. Activities of literacy coaches.

focus of the high school and to discuss strategies they can use in their instruction. Coach conducts a book club for parents and students, in which they discuss a specific novel that has been read by the group.)

Visiting classrooms. Coach observes in the classrooms as a means of learning more about how instruction is being provided. Generally, this includes three steps: a preconference with the teacher to set a goal for the observation, the actual observation, and a postconference in which the teacher and coach meet to discuss what was seen. (Example: Teacher asks coach to observe how he or she is conducting a discussion group: Is the teacher involving all students? What is the nature of the questioning? Coach discusses the focus of the observation, observes, and then holds a debriefing meeting in which coach and teacher discuss what was seen. Most frequently, there is follow-up to this that includes other coaching activities.)

Conducting professional development sessions. Coach provides information and involves teachers in various activities about a specific topic or a set of strategies. (Example: Coach is responsible for planning and leading a professional development day, which is focused on improving comprehension of students in all content areas.)

Participating in one's own professional growth. Coaches attend meetings to increase their knowledge and understanding of literacy instruction and assessment, or how to coach effectively or meet with other coaches or mentors. (Example: Coach attends meetings about how to use data for instructional decision making.)

Performing administrative tasks. Coaches document coaching efforts, work with scheduling, arrange visits for educators.

FIGURE 14.1. *(continued)*

To accomplish this role, coaches must understand the dynamics of school change. In their discussion of school change, Hall and Hord (1987) note that the concerns of those involved in change efforts transition from an awareness level (little concern about or involvement with the innovation) through concerns about self (how will this affect me?) to task concerns (how to do this) to impact concerns (how will this affect students?). These stages are evident in the responses teachers give to coaches when asked how they (the teachers) might address literacy issues as part of their instructional practices (see Figure 14.2). Coaches must understand that because teachers are at various stages, they must differentiate the ways in which they work with individual teachers. Teachers will respond if coaching is adjusted to meet their needs and interests.

Awareness level: This has no relevance for me. My focus is on the ability of my students to meet my expectations and learn all they can in my U.S. history course. Of course, they can't read the book, but I hold their attention when I lecture and they do take notes. I just can't use the textbook! Are there really ways you can help me to do that?

Concerns about self: Well, I'm not certain whether I can put them in groups. It seems as though it will take a lot of time—and what will they actually learn? I'm really not accustomed to group work in my classroom.

Task concerns: Okay, you convinced me that this group work has some merit if I structure it carefully and provide guidance. But I'm not really sure how to do this. What do you mean by "Think, Pair, Share"? Won't it be too noisy? Can you help me think about the kinds of tasks I should give my students? How do I structure the activities—and what activities are available?

Impact concerns: How can we gather information that will help me determine what the students have learned? I'd like to see how this works with this lively group of 10th graders. I know it's hard to get their attention, and I must admit that I've seen a difference in their motivation to learn. It's been great to have them ask questions and raise issues. But are they learning as well or even more?

FIGURE 14.2. Examples of levels of concern.

5. *Coaching is cooperative, collaborative, and collegial.* Although the first four assumptions hint at the importance of collaboration, this assumption is so important that it needs to be mentioned specifically. Coaches who are seen as functioning in a monitoring, evaluating, or supervising role will not be successful as coaches. The coaching role does put the coach in a somewhat unusual position in a school—neither administrator nor classroom teacher. Success requires coaches to build relationships with teachers so that they can work together on concerns. As a high school coach once said to me, "Acting as an evaluator will kill you." Although this statement is true for coaches at all levels, it is probably even more relevant at the middle and high school levels where the teachers see their major responsibility as facilitating students' learning of content and concepts in a specific discipline (e.g., science, social studies, math). It is the coach's role to help content experts understand how literacy instruction can be integrated into their teaching repertoires and actually aid them in achieving their goals.

All of these assumptions place the literacy coach in a central position in middle and high schools. Although coaches may at times work with students to help them understand how to prepare for a state assessment test, or with parents to provide advice about how they can support their children's learning, their key role is to support teachers' understanding of how to provide effective instruction that takes advantage of the teachers' knowledge of content and the coaches' understanding of how various literacy instructional strategies can augment and facilitate instruction. This is especially important when teachers have concerns about how to meet the needs of those students who struggle to read the content textbook or who have difficulty completing assignments that require extensive reading or writing.

Unique Features of Literacy Coaching in Middle and Secondary Schools

Although there is much that is similar about coaching at all the grade levels, there are also some differences between coaching at the elementary and the upper grades. First and foremost, teachers at the upper levels may not be as knowledgeable about literacy instruction, and unlike teachers at the primary level, they do not see literacy as their primary responsibility. Moreover, middle and high school teachers may be working with 120 or more students a day, unlike teachers at the elementary level who may have fewer than 30 students in their classrooms. Coaches working at the middle or secondary levels, therefore, may need to spend more time developing the rationale for integrating literacy into content-area instruction and establishing the relevance of such instruction. They may also have to provide background knowledge about literacy assessment and instruction to assist teachers in understanding how such instruction can be an integral part of classroom practices.

The other distinguishing feature of coaching at the middle and secondary levels has to do with the knowledge and skills essential for effective coaching. At the elementary level, many literacy coaches come to their positions with an in-depth understanding of literacy instruction and assessment; some have reading specialist certification and others are seasoned literacy teachers. At the middle and secondary levels, the literacy coach has to have that same in-depth understanding of literacy and, in addition, be knowledgeable about content-area demands. The *Standards for Middle and High School Literacy Coaches* (International Reading Association [IRA], 2006) developed by the IRA in collaboration with the NCTE, National Council of Teachers of Mathematics (NCTM), National Science Teachers Association, and the National Council for the Social Studies, provides excellent insights about coaching at those levels. The authors indicate that the document "represents an ideal" (p. 5); coaching standards are divided into two parts—leadership standards and content-area literacy standards. The leadership standards apply to coaching across all content areas, and the content-area literacy standards are specific to the demands of the various content areas. The successful coach, at the middle and secondary levels, must recognize that although there may be some "generic" strategies that can be used across disciplines, each content area has demands specific to that discipline. Students must learn to read science texts like a scientist, social studies text like a historian, and so on.

This need to understand the demands of the disciplines is one that has important implications for those selecting, as well as those wanting to be, literacy coaches. Teachers often ask whether coaches should be reading specialists. Certainly, literacy coaches must have the knowledge and skills identified in the position statement of the IRA (International Reading Association, 2004). And although reading specialist certification is the ideal or the "gold standard" (Frost & Bean, 2006), coaches at the middle and high school levels often gain their understanding of literacy assessment and instruction from the professional development provided as part of the literacy initiative in the school. For example, in the Pennsylvania High School Coaching Initiative (PAHSCI; n.d.), coaches learn about effective literacy instruction by participating in professional development provided by the Penn Literacy Network (n.d.). They are also provided with a mentor who meets with them monthly. In such cases, coaches may be especially strong teachers from one of the content areas who are willing to learn essential literacy skills and competencies. The potential coach brings strong content knowledge to the table and supplements that with professional development in literacy instruction. The reverse can be true as well. A coach who is a reading specialist and brings deep knowledge about literacy instruction and assessment to the position, can learn more about content demands by working with the content teacher to gain an understanding of how content and literacy demands can be meshed. Again, the "ideal" is an individual who has reading specialist certification, the ability to work well with adults, leadership skills, and an understanding of the various content fields and their demands. In May 2006, the Board of the IRA passed a resolution that reiterated its position on the importance of reading specialist certification for the "highly qualified" literacy coach. We do need empirical evidence, however, about how the qualifications of coaches affect what they do and how they do it. We also need to be certain that coaches receive the professional development and ongoing support they need in order to function effectively.

Examples of Coaching at the Middle/High School Levels

In this section two different models are offered to illustrate the diversity in how coaching can be implemented in schools. Certainly, there are other models or initiatives that are occurring across the country. These two, however, demonstrate some of the similarities and differences that exist.

Pennsylvania High School Coaching Initiative (PAHSCI)

The PAHSCI coaching initiative, launched by the Annenberg Foundation and the Pennsylvania Department of Education in 2005–2006, is a 3-year initiative that places one literacy and one math coach for every 600 students in 26 high-need high schools in Pennsylvania. Other partners in this effort are the University of Pennsylvania's Penn Literacy Network, Foundations, Inc., Research for Action, and the Philadelphia Foundation. The program goals, similar to those of other models, include improving student performance and preparing students for the workforce through literacy, training teachers as coaches, developing professional communities of learners, building capacity in Pennsylvania for sustainability and expansion of the model, and generating a research base of effective job-embedded professional development for instructional coaching. Some of the key dimensions of this project include a strong literacy framework that supports coaching, training, and mentoring for coaches and an emphasis on working with leadership in the schools. Additional information about PAHSCI can be found at *www.pacoaching.org*.

Qualifications of Coaches

The Pennsylvania Department of Education wrote a job description based on the Standards draft document written by NCTE/IRA. Each district selected its own coaches; some leeway was provided, given the difficulties in finding individuals who met qualifications or who wanted to serve in such a role. The project leaders wanted coaches who had excellent interpersonal skills and strong content knowledge and who saw themselves as leaders, and as learners (personal conversation with Ellen Eisenberg, Executive Director, PAHSCI, March 20, 2007).

Training for Coaches

Coaches and school leaders attended a total of 9 days of professional development work related to academic literacy and coaching during the summer and early fall months. Professional development related to literacy was provided by the Penn Literacy Network (PLN, n.d.), and Foundations, Inc., provided training in the area of instructional coaching and mentoring. Coaches and principals also received ongoing technical support throughout the year from mentors, who visited each district four times a month, and in three networking sessions per year. Three mentors were assigned to each school: One was assigned to work with the literacy coach, another with the math coach. The third mentor worked with the principal and other administrators to help them understand the key roles of coaches and to serve as a buffer when coaches were experiencing difficulties. These mentors also participated in and facilitated the professional development training for coaches.

Role of the Coach

The coaches in PAHSCI schools facilitate in-class coaching and modeling, peer collaboration, and teacher training in order to improve teaching and learning at their schools. They work with teachers in one-on-one coaching, in small-group collaboration, and with whole groups that focus on a specific topic or issue. They begin by helping teachers understand the goals of the initiative and what the coaches' role might be. The emphasis is on working as partners with teachers to help students learn. Coaches implement a B, D, A (before, during, and after) model of coaching: They co-plan *before* the coaching session, at which time teachers and coaches decide the focus of the coaching session; they visit in classrooms and either co-teach, model, or watch the teacher practice his or her craft; and coaches and teachers debrief *after* the classroom visitation to discuss areas of strengths and areas of need. Together, coaches and teachers prioritize the areas of focus and collaboratively decide how to approach the identified needs. Although a school working in this project has made a commitment to schoolwide involvement, PAHSCI leaders suggest that coaches begin with those teachers who are most interested and willing to work with a coach. Administrators and coaches are discouraged from focusing on resistant teachers. The coach, who is a peer of the teachers, is not to be seen as an evaluator; the emphasis is on collegiality and collaboration.

Research Efforts

The project has a comprehensive approach to evaluation (PAHSCI, n.d.). Qualitative data are being collected that help to explain student achievement, participant knowledge and practice, and changes in school culture and capacity. Quantitative data are also being analyzed to determine the extent of implementation of coaching interventions and to relate this to achievement gains.

Collaborative Coaching and Learning

The Collaborative Coaching and Learning (CCL) initiative began in 1996 in Boston and has evolved over time (CCL, n.d.). Initially, teacher involvement was voluntary, and coaches were usually in a school only 1 day each week. Given some dissatisfaction with the efficiency of this initial approach, changes were made in the initiative.

Leaders of the CCL were influenced by Lucy Calkin's work with Readers' and Writers' Workshop, especially the notion of teachers learning together. The initiative is implemented in elementary, middle, and high schools in Boston, where a cohort of either grade-level, departmental, or interdisciplinary teachers, meets weekly for 9 weeks for about 2 hours each week. The cohort group members, working with a coach, develop a course of study, setting goals for themselves. They talk about what they are reading, construct model lessons, and demonstrate these in a lab setting. Most frequently, the coach models first, after which any teacher may volunteer to demonstrate a model lesson which is observed by cohort members. The observation is preceded by a conference and followed by a meeting at which teachers and coach debrief about what was observed. The coach is also available to meet individually with teachers in the cohort as they try new strategies. At the end of the 9-week cycle, new teachers are identified to begin a new cycle. Although there is provision for one-on-one coaching, the inquiry and lab periods require the teachers and coach to work collaboratively.

Qualifications of Coaches

Potential CCL coaches are required to write an analysis of a videotaped classroom lesson and to submit a writing sample. They need to have a minimum of 3 years of teaching experience, a knowledge of literacy, understanding of test data, and demonstrated leadership abilities to mentor teachers and lead professional development activities.

Training of Coaches

New coaches enroll in a course that is offered every fall. They conduct periodic professional self-assessments to identify their needs and then set goals to address targeted areas. Coaches also receive 15 hours of professional development in literacy each month. They are mentored on a regular basis by district personnel and provided feedback about their work.

Role of Coaches

As mentioned previously, in the CCL model coaches both conduct collaborative (group) coaching and provide one-on-one support to teachers. They assist the cohort of teachers in collaboratively selecting a focus for the 9-week course of study, often by analyzing school data. The inquiry sessions, facilitated by coaches, are discussions about the readings and lessons developed by teachers. Coaches and teachers co-construct lessons, and coaches demonstrate the initial lessons until teachers feel comfortable teaching in the lab setting.

Research

The CCL has been evaluated extensively over time by evaluators from Education Matters, a not-for-profit firm specializing in evaluation studies about school reform and change. In their Report of Year II, Neufeld and Roper (2003) indicated that the CCL was seen as a valuable model of professional development. They found that over time there were increases in teachers' participation in determining the focus of their work and in reflecting on both their own teaching and that of others. Some teachers were still resistant to teach in front of their colleagues, but there has been an increase in the establishment of a collaborative culture in the schools. According to Neufeld (2006), there are still challenges to be addressed, specifically, the inconsistency in implementation of CCL across the district. More information about CCL can be found at *www.literacycoachingonline.org/programs/database/1166834992.html*.

The two models described here illustrate some of the differences that can exist in the way in which literacy coaching is implemented in schools. In both models, however, one sees an emphasis on a literacy framework (beliefs or assumptions about literacy learning), and there are guidelines about coach qualifications, procedures for how coaches are to work with teachers, and a comprehensive evaluation plan that enables the districts or schools to learn from what they are doing. Although only two coaching models are described, there are many more such models. The website *www.literacycoachingonline.org* provides other examples and sources that may be helpful to those interested in literacy coaching at the secondary levels. The vignette in Figure 14.3 describes a hypothetical day in the life of a literacy coach and, indeed, is a compilation of what several literacy coaches have shared about how they spent their days. Each coach has said that there is no typical day.

Guidelines for Coaching: Advice from the Field

There are many excellent books and articles written by those who have studied coaching and by those who have been coaches themselves. A list of these resources and some websites that may be helpful to those interested in coaching at the middle and high school levels appears at the end of this chapter in Appendix 14.1. Below are several essential guidelines that come from coaches in the field with whom I have worked, and from my own

7:30 A.M. Met with ninth-grade English teacher to finish the co-planning for the lesson to be co-taught in second period. Focus on writing group summaries. Teacher indicates that there are three students who are reading "way below" grade level and have trouble reading the text. Coach and teacher agree to use "collaborative" grouping so that these struggling readers can work with both average and proficient readers.

8:00 A.M. Gathered materials; checked e-mail; reviewed schedule.

Period 1. Met with ELLs (English language learners) teacher who wants to work on writing with her students. She is concerned that these students have some technical writing problems; in addition, they don't seem to see the value of writing. Coach agrees to come into the class to do a model lesson on why writing is important and how it can help students learn more effectively. (Teacher and coach agree that this would be a first step in helping students improve their writing skills.) Lesson to be taught on Wednesday.

Period 2. Co-taught lesson on writing group summaries in ninth grade English class. Students had just finished reading *I Know Why the Caged Bird Sings* by Maya Angelou. Teacher leads a whole-class discussion about the book, focusing on individuals' reactions to the text. Then coach talks to students about what a summary is and what makes an effective summary. He then asks students to work in collaborative groups of four to write a summary of their reading. Their goal is to write a summary that would encourage others to read the text. The plan is for students to share their summaries in tomorrow's class. Coach and teacher walk from group to group, interacting and making suggestions. Coach takes notes about the type of work being done by the three students who have some reading difficulties. Notices that in two of the groups, the students are able to actively participate, whereas in the third group, the struggling reader is a nonparticipant.

Period 3. Meeting with business education teacher who wants to do a unit on entrepreneurs. Discuss ways in which the teacher can introduce new vocabulary to the students. Teacher recognizes that all students in that particular class need additional instruction with vocabulary concepts if they are going to be able to read assigned materials. Coach and teacher decide on the use of a concept map to introduce vocabulary and then to have a self-choice activity (students are to identify six words and find definitions). Teacher and coach co-plan the lesson. Business education teacher indicates she wants to try this out and then will let the coach know what happens.

Period 4. Lunch and informal chat with the principal about the professional development day to be held the following week. Principal and coach discuss

(continued)

FIGURE 14.3. A day in the life of a Sam, a high school literacy coach. (Subtitle: There is no typical day!)

plans that require the coach to lead a session on how teachers can promote active engagement in the classroom. Principal believes that the teachers are having difficulty moving from a whole-class, lecture approach to more small-group, differentiated instruction. Principal is committed to the overall emphasis on incorporating literacy into the various content areas.

Period 5. Group meeting with a small team of volunteer teachers from various content areas (English, foreign language, algebra, and psychology) who are interested in lesson study. Coach provides soft drinks and cookies, and teachers come in eager for the chance to talk and relax. These volunteers have agreed to have their lessons videotaped and discuss the logistics of this planning. They also set the ground rules in regard to who sees the tape and how it is to be used. The time goes quickly because teachers are eager to talk about what they will do during this videotaping and subsequent discussion about the lesson.

Period 6. Coach has a debriefing meeting with the English teacher with whom he taught this morning. Coach and teacher agree that the discussion portion of class went well. Students were reflective and able to identify important aspects of the book. Coach and teacher were also pleased with the ways the students worked in small groups; they were actively involved, except for the one student. Coach suggests that the teacher do some regrouping; in addition, teacher and coach decided to talk to the counselor about this student to get more information. Coach and teacher were concerned that the students were experiencing difficulty in writing summaries. They decided that they could best help students think about effective summaries by asking students to write their summaries on overhead transparencies; this would be followed by a class discussion about why the various pieces were examples of good summaries and how each could be improved. Teacher asks coach to lead that discussion and indicates that she would interject when it seemed necessary or appropriate. Teacher indicates that she is appreciative of coach's willingness to work through this with her.

Period 7. Coach goes back to his office; checks e-mail and messages (has one from a parent of a struggling reader and three from various teachers who want to see him). He quickly organizes materials for the following day and then goes to the classrooms of the three teachers with his calendar to schedule times to see them.

After school. Coach goes through his resources to locate materials for the foreign language teacher, who is excited about using some new vocabulary strategies. Coach realizes that he needs to take some materials home to begin planning for the professional development day.

FIGURE 14.3. *(continued)*

work as a researcher and as an external coach, working with teachers in the field.

Guideline 1: Identify What Is Non-Negotiable

One of the difficulties that often arise is that coaches, teachers, and administrators are not certain about the role of a coach. Should a coach work with students, as well as with teachers? How and how often? Can administrators assign coaches to study hall or bus duty? With which teachers should the coach work? How does the coach communicate with the principal and what information is communicated? Although the answers to these questions may differ somewhat depending on the specific program, there should be some "musts" that are identified and communicated to all in the school, if possible, before coaching is implemented. In some programs, coaches are never assigned to work with students on an ongoing basis, although they often work with students when they are modeling or co-teaching. In others, a coach may have teaching responsibilities for part of the day. There needs to be a clear understanding of what a coach's responsibilities are.

Moreover, because coaches are generally considered to be "teachers," they may be assigned "typical" duties of teachers. Coaches, however, should not be pulled into full-day service such as substitute teaching for an absent teacher, just because they seem to have flexible time. If ground rules are established before it begins, the coaching program has a better chance of being effective and school personnel have a clearer understanding of what coaches are to do—and not do.

Guideline 2: Take Time to Develop Relationships Built on Trust

The role of coach is an ambiguous one. Generally, classroom teachers do their work behind closed doors, or in what could be called a culture of isolation. If they experience instructional or management problems, they can ask their peers or an administrator for advice. Literacy coaches, therefore, must establish themselves as members of the school community and help teachers understand how they can support teachers' efforts. Too often, teachers are not certain of how to work with a coach. An initial step is to discuss the existing possibilities or options for a coach—serving as a resource, helping teachers solve problems, and providing specific feedback about aspects of classroom instruction. One teacher who spoke positively about the coach in her school stated, "We talked about the possibility of my using a novel in my French class and how I could do this. I was really excited. By the following Tuesday, I had the books I needed in my classroom. She is a gem!" Several of the following guidelines provide specific ideas for building trust.

Guideline 3: Offer Opportunities for Choice

Although it is tempting for coaches to want to make decisions about instructional goals, and how to address them, giving teachers opportunities to identify their own needs, using available data or other information, creates a more collegial relationship that may enable them to work more effectively with each other. Moreover, the teacher who has identified the goals or needs may be more inclined to follow through with implementing specific strategies. Choice is important.

Guideline 4: Confidentiality Is a Key to Success

Although coaches can hear and see many things as they work with teachers, they must not discuss with others any aspect of what they know. For example, coaches cannot participate in talk in the teachers' lounge about a teacher's difficult students or the teacher's difficulty with students. The only time that coaches should talk about the experiences of a specific teacher is when they ask that teacher for permission to share his or her good work.

Coaches who have accepted positions in schools in which they have taught often find it difficult to maintain this confidentiality. After all, they have been working as teacher colleagues. As coaches, however, they should not share information about what they have seen in classrooms with other teachers or with administrators. Likewise, coaches should not share with teachers confidential information that has been discussed in meetings with administrators. In fact, as one coach said, "You are in no-man's-land. You can't talk to teachers and you can't talk to administrators. Thank goodness for the other coach!"

Guideline 5: Coaches Are Not Evaluators; Rather, They Are There to Provide Support

As already mentioned, coaching is not an evaluative activity. Coaches are in the schools to facilitate student learning by supporting teachers' instruction. Because administrators may not understand the role of a coach, they may ask coaches to make judgments about the teaching of specific teachers. Likewise, if coaches see problematic instruction, they may want to talk about it with an administrator. Such interactions will quickly change the coaching dynamics. Coaches and administrators must recognize early on that a coach's role will be severely diminished if such interactions occur. It is the administrator's role to evaluate instruction; coaches are there to support teachers in their work. This does not mean that coaches do not talk with administrators about the "general" curriculum or instructional need for improving a specific aspect of literacy instruction. Certainly, coaches will need the support of the administration if they want to schedule a general meeting to discuss ways to improve questioning skills or to address the need for active engagement in the classrooms. But coaches should not identify specific teachers who may have difficulties; they should instead focus on the needs of a grade level or a content field. Cathy Toll's article, "Separating Coaching from Supervising" (2004) offers more specifics about the difference between coaching and supervision and can be beneficial for coaches as well as school administrators.

Guideline 6: Work with All Teachers

All teachers, even the very best, can benefit from interacting with another adult about instruction. Sometimes excellent teachers need the positive recognition that comes from such interaction. At other times, these excellent teachers are excited about the opportunity to try some new strategies to become even more effective. While I was visiting a high school in the PAHSCI project, a teacher mentioned that the coach had made all the difference and commented, "I wasn't totally burned out, but I was crinkly around the edges. Now I'm really excited about teaching." By working with all teachers, literacy coaches avoid being identified as individuals who are there to "fix" the poor teachers. When a coach works with teachers who are seen by their peers as excellent teachers, other teachers may be more comfortable expressing a willingness to collaborate with the coach.

Guideline 7: Begin with the Willing

Although coaches want to eventually work with all teachers, a coach who is new to a school or the position should begin by working with volunteers. There is so much to learn about the school and the various content areas, that beginning with volunteer teachers enables coaches to "test their wings." Success with volunteers often creates an interest and willingness in others to become involved. During the initial stages of coaching, coaches need time to gain insights about the culture of the school, including what is generally acceptable and what is not. For example, in some schools union agreements specify that teachers are not required to stay after school beyond a certain time period or that classroom observations are to be conducted only by administrators unless a teacher makes a request for another person to come into the classroom.

Guideline 8: Differentiate Coaching Based on Needs of Students and Teachers

The needs of students as identified by teacher observations and results of various tests should play a key role in the focus or content of coaching. At the same time, teachers, like their students, require and benefit from different approaches to coaching. Some teachers may want to co-plan with the coach and then teach the lesson independently; others may want to co-plan and co-teach, taking time after the lesson to discuss what went well and what can be improved. Some teachers actually want to have the coach observe the instruction and provide feedback, although this may not occur until after the coach has done some initial work with the teachers.

Teachers may only want to problem solve with the coach about specific ideas for instructional change, especially for students who are experiencing difficulty. In these cases, coach and teacher may talk about the test data that are available for students in that class. For example, after seeing some students' poor reading comprehension scores on the state reading test, one English teacher worked with the coach to develop lessons that focused on helping students remember what they were learning from text. The coach and the teacher discussed two major strategies: small-group discussion of key ideas that students had identified independently and group writing of summaries. They co-planned the first lesson, and the teacher decided that she would appreciate the coach's help in co-teaching it. They then discussed how they would share responsibilities for that lesson. What started as a problem-solving situation evolved into a series of activities, from co-planning to co-teaching. This, of course, was followed by a debriefing conversation, in which the coach and the teacher talked about what worked well and what needed to be changed.

What is important here is that coaches recognize that teachers, like their students, differ in their beliefs about teaching and learning, their knowledge, and their approaches to learning (and to coaching). These differences need to be acknowledged, respected, and appreciated.

Guideline 9: Know Yourself

As they interact with many different individuals over a school day or week, it is crucial for coaches to have some understanding of their own beliefs about teaching and learning—about what effective classroom instruction looks like. Some coaches admit that although they would have a much better organized classroom with more structure, the teacher they are visiting gets results with a different approach. Coaches cannot, nor should they attempt to, "clone" themselves. Differences in beliefs about practice, if not respected, can cause conflicts and lessen any opportunity for coaching. At the same time, honest discussion about such differences can often provide a means of getting to the basic issue—how we can together provide effective instruction for students.

Taking time to self-assess your skills and competencies can be helpful; a self-assessment instrument is available on the Literacy Coaching Clearinghouse website (*www.literacycoachingonline.org*). Some coaches find it useful to "coach" each other by sitting in on coach–teacher conversations and reflecting on what occurred in the discussion.

Conclusion

At the present time, literacy coaching is seen as an approach for providing school-based professional development that can ultimately have a positive effect on student learning. It is currently being implemented extensively at the middle and high school levels to provide all teachers with a better understanding of how they can improve content-area learning by using effective literacy-based strategies. There is no one best approach to coaching. Schools developing a coaching model should take into consideration their needs relative to teachers and students. Coaches have an especially important role in helping teachers meet the needs of their struggling readers, while at the same time assisting teachers in improving instruction for all students. We know that there are some "essentials" for effective coaching, which include having a qualified coach who has the knowledge, skills, and interpersonal skills necessary to work with other adults as a colleague; recognizing that coaching will not be successful if it is seen as an "evaluative " process; and understanding that coaching is not a "quick fix." There is some evidence that such an approach can work: Teachers, overall, seem to value literacy coaching, and coaching results in changes in classroom instruction and practices. At the same time, there is a need for more research about the effects of coaching on student achievement and the features of coaching that are essential to support and nurture middle and high school teachers.

Acknowledgments

I would like to acknowledge the contributions of several secondary literacy coaches in Pennsylvania; each has helped me get a better sense of how literacy coaches function to promote teacher learning and student achievement in their schools: Judy Berg, Literacy Coach, Lancaster School District; David Cohn, Philadelphia School District; Angie Dexheimer, Scranton School District; Michele McClendon, Pittsburgh Pubic Schools; and Dorothy Wood, Hazelton School District. Special thanks to Diane Hubona, literacy coach, and Lisa Hartsock, math coach, at Bellwood-Antis High School in Pennsylvania. During the day that I spent at Bellwood-Antis High School with Diane and Lisa and their administrators and teachers, I saw the potential of coaching for improving instruction and learning in action.

I also acknowledge the contributions and support of Ellen Eisenberg, Project Director for PAHSCI.

References

American Educational Research Association, (2005). *Research points: Teaching teachers: Professional development to improve student achievement* (Vol. 3, issue 1) [Brochure]. Washington, DC: Author.

Biancarosa, G., & Snow, C. (2004). *Reading Next: A vision for action and research in middle and high school literacy.* Washington, DC: Alliance for Education.

Coggins, C., Stoddard, P., & Cutler, E. (2003, April). *Improving instructional capacity through school-based reform coaches* (ERIC Document Reproduction Service No. ED478744). Presented at the annual meeting of the American Educational Research Association, Chicago.

Collaborative Coaching and Learning (CCL). (n.d.). *Literacy coaching program details.* Retrieved February 15, 2007, from *www.literacycoachingonline.org/ programs/database/1166834992.html.*

Costa, A., & Garmston, R. (2002). *Cognitive coaching: A foundation for renaissance schools* (2nd ed.). Norwood, MA: Christopher-Gordon.

Feldman, J., & Tung, S. (2002). *The role of external facilitators in whole school reform: Teachers' perceptions of how coaches influence school change.* Boston: Center for Collaborative Education (ERIC Document Reproduction Service No. ED470680).

Frost, S., & Bean, R. M. (2006). *Qualifications for literacy coaches: Achieving the gold standard.* Retrieved February 13, 2007, from *www.literacycoachingonline. org/briefs/LiteracyCoaching.pdf.*

Fullan, M. (2001). *Leading in a culture of change.* San Francisco: Jossey-Bass.

Hall, G. E., & Hord, S. M. (1987). *Change in schools: Facilitating the process.* New York: State University of New York Press.

International Reading Association. (2004). *The role and qualifications of the reading coach in the United States: A position statement of the International Reading Association* [Brochure]. Newark, DE: Author.

International Reading Association. (2006). *Standards for middle school and high school literacy coaches.* Newark, DE: Author.

Joyce, B., & Showers, B. (2002). *Student achievement through staff development.* Alexandria, VA: Association for Supervision and Curriculum Development.

National Council of Teachers of English. (2004, May). *A call to action: What we know about adolescent literacy and ways to support teachers in meeting students' need: A position/action statement from NCTE's Commission on Reading.* Available: *www.ncte.org/about/over/positions/category/read/118622. htm.*

National Staff Development Council. (2001). *Learning.* Retrieved September 1, 2005, from *www.nsdc.org.*

Neufeld, B. (2006). *Summary of the report: Instructional improvement in the Boston public schools: 1996–2006.* Available: *www.renniecenter.org/research_ docs/Summary-Instruction.pdf.*

Neufeld, B., & Roper, D. (2003). *Expanding the work: Year II of collaborative coaching and learning in the effective practice schools.* Cambridge, MA: Education Matters (ERIC Document Reproduction Service No. ED480874).

Penn Literacy Network. (n.d.). *www.gse.upenn.edu/pln.*

Pennsylvania High School Coaching Initiative. (n.d.). *High school coaching initiative*. Retrieved February 13, 2007, from *www.pacoaching.org/index.php? option=com_content&task=view&id=35&Itemid=63*.

Poglinco, S., Back, A., Hovde, K., Rosenblum, S., Saunders, M., & Supeovitz, J. (2003). *The heart of the matter: The coaching model in America's choice schools*. Philadelphia: University of Pennsylvania, Consortium for Policy Research in Education. Retrieved February 13, 2007, from *www.cpre.org/ Publications/AC-06.pdf*.

Readance, J. E., Bean, T. W., & Baldwin, R. S. (2004). *Content area literacy: An integrated approach* (6th ed.). Dubuque, IA: Kendall/Hunt.

Spillane, J. P., & Louis, K. S. (2002). School improvement processes and practices: Professional learning for building instructional capacity. In J. Murphy (Ed.), *Educational leadership challenge: Redefining leadership for the 21st century* (pp. 162–176). Chicago: University of Chicago Press.

Taylor, B. M., Pearson, P. D., Peterson, D. S., & Rodriguez, M. C. (2005). The CIERA school change framework: An evidence-based approach to professional development and school reading improvement. *Reading Research Quarterly, 40*(1), 40–69.

Toll, C. A. (2004). Separating coaching from supervising. *English Leadership Quarterly, 27*(2), 5–7.

Toll, C. A. (2005). *The literacy coaches' survival guide: Essential questions and practical answers*. Newark, DE: International Reading Association.

Walpole, S., & McKenna, M. (2004). *The literacy coach's handbook: A guide to research-based practice*. New York: Guilford Press.

Appendix 14.1. Additional Resources for Effective Literacy Coaching

Barkley, S. G. (2004). *Quality teaching in a culture of coaching.* Lanham, MD: Scarecrow Press.

Graham, S., & Perin, D. (2007). *Writing Next: Effective strategies to improve writing of adolescents in middle and high schools.* Washington, DC: Alliance for Excellent Education. *www.all4ed.org/publications/WritingNext/WritingNext. pdf.*

National Association of Secondary School Principals. (2005). *Creating a culture of literacy: A guide for middle and high school principals. www.principals.org/ s_nassp/sec.asp?CID=62&DID=62.*

Puig, E. A., & Froelich, K. S. (2006). *The literacy coach: Guiding in the right direction.* Boston: Addison-Wesley.

Sturtevant, E. (2003). *The literacy coach: A key to improving teaching and learning in secondary schools.* Washington, DC: Alliance for Excellent Education. *www.all4ed.org/publications/LiteracyCoach.pdf.*

Sweeney, D. (2003). *Professional development by and for teachers: Learning along the way.* Portland, ME: Stenhouse.

Toll, C. A. (2007). *Lenses on literacy coaching: Conceptualizations, functions, and outcomes.* Norwood, MA: Christopher-Gordon.

Websites

www.literacycoachingonline.org
www.pacoaching.org
www.readwritethink.org

CHAPTER 15

Keeping Parents Involved in Their Children's Education during the Middle and High School Years

Laurie Elish-Piper

P arent involvement is relatively commonplace during the preschool and elementary years; however, it is rare in many middle and high schools. At-home reading programs, family literacy nights, and weekly classroom newsletters are the norm for students in many preschool and elementary classes, but these practices do not seem to fit in classrooms with adolescents. As students enter adolescence, it is still important for parents to be involved with their schooling. Although parent involvement does and should look very different in middle and high school than it does during the elementary years, it still offers many benefits for older students, especially those students who find reading and learning difficult. Furthermore, the common belief that parents are not interested in participating in their adolescents' schooling runs counter to observations of the hundreds of parents who show interest through such activities as attending school sporting events, concerts, plays, competitions, and fund-raisers. Clearly, many parents of middle and high school students are willing and able to participate in their children's schooling; they may just be awaiting the invitation to become involved.

This chapter summarizes the research on and identifies aspects of parent involvement that are productive, manageable, and effective with older students. In addition, the needs of struggling readers and practical suggestions for teachers who want to increase parent involvement during the middle and high school years are described. It is important to note that although the term *parent* is used in this chapter and in the professional literature, there are many adults who function in parenting roles for teens, including grandparents, aunts, uncles, older siblings, foster families, and other adults. In this chapter the term *parent* refers to any responsible adult who cares for and supervises a teen.

What Does the Research Say about Parent Involvement and Older Students?

Parent involvement during the middle and high school years affects many aspects of students' education (Sanders, Epstein, & Connors-Tadros, 1999). Although parents can participate in their children's education in many ways, the impact is seen primarily in regard to three outcomes related to schooling: academics, attitudes and behavior, and expectations and aspirations.

Academics

Students whose parents participate in their education tend to have more academic success in school than their peers whose families are not involved (McCarthey, 2000). Some of the specific benefits for adolescents when their families are involved in their schooling are higher grade point averages, higher test scores on both standardized and classroom assessments, enrollment in more challenging academic courses and programs, more classes passed, more credits earned toward graduation (Henderson & Mapp, 2002), and higher graduation rates (Gutman & Midgley, 2000; Sanders & Herting, 2000). Parent support and participation in education is also correlated to lower levels of in-grade retention and decreased dropout rates (Miedel & Reynolds, 1999; Trusty, 1999; Yonhezawa, 2000). More specifically, in schools where teachers reported high levels of outreach to parents, test scores grew 40% more than in matched schools that reported low levels of parent outreach (Henderson & Mapp, 2002). Furthermore, the longer families stayed involved, the more students' grades and teacher ratings increased, indicating that parent involvement can have a cumulative effect that accrues over time (Jordan, Orozco, & Averett, 2002). For example, students whose parents participated in their education throughout elementary, middle, and high school tended to be more successful than those whose parents participated only occasionally or not at all during their school years. The effects of parent involvement reached even beyond middle and high school, as reported by Trusty (1999), who found that the level of parent support and participation in eighth grade was related to students' progress toward completing a bachelor's degree 2 years after high school graduation. In other words, parent involvement forms a foundation that can support students as they pursue educational goals even after high school graduation.

Although all students benefit when their families participate in their education, students who struggle with learning and reading tend to make the greatest academic gains on tests and in schoolwork (Jordan et al., 2002). Because struggling readers are more likely than their higher-achieving peers to drop out of school and not graduate, parent support related to the value of staying in school has the greatest impact on this group of adolescents (Jordan et al., 2002).

A meta-analysis of 25 research studies on parent involvement and student achievement found that the relationship between parent involvement and students' academic achievement is close to $r = .30$, which means that students from families with strong parent involvement had a success rate in school that was 30% higher than their peers whose parents were less involved (Fan & Chen, 1999). Clearly, the research indicates that parent involvement makes a significant contribution to student academic outcomes in middle and high school.

Attitudes and Behavior

Parent involvement also affects other aspects of students' schooling beyond grades. For example, parent involvement is related to better school attendance (Henderson & Mapp, 2002) and greater preparedness for classes (Simon, 2004). In addition, adolescents who have strong support at home also tend to be less disruptive in school (Gutman & Midgley, 2000; Sanders & Herting, 2000) and have more positive attitudes toward school. When parents discuss assignments and understand teacher expectations for homework, students tend to have more positive attitudes toward school (Ho Sui-Chu & Willms, 1996; Shumow & Miller, 2001). Furthermore, the more that parents were involved at home in their children's education, the more students reported believing that it was important for them to perform well in school (Shumow & Miller, 2001). In addition, students whose parents participated in their schooling tended to have greater motivation and more positive student–teacher relationships, which led to improved effort and engagement in classes (Palenchar, Vondra, & Wilson, 2001; Sanders, 1998). In schools with high levels of parent support and participation, more positive school climates were reported (Desimone, Finn-Stevenson, & Henrich, 2000). These affective and contextual aspects of education (i.e., attitude, behavior, and school climate) provide the foundation for students to succeed in school. With struggling middle and high school readers, these foundations are of critical importance because to succeed, students must believe they can learn; they must behave in a manner that demonstrates this self-belief; and they must feel safe, comfortable, and supported in their schools and classrooms. When these pieces are in place, struggling readers are more likely to be successful (Desimone et al., 2000).

Expectations and Aspirations

Students whose parents are supportive of learning and schooling are more likely to graduate from high school, attend college, and earn a college degree (Gutman & Midgley, 2000; Sanders & Herting, 2000). In general, parents' aspirations and expectations for their children have a significant effect on students' performance in school and beyond (Fan & Chen, 1999). When parents set high expectations and encourage their children to aspire to reach high goals, they are more likely to do so. Parents who are very involved with their children's schooling tend to help their children plan their educational programs to include more challenging courses of study, which allow them to set and pursue higher academic goals (Ho Sui-Chu & Willms, 1996).

The benefits of parent involvement for middle and high school readers are numerous. In a national survey conducted by Metropolitan Life Insurance Company (1998), however, 75% of parents of middle and high school students reported that their children's schools had not contacted them to offer options for parents to participate in their teens' schools. This finding is an interesting one in light of another result from the study, which stated that students, parents, and teachers all agreed that parent involvement was very important for students' successes in school. Given the many benefits of parent involvement for middle and high school readers, the question is not whether parents should be involved in their children's schooling; rather, the question is how to determine what parent involvement looks like in light of the changing developmental stages and needs of adolescents and the structure of middle and high schools.

Identity Development

Adolescent students in the middle and high school years go through an important developmental process of identity development that is an essential step toward adulthood. During this process adolescents commit to who they are and want to be, or how they see themselves. This essential milestone is the key to becoming an adult (Erikson, 1968). Because of the need to develop a solid self-identity, many adolescents distance themselves from their parents to assert that they are separate individuals who make their own decisions in life. This process is essential for developing into a healthy adult; however, it presents challenges for home–school connection initiatives.

Because of these important developmental considerations, effective parent involvement efforts at the middle and high school levels look different from traditional practices used in the elementary school. During the elementary years, for example, parents often work in the roles of teachers or tutors for their children by completing homework assignments side by side, studying school subjects together at home, and engaging in shared reading. Teachers of younger children also tend to offer home–school connection ideas to parents, who then take on the leadership role for teaching their children at home (Christenson & Sheridan, 2001). Once students approach adolescence, effective parent participation in school shifts from the "parent as teacher or tutor" role to "parent as coach, mentor, or supporter" role. At the middle and high school levels, teachers may discuss with students how parents can support learning at home; students then serve as mediators by sharing this information with their parents (Epstein, Simon, & Salinas, 1997). This change in the parents' role is often necessary as middle and high school students encounter school subjects and assignments that may exceed their parents' comfort levels or expertise (e.g., algebra, chemistry, foreign languages). As parents shift to a coaching, mentoring, and supporting role, they can continue to be involved while at the same time allowing their teenage children the space and opportunities needed to grow and develop toward adulthood (Catsambis, 1998).

A Framework for Parent Involvement in Middle and High School

Before educators can reach out to parents to build home–school connections, four foundational issues must be addressed (Christenson & Sheridan, 2001). These issues are the *approach*—the framework for interactions with families; *attitudes*—the values and perceptions educators in the school hold in regard to family–school relationships; *atmosphere*—the climate in the school for families, students, and educators; and *actions*—strategies for building shared responsibility for student learning. Each of these components is defined and explained in Figure 15.1.

By addressing these issues, educators can create a context that supports effective parent involvement at the middle and secondary levels. The first three components—approach, attitudes, and atmosphere—focus on the beliefs and expectations that teachers and administrators hold in regard to parent involvement. These components are essential for creating a climate where parents, students, and teachers feel comfortable, safe, and valued. Through professional discussions about these components during faculty meetings, team meetings, and department meetings, educators can lay

APPROACH: *The framework for interactions with families*
- Mutually shared goals for students' learning
- Belief that parent involvement is important
- Belief that working together will benefit students' learning
- Recognition of contributions of in- and out-of-school experiences for students' learning

ATTITUDES: *The values and perceptions held about family–school relationships*
- Mutual respect across home and school
- Positive perspective that focuses on school, family, and student strengths
- A nonblaming, no-fault, problem-solving approach
- Willingness to listen, respond, and work together for the good of the student
- Belief that "We're in this together for the good of the student."

ATMOSPHERE: *The climate in schools for families, students, and educators*
- Welcoming, respectful, inclusive, supportive environment for *all* students and families
- Multiple communication methods to reach all families
- Trust and collaboration—"We learn from each other."
- Meaningful ways and flexible options for family involvement

ACTIONS: *Strategies for building shared responsibility for student learning*
- Information about school policies and practices shared with families in accessible ways
- Mechanisms for using family input to modify school policies and practices
- Support and resources for creating and maintaining family–school partnerships
- Partnership approach rather than traditional approach to involvement
- Ongoing efforts to involve *all* families in meaningful ways

FIGURE 15.1. A framework for parent involvement. Adapted from Christenson and Sheridan (2001). *Schools and families: Creating essential connections for learning.* New York: Guilford Press. Copyright 2001 by The Guilford Press. Adapted by permission.

the foundation that acknowledges the importance and value of parent involvement for their students. The final section of Figure 15.1 focuses on actions—what educators can do to involve parents in their sons' and daughters' education. These actions are the specific events, strategies, and interactions that educators can use to engage parents in their teens' education and schooling. The rest of this chapter presents specific actions that educators can take to get parents involved with their children's education at the middle and high school levels.

Actions to Promote Meaningful, Manageable, Effective Parent Involvement at the Middle and High School Levels

Educators can take many actions that may promote stronger ties between home and school in middle and high schools; however, those that build on the research cited in the opening sections of this chapter offer the most promise for promoting positive outcomes for middle and high school students, especially struggling readers. This part of the chapter focuses on the following areas: establishing effective communication between home and school; helping parents support learning through organization, motivation, and preparation; fostering a reading climate at home; promoting parent–child discussions about school; coaching at home for homework and studying; and school-based outreach efforts.

Effective Communication between Home and School

When parents know homework expectations and school and classroom policies, their sons and daughters are more likely to be prepared for and succeed in class. Through the use of effective home–school communication, a safety net can be constructed to support students, especially those who find school difficult (Christenson & Sheridan, 2001).

Newsletters

Newsletters are not just for elementary classrooms, although they are much more common at that level. There are two main purposes for parent newsletters: to inform parents about what students are studying and expected to do in class, and to offer suggestions for ways parents can support students in school (e.g., at-home study tips, the importance of talking about school at home, the importance of letting adolescents know that school and learning are valued by the family) (Bass, Dasinger, Elish-Piper, Matthews, & Risko, 2008).

The newsletter can be adapted for middle and high school in a beginning-of-the-year letter in which teachers introduce themselves; describe key information about their classes; and provide contact information so parents (and students) know how to handle questions about such classroom issues as assignments, due dates, grades, tests, makeup work, and major projects. Such letters can be distributed when students receive their class schedules, or they can be sent through "snail mail" prior to the start of the school year. Susan Williams, an experienced middle school language arts teacher, sends such a letter to all of her incoming eighth-grade students approximately 1 week before school starts. She asks students to share it with their parents and to write her response letters telling her a bit about themselves and their families. The letters are due at the end of the first week of school, and she gives homework credit to students who write responses. According to Ms. Williams, this activity is one of the most effective ways to connect with the large number of her students and their families.

Newsletters can be sent several times throughout the year, but the plan for this must be realistic, especially for teachers who teach various classes and levels. For example, a middle school teacher in a team setting in which several teachers from different disciplines work together with the same group of students may find that a monthly newsletter works well. However, a high school English teacher who teaches 150 different students each day may find that sending home a newsletter once per quarter is more manageable.

The format for the newsletter is another consideration. Should it be a printed newsletter distributed to students to take home, a posted newsletter on the school website, an e-mailed newsletter sent to parents' e-mail addresses, or a printed newsletter sent via snail mail? Which would be the most appropriate option in your school? Which option would parents prefer?

For teachers who prepare their own newsletters, the following tips may be helpful to increase the likelihood that the newsletters are actually read by parents. First, remember the dollar bill rule (Parent Institute, 2002). The dollar bill rule states that a dollar bill placed anywhere on the page of a newsletter should touch some graphic element such as a picture, headline, box, or bullet point to ensure that the text is not too dense or overwhelming for parents to read. For example, instead of writing several paragraphs about an upcoming project, a more reader-friendly way to present the information in a newsletter is to use a bulleted list of key items or to include a diagram showing the important information. With a limited amount of text and the inclusion of graphics, newsletters can be read much more quickly and efficiently by busy parents (Parent Institute, 2002). Second, keep the reading level low enough (aim for a fourth- to sixth-grade reading level) so that most parents can read a newsletter easily and quickly. The "tools" feature on most word processing programs can calculate a readability level of a document. Third, when it comes to newsletters, less is more. Keep the newsletter limited to one or two pages in length to make it manageable for parents to read.

Professionally written newsletters with general tips and ideas for parents and families are also available for schoolwide use at the middle school and high school levels. Samples and ordering information for can be found on the Parent Institute website located at *www.parent-institute.com*.

Positive and Supportive Communication

Although group communication offered by print or electronic newsletters is a great way to get information to a large number of parents in an efficient manner, personalized communication is also important for building home–school connections. When students are doing well, teachers might contact parents to share the good news, perhaps by adding brief positive notes to report cards and progress reports that parents must review and sign. Some teachers find that making three "quick calls" each day allows them to leave short phone messages to let parents know of their children's progress. For example, a teacher may call and leave the following message, "Hello, this is Miss Sommers from Taft High School. I have good news. Jordan passed the history test today! I just wanted to share the great news. Keep up the good work!" The parents of many struggling readers are accustomed to receiving only negative communications from school, and upon receiving a positive comment such as "Jake had perfect attendance this quarter," "Sabir has done a great job debating issues in our class," or "Ronzell has used the Internet effectively for his research project" parents (and adolescent students) will feel a sense of pride and competence, which can lead to increased connections between home and school and the increased engagement of students (Smith & Wilhelm, 2004).

Personalized communication is also important when students begin to experience difficulty in a class. This can be done through phone calls, e-mail messages, or periodic progress reports. Informing parents early on that their son or daughter is earning a low grade in class can provide time and opportunities for students to improve before report cards are issued. A common complaint from the parents of struggling readers is that by the time they see the failing grade on the report card, it is too late to address the issue.

When teachers need to contact families to address student performance, motivation, behavior, or engagement in the classroom, applying the "my son or daughter test" is a good way to frame the conversation in a positive, supportive manner. In other words, if a teacher tries to think about the situation as if the student were his or her own son or daughter, the result is likely to be more empathetic and effective (Canter & Associates, 1999). Rather than calling to inform a parent that "David hasn't turned in homework for 2 weeks, he failed the last exam, and he is getting an F in English class," the teacher can use the "my son or daughter test" to rephrase the situation by saying, "I am concerned that David is having a difficult time in my English class. For the past 2 weeks he hasn't turned in his homework, and he did poorly on the last test. If he continues in this way, he will earn a very low grade for this quarter. I think that if we all work together, we can figure out a way to help David improve his grade in class. Here are some ideas I have that may be helpful." In the first example, the teacher simply reports the situation, whereas in the second situation the teacher focuses on inviting the parent to work with her (and the student) to try to improve the situation. In other words, the first example focuses on problem reporting, whereas the second example focuses on problem solving. Especially when reaching out to the parents of struggling readers, it is most effective to adopt the problem-solving stance.

When initiating communication with parents, teachers must also consider language issues, as some parents may speak a language other than English and some may have low levels of literacy themselves (Smith & Elish-Piper, 2002). Two basic suggestions to address these challenges are to locate bilingual individuals in the school or community who can translate written materials and arrange for interpreters for parent–teacher conferences when language is an issue, and to prepare all written materials to be shared with parents so they are clear, concise, and easy to read.

Sharing Insider Information

Insider information focuses on how the school works, the resources available to struggling readers and how to access them, how to advocate for extra help for students, teacher expectations, and how to support struggling readers at home. Teachers and school administrators have this knowledge, but it is often not available to parents, and it does make a difference to middle and high school students' achievement. For example, a parent recently called the Reading Clinic where I work. The parent reported, "My daughter will not be allowed to go on to high school if she can't reach a Lexile level of 1,000 by the end of the year. I want to help, but I don't even know what a Lexile is, let alone how to help her." The mother then went on to explain that the teacher had reported, "I have 150 students, and if you can't help your daughter at home there is nothing more I can do here at school." This is the unfortunate reality for the parents of some struggling middle and high school readers. It is also a reality that many middle and high school teachers feel overwhelmed in trying to provide support for large numbers of students who have varied needs. Although this parent was savvy enough to contact the local university Reading Clinic to get information and support for her daughter, many parents are unable or unaware of how to secure such assistance and information.

Insider information can be shared in typical ways such as via newsletters, phone calls, e-mails, in conferences, and at open houses. Teachers can also prepare FAQ (Frequently Asked Questions) sheets for parents that list common problems and useful solutions parents can pursue (see Figure 15.2). They can be posted on the school website, included in the parent handbook, distributed at orientation, and included with report cards, perhaps in several languages represented at the school. When teachers feel that they are working at capacity and cannot personally provide additional assistance to students outside class time, they can help struggling readers

Frequently asked question (FAQ)	Suggestions/resources
My child has a hard time understanding reading assignments. What can I do to help?	Provide a quiet time for your child to read assignments at home. Have your child divide the reading assignment into parts that will take about 10–15 minutes to read. At the end of each part, ask your child to tell you about what was read. Have your child take a break after each part to improve focus and concentration.
	Contact your child's teacher to find out if the reading assignment is available on tape or CD. If so, your child may be able to listen to the assigned reading to improve understanding. Call the school office at 555-6666 to contact the teacher.
	Encourage your child to participate in the before-school peer tutoring program for help with reading assignments. Your child can sign up for peer tutoring in the school library at the main desk.
	After-school reading tutoring programs are offered at these locations: Main Community Center, 555-1212; Central University Reading Clinic, 555-2222; Good Shepherd Church, 555-3333; and Downtown YMCA, 555-4444. Consider signing up your child for tutoring at one of these programs.
	If your child has not been tested by the school reading specialist, discuss this option with your child's counselor. The counseling office can be reached at 555-5555.

FIGURE 15.2. Sample FAQ sheet for parents of students with reading difficulties.

and their parents simply by making them aware of after-school academic programs, community-based tutoring programs, supplemental materials such as books on tape or websites that provide reinforcement or practice activities, peer tutoring programs, and other existing resources and services that may be useful.

Teachers can also share specific information that is most likely to support positive outcomes for students, especially struggling readers. When deciding what to include or exclude in a parent communication, emphasize those types of information that are most likely to make a difference (see Figure 15.3).

- How parent involvement makes a difference for student success—a summary of the research
- What to expect during the transition to middle school or high school
- Planning the school course of study
- Study strategies and approaches that work
- Preparing for college (financial aid, ACT/SAT, scholarships, role models)
- How to get information and support at the school and in the community

FIGURE 15.3. Information to share with parents that makes a difference for student learning.

Helping Parents and Students Use Effective Study Strategies at Home

Many middle and high school students lack organizational skills and come to class unprepared. The challenge is often greater for struggling readers, who may misplace assignments, forget to take books home to study for a test, or show up with the wrong materials for class on a regular basis. Although these problems may frustrate the student (and perhaps even the teacher and parent), the real issue is that poor organization and preparation cause struggling readers to miss instruction, fall behind in class, and earn lower grades. For these reasons, teachers may want to help parents learn to coach their struggling readers at home to build these basic life skills of organization and preparation.

Organizing Assignments

Students and their parents may not be aware of the importance of good organizational skills for success in middle and high school. Teachers, however, often cite organization as one of the most important skills students need for success in school. At the beginning of the year, explain to students (and share with parents) the importance of having a calendar to record homework assignments, test dates, and other useful information. Some schools require students to purchase a school planner as part of their book rental fees, but other schools do not have such provisions in place. Depending on the school, many students may have cell phones with planners, Palm Pilots, or day planners. Some teachers provide a weekly template that students fill in with assignments and notes and store in their class folders. Other teachers post calendars on their websites for students and parents to access. Especially at the middle school level when students are just learning to take responsibility for keeping track of assignments from different teachers, a few minutes spent at the end of class to record their assignments and organize materials is a very simple way to promote the development of students' organizational skills. Regardless of the type of calendar or planner used, it is important for students and parents to understand the value of this tool for keeping students organized.

Students who struggle with learning and reading often have difficulty with other aspects of organization. Offering students and parents suggestions such as color coding classes (red folder and spiral notebook for English, green folder and binder for science, orange folder and notebook for social studies, and so on) is a simple yet effective method for promoting organizational skills. If organizational challenges are a serious concern in a school, a team of teachers may collaborate to prepare a FAQ sheet (see Figure 15.2 for a sample FAQ sheet) about helping students with organizational issues.

Establishing Study Times

Many parents insist that their adolescents study for extended periods of time, especially if they have earned low grades in school. This approach may seem logical; however, it is actually not effective (Luzzo & Spencer, 2002). Teachers can let parents and students know that 20 minutes is the most effective time block for most homework or studying sessions. By breaking long assignments into smaller parts that can be completed in 20 minutes or less, the student will be able to focus full attention on the assignment. By taking breaks after 20 minutes, the student can keep the mind sharp and attention focused. Sharing this information via newsletters, an open house, or FAQ sheets can help parents understand the appropriate expectations for study times for their teens.

Creating an Effective Study Environment

Encourage parents to have their sons and daughters think about where and when they do their homework. By selecting a time and location with few distractions, students will be able to focus and complete tasks more effectively. Noise level and lighting are other considerations. Many students complete their homework on the computer, but this format can also be distracting if they are engaged in instant messaging, downloading music, and surfing the Internet while completing assignments. Encourage parents to talk to their adolescents about selecting effective study conditions and what these might be. Teachers can let parents and students know that optimal study conditions vary from one person to the next, and the goal is to find conditions that are effective for the individual. Suggestions about effective study conditions can be shared in a newsletter, on the school website, during conferences, or in other communications with parents.

Helping Parents Create
a Positive Learning Climate at Home

Parents can do many things to help their teens do well in school, even those parents who may speak a language other than English, who may have low literacy levels themselves, who may have long work hours that keep them away from the home for extended periods, or who face other challenges.

Many struggling middle and high school readers do not find reading interesting or engaging, and they avoid it as much as possible. This logical response to an activity that is difficult poses further problems, however. The more these students avoid reading, the farther they fall behind. This phenomenon is explained by the Matthew Effect (Stanovich, 1986), which suggests that good readers get better because they practice, and they practice because they feel good about their reading. However, struggling readers do not practice, and therefore their reading does not improve. Furthermore, as their peers advance their reading skills while the struggling readers stay at the same level, the gap between the struggling readers and their peers widens. Because there are only a limited number of hours in a school day, it is important for teachers to provide suggestions to parents for ways to promote reading at home by creating a positive reading climate (Elish-Piper, 2004). Teachers may share the suggestions in Figure 15.4 with the parents of their struggling readers.

Encouraging Discussions
between Parents and Adolescents about School

One of the most significant ways that parents can support their children in middle and high school is to discuss school together. Teachers can make parents aware of how simple discussions about school really can make a difference in how middle and high school students, especially struggling readers, view school and its importance in their lives. Encourage parents to ask their sons and daughters, on a regular basis, how they are doing in school. Emphasize that this question should lead to a discussion, not an interrogation, and can focus on such things as what the teen is learning in school, successes, challenges, goals, and interesting experiences. These conversations can occur at breakfast, during dinner, while driving together, or on the phone. The important thing is for parents and teens to talk to each other about school. Teachers may consider adding an item to homework assignments on a regular basis to encourage such discussions. For example, a teacher may add this item: "Talk to a member of your family about this assignment. Ask the family member to write one comment and one question about this assignment at the top of the page." By formalizing these dis-

✓ Let adolescents see you and other adults reading for fun.

✓ Subscribe to a magazine for your teen.

✓ Share newspaper stories with your teen and discuss them during dinner or at other times.

✓ Choose a special book as a gift for your teen (e.g., think about the teen's interests, such as music, celebrities, hobbies, sports, science fiction, humor, fashion, technology, etc.).

✓ Take your teen to a bookstore often and encourage him or her to select interesting reading materials.

✓ Encourage and acknowledge the many types of reading your teen does (e.g., school assignments, Internet sites, how-to instructions, e-mail, instant messaging, magazines, etc.).

✓ Encourage your teen to read to younger brothers, sisters, or other children.

✓ Help your teen choose reading materials about the future (colleges, careers, current issues).

✓ Avoid arguing with your teen about reading! Try to keep finding ways to show your teen how important and enjoyable reading can be.

FIGURE 15.4. Creating a reading climate at home for middle and high school students. Adapted from Elish-Piper (2004). Copyright 2004 by the Illinois Reading Council. Adapted by permission.

cussions, teachers may be able to nudge parents and teens to discuss school assignments more often.

Stressing Excellence, Not Perfection

Many struggling middle and high school readers feel overwhelmed by the demands of school and assigned reading materials. Teachers must help parents (and their teens) understand that excellence, not perfection, is the goal. Although parents and teachers want teens to do their best, mistakes are a normal part of learning and striving for perfection is unrealistic and stressful. By working toward improvement, teens can do their best, and parents and teachers can help students to see their growth and improvement over time. Teachers, parents, and students may consider setting realistic goals collaboratively and then working together to reach them. Striking a balance between high expectations and reality is difficult, but it is of critical importance for adolescents who are establishing their identities and are most motivated by engaging in pursuits in which they feel competent. If teens are held to unrealistic expectations, they may become frustrated and begin to shut down in the particular academic area (Smith & Wilhelm, 2004).

Encouraging Family Learning Activities

Share information with students and their parents about educational opportunities available for families outside school, such as special exhibits, interesting television programs, and community events that may provide a foundation that can be helpful in school. For example, the background information gained by attending a community fine arts show may help a student understand the content of an art class. Or watching the State of the Union speech with their parents may provide students with background knowledge for the study of current events in a high school government or civics class (Marzano, 2004).

Providing Parental Support for Challenging School Assignments

In the elementary school years, parents may be asked to assist their child in an area of the curriculum in which the child is struggling. Such a request can be problematic for parents who are unfamiliar with the content area being studied. For example, a colleague recently approached me to vent about how frustrated she was with her high school son's struggles in chemistry. She explained, "I've tried to help teach him with chemistry, but I couldn't understand the assignments. I tried to read the chapters, but I couldn't figure them out either. We always ended up in a fight, so it was a total loss." As middle and high school students study more complex content, it is less likely that their parents will be able to assist them. Teachers are encouraged, therefore, to share some useful strategies and tips with their students' parents for coaching and encouraging their children to complete their assignments, rather than expecting parents to shoulder the responsibility of providing the instruction.

Teachers Involve Parents in Schoolwork

The Teachers Involve Parents in Schoolwork (TIPS) approach to interactive homework does not require parents to know about the content of an assignment or to help students complete the task. This approach to homework has been correlated with improved student academic achievement in the middle school grades (Epstein et al., 1997). With TIPS, teachers assign homework that requires students to demonstrate or discuss some aspect of their learning with a family member. This involvement may include interviewing family members, discussing real-world applications of content, or gathering family input into texts the students write. During the TIPS process, parents monitor and support their children, but they are not expected to teach content, read assignments, or direct projects because those responsibilities belong to the students. Each TIPS assignment also includes a section for home–school communication in which family members are asked to share observations, comments, or questions regarding the assignment. Teachers typically assign TIPS activities no more than once per week, giving 2 or more days to complete the assignment to accommodate busy family schedules. More information on this approach to homework and sample TIPS lessons can be found at the TIPS website sponsored by the National Network of Partnership Schools, *www.csos.jhu.edu/p2000/tips/ TIPSmain.htm.*

Additional Strategies to Help with Challenging Assignments

What else can teachers do to help parents to assist their teens at home when parents find the content, strategies, or assignments challenging? Grabarek (2006) suggests using trigger questions and identifying and accessing resource help to assist teens when they are experiencing difficulty with their homework or studying (see Figure 15.5). This approach is also helpful for struggling readers, who may find that the framework helps them focus their attention on key parts of a text or assignment.

Teachers may demonstrate this approach to parents during an open house, explain the steps during conferences, write a step-by-step process in a newsletter, offer an evening workshop on study tips for use at home, or teach the approach to students and ask them to teach it to their parents. See Figure 15.5 for suggestions on using this approach.

Another general study strategy that can help all adolescent students, especially struggling readers, and bring order to their understanding of a reading assignment is the 3-2-1 strategy (Zygouris-Coe, Wiggins, & Smith, 2004/2005). At the end of a reading assignment or homework assignment, students are encouraged to stop and tell a family member three things they learned, two key vocabulary terms they learned, and one question they still have. This strategy is one that teachers can model in the classroom and then ask students to discuss and use with their parents. The main benefits of the 3-2-1 strategy are that it can be applied to any content area, requires no preparation on the parent's part, and helps the student focus on key ideas and information.

Inviting Parents into the School to Build Home–School Connections

Thus far this chapter has emphasized the types of things parents can do at home in the course of their daily lives to support their teens' learning, and the types of information teachers can share to promote parent participation

Trigger Questions
- Parent asks a question to help the student make a connection between new problems or tasks and what he or she has learned before.
  - Did your teacher talk about this in class today? What do your notes say?
  - What do you know about this topic already? Write it down.
  - How does _____ relate to what you did yesterday in class?
  - What does your textbook say about _____?

Identify and Access Resource Help
- Does the student have the book(s) and other supplies needed to complete the assignment?
- Does the student know where to look in the book for useful information (index, glossary, table of contents, bold-faced words, etc.)?
- Is there a family member, friend, or other person who can serve as a content expert to help with the assignment?
- If the student and parent do not understand the assignment or the content, what targeted question(s) can the student ask the teacher in school the next day?
- Is the student spending unproductive hours searching the Internet for information?
- Are there libraries, community resources, or school support that would be helpful to the student?

FIGURE 15.5. General strategies to help with homework (when parents don't know or understand the content). Adapted with permission from Grabarek (2006).

at home. Another successful approach to parent involvement is to invite parents into the school for special events.

One Book Program

Many cities and towns are involved in "One Book" programs, in which interested individuals read the same book and participate in discussions about it. Middle and high schools are now adapting this activity to their settings by engaging students, teachers, and parents with the same book. For example, if the book *The Namesake* (Lahiri, 2004) is selected at a high school, the book (and the audio version for those who prefer to listen to the book) can be read and meetings may be held afterward to discuss the book. If the book has also been made into a movie, participants may be invited to view and compare the two versions. *To Kill a Mockingbird* (Lee, 1960), *Seabiscuit* (Hillenbrand, 2002), and *The Namesake* (Lahiri, 2004) are good examples for this type of activity. The One Book program can be implemented schoolwide, by grade level, or by an individual teacher. The shared experience of reading the same book can be powerful for bonding teens, their parents, and their teachers. In lower-income areas where it may be difficult for families to obtain copies of the book, grants and collaborative relationships with the public library may allow all interested families to access the book and/or audio version, if available, free of charge.

Learning Celebrations

Learning celebrations highlight student learning and projects. For example, in conjunction with a study of astronomy, high school students collaborated with university researchers to analyze complex data and then participated in community "star parties" that were held to invite astronomy enthusiasts and families to share their learning and to pursue questions of mutual interest (Alvarez, 1996). Such celebrations can easily be adapted to other areas of the curriculum such as the fine arts, literature, or physical education/fitness.

Family Literacy Nights

Family literacy events have become popular for younger children; however, this approach also holds promise at the middle and high school levels. Families can be invited to spend an evening at the school browsing at a book fair, listening to local authors discuss their books and writing processes, watching local celebrities do dramatic readings of their favorite books, listening to a professional storyteller, or watching students do skits about books they have recently read. Art students might create an exhibit about books; the band or a choral group could give a performance related to a book or an aspect of reading, and a theater club might perform scenes from famous books. Involving many students in Family Literacy Night performances, demonstrations, and exhibits, encourages more families to attend. The first Family Literacy Night at school might be held in October during Teen Read Week. This week is sponsored by the American Library Association (*www.ala.org/ala/yalsa/teenreading/trw/teenreadweek.htm*) and includes a number of school activities related to reading.

Funds of Knowledge

Middle and high school teachers are finding that their students come from increasingly diverse backgrounds. A "funds-of-knowledge approach" (Hidalgo, Sui, & Epstein, 2004, p. 711) creates a multicultural climate that invites all families to participate in their teens' learning. In this approach teachers create lessons that draw on knowledge sources in families, incorporate multicultural literature and texts, and include parents and others from the community as intellectual resources for the classroom. In the funds-of-knowledge approach, the teacher serves as an ethnographer or cultural anthropologist to learn about the types of knowledge and re-sources available in the homes and community of his or her students (González, Moll, & Amanti, 2005). The teacher then uses this knowledge to make connections to the curriculum with the students and their families. Guest speakers can be invited to the classroom to share their life experiences, travels, hobbies, or cultures. Possible topics for presentations, demonstrations, and displays include careers, music, horticulture, art, drama, and crafts (Kyle, McIntyre, Miller, & Moore, 2006). As a concluding activity, the school can host a community learning celebration that highlights the many talents and experiences of community members and families (McIntyre, Kyle, Moore, Sweazy, & Greer, 2001).

Conclusion

Parents' participation in their children's schooling is an important contributor to student success during the adolescent years and beyond. By balancing the benefits of parent involvement approaches that are supported by research with the developmental changes and needs of middle and high school students, educators can help teens and parents work collaboratively to support student learning and success. The ideas offered in this chapter are supported by research and have been used successfully in many middle and high schools. However, the particular aspects of each school community must be noted. Thus, teachers and administrators may find some of the suggestions more appropriate for their students and families than others. In addition, modifications of some of the ideas may be necessary to fit the realities or needs of a particular school community. The real issue is not which strategies for promoting parent involvement are implemented, but rather that all middle and high school teachers work collaboratively with parents to support students' learning and success.

References

Alvarez, M. C. (1996). Explorers of the universe: Students using the World Wide Web to improve their reading and writing. In B. Neate (Ed.), *Literacy saves lives* (pp. 140–145). Winchester, UK: United Kingdom Reading Association.

Bass, J., Dasinger, S., Elish-Piper, L, Matthews, R., & Risko, V. (2008). *A declaration of readers' rights: Renewing our commitment to students*. Boston: Allyn & Bacon.

Canter & Associates (1999). *First-class teacher: Success strategies for new teachers*. Santa Monica, CA: Author.

Catsambis, S. (1998). *Expanding knowledge of parental involvement in secondary education—Effects on high school academic success.* CRESPAR (Center for Research on the Education of Students Placed at Risk; Report No. 27). Retrieved April 1, 2006, from the Johns Hopkins University website: *www. csos.jhu.edu/crespar/Reports/report27entire.htm.*

Christenson, S. L., & Sheridan, S. M. (2001). *Schools and families: Creating essential connections for learning.* New York: Guilford Press.

Desimone, L., Finn-Stevenson, M., & Henrich, C. (2000). Whole school reform in a low-income African American community: The effects of the CoZi Model on teachers, parents, and students. *Urban Education, 35,* 269–323.

Elish-Piper, L. (2004). Helping parents support their children as readers at home. *Illinois Reading Council Journal, 32*(3), 17–29.

Epstein, J. L., Simon, B. S., & Salinas, K. C. (1997). Involving parents in homework in the middle grades. *Research Bulletin, 18.* Retrieved May 24, 2005, from *www.pdkintl.org/edres/resbul18.htm.*

Erikson, E. H. (1968). *Identity: Youth and crisis.* New York: Norton.

Fan, X., & Chen, M. (1999). *Parental involvement and students' academic achievement: A meta-analysis.* Arlington, VA: National Science Foundation.

González, N., Moll, L. C., & Amanti, C. (2005). Introduction: Theorizing practices. In N. González, L. C. Moll, & C. Amanti (Eds.), *Funds of knowledge: Theorizing practices in households and classrooms* (pp. 1–28). Mahwah, NJ: Erlbaum.

Grabarek, K. (2006). *Staying involved: Approaches to helping our middle school and high school students learn.* Retrieved April 7, 2006, from the Parent Academic Resources Incorporated website: *www.academicresources.org/learning. html.*

Gutman, L. M., & Midgley, C. (2000). The role of protective factors in supporting the academic achievement of poor African American students during the middle school transition. *Journal of Youth and Adolescence, 29,* 223–248.

Henderson, A. T., & Mapp, K. L. (2002). *A new wave of evidence: The impact of school, family, and community connections on student achievement.* Austin, TX: National Center for Family and Community Connections with Schools.

Hidalgo, N., Sui, S.-F., & Epstein, J. (2004). Research on families, schools, and communities: A multicultural perspective. In J. A. Banks & C. A. M. Banks (Eds.), *Handbook for research on multicultural education* (pp. 631–655). San Francisco: Jossey-Bass.

Hillenbrand, L. (2002). *Seabiscuit.* New York: Ballentine.

Ho Sui-Chu, E., & Willms, J. D. (1996). Effects of parental involvement on eighth-grade achievement. *Sociology of Education, 69,* 126–141.

Jordan, C., Orozco, E., & Averett, A. (2002). *Emerging issues in school, family, and community connections.* Austin, TX: National Center for Family and Community Connections with Schools.

Kyle, D. W., McIntyre, E., Miller, K. B., & Moore, G. H. (2006). *Bridging school and home through family nights.* Thousand Oaks, CA: Corwin.

Lahiri, J. (2004). *The namesake.* New York: First Mariner Books.

Lee, H. (1960). *To kill a mockingbird.* New York: HarperCollins.

Luzzo, D. A., & Spencer, M. K. (2002). *Overcoming the hurdles to academic success: Strategies that make a difference.* Boston: Houghton Mifflin.

Marzano, R. J. (2004). *Building background knowledge for academic achievement.* Alexandria, VA: Association for Supervision and Curriculum Development.

McCarthey, S. J. (2000). Home–school connections: A review of the literature. *Journal of Educational Research, 93,* 145–153.

McIntyre, E., Kyle, D., Moore, G., Sweazy, R. A., & Greer, S. (2001). Linking home and school through family visits. *Language Arts, 78,* 264–272.

Metropolitan Life Insurance Company. (1998). *The Metropolitan Life survey of the American teacher: Building family–school partnerships.* Retrieved May 24, 2005, from *www.metlife.com/WPSAssets/17708507701018400929V1Flifesurv-98.pdf.*

Miedel, W. T., & Reynolds, A. J. (1999). Parent involvement in early intervention for disadvantaged children: Does it matter? *Journal of School Psychology, 37,* 370–402.

Palenchar, D. R., Vondra, J. I., & Wilson, J. A. (2001). *Parental involvement and early school functioning.* Paper presented at the annual meeting of the American Educational Research Association, Seattle, WA.

Parent Institute. (2002). *68 parent involvement ideas that really work.* Retrieved December 21, 2006, from *www.par-inst.com.*

Sanders, M. G. (1998). The effects of school, family, and community support on the academic achievement of African American adolescents. *Urban Education, 33,* 385–409.

Sanders, M. G., Epstein, J. L., & Connors-Tadros, L. (1999). *Family partnerships with high schools: The parents' perspective.* Baltimore: CRESPAR (Center for Research on the Education of Students Placed at Risk; Report No. 32). Retrieved March 22, 2006, from the Johns Hopkins University website: *www.csos.jhu.edu/crespar/Reports/report32entire.htm.*

Sanders, M. G., & Herting, J. R. (2000). Gender and the effects of school, family, and church support on the academic achievement of African-American urban adolescents. In M. G. Sanders (Ed.), *Schooling students placed at risk: Research, policy, and practice in the education of poor and minority adolescents* (pp. 141–161). Mahwah, NJ: Erlbaum.

Shumow, L., & Miller, J. D. (2001). Parents' at-home and at-school academic involvement with young adolescents. *Journal of Early Adolescence, 21,* 68–91.

Simon, B. S. (2004). High school outreach and family involvement. *Social Psychology of Education, 7,* 185–209.

Smith, M., & Wilhelm, J. D. (2004). "I just like being good at it": The importance of competence in the literate lives of young men. *Journal of Adolescent and Adult Literacy, 47,* 454–461.

Smith, M. C., & Elish-Piper, L. (2002). Primary-grade educators and adult literacy: Some strategies for assisting low-literate parents. *Reading Teacher, 56,* 156–165.

Stanovich, K. E. (1986). Matthew effects in reading: Some consequences of individual differences in the acquisition of literacy. *Reading Research Quarterly, 21,* 360–406.

Trusty, J. (1999). Effects of eighth-grade parental involvement on late adolescents' educational experiences. *Journal of Research and Development in Education, 32*, 224–233.

Yonhezawa, S. (2000). Unpacking the black box of tracking decisions: Critical tales of families navigating the course of placement process. In M. G. Sanders (Ed.), *Schooling students placed at risk: Research, policy, practice in the education of poor and minority adolescents* (pp. 109–140). Mahwah, NJ: Erlbaum.

Zygouris-Coe, V., Wiggins, M. B., & Smith, L. H. (2004/2005). Engaging students with text: The 3-2-1 strategy. *Reading Teacher, 58*, 381–384.

CHAPTER 16

"But I'm Not Going to College!"

DEVELOPING ADOLESCENTS' LITERACY FOR THE 21ST-CENTURY WORKPLACE

Jill Lewis

Earning a college degree has become the gold standard requisite for realizing the American Dream. Meeting this standard has become increasingly possible, and greater accessibility to higher education through a variety of mechanisms since 1960 has increased enrollment. In fact, in 1999 the National Center for Education Statistics (NCES) found that during the previous 40 years enrollments at 4-year colleges had doubled, and at community colleges it had increased fivefold, a tribute to the open admissions policies at most 2-year institutions. Further, in the belief that a more rigorous curriculum will provide more students the skills they need to attend college, there is a recent trend among states to use college prep programs as the "default" programs for all high school students (Camara, 2003). The media are replete with ads targeted at parents who recognize the value of higher education and are trying to figure out how to pay college costs for their children, and questions about the affordability of a college education frequently make headline news.

It seems the conventional wisdom is that college is necessary for a positive economic future. This belief is borne out by income comparisons between those who attend and complete college and those who don't. For instance, recent U.S. Census Bureau (2006) data continue to demonstrate the labor market value of a college education. Workers with a bachelor's degree earned, on average, $51,206 a year, whereas those with a high school diploma averaged only $27,915 annually. Moreover, workers with advanced degrees earned an average yearly salary of $74,602, and workers without a high school diploma averaged $18,734 a year.

The reality, though, is that not all good jobs require a college degree. Rosenbaum (2004) points out:

> College degrees do not always have payoffs. And, college degrees are not required to enter many rewarding jobs, including construction trades, clerical and administrative support, auto and airplane mechanics, printing, graphics, financial services, and many government and social services. Union electricians, machinists, tool and die makers, and sheet-metal workers, for instance, have high-demand skills, excellent benefits, good working conditions, and annual salaries that often exceed $45,000 by age 28 (and are much higher with overtime. (¶2)

So should all young people go to college? Maybe. Maybe not. In any case, the reality is that they don't. And for us to plan middle and high school instruction only with *college for all* as the goal denies many adolescents access to skills they will need once they leave high school, including skills for the workplace.

This chapter does not argue with the importance of increasing opportunities for students to attend college or with the value of a higher education and obtaining a degree. It also recognizes that there are values to a college education that cannot be measured by dollars earned. Rather, the purpose here is (1) to provide evidence that not all students go to college and that even among those who do, not all complete degree requirements; (2) to argue that we, therefore, must prepare students for the workplace while they are in middle/high schools; and (3) to offer examples of curriculum elements that can satisfy the need for workplace literacy development with adolescents, especially for struggling readers.

High School Graduation and Dropout Data

High school graduation rates have been used as indicators of success by school districts across the country. Unfortunately, nationwide large numbers of students do not finish high school. A recent study from Editorial Projects in Education reports that only 69.9% of students nationwide graduate from high school with a regular diploma (Swanson, 2006). In a recent PBS Online NewsHour, Jay Greene (2006) noted, "We hit actually a peak in national graduation rates in 1979 at 76 percent, and now it's slipped down to about 70 percent. There were 2.7 million high school diplomas awarded in 2003 by public high schools. And, according to the census, there were about four million kids who could have been in that cohort to graduate, so about 70 percent" (¶.32).

Among minority students, data on high school graduation with a regular diploma are even more disturbing. In 2002–2003 only 51.6% of African American students, 55.6% of Hispanic students, and 47.4% of American Indian students graduated with a regular diploma, in contrast to 77% and 72.7% of Asian and European American students, respectively. Gender differences for high school graduation are also of concern when we look at minority groups, with African Americans showing the widest disparity: 57.8% for females and only 44.3% for males (Swanson, 2006).

Determining the percentage of students who drop out of high school is more complex than determining the percentage of those who do not graduate with a regular diploma. National data are imprecise at best. States currently use different formulas for determining the dropout rate, resulting in different graduation rates for different geographic areas. Many states base their figures on the percentage of students who leave high school each year without obtaining a secondary school credential or without enrolling in another educational program. But students often leave a district, moving to enroll in another school system either in or out of state, and tracking these students may be difficult. Others may enroll in general equivalency diploma (GED) programs, but schools may not receive enrollment information on their former students, and states vary insofar as the date by which a student must enroll in another educational program in order to be considered as "still attending." Still others may or may not be included in the dropout count if they leave school during the summer or get married, and those students who enter college after 3 years of high school may or may also not be included. The dropout rate of Hispanic students is particularly severe. Among those ages 16–24, Hispanic youth accounted for 40% of all high school dropouts in 2004. However, they made up only 17% of the total youth population (Child Trends, 2006).

Although some states have reported declines in their dropout rates, this is not necessarily a good sign. According to Western and Pettit (2002), a recent decrease in dropout rate is at least in part related to the dramatic increases in incarceration rates among African American high school dropouts since 1980, which takes them out of the civilian noninstitutionalized population on which these estimates are based.

Further complicating the data is some evidence that low-achieving students are being pushed out of high schools because of the effect their low scores have on a school's Adequate Yearly Progress and the subsequent penalties the school will face unless the scores improve. Orfield, Losen, Wald, and Swanson (2004) offer narratives from students in Alabama, Florida, New York, Illinois, and Mississippi who have either dropped out or have felt "pushed" out of school. They note, "Several of these stories illustrate the 'dark side' of high-stakes testing policies. Many of these students and their families express shock and dismay when they are told they will not be allowed to return to school or to graduate because of their poor test performance" (p. 3).

The need for transparency and consistency in the data is evident, and in July 2005, 45 governors and 12 national organizations signed onto *Graduation Counts: A Compact on State High School Graduation Data.* The signers of this agreement would use a common definition for their high school graduation rate. At the press conference celebrating the signing, National Governors Association chairman Mark Warner commented, "Because of the inconsistent quality of state data on graduation and dropout rates, many states cannot account for the status of their students as they progress through high school and beyond. The historic compact we signed today will help address this problem" (National Governors Association, 2005).

There are multiple reasons for students to drop out of school. In a recent survey of high school dropouts, two-thirds of those interviewed said that they would have worked harder if more had been required of them, and 70% of these former students were confident that they could have graduated if they had tried harder (Bridgeland, DiJulio, & Morison, 2006). From these students' comments, it appears that even they are blaming the victim, but more than one in every four high school seniors nationwide read at a level less than *proficient* on the Nation's Report Card (NCES, 2007) and their trying harder is not equivalent to getting some real help.

Economic, social, and educational factors surely all contribute to the dropout rate, and education reformers and schools have sought ways to keep adolescents in school. Nevertheless, despite their efforts and despite differences among ethnic groups and differences in results from the various formulas used, what we can say with certainty is that many students do not complete high school or graduate with a regular high school diploma. And although numbers differ somewhat and causes for not finishing high school vary, the point here is that not all students go on to college, and thus educators must prepare those who don't for the workplace that they will enter during their adolescent years.

College Completion Data

Another population we must address as we consider adolescent literacy curricula for middle and high schools is those students who do graduate high school with a regular diploma and attend college but who do not obtain a college degree. The percentage of high school graduates going on to college affects national high school rankings and property values, and high-achieving schools are sure to tout their success. What is not advertised and also not tracked by high schools is the percentage of students from any particular high school who begin college but do not complete their studies and do not obtain a degree. This number is large.

Various explanations are offered for noncompletion. Achieve, Inc. (Peter D. Hart Research Associates/Public Opinion Strategies, 2005) suggests that some noncompletion can be attributed to a lack of rigor in the high school curriculum. Others point to family income or parents' level of education. One study also examined college completion alongside college transfer rates and need for remedial course work at college (Camara, 2003) and found that 64% of traditional college students (high school graduates who enroll in college full-time immediately after high school) attained a BA degree in 6 years or less from a 4-year institution, versus 55% of all freshmen. Analysis by gender also yields differences in college completion. Census data released in February 2006 show that 31% of women ages 25–29 had attained a bachelor's degree or higher, whereas only 26% of comparable men held postsecondary degrees (U.S. Census Bureau, 2006).

For a variety of personal and economic reasons, many students start college several years after high school graduation, and many students take more than the traditional 4 years to complete a college education. Thus NCES (U.S. Department of Education, 2004) studied the college completion rate of 25–29-year-olds and found an increase from 22% in 1985 to 29% in 2000. This is still a small percentage graduating, and there has been no measurable difference since 2000. The study also reported that although increasing numbers of high school graduates attend college, many neither start nor complete college.

Thus, we have considerable evidence that large numbers of high school students drop out of high school, graduate from high school but do not go on to college, or begin college but do not complete their college education. It behooves us, then, to prepare students for multiple paths into adulthood and the workplace, even though a particular path may be less than we wanted for our children and less than they might have obtained under other circumstances. This should not be interpreted as a lack of faith in the capacity of children to succeed. Rather, it should be considered as an attempt to achieve balance between our hopes for all children and the reality.

Workplace Literacy as Part of the Middle/Secondary School Curriculum

Educators are familiar with the corporate sector's dissatisfaction with the skills students have when they graduate high school. *A Nation at Risk* (National Commission of Excellence in Education, 1983) is often considered the first wake-up call for the need for education reform, with the Sec-

retary's Commission on Achieving Necessary Skills (SCANS) of 1991 continuing the call for change. The Standards movement followed, and schools
continued to attempt to meet the challenges posed by the corporate community. But employers are not yet satisfied with the results, and recent
trends are even more unsettling for them. A recent report, *America's Perfect
Storm: Three Forces Changing our Nation's Future*, describes three powerful changes in American society, the confluence of which will create
economic disaster unless there are significant and immediate education
reforms: a shifting labor market wherein education and skills are increasingly valued; a changing demographic including a rapid-growing Hispanic
population; and significant disparities in reading and math skills, particularly along racial and socioeconomic lines (Kirsch, Braun, Yamamoto, &
Sum, 2007). It is with an eye on the need for reform, coupled with the realities of high school graduation, drop out rates, and noncompletion of college, that this section addresses literacy. It describes how teachers can meet
the need to have high expectations for students and encourage students to
reach their fullest potential, while simultaneously preparing students for
what is needed in the workplace—an environment many will enter sooner
rather than later.

High School Reform and Literacy for the Workplace

Some broad-based strategies have become recent hallmarks of high school
reform, and these may affect high school graduation and dropout rates.
They include career-focused tracks or career academies, student-driven
action plans, individual graduation plans that blend academics and other
learning experiences, and more rigorous course work and personalized
daily schedules for struggling students (Education Trust, 2005). Smaller
schools are becoming more popular, and studies suggest that they improve
student achievement (Wasley et al., 2000). Individualized career-oriented
learning programs tailored to students' learning needs and career plans are
also gaining traction, and vocational education has lost some of the stigma
it once had as the "track" for less capable students (Aratani, 2006). These
are large-scale initiatives, but they do not address needs at the classroom
level. What can we do during our daily instruction that will contribute to
the students' preparedness for work while simultaneously providing the
rigor and skills necessary for education beyond high school?

There are several reliable sources to which we can turn to determine
what is needed in literacy curriculum reform in order to prepare students
for entrance to the workplace after high school or even before high school
graduation. The first source is the business community's own input on
what it says it needs from its employees. This can be considered a reliable
source because it is in the business community's self-interest to describe
accurately what it needs from employees. According to a recent survey con-

ducted by the Partnership for the 21st Century, the nation's new workforce entrants are "woefully ill-prepared for the demands of today's and tomorrow's workplace," and there is considerable concern about the new workers who will replace retiring baby boomers (Casner-Lotto & Barrington, 2006). Some of the findings from the Executive Summary of this survey appear in Table 16.1, and they are critical for understanding what it is employers want in employees, including employees who have not attended college or completed a college education. Numbers on the table represent percentages of employers who believe a particular ability is important for high school, 2-year college, or 4-year college graduates to have.

Employers who were interviewed for the Partnership survey expressed great concern about the deficiencies of high school graduates. According to these employers, 42% of graduates were "deficiently prepared, with 80.9% deficient in written communication, 70.3% deficient in professionalism and 69.6% deficient in critical thinking" (Casner-Lotto & Barrington, 2006, p. 1). Respondents also said that critical thinking (77.8%) and creativity/ innovation (73.6%) would become increasingly important. Although the Partnership recognized the strategic role the corporate sector played in preparing students for work, more than three-fourths of the respondents held K–12 educators responsible for developing a ready workforce. Researchers for the American Diploma Project found similar weaknesses in high school graduates, noting "literacy and critical-thinking skills as much more important than job-specific or computer skills" (American Diploma Project, 2004, p. 3).

Students can also provide important information about their readiness for work. Achieve's study (Peter D. Hart Research Associates, 2005) of 1,487 recent high school graduates, 400 employers, and 300 college instructors found that 39% of recent graduates who entered the workforce without earning a college degree say that there were gaps in their prepara-

TABLE 16.1. Top Five Most Important Skills

	High school graduates	Two-year college graduates	Four-year college graduates
Professionalism	80.3	83.4	93.8
Teamwork	74.7	82.7	94.4
Oral communication	70.3	82.0	95.4
Ethics and social responsibility	63.4		
Reading comprehension	62.5	71.6	
Critical thinking		72.7	92.1

Note. From Casner-Lotto and Barrington (2006). Reprinted with permission from The Conference Board, Inc.

tion for what is expected of them in their current jobs. Employers who also estimate that 39% of recent high school graduates are unprepared for entry-level jobs confirm the students' self-assessment.

Literacy for the Workplace: Classroom Strategies

There are areas in which academic literacy (Lewis, 1996, 2007a, 2007b) and workplace literacy overlap. For instance, all students in middle/secondary schools should be engaged in activities that develop their abilities to think critically to solve problems. But there are unique features of literacy needed in the workplace that often go unnoticed and unaddressed in the middle/secondary school. What would middle and high school curricula look like if these features were added? How can we align some of a curriculum with employer expectations? Although the following discussion doesn't offer all possible strategies for all content fields, it does provide enough suggestions to give a flavor of what is needed. Some suggestions may seem rudimentary, perhaps unsophisticated for middle and high schoolers. However, the recent National Assessment of Educational Progress (NAEP) scores of 12th graders, in which the average reading score for 12th graders in 2005 was the lowest since 1992 (NCES, 2007), confirm that middle and high school teachers must address large numbers of struggling readers, helping them to access and utilize texts similar to those that they will encounter in the workplace. As Lewis (2007b) has noted, our teaching must begin where the students are but demonstrate how to move beyond their existing knowledge to formulate new understandings. In this section we look at five dimensions of literacy that we can develop in all middle/secondary classrooms with the workplace in mind, which do not water down content but can add to the students' repertoire of literacy skills: reading comprehension, oral communication, written communication, teamwork, and creativity/innovation. These suggestions can be woven into teachers' daily plans.

Workplace Literacy and Reading Comprehension

Several aspects of reading comprehension must be addressed that have particular relevance for the workplace and regardless of a student's career aspirations. These include summarizing/restating written and spoken texts, evaluating sources of information, interpreting and responding to visual messages, following directions, and reading documents. To address several of these comprehension skills, Lewis (2007a) offers activities that can occur in any content classroom.

Summarizing/Restating Written and Spoken Texts

The ability to summarize and restate ideas is needed for the workplace where information is communicated from one employee to another, perhaps from a superior to an employee, who in turn may need to communicate it to others. For practice, students can identify the essential elements of the original ideas and put these into concise, easily remembered language. Content teachers find that initially using short pieces of text, and gradually progressing to longer ones, is especially beneficial to struggling readers, following this procedure:

> Choose written text that contains complex ideas and language. Select two or three key sentences from the text that students will need to rewrite in their own words after they have read the text. They may do this with a partner or a small group. The class should compare responses to (1) confirm comprehension of complex ideas; (2) recognize multiple ways the same idea can be expressed; (3) develop new academic vocabulary. If students' have changed the meaning of the text, discuss where the confusion may have occurred and have students revise their original re-written sentence. Students can partner to create sentences or to compare their writing prior to class review. After working with single sentences that contain complex ideas, students should be able to transition to creating summaries of texts of increasing complexity and length. (Lewis, 2007a, p. 157)

A similar process can be used for restating/summarizing oral communications, beginning with brief conversations, such as a telephone conversation, and then going on to a longer communication that would be similar to a meeting in the workplace, for which students might take notes and then summarize the key points of the meeting.

Evaluating Sources of Information

The workplace can be rife with rumors, and students need to know that news or rumors they hear at work should be carefully considered before being accepted as "truth." When is something most likely fact? When is it opinion? Young workers are undergoing a transition in their ability to evaluate and make judgments about ideas (see Lewis & Dahbany, Chapter 1, this volume). We can help them become more proficient at determining whether something is believable through a few short activities, each of which can be designed for particular subject areas.

To begin, teachers can draw distinctions between different types of false ideas students may encounter in texts, friends, all forms of media (including the Internet), and in the workplace. At the website *www. About.com*, students can access information about four types of false ideas: Hoax = false, deliberately deceptive information; UL = urban legend—a

popularly believed narrative, typically false; Rumor = anecdotal claims—
may be true, false, or in between; Junk = flotsam and jetsam of the Net. At
this website, students can also learn how a rumor may become a legend:

> It's typical for the content of rumors, hoaxes, and urban legends to undergo
> changes as they pass from person to person (or inbox to inbox, though texts
> forwarded via e-mail tend to vary less than orally transmitted versions). Vari-
> ants emerge for a couple of reasons. For one, as anyone who has ever played
> the children's game called "Telephone" can attest, perception and memory can
> be fallible, and people tend to misremember and/or misreport what they've
> heard. For another, it's simply in the nature of storytelling and storytellers to
> "creatively enhance" the details of a yarn to make it more scary, more funny,
> or more believable. (Urban Legends, n.d., ¶3)

Students can identify and discuss rumors, hoaxes, and urban legends
they've heard. Examples offered at *www.About.com* include the following:
AOL is planning to eliminate unlimited access; parking lot thieves knock
out their victims by convincing them to sniff ether-laced perfume; cell
phones cause gas station explosions. Students might conduct research to
find the origin of these stories.

A second suggested strategy for developing reading comprehension
useful for the workplace encourages students to analyze the basis of opinions and to avoid accepting only those opinions that confirm students' current beliefs or ignoring evidence that does not agree with their current
thinking. Lewis (2007a) identifies three types of opinions that differ
because of the level of expertise on which each is based: Expert Opinion,
Informed Opinion, and Unsupported Opinion. Teachers can provide students with the characteristics and examples of each of these. For instance,
Expert Opinion usually has firsthand research as a basis for opinion, as in
the case of a jazz historian writing about the influence of John Coltrane or
an archeologist offering an opinion about how the pyramids were built.
Informed Opinions often make references to reliable data sources, findings
from experts, or historical references; they may also use visual aids to support their ideas. Unsupported Opinions include sweeping generalizations,
stereotypes, and unsupported claims (Lewis, 2007b).

Once students are able to distinguish between different types of opinions, they can look for examples of these in content texts, including newspapers and Web texts. Students may also be given statements and asked
to explain what would be needed to make each statement an Expert,
Informed, or Unsupported Opinion. For example, the statement "People
who purchase hybrid cars buy them because they care about global warming" lends itself to different opinions. Students may suggest for Expert
Opinion, "I interviewed 20 hybrid car owners, and 36% of them said they
purchased the car because of their concern about global warming"; for
Informed Opinion they could create a sentence such as, "*Time* magazine

reported that its survey of car dealers and hybrid car owners found that more often than not, individuals bought hybrid cars because of concerns about global warming"; an Unsupported Opinion may possibly be, "I think people buy hybrid cars out of concern for global warming." When students work with texts, encourage continued application of these distinctions.

Interpreting and Responding to Visual Messages

A third comprehension skill critical to success in the workplace and that can easily be incorporated into content-area lessons is the ability to interpret visual messages accurately and to respond to and create such messages. Lewis (2007a, 2007b) notes that any time students encounter graphic aids in their textbooks, teachers have an opportunity to teach comprehension strategies. Such visuals may include bar charts, pie charts (or circle graphs), flowcharts, time lines, tables, line graphs, diagrams, photographs, maps, or artwork. After identifying the key features of the visual they want to share with students, teachers can discuss the graphics in ways that will direct students to closer inspection of the visual and facilitate comprehension. For example, a teacher may ask students to:

1. Determine whether a visual supports a particular quote from a text.
2. Add to the visual another detail from the text in which it is found.
3. Give their personal response to the visual.
4. Find two visuals on the same topic and note any differences they see in the ways information on the same topic is portrayed on these.
5. Explain how the purposes of two visuals on the same topic differ.
6. Discuss how the visual helps them to better understand their world.
7. Discuss how the visual helps students to comprehend the text.
8. Make predictions about the percentages that will be included to complete this visual. (To do this, leave off some data from the visual.)
9. Draw inferences from this visual.
10. Draw conclusions from this visual.
11. Paraphrase or summarize this visual.
12. Explain the different parts of this visual related to each other.
13. Use this visual to create questions for a quiz.
14. Draw a sketch, graph, chart, or table for the information here.
15. Discuss two (2) things that visual A tells you more easily than graph B, and what visual B tells you more easily than visual A. (To do this, select two visuals from the same text where similar information is displayed differently.) (Lewis, 2007a, pp. 157–158)

Workplace Literacy and Oral Communication

Increasingly, employees need to communicate with each other. This requires effective speaking and listening skills as well as the ability to interpret non-verbal communication. To get students better prepared for communication in the workplace, teachers may begin with a simple diagram of the communication process illustrating the listening/speaking cycle. Many students can no doubt provide examples of times when they were speaking and thought they were not being heard. Encourage them to discuss issues of respect, clarifying, feedback, and tone.

Oral communication experiences most relevant for the workplace include individual presentations, small-group discussion, and interviews. Purposes for listening can include learning new information, following directions, and sharing work assignments. Students must learn to develop the ability to develop criteria for effective communication and to assess their own performance as well as that of others. Practice in recognizing and interpreting nonverbal communication will also be valuable.

Developing Speaking Skills

According to the U.S. Bureau of Labor Statistics (2005) many of the jobs available to students who do not attend or complete college will be in service sector positions, such as filled by cashiers, retail salespersons, combined food preparation and serving-related workers, waitstaff member, office clerks, customer service representatives, and child care workers. There are many activities students in middle and high schools can do to prepare for effective communication in these situations. Role playing, for instance, can address issues of student diction, eye contact, grammar, and appropriate responses to customer questions and comments. Such activities can be designed to address content while developing speaking skills. For example, a student may pose as a travel agent and another student may be interested in visiting a certain place, which can form the basis of a geography lesson. The two students can exchange questions and answers about the region to be visited to reinforce their geographical knowledge while also attending to effective communication.

Whether students are interviewing for college entrance or for the workplace, practice in having an interview can be truly valuable and can generate good student participation. At *www.tfpl.com/temporary_recruitment/candidates/ccv___interviews.cfm*, students can learn how to handle themselves, prepare for certain types of questions, manage individual as well as group interviews they may have, and what to do if a question arises that suggests an attempt to get information that may lead to discrimination, such as marital status, sexual preference, age, or disability. Students may not be aware of the obligations employers have in this regard when they are looking for new hires.

Any individual who is successful in the workplace, even a person without a college degree, has the possibility of advancing to a position requiring increasingly sophisticated communication skills. In Chapter 1 of this book,

Lewis and Dahbany direct readers to a rubric to use for evaluating presentations (p. 22). This rubric works equally well for simulations of workplace presentations, such as training sessions (students in a science class may conduct "training" on how to perform an experiment), explaining new software (in the students' computer class), or introducing bookstore employees to an author's new book that has just been received.

Improving Listening Skills

Teachers are all too familiar with adolescents who are physically present in class but appear mentally absent. Helping students to develop an awareness of the indicators of effective listening gives them a greater chance of full participation in the workplace and less likelihood of making mistakes because they have failed to hear a directive from a superior. Students can be provided an inventory to assess their listening behaviors (see Figure 16.1) and can set goals for improvement. Their inventories might be used for several classes; this can help students to realize the correlation between listening and achievement in class.

Nonverbal Communication

Communication is also affected by nonverbal information the speaker and listener provide. Some estimate that as much as 93% of our communication is nonverbal. Although it is difficult to verify the accuracy of this figure, an awareness of one's own nonverbal communication as well as that of others is important in any job situation. Nonverbal communication usually refers to body language, which generally includes eye contact, gestures, posture, dress, expression, and personal space. Links to a wide variety of information about nonverbal communication can be found at *www3.usal.es/~nonverbal/miscellany.htm*. Having students analyze teachers' nonverbal cues, using a form similar to that shown in Figure 16.2, can help them to develop an awareness of nonverbal communication. Of course, students would need permission to do this, but it can generate interesting discussion.

Communication issues that are prevalent in high school also provide opportunities to discuss how similar problems may occur in the workplace and that the strategies students use to cope with these issues while still in school can be beneficial upon graduation. These issues include learning how to say "no" without offending anyone; dealing with aggressive or hostile individuals; building trust and confidence; and setting boundaries for how others may speak to them. Students' personal experiences in handling these situations, along with role play, offer good opportunities for developing communication skills.

DIRECTIONS: The survey that follows asks a series of questions that you should answer on the basis of your experiences and your knowledge of yourself. Think for a few minutes about each question before you rate yourself. Be as truthful as possible. The information you obtain is to be used for your own benefit. It is not a test! You will not be graded on your answers.

SURVEY OF LISTENING BEHAVIORS				
Directions: For each item, circle the number that you feel best describes you as you are now. (1 = not true of me at all; 4 = very true of me)				
1. I spend a lot of time planning what to say back to someone when he or she is talking to me, rather than listening to what the person is saying.	1	2	3	4
2. I don't like pauses in conversation and usually fill in someone else's words when the person pauses to think.	1	2	3	4
3. I focus on the speaker and don't let my mind drift off.	1	2	3	4
4. I get distracted when I listen and glance at the clock or my watch, the T.V., or anything else around me.	1	2	3	4
5. I show interest and attention by leaning in toward the speaker.	1	2	3	4
6. I avoid monopolizing or taking over the conversation and let the other person talk.	1	2	3	4
7. I get fidgety when listening and move around a lot.	1	2	3	4
8. I use encouraging and complimentary words to show my feelings toward the speaker.	1	2	3	4
9. I am able to ask questions if I don't understand what the speaker is saying.	1	2	3	4
10. I am quick to offer solutions to the speaker's problems.	1	2	3	4
11. I get annoyed when the speaker doesn't follow my advice.	1	2	3	4
12. I try to follow the speaker's ideas and to check that I understand the conversation.	1	2	3	4
13. I believe I use effective listening skills.	1	2	3	4
14. I believe my listening skills will be effective in my career.	1	2	3	4

(continued)

FIGURE 16.1. Listening survey. Adapted with permission from MacKenzie (2006).

Now analyze the results of your survey. Item numbers appear below for Effective Listening Behaviors and Ineffective Listening Behaviors. Put your score for each next to the number of the item.

Effective Listening Behaviors: 3 ___ 5 ___ 6 ___ 8 ___ 9___ 12___ 13___ 14___

Ineffective Listening Behaviors: 1 ___ 2 ___ 4___ 7 ___ 10 ___ 11___

Did you have many 1s for the Ineffective Listening Behaviors and many 4s for the Effective Listening Behaviors?

Assessing Your Listening Behavior

1. Based on the information you've obtained from this survey, what are your areas of greatest confidence? _____

2. In a few sentences, describe the listening goals you would like to achieve this year.

_____

_____

_____

FIGURE 16.1. *(continued)*

Workplace Literacy and Written Communication

As noted earlier, the business community has been disheartened by the poor writing skills of their recent employees. One of the reasons for this lack may have to do with the students' writing experiences in middle and high school. Typically, adolescents receive considerable practice in writing persuasive essays and occasionally are asked to write a letter, a personal essay, or a set of directions for others to follow. But writing needs for the workplace are somewhat different from these typical assignments, especially for entry-level employees. While still in middle/high school, students can become familiar with some writing formats that are encountered more often in the workplace, such as letters of introduction, memos, e-mail, and resumes.

Letters of Introduction

A letter of introduction is often used when a prospective employee is applying for a job, and it would be included with a resume. Students can practice writing letters of introduction by preparing one for a teacher of almost any class they are taking. The message would include the student's (1) reasons for taking the class, (2) career goals, (3) a brief description of any work

Directions: Complete this activity for one of your teachers. For each category
write a few sentences that characterize your teacher's nonverbal behavior.
Then explain how these characteristics affect you as a listener.

1. EYE CONTACT

_____

_____

_____

2. GESTURES

_____

_____

_____

3. POSTURE

_____

_____

_____

4. DRESS OR PHYSICAL APPEARANCE

_____

_____

_____

5. VOCAL EXPRESSION

_____

_____

_____

6. PERSONAL SPACE

_____

_____

_____

WHAT ELSE DO YOU NOTICE ABOUT THIS TEACHER'S COMMUNICATION
STYLE THAT AFFECTS YOU AS A LISTENER?

_____

_____

_____

FIGURE 16.2. Analyzing nonverbal behavior.

experience, (4) favorite activities, (5) an assessment and discussion of the student's current communication skills, including strengths and weaknesses, and (6) a brief discussion of the student's familiarity with e-mail and other communication technologies. Before students write their letters, the class might discuss why each of these elements would be important in a letter of introduction. The final result might look like Figure 16.3.

Writing Business Memos

Most businesses use online or hard copy one-page memos to communicate with employees and reduce meeting time. Knowing the various components of a business memo can enable students to read as well as to write them, should the need arise. Entry-level employees can anticipate receiving memos from coworkers, including upper management and colleagues who work in the same department, as well as employees who are located elsewhere in the company. Effective business memos communicate simply, using primarily declarative sentences so that readers can quickly understand what is required. Teachers can have students write memos related to group projects to inform each other about aspects of the group work such as meeting places and times, what to bring to a meeting, what the objectives will be, what the roles of group members will be. The standard format for the memo described here can be used for a group presentation being planned on *metamorphosis*.

In the "To" section, the author writes the membership of the group project, such as *Team Members for Metamorphosis Presentation*. If the memo is from the team leader, that job title comes after the student's name—for example, *Wilma Johnson, Team Chairperson*—and if the memo is typed, the chairperson initials the typed name. The date is the date the memo is written, and the subject line is specific, such as *Next Team Meeting Date and Responsibilities*, as in the following example:

MEMORANDUM

TO: (readers' names and job titles, or team or group name)

FROM: (your name and job title)

DATE:

SUBJECT: (specifically what the memo is about)

The contents of memos vary, but the structure usually includes an opening section that states any issues that may be addressed in the memo. For instance, the team may have agreed to meet once a certain period of time has passed, or there may be a need to review the assignment. Next, the purpose for the memo is stated, which in this case is to set a meeting date to make and sure that the assignment is understood and all roles for the pro-

MILES WALKER
29 Finderne Street
Jersey City, NJ 07305
555-126-3454

February 26, 2008

Mrs. Lisa Moore, Teacher
Snyder High School
1076 Kennedy Blvd.
Jersey City, NJ 07305

Dear Mrs. More:

SUBJECT: STUDENT INTRODUCTION

At your request, I am providing you with additional information about my life
and goals. Thank you for the opportunity to share this information.

- **Why I'm Taking ART II:** I consider myself a serious art student. I like to
  paint and draw and have used pastels and oils to create different works. I
  think this class will help me to improve my artwork.
- **My Career Goals:** I am undecided right now, but I do plan to do
  something in the arts.
- **Employment History:** I have worked part-time the past 17 months for
  McDonald's as a cashier.
- **Communication Skills:** I feel I speak clearly and have a nice voice. I like
  speaking to the customers, and they seldom ask me to repeat anything. I
  consider myself friendly. I am a decent writer, but could use more
  instruction.
- **Technology:** This is my strongest area; you might even call me a
  "computer geek." Composing technomusic is a hobby of mine. I have a great
  deal of experience with Internet use, including search engines and e-mail.

If you need additional information, please let me know. I look forward to the
class and believe I will learn a lot this year.

Sincerely,

Miles Walker

FIGURE 16.3. Sample letter of introduction.

ject are clear. The memo's closing summarizes what was said and the action that should follow, such as the date, time, and location of the meeting. A courteous "thank you" at the end of a memo is always valued. Until recently, memos were not signed; sometimes the author initialed the "From" section. Increasingly, though, a signature does appear at the end of a memo, under a typed signature, so students can be given the option of providing the signature either way.

Writing E-Mail

E-mail has become the standard communication form in many businesses, even between coworkers whose desks are next to each other. This is a quick means of communicating and provides a paperless method for retaining and filing documents. Unfortunately, students have often developed a set of bad habits that, if unchecked, can follow them into the workplace with negative consequences. It is important to remind students about the uses of e-mail in the workplace:

- If e-mail is written on a company machine, it is not yours alone.
- E-mail is not private. Don't say things you will regret.
- Personal e-mail should not be done during paid work time.
- Avoid "flaming" in e-mail. Keep your tone professional.
- Anything you say in e-mail can be forwarded to another person, so be careful about what you write.
- Abbreviated "e-mail-eze" is not acceptable for professional e-mails (e.g., *bcuz, lol*).
- E-mail should not substitute for one-on-one communication.

In all content fields, students can practice sending e-mail to teachers and fellow students that reflects these considerations. They can also discuss the benefits of e-mail and how it differs from face-to-face communication. Teachers may ask students whether they would prefer to receive grades by e-mail, regardless of the grades they receive, and point out how negative e-mail may be better delivered in person. Ask how they handle e-mail that angers them, and teach the 24-hour rule: waiting at least 24 hours before responding to e-mail that upsets them. Ask whether they have ever received e-mail that was confusing or misunderstood and how they handled such communication. Describe how assignments sent by e-mail need to be written (and draw parallels to work assignments), as well as how to get clarifications. First impressions drawn from e-mail can be shared: How do tone, spelling, and format affect the students' reactions? These brief discussions can prepare students for professional and responsible use of e-mail in the workplace.

Writing Resumes

A resume, an often overlooked writing form, is important to a student's future. Adolescents who do not plan to attend college, who do not complete their high school education, or who start college but do not earn a degree often do not have any preparation for writing a resume. Students can be introduced to this writing format by creating resumes for historical figures, literary characters, scientists, artists, or any significant individual in a content field. Using resources found on the Internet and elsewhere, students can research these individuals and create resumes that follow resume-writing guidelines. They can then develop personal resumes to highlight their individuality, yet conforming to resume style. They can learn about proofreading, honesty, relevance of skills and past accomplishments, and accuracy. Sample resume formats can be found at *www.jobsearch. about.com/od/resumes/p/resumetypes.htm*. An example of a resume for a student applying for a part-time job is shown in Figure 16.4.

Workplace Literacy and Teamwork

Many students have already experienced teamwork in some of the workplaces where they have held jobs, such as at McDonald's or in a store at a mall. As mentioned earlier, employers depend heavily on the ability of their employees to work in teams, and yet the workforce is not meeting employers' needs in this regard. There is a rapidly growing need for employees to work collaboratively in the workplace, and teamwork is dependent on effective communication. Increasingly, the workplace also requires collaboration between experts from many different fields. Costa (n.d.), notes,

> Cooperative humans realize that all of us together are more powerful—intellectually and/or physically—than any one individual. Probably the foremost disposition in our post industrial society is the heightened ability to think in concert with others; to find ourselves increasingly more interdependent and sensitive to the needs of others. Problem solving has become so complex that no one person can go it alone. No one has all the data needed to make critical decisions; no one person can consider as many alternatives as several people can. (p. 13)

The value of teamwork has long been recognized. Johnson and Johnson (1986) found persuasive evidence that cooperative teams achieve at higher levels of thought and retain information longer than students who work quietly as individuals. Students are capable of performing at higher intellectual levels when asked to work in collaborative situations than when asked to work individually (Vygotsky, 1978). Equally, teamwork can provide the means for developing leadership, building relationships, and enhancing communication skills.

ALLISON GRAHAM
12 Stirrup Court
Somerville, NJ 08816
(555) 686-1325
E-mail: agraham16@aol.com

Objective: **To obtain a part-time job after school and weekends**

PERSONAL TRAITS

Honest and trustworthy.   Dependable.   Cooperative.   Willing to learn.

OUT-OF-SCHOOL WORK EXPERIENCE

2006–2007 Waitress & Cashier (*Fondue Café*)
Worked in local restaurant
Waited tables during rush hour
Cashier

2005–2007 Babysitter
Babysat for children ages 3, 4, and 6 in neighbor's home

2005–2007 Artist and poet
Combined my artwork and poetry to produce material for sale at craft shows.

IN-SCHOOL WORK EXPERIENCE

2006–2007 President, School Honor Society
Provide Society members with direction on school projects, including book club sales,
school store, and bake sales.
Meet with school administration to discuss classes and curriculum

2005–2007 Founder and President, School Poetry Club
Meet weekly to prepare *Rainbow*, the new school poetry magazine

Education: High school graduation—June 2008. AP classes in Music, English, Art History
Summer Gifted and Talented Program, Bryn Mawr College, Bryn Mawr, PA, July 2006

FIGURE 16.4. Student's part-time job resume.

Many teachers are familiar with research on teamwork and do engage students in small-group work and this kind of activity. Examples of small-group activities are provided throughout this book. However, both students and teachers sometimes comment that during group work, it is often only one or two students who "carry" the group. Others do little, which seems unfair and makes grading group projects difficult. Thus, although students are placed in groups, not all participate and not all learn to become effective team members. One answer to making the process of good teamwork more accessible to students is to have them complete a rubric (see Figure 16.5) to evaluate their own efforts in the group as well as those of other team members. This experience addresses the need for all students to learn that they have a responsibility to contribute to the team while also calling their attention to the features of effective group work.

Workplace Literacy and Creativity/Innovation

Although the business community does not recognize the need for employees with only a high school degree or less to have sophisticated thinking skills, it is evident that success in the workplace is often dependent on being able to "think outside the box." Highly creative individuals, such as Einstein, Newton, and DaVinci, had new ways of looking at things and frequently suggested alternatives for solving problems. This is a highly usable skill in the workplace, which may go unnoticed until a real problem arises, but creative workers use it almost every day. Think about the example RAFT activity in Chapter 1 of this book, designed to develop students' ability to understand multiple perspectives. Individuals who are creative are able to do that—they can reflect on how something may appear to someone else. A flexible salesperson, for example, is able to consider the value of a product to a customer, even if that customer's tastes, needs, and lifestyle are very different from the salesperson's. A creative salesperson can also encourage the customer to think about a product from a new perspective, perhaps a product the customer never thought he or she needed and now absolutely must have. Innovative workers can also look at a situation, such as a restaurant's food service, and identify ways in which the restaurant might provide it more efficiently or offer better service. There are strategies for promoting creativity and innovation in the classroom without sacrificing curriculum.

Creative Questioning

Teachers can promote creativity in their classrooms by eliminating forced-choice answers to test questions and by promoting open-ended class discussions that encourage students to think about possibilities. Questions that ask students to think about incongruent possibilities and "What would

This checklist is used to assess and give feedback on daily student performance in a team.

Contribution to Group's Tasks and Completion of Personal Tasks				
• Participates actively				
• Models caring about goals				
• Helps direct the group in setting goals				
• Does not impede the group's goal setting				
• Helps direct group in meeting goals				
• Does not distract the group from meeting its goals				
• Thoroughly completes assigned tasks				
Discussion Skills and Active Listening				
• Shares many ideas related to the goals				
• Encourages all group members to share their ideas				
• Empathetic to other people's feelings and ideas				
• Listens attentively to others				
Contribution to Group's Evaluation, Problem Solving and Cohesion				
• Encourages group members to evaluate how well they are working together				
• Involves the whole group in problem solving				
• Actively participates in helping group members to work better together				

FIGURE 16.5. The effective team member: A checklist. Adapted by Hilary McLeod, Peel District School Board, from the *Bellingham Schools Home Page*, Kulshan Middle School. *schools.tdsb.on.ca/riverdale/welcome/guidance/curriculum/careerstudy/handouts/handout02.htm.*

happen if" generate creative thought. Teachers can also invite students to ask questions that yield creative responses. The broader the question, the fuller the answers generated and the richer the possibilities that may evolve. Nancy Pearl offers an interesting example. In 1996, Pearl, then executive director of the Washington Center for the Book (WCB) at the Seattle Public Library, asked the question, "What if everybody in Seattle read the same book?" This evolved into the If All of Seattle Reads the Same Book project. Since then, more than 50 cities, counties, or states have begun programs that encourage members of a community to read the same book at the same time and then discuss it in numerous venues. An art instructor, Marvin

Bartel (2004/2006), designed a set of questions to promote students' creative thinking about their work. Figure 16.6 provides an adaptation of Bartel's work for teachers of all content fields. The questions generate thoughtful responses about the resources used, the effect on the audience, and the students' own thinking processes as they progressed.

Brainstorming and Problem Solving

Brainstorming ideas in small groups is a valuable activity for developing innovative thinking. Cullen (1998) explains:

> Brainstorming is an activity used to generate ideas in small groups. The purpose is to generate as many ideas as possible within a specified time-period. These ideas are not evaluated until the end and a wide range of ideas is often produced. Each idea produced does not need to be usable. Instead, initial ideas can be viewed as a starting point for more workable ideas. The principle of brainstorming is that you need lots of ideas to get good ideas. (¶1)

Creating a mind map, sometimes called a web, semantic map, or a semantic web, is an excellent strategy for generating multiple thoughts on a particular topic. Michalko (1994) uses a variation of this, the Lotus Blossom activity, wherein students freely associate links between the ideas generated on one theme or problem, and new ideas and connections are generated. Michalko explains, "This exercise involves starting with a central theme or problem and working outward, using ever-widening circles or 'petals.' Central themes lead to ideas that themselves become central themes, and so forth. The unfolding themes trigger new ideas and new themes." He offers an example of how this strategy worked for an unemployed marketing executive, illustrating how value can be added to ideas if we let the creative process flow. Using the Lotus Blossom exercise to generate ideas that he needed to land a job, his central theme was "job." One of the ideas surrounding this central box was "create a resume." "Resume" then became a new central theme, and, by generating new ideas and connections around this theme, he came up with a number of variations on the idea of a resume. "For example, he took out ads in several papers with the bold headline '$50,000 Reward.' The fine print below explained that an employer could save $50,000 by not paying a headhunter to find a person with his marketing talents. When interested employers called the number listed in the ad, they heard a recording of his resume. He received 45 job offers" (Michalko, 1994, ¶9).

Similarly, teachers can promote creativity and innovation by encouraging students not to settle on their first answer to solve a problem. Either individual students or small groups can be given a problem to solve, with their task being to suggest as many ways as possible to solve it. This can be

Thinking Questions (for the art class)	Thinking Questions (for other classes)
Materialization of thought and feeling	**Materialization of thought and feeling**
What would be a wrong material for this work? Why would it be wrong? What materials could I compare in order to see which I think is best? How am I changing the look because of the _____ I am using? How do I select materials to say what is important to me? Which other materials should I try using for this work?	These questions can also be applied to resources students plan to use for a project, equations for a math problem. Change "look" to "focus."
Considering innovation If students make too many cliché subjects, post and ask questions of this kind: What am I doing in this artwork that I never tried before in another artwork? What is the opposite of the effect that I am trying to get? How is my work different from anything I have ever seen done by others? What would my work sound like as music? What instruments would play it? What things do I try before I am satisfied with my discoveries? How can I work with fewer distractions so my ideas can flow better? What can I do to change these materials so they include a surprise?	Most of these questions work in all content fields. Change "artwork" to the appropriate format, e.g., project, presentation, research paper.
Considering my growth and abilities Use these questions to encourage new learning: What should I sketch or practice to figure out how I want something to look? What are the parts that are more challenging than what I usually do? What skills am I practicing and learning as I create this artwork?	Most of these questions are appropriate for all content fields. If needed, change "sketch or practice" to "write" wherever needed; change "artwork" to the format being used.

(continued)

FIGURE 16.6. Thinking questions for all classes. Adapted with permission from Bartel (2004, updated March 18, 2006).

Considering the quality of my work

Use these questions to encourage more imaginative thinking about the possibilities:

What things can I repeat but also change to give motion in my work?

How can I have less motion in the work?

What things could be made bigger and what parts could be made smaller?

What parts are most apparent to somebody seeing this work for the first time?

What parts seem heaviest and what parts lightest?

How can I make my lines and edges lively?

How can I make them calm?

How can I show fastness and slowness in my work?

How do I show that I care about my work, or that I do not care?

If I am tight, how can I become loose and flamboyant?

How can I make my colors really stand out? How could I really blend them?

How can I make everything look flat and without any depth?

Do I want the piece to be realistic, fantastic, expressive, formal, or a mixture of styles?

Do I want my work to make a statement or to ask a question?

What can I hide in my work to give it secret magic and mystery?

How can I provide hints and clues in my work?

Although many of these questions seem specific to art, they can be revised for other content fields. The idea is to get students to think of ways their work may be more distinctive. For example, if writing a persuasive essay, a student may ask, "What things should I emphasize more to make a stronger argument?" The questions about tone in art can be revised, if needed, to ask about tone in other types of materials the student is preparing.

Reflection and anticipation

Use these questions to inculcate thinking ahead to the next learning opportunity:

What questions did I ask myself as I worked that were not on this list?

What ideas would I not have thought of without doing this work?

What did I learn today by doing this artwork?

What are some other questions every artist should ask?

What important ideas were purposely omitted from this work?

What do I need to do next?

Nearly all of these questions work for all content fields.

FIGURE 16.6. *(continued)*

a math problem, a science lab experiment, getting information about music preferences from students at their school, or changing the school cafeteria's lunch selections. Once students think of several possibilities for solving the problem, consider whether (1) some ideas may be combined for even greater effectiveness, or (2) it may be helpful to think in opposites, such as what can be done to ensure that the cafeteria never changes its food choices.

Concluding Comments

Teaching adolescents in middle/high schools with an eye toward workplace literacy lends itself to some unique classroom opportunities that can serve all students well. Teaching in this way does not mean that students will never encounter (or never grow to love) great literary works or the fascinating worlds of physics or political science available in middle/high school classrooms through the United States. It does challenge teachers, however, to take seriously the task of preparing *all* students for their futures, realizing how different the future may be for each adolescent we teach.

References

American Diploma Project. (2004). *Ready or not: Creating a high school diploma that counts.* Retrieved January 20, 2007, from *www.achieve.org/files/ADPreport_7.pdf.*

Aratani, L. (2006, March 12). Vo-tech as a door to college. *The Washington Post,* p. C11. Retrieved January 22, 2007, from *www.washingtonpost.com/wp-dyn/content/article/2006/03/11/AR2006031101158.html.*

Bartel, M. (2004, updated March 18, 2006). *Encouraging creative thinking with awareness questions.* Retrieved March 2, 2007, from *www.bartelart.com/arted/questions.html.*

Bridgeland, J., DiJulio, J., & Morison, K. B. (2006). *The silent epidemic: Perspectives of high school dropouts.* Washington, DC: Civic Enterprises. Retrieved January 18, 2007, from *www.gatesfoundation.org/nr/downloads/ed/TheSilentEpidemic 3-06FINAL.pdf.*

Camara, W. J. (2003). *College persistence, graduation, and remediation.* The College Board. Retrieved March 16, 2006, from *www.collegeboard.com/repository/rn19_22643.pdf.*

Casner-Lotto, J., & Barrington, L. (2006, October). *Are they really ready to work?: Employers perspectives on the basic knowledge and applied skills of new entrants to the 21st century U.S. workforce.* Executive Summary. The Conference Board, Partnership for 21st Century Skills, Corporate Voices for Working Families, Society for Human Resource Management. Retrieved February 21, 2007, from *www.cvworkingfamilies.org/downloads/Business%20and%20 Education%20Executive%20Summary.pdf.*

Child Trends. (2006). *High school dropout rates.* Retrieved February 20, 2007, from *www.childtrendsdatabank.org/pdf/1_PDF.pdf.*

Costa, A. L. (n.d.). *Components of a well developed thinking skills program.* Retrieved January 14, 2007, from *www.newhorizons.org/strategies/thinking/costa2.htm.*

Cullen, B. (1998). Brainstorming before speaking tasks. *Internet TESL Journal,* 4(7). Retrieved February 10, 2007, from *iteslj.org/Techniques/Cullen-Brainstorming/.*

Education Trust. (2005, November). *Gaining traction, gaining ground: How some high schools accelerate learning for struggling students.* Washington, DC: Author. Retrieved December 18, 2006, from *www2.edtrust.org/NR /rdonlyres/6226B581-83C3-4447-9CE7-31C5694B9EF6/0/GainingTractionGainingGround.pdf.*

Greene, J. (Originally aired June 27, 2006). High school drop-out rates rise. *PBS The Online NewsHour.* Retrieved February 20, 2007, from *www.pbs.org/newshour/bb/education/jan-june06/dropout_06-27.html.*

Johnson, D. W., & Johnson, R. T. (1986). *Circles of learning: Cooperation in the classroom.* Edina, MN: Interaction Book Company.

Kirsch, I., Braun, H., Yamamoto, K., & Sum, A. (2007, January). *America's perfect storm: Three forces changing our nation's future.* Princeton, NJ: Educational Testing Service. Retrieved February 21, 2007, from *www.ets.org/Media/Education_Topics/pdf/AmericasPerfectStorm.pdf.*

Lewis, J. (2007a). Academic literacy: Principles and learning opportunities for adolescent readers. In J. Lewis & G. Moorman (Eds.), *Adolescent literacy: Policies and promising practices* (pp. 143–166). Newark, DE: International Reading Association.

Lewis, J. (2007b). *Academic literacy: Readings and strategies* (4th ed.). Boston: Houghton Mifflin. (1996 rev.)

MacKenzie, S. (2006). *Is your communicating as good as your driving!* Retrieved February 12, 2007, from *www.powerlife-solutions.com/features/articles-driving.html.*

McLeod, H. (n.d.). *The effective team member—A checklist.* Retrieved March 3, 2007, from *schools.tdsb.on.ca/riverdale/welcome/guidance/curriculum/careerstudy/handouts/handout02.htm.*

Michalko, M. (1994). *Lotus Blossom technique.* Retrieved March 6, 2007, from *members.optusnet.com.au/~charles57/Creative/Techniques/lotus.htm.*

National Center for Education Statistics. (1999). *Digest of educational statistics 1999.* Washington, DC: U.S. Government Printing Office.

National Center for Education Statistics. (2007, February). *The nation's report card: 12th-grade reading and mathematics 2005* (NCES2007-468). Retrieved March 1, 2007, from *nces.ed.gov/nationsreportcard/pdf/main2005/2007468.pdf.*

National Commission on Excellence in Education. (1983). *A nation at risk: The imperative for educational reform.* Washington, DC: U.S. Government Printing Office.

National Governors Association. (2005, July 17). *Governors sign compact on high school graduation rate at annual meeting.* Retrieved February 13, 2007, from *www.nga.org/portal/site/nga/menuitem.6c9a8a9ebc6ae07eee28aca9501010a0/ ?vgnextoid=f599184d94525010VgnVCM1000001a01010aRCRD&vgnextcha nnel=4b18f074f0d9ff00VgnVCM1000001a01010aRCRD.*

Orfield, G., Losen, D., Wald, J., & Swanson, C. B. (2004). *Losing our future: How minority youth are being left behind by the graduation rate crisis.* Cambridge, MA: The Civil Rights Project at Harvard University. Contributors: Advocates for Children of New York, The Civil Society Institute. Retrieved January 17, 2007, from *www.urban.org/UploadedPDF/410936_LosingOurFuture.pdf.*

Peter D. Hart Research Associates/Public Opinion Strategies. (2005). *Rising to the challenge: Are high school graduates prepared for college and work? A study of recent high school graduates, college instructors, and employers.* Washington, DC: Achieve Inc. Retrieved from *www.achieve.org/files/pollreport_0.pdf.*

Rosenbaum, J. E. (2004, Spring). All good jobs don't require a college degree. *American Educator.* Retrieved February 5, 2007, from *www.aft.org/pubs-reports/american_educator/spring2004/collegedegree.html.*

Secretary's Commission on Achieving Necessary Skills. (1991). *What work requires of schools: A SCANS report for America 2000.* Washington, DC: U.S. Department of Labor.

Swanson, C. B. (2006). *Diplomas count: An essential guide to graduation policy and rates.* Retrieved June 26, 2006, from *www.edweek.org/ew/toc/2006/06/ 22/index.html.*

Urban Legends. (n.d.). *The knockout perfume.* Retrieved February 24, 2007, from *urbanlegends.about.com/library/weekly/aa052400a.htm (¶3).*

U.S. Census Bureau. (2006). *www.census.gov/Press-Release/www.releases/archives/ education/004214.html.*

U.S. Department of Education, National Center for Education Statistics. Digest of education statistics. (2004). Based on U.S. Department of Commerce, Census Bureau, Current Population Surveys (CPS), March, various years. Retrieved from NCES Youth Indicators, 2005. Retrieved February 6, 2007, from *nces.ed.gov/programs/youthindicators/Indicators.asp?PubPageNumber=20.*

U.S. Department of Labor Bureau of Labor Statistics. (2005, December 20). Tomorrow's jobs. In *Occupational Outlook Handbook,* pp. 1–8. Retrieved January 28, 2007, from *www.bls.gov/oco/oco2003.htm.*

Vygotsky, L. (1978). *Mind in society: The development of higher psychological processes.* Cambridge, MA: Harvard University Press.

Wasley, P. A., Fine, M., Gladden, M., Holland, N. E., King, S. P., Mosak, E., et al. (2000). *Small schools: Great strides.* Retrieved November 24, 2006, from *www.bankstreet.edu/gems/publications/smallschools.pdf.*

Western, B., & Pettit, B. (2002). Beyond crime and punishment: Prisons and inequality. *Contexts, 1,* 37–43. Retrieved January 19, 2007, from *www. childtrendsdatabank.org/indicators/1HighSchoolDropout.cfm, p. 4.*

Index

341